Everyday Spelling

Authors

James Beers • Ronald L. Cramer • W. Dorsey Hammond

**S F
A W**

Scott Foresman
Addison Wesley

Editorial Offices: Glenview, Illinois • New York, New York
Sales Offices: Reading, Massachusetts • Duluth, Georgia • Glenview, Illinois
Carrollton, Texas • Menlo Park, California

1-800-552-2259

http://www.sf.aw.com

■ ACKNOWLEDGMENTS

TEXT

p. 17: "A dry leaf. . ." from *More Cricket Songs* Japanese haiku translated by Harry Behn. Copyright © 1971 by Harry Behn. Used by permission of Marian Reiner; "Clink!" by Kazue Mizumura from *Flower, Moon, Snow* by Kazue Mizumura. Copyright © 1977 by Kazue Mizumura. Reprinted by permission of HarperCollins Publishers.

ILLUSTRATIONS

pp. 12, 35, 37, 38, 43, 115, 116, 117: Paul G. Somers; **pp. 12, 13, 15, 18, 19, 23, 27, 31, 33, 44, 70, 96, 122, 148:** David Wink; **pp. 14, 40, 66, 92, 118, 144:** Lloyd Brooks; **pp. 14, 21, 66, 80, 129, 151:** Randy Chewning; **pp. 16, 28:** Laura Derichs; **pp. 17, 35, 36, 63, 88, 98:** Roger Chandler; **pp. 17, 29, 125, 137, 147, 155, 163, 226, 227:** Steven Mach; **pp. 17, 35, 36, 63, 73, 88, 98, 99, 121, 133, 159:** Yoshi Miyake; **pp. 20, 94, 138, 159:** Paul Sharp; **pp. 22, 48, 50, 74, 76, 100, 126, 152:** C. K. Poedtke; **pp. 24, 68:** Ellen Gould; **pp. 25, 54, 81, 106:** Richard Syska; **pp. 26, 52, 78, 104, 130, 156:** Thomas Kovacs; **pp. 30, 56, 82, 108, 134, 160:** John Margeson; **p. 32:** Barbara Samanich; **pp. 33, 69, 121, 154:** Corasue Nicholas; **pp. 34, 60, 61, 114, 124, 125, 138, 147, 164, 167:** Joe Rogers; **pp. 34, 60, 86, 112, 138, 164:** Maria Stroster; **pp. 38, 39, 41, 45, 49, 53, 57:** Kathy Petraukas; **p. 42:** Mary Francis Gregory; **pp. 43, 55, 139, 146:** Mary Jones; **pp. 46, 102:** Susan Shipley; **pp. 47, 59:** Mary Lynn Blasutta; **pp. 51, 81:** Gwen Connelly; **pp. 51, 142, 143, 145, 149, 153, 157, 161:** Jared Lee; **p. 58:** Randy Verougstraete; **p. 72:** Craig Rex Perry; **pp. 77, 103, 111:** Patti Green; **pp. 84, 85, 110, 112, 129, 141, 165:** Teresa Jonik-Heine; **p. 85:** Susan Swan; **pp. 90, 91, 93, 97, 101, 105, 109:** Kelly Hume; **pp. 99, 120:** Terry Sirrell; **p. 107:** Paul Moch; **p. 113:** Marianne Wallace; **pp. 116, 119, 123, 127, 131, 135:** Marcy Ramsey; **p. 118:** Patricia Barbee; **p. 128:** Kees de Kiefte; **p. 132:** Eldon Doty; **pp. 136, 158:** Harry Roolaat; **pp. 150, 162:** Mary Jo Phelan; **p. 163:** Jack Wallen; **p. 166:** Rebecca Brown; **pp. 170, 171:** Scott McKowen; **pp. 172, 173, 190, 191, 214, 215:** John Sandford; **pp. 174, 175, 196, 197, 202:** Chris Sheban; **pp. 182, 183:** Joel Spector; **pp. 184, 185, 187, 195, 201, 222, 223:** Three Communication Design; **pp. 198, 199, 207:** Ka Botzis; **pp. 204, 205:** Susan Spellman; **pp. 212, 213:** Franklin Hammond; **pp. 216, 217:** Lance Jackson; **pp. 218, 219:** Lisa Adams; **pp. 224, 225:** LeeLee Brazeal; **pp. 228, 229:** Paul Dolan

PHOTOGRAPHS

p. 95TL: Joe Viesti/Viesti Associates, Inc.; **p. 95BC:** Trevor Page/Hutchinson Library; **p. 95R:** Bavaria/Viesti Associates, Inc.; **p. 171:** Courtesy Museum of New Mexico Neg. #35614; **p. 175T:** Connie Geocaris/Tony Stone Images; **p. 175C:** Richard Bradbury/Tony Stone Images; **pp. 176, 177, 181C:** Alinare/Art Resource; **p.181T:** Scala/Art Resource; **p. 181B:** Erich Lessing/Art Resource; **pp. 182, 207, 211, 288T, 302B:** Courtesy NASA; **p.183:** Elizabeth Harris/Tony Stone Images; **p. 187:** Superstock; **p.193:** Roger Ressmeyer/Starlight; **pp. 194, 195, 196, 197:** William E. Ferguson; **p. 197:** Field Museum of Natural History, artist Charles R. Knight; **p. 200:** UPI/Bettmann; **p. 201:** Paul Scott/Sygma; **p. 203:** L. J. Fineman/FPG; **pp. 206, 207:** Science Graphics, Inc.; **p. 219:** Culver Pictures; **pp. 222, 223:** Three Communication Design; **pp. 254, 255B, 264T, 280T, 285B, 290, 292, 293B, 309:** Cynthia Clampitt; **p. 255T:** Courtesy Ford Motor Company; **p. 256T:** Courtesy French Government Tourist Office; **pp. 267, 279B:** Library of Congress; **p. 275B:** Field Museum of Natural History; **pp. 276T, 278B, 291T, 293T, 303, 310T:** Catherine Koehler; **p. 278T:** Courtesy The American Red Cross; **p. 283T:** Michael D. Sullivan; **pp. 283B, 301:** Courtesy U. S. Geological Survey; **p. 284:** From *Little Women* by Louisa May Alcott, illustrated by Louis Jambor. Copyright © 1947 by Grosset & Dunlop. All rights reserved. Used by permission. **p. 287:** Egon Bork; **p. 288B:** Courtesy WGN News; **p. 289B:** Courtesy Hale Observatories; **p. 308:** Courtesy Texas Department of Public Safety

Unless otherwise acknowledged all photographs are the property of Addison-Wesley Educational Publishers Inc.

CONTENTS

■ CONTENTS

UNIT 3

CONTENTS

UNIT 6

Cross-Curricular Lessons

✋ SOCIAL STUDIES

🍎 HEALTH

💡 SCIENCE

CONTENTS

✳ FREQUENTLY MISSPELLED WORDS!

Lots of words on your spelling lists are marked with green asterisks ✳ These are the words that are misspelled the most by students your age.*

Pay special attention to these frequently misspelled words as you read, write, and practice your spelling words.

a lot	our	we're	themselves	don't
too	probably	again	then	elementary
it's	they're	clothes	always	especially
because	until	didn't	awhile	field
that's	different	everybody	Christmas	Florida
their	really	off	doesn't	friend
there	usually	TV	except	grabbed
you're	beautiful	myself	outside	since
favorite	college	basketball	when	something
were	they	let's	whole	swimming
everything	through	there's	beginning	
finally	where	which	business	

* **Research in Action** is a research project conducted in 1990–1993. This list of frequently misspelled words is one result of an analysis of 18,599 unedited compositions. Words are listed in the order of their frequency of misspelling.

STRATEGY WORKSHOP

Developing Spelling Consciousness

DISCOVER THE STRATEGY We all misspell words like these—words we know how to spell, or ought to.

to	they	friend	we're
too	when	whole	where
our	until	didn't	grabbed
off	which	Florida	
then	were	TV	

In this book they're called **frequently misspelled words.** They're words that are misspelled over and over by students your age.

1. miss pell
2. notice
3. conclusionesses

Which three words did the writer misspell in the car wash notice above? Find them and write them correctly.

Misspelling these words makes us look bad because they're basically easy words. Some we never learned to spell correctly. Others we know but never notice. If we could only learn to "see" are mistakes, we'd catch them. (Did you catch the misspelling in that last sentence?)

We need to make ourselves aware of these words. We need to develop our **spelling consciousness.**

I.N.C

TRY IT OUT Proofread this set of directions. Find the eight misspellings of short, simple words, and write each word correctly. *Hint:* Proofread for meaning too. A word that looks like it's spelled right may actually be the wrong word.

4. _____

5. _____

6. _____

7. _____

8. _____

9. _____

10. _____

11. _____

> Directions to the campsite ↓
>
> 🚗 Exit the highway at exit 7. ➡ Than drive untill you see a billboard wich advertises trips to florida. 🌴 Did'nt you say you where going there soon? Anyway, that's were you turn right.
>
> ➡ Turn left wen the road ends. It's right there.

LOOK AHEAD You'll find more **frequently misspelled words** ✳ in the lessons that follow. Each one is marked by the symbol you see here. You'll also find them in proofreading exercises. Look through the lists for the next five lessons and write down any frequently misspelled words that are spelling problems for you.

1. _____

2. _____

3. _____

Getting Letters in Correct Order

SPELLING FOCUS

Watch for letter combinations that are hard to keep in order. Pay close attention to those parts: **p<u>oe</u>try, thr<u>ough</u>, b<u>ui</u>lding**.

■ **STUDY** Say each word. Then read the sentence.

1. *p<u>oe</u>try*   Let's read a book of **poetry.**
2. *b<u>eau</u>tiful* ✳   Red roses look **beautiful** to me.
3. *thi<u>r</u>teen*   Ali is **thirteen** years old today.
4. *ton<u>gue</u>*   A frog's **tongue** is sticky.
5. *pi<u>e</u>ces*   Pick up the sharp **pieces** of glass.
6. *n<u>ei</u>ghborhood*   Welcome to our **neighborhood.**
7. *th<u>ou</u>sand*   A **thousand** voices cheered.
8. *thr<u>ough</u>* ✳   Pups tumbled **through** the door.
9. *unus<u>ua</u>l*   That striped lizard is **unusual.**
10. *b<u>ui</u>lding*   It was cool in the brick **building.**

11. *li<u>ce</u>nse*   My sister got her driver's **license.**
12. *remod<u>el</u>*   We will **remodel** the kitchen.
13. *grat<u>e</u>ful*   I am **grateful** for your gift.
14. *en<u>e</u>my*   Make a friend, not an **enemy.**
15. *inst<u>r</u>ument*   A trumpet is a brass **instrument.**
16. *p<u>er</u>form*   The clowns **perform** magic tricks.
17. *p<u>re</u>fer*   I **prefer** bagels to muffins.
18. *jud<u>ge</u>d*   Ms. Li **judged** the talent contest.
19. *ad<u>j</u>usted*   I **adjusted** the safety belt to fit.
20. *sol<u>di</u>er*   The tin **soldier** was painted blue.

■ **PRACTICE** First write the words you think are easy to spell. Then write the ones that are harder for you to spell. Take care as you write each word.

■ **WRITE** Choose ten words to write in sentences.

1. _____
2. _____
3. _____
4. _____
5. _____
6. _____
7. _____
8. _____
9. _____
10. _____
11. _____
12. _____
13. _____
14. _____
15. _____
16. _____
17. _____
18. _____
19. _____
20. _____

CHALLENGE!

preliminary
tremendous
mediocre
perception
neutrality

✳ **WATCH OUT FOR FREQUENTLY MISSPELLED WORDS!**

SYNONYMS   Write a list word that means the same as each word below.

1. poems
2. parts
3. adapted
4. rare
5. tool
6. lovely
7. act
8. thankful
9. finished
10. structure
11. foe
12. desire

CONTEXT CLUES   Write the list word that best completes each sentence.

13. Rosa's father was a ___ in the Persian Gulf War.
14. The house was old and run-down, so they decided to ___ it.
15. My older sister just got her driver's ___.
16. Toshio is ___ years old.
17. The doctor said, "Open your mouth and stick out your ___."
18. The contest was ___ by a panel of experts.
19. The streets are always crowded in the ___ where David lives.
20. That painting is worth a ___ dollars.

STRATEGIC SPELLING

Developing Spelling Consciousness

We sometimes misspell familiar words that we shouldn't miss. Proofread the passage. Find the four misspelled words and write them correctly.

It's been six weeks since we moved here, and I guess it's not so bad. We ride our bikes throw the park every day. The flowers in the park are beutiful! I miss my frend Shannon, but she has promised to come visit soon. I hope she brings her bike wen she comes!

21. _____
22. _____
23. _____
24. _____

1. _____
2. _____
3. _____
4. _____
5. _____
6. _____
7. _____
8. _____
9. _____
10. _____
11. _____
12. _____
13. _____
14. _____
15. _____
16. _____
17. _____
18. _____
19. _____
20. _____

FREQUENTLY MISSPELLED WORDS ✻ FREQUENTLY MISSPELLED WORDS ✻

Try saying *beautiful* this way: *bea-u-ti-ful*. It will remind you to write an **e** and a **u.** Then you have to remember to put an **a** between them!

PROOFREAD FOR CAPITALIZATION

Capitalize nouns that name a particular person, place, day, or month. Do not capitalize seasons of the year. For example:

The neighborhood art fair held each Summer along the Fox River opens july 2.

Check Proper Nouns Read each sentence. Correct the words that should be capitalized. If a sentence is correct, write "Correct."

1. The art fair will run thursday through Sunday.
2. This unusual event is open to all silver City residents.
3. Come to the building at 610 Maple street.
4. The art will be judged by Miguel ramos.
5. Mr. Ramos has lived in our city for thirteen years.

1. _____

2. _____

3. _____

4. _____

5. _____

PROOFREAD AN ANNOUNCEMENT Find the five
misspelled words in this announcement and write them correctly. Also fix three capitalization errors.

> For our first concert this fall, Madhu Shankar will preform at the school auditorium saturday. Ms. shankar plays the sitar, an unusal instrument from india. We are greatful to Ms. Shankar for agreeing to play this beatiful music. Everyone in the nieghborhood is invited to attend.

Word List

license	thousand
remodel	neighborhood
grateful	perform
poetry	soldier
enemy	pieces
judged	through
beautiful	unusual
thirteen	prefer
instrument	building
tongue	adjusted

Personal Words

1. _____

2. _____

WRITE AN ANNOUNCEMENT Write an announcement for
a school event. Use three spelling words and a personal word.

 **Review**

poetry	neighborhood
beautiful	thousand
thirteen	through
tongue	unusual
pieces	building

MAKING INFERENCES   Write the list word that is missing from each person's statement.

1. Nurse: "Keep the thermometer under your ___."
2. Chef: "I'll cut this pie into eight ___."
3. Architect: "This is our town's tallest ___."
4. Usher: "Section four is ___ that gate."
5. Teacher: "Can you name the ___ original colonies?"
6. Mayor: "Get to know the people in your ___."
7. Mechanic: "That engine is making an ___ noise."
8. Auctioneer: "Do I hear three ___?"
9. Announcer: "Our guest will read some of her ___."
10. Camper: "Nothing's more ___ than the great outdoors."

1. _____
2. _____
3. _____
4. _____
5. _____
6. _____
7. _____
8. _____
9. _____
10. _____

Multicultural *Connection*

POETRY   People in every culture write poetry. These poems all describe nature.

TWO HAIKU

A dry leaf drifting
down to an icy torrent
clings to a green rock.
—Bokusui *(Japanese)*

Clink!
An iced branch falls.
I see the shattered moonlight
Scatter at my feet.

—Kazue Mizumura
(Japanese American)

SPRING SONG

As my eyes search the prairie
I feel the summer in the spring.
—*Chippewa*

Complete each sentence with one of the words in the box.

haiku	prairie	traditional

1. The Chippewa still remember when much of North America was a flat land of endless grass, called the ___.
2. A Japanese poem about nature, with two lines of five syllables and a middle line of seven syllables, is called ___.
3. In her poetry, Kazue Mizumura combines modern experiences with a classic, ___ art form from Japan.

1. _____
2. _____
3. _____

Short Vowels

SPELLING FOCUS

Short **a** is usually spelled **a**: **admire**. Short **e** is usually spelled **e**: **method**. Short **i** is usually spelled **i**: **swimming**. Short **o** is usually spelled **o**: **modern**. Short **u** is usually spelled **u**: **clumsy**.

STUDY   Say each word. Then read the sentence.

1.	admire	I **admire** your bravery.
2.	canyon	A **canyon** has steep sides.
3.	lemonade	She drank a glass of **lemonade.**
4.	method	Use this **method** to learn music.
5.	distance	We saw a forest in the **distance.**
6.	swimming ✳	Let's go **swimming** in the lake.
7.	modern	Kelly took a class on **modern** art.
8.	comedy	One of the movies is a **comedy.**
9.	husband	They are **husband** and wife.
10.	clumsy	The **clumsy** puppy fell in a heap.
11.	magnify	Telescopes **magnify** the stars.
12.	cannon	Smoke poured from the **cannon.**
13.	decorate	We should **decorate** for the party.
14.	strict	Our teacher's rules are **strict.**
15.	injury	Your ankle **injury** looks painful.
16.	tissue	He blew his nose with a **tissue.**
17.	honesty	She was trusted for her **honesty.**
18.	property	He bought **property** near the sea.
19.	hundredth	The **hundredth** customer won.
20.	dungeon	Beneath the castle lay a **dungeon.**

PRACTICE ▪ Write four words with **short a**
▪ three words with **short e**   ▪ four words with **short o**
▪ five words with **short i**   ▪ four words with **short u**

WRITE   Choose two sentences to write a dialogue.

1. _____

2. _____

3. _____

4. _____

5. _____

6. _____

7. _____

8. _____

9. _____

10. _____

11. _____

12. _____

13. _____

14. _____

15. _____

16. _____

17. _____

18. _____

19. _____

20. _____

CHALLENGE!

adequate
reconcile
insulation
reluctant
thunderstorm

✳ **WATCH OUT FOR FREQUENTLY MISSPELLED WORDS!**

WORD MATH   Answer each problem with a list word.

1. lemons + water + sugar =
2. partner + male + married =
3. prison + dark + underground =
4. moving + stiff + awkward =
5. valley + narrow + deep =
6. theater + humorous + happy ending =
7. paper + soft + absorbent =
8. land + buildings + objects + owned =
9. fairness + truthfulness + uprightness =
10. manner + plan + order =

ANALOGIES   Write the list word that completes each analogy.

11. Ugliness is to deface as beauty is to ____ .
12. Measles is to disease as broken leg is to ____ .
13. Villain is to despise as hero is to ____ .
14. Gigantic is to reduce as tiny is to ____ .
15. Land is to hiking as water is to ____ .
16. One is to first as one hundred is to ____ .
17. Generous is to selfish as lenient is to ____ .
18. Pony Express is to old-fashioned as fax machine is to ____ .
19. Inches are to miles as closeness is to ____ .
20. Transportation is to train as weapon is to ____ .

STRATEGIC SPELLING

Seeing Meaning Connections

Words related to decorate
redecorate
decor
decorator
decorative

Complete each sentence with a word from the box.

21. Kristie didn't like her bedroom's

_____ .

22. She decided to _____

the bedroom in a new style.

23. Kristie called an interior _____ for advice.

24. He suggested a _____ wallpaper.

1. _____
2. _____
3. _____
4. _____
5. _____
6. _____
7. _____
8. _____
9. _____
10. _____
11. _____
12. _____
13. _____
14. _____
15. _____
16. _____
17. _____
18. _____
19. _____
20. _____

Take a Hint
To spell *comedy*, remember this:
Co**me**dy isn't funny unless you include **me.**

☰	Make a capital.
/	Make a small letter.
∧	Add something.
ℰ	Take out something.
⊙	Add a period.
¶	New paragraph

PROOFREAD FOR PUNCTUATION

Use commas to separate items in a series. Add a comma between the day and the year of a date. For example:

> No swimming, boating, or fishing allowed until May 28, 1997.

Check for Commas Read each sentence. Write the word or number where a comma should be placed.

1. Dogs cats, and other pets are not allowed on the beach.
2. The lemonade stand opens June 1 1997.
3. We are not responsible for lost damaged, or stolen property.
4. Swimming lessons are on Mondays Tuesdays, and Fridays.
5. The beach closes for the season on September 5 1997.

1. _____

2. _____

3. _____

4. _____

5. _____

PROOFREAD RULES
Find the five misspelled words in the rules and write them correctly. These errors may be list words or words you learned before. Also fix three comma errors.

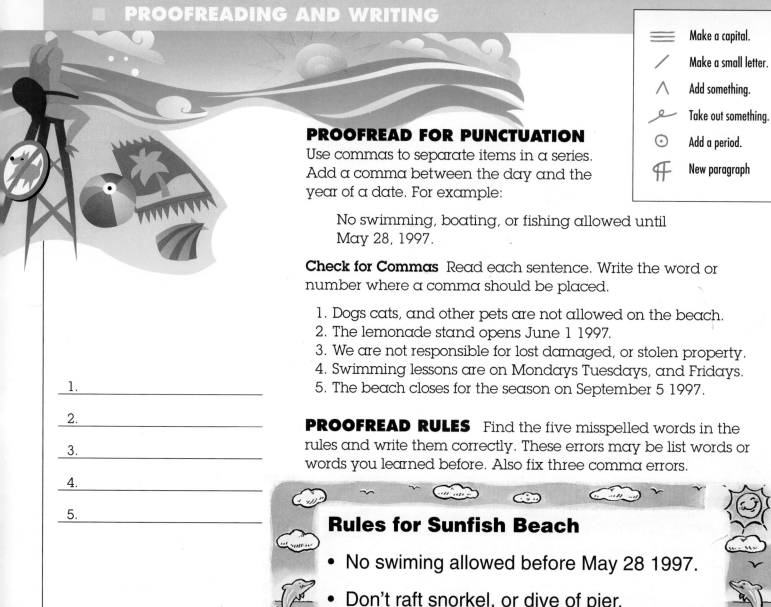

Rules for Sunfish Beach

- No swiming allowed before May 28 1997.

- Don't raft snorkel, or dive of pier.

- To prevent enjury, throw glass plastic, and aluminum trash in recycling bins behind the main bilding.

- Be aware of your distance from shore.

- Fines given for damage to praperty.

Word List

magnify	swimming
canyon	tissue
admire	honesty
cannon	property
lemonade	modern
method	comedy
decorate	husband
strict	clumsy
injury	hundredth
distance	dungeon

Personal Words

1. _____

2. _____

WRITE RULES
Write rules for a place where you have fun or play sports. Use three spelling words and a personal word.

Review

admire	swimming
canyon	modern
lemonade	comedy
method	husband
distance	clumsy

ANTONYMS   Write the list word that means the opposite of each word below.

1. old-fashioned
2. tragedy
3. dislike
4. graceful

1. new fashioned
2. ~~enemy~~
3. ~~admire~~
4. ~~clumsy~~

DEFINITIONS   Write the list word that matches each clue.

5. space between
6. a narrow valley
7. a married man
8. way of doing something
9. moving along in the water
10. a drink made from juice

5. distance
6. method
7. husband
8. modern
9. swimming
10. lemonade

Word *Study*

LATIN ROOTS: *magni*   Many English words are built on Latin roots. For example, the list word *magnify* comes from the Latin root **magni,** which means "great" or "large."

magnify	magnitude
magnificently	magnate
magnanimous	

Complete the word web with the **magni** words in the box. Use your Spelling Dictionary if you need help.

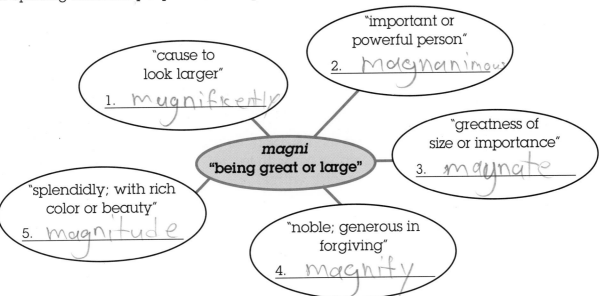

"cause to look larger"
1. magnificently

"important or powerful person"
2. magnanimous

"greatness of size or importance"
3. magnate

"splendidly; with rich color or beauty"
5. magnitude

"noble; generous in forgiving"
4. magnify

magni
"being great or large"

21

Words with ei and ie

Long **e** can be spelled **ei** and **ie**: c<u>ei</u>ling, f<u>ie</u>ld.

■ **STUDY** Say each word. Then read the sentence.

1.	ceiling	Streamers hung from the **ceiling.**
2.	receipt	Get a **receipt** when you pay.
3.	deceive	Never **deceive** your friends.
4.	neither	She called **neither** one of us.
5.	field ✱	A scarecrow stood in the **field.**
6.	achieve	Work hard to **achieve** your goals.
7.	belief	Our **belief** gives us strength.
8.	brief	After a **brief** wait, the train left.
9.	relief	It is a **relief** to be home again.
10.	apiece	Limes are just ten cents **apiece.**

11.	leisure	We play ball in our **leisure** time.
12.	protein	Beans and meat contain **protein.**
13.	receiver	Speak into the telephone **receiver.**
14.	seize	The army fought to **seize** the fort.
15.	conceited	The handsome man was **conceited.**
16.	shield	The porch will **shield** us from the sun.
17.	niece	Annie sent her new **niece** a rattle.
18.	diesel	A **diesel** truck honked its horn.
19.	grief	Tears of **grief** wet his cheeks.
20.	yield	Soldiers won't **yield** the fort.

■ **PRACTICE** Sort the words by writing
- eleven words with **ie**
- nine words with **ei**

■ **WRITE** Choose two sentences to include in a paragraph.

1. _____
2. _____
3. _____
4. _____
5. _____
6. _____
7. _____
8. _____
9. _____
10. _____
11. _____
12. _____
13. _____
14. _____
15. _____
16. _____
17. _____
18. _____
19. _____
20. _____

CHALLENGE!

deceitful
conceivable
retrieval
unwieldy
grievance

✱ **WATCH OUT FOR FREQUENTLY MISSPELLED WORDS!**

COMPLETE A POEM Complete the poem with list words.

I went to the store with my youngest niece.
We saw some bugs, five cents (1) .
I told my niece, "It's my belief
that bugs will only bring us (2) ."
My (3) replied, to my relief,
in words as kind as they were (4) ,
that she had two bugs at home in a box
and (5) of them was fun to watch.

CONTEXT CLUES Write the list word that completes
each sentence.

6. The farmer plowed the ____ before planting corn.
7. Do you have any evidence for that ____?
8. A cold drink provides some ____ from the summer heat.
9. Eva tried to ____ her skin from the sun with a hat.
10. I refuse to ____ to your demands.
11. With hard work and patience, you can ____ great things.
12. That truck runs on ____ fuel.
13. I held the telephone ____ up to my ear and listened.
14. Melvin had a ____ that proved he had paid for his ticket.
15. Ed, a modest person, never acts ____ about his good grades.
16. When I throw you the rope, ____ it with both hands.
17. The room was painted red, from the floor to the ____.
18. Tell the truth and don't ____ us about your plans.
19. After your work is done, do you have the ____ to play?
20. Meat, beans, and cheese are good sources of ____.

1. _____
2. _____
3. _____
4. _____
5. _____
6. _____
7. _____
8. _____
9. _____
10. _____
11. _____
12. _____
13. _____
14. _____
15. _____
16. _____
17. _____
18. _____
19. _____
20. _____

STRATEGIC SPELLING

Using the Problem Parts Strategy

Write four list words that are hard for you. Underline the part of
each word that gives you problems. Picture the words. Focus on
the problem parts.

21. _____   23. _____

22. _____   24. _____

*FREQUENTLY MISSPELLED WORDS * FREQUENTLY MISSPELLED WORDS *

Some students have
trouble spelling *field*. To
help you remember to spell
the **long e** sound with **ie,**
think of *a field on fire*.

⟹	Make a capital.
/	Make a small letter.
∧	Add something.
ℯ	Take out something.
⊙	Add a period.
⸠	New paragraph

PROOFREAD FOR USAGE When comparing two things, use **-er** or *more*. When comparing more than two things, use **-est** or *most*. Never use both together. For example:

Tuesday was the ~~warmest~~ warmer of the last two days, but it was also the ~~most~~ rainiest day this week.

Check Comparatives and Superlatives Read each sentence. Fix any mistakes with words that compare things.

1. The heavier rainfall all week occurred Tuesday.
2. Tuesday's brief storm was more worse than Monday's storm.
3. This thunderstorm was the most destructive of the two.
4. Thursday was the most coldest day this week.
5. Friday will be the better day this week for leisure activities.

1. _____
2. _____
3. _____
4. _____
5. _____

PROOFREAD A WEATHER REPORT Find five misspelled words and write them correctly. Some may be words you learned before. Fix three comparative or superlative adjectives.

> Today was the colder of the last three days, with breif showers. However, were going to have releif from the rain soon. Friday and Saturday should be good days for liesure activities. Niether day will be cold. Friday will be the most sunniest day this week, with the most highest temperatures.

Word List

leisure	seize
shield	yield
achieve	diesel
niece	grief
belief	relief
protein	neither
field	brief
receipt	conceited
deceive	apiece
receiver	ceiling

Personal Words

1. _____

2. _____

WRITE A WEATHER REPORT Report on the weather in your area. Use two spelling words and a personal word.

Review

DEFINITIONS   Write the list word that matches the clue.

1. for each one
2. get by effort
3. not either
4. opinion
5. open country

6. use deceit
7. surface opposite the floor
8. lasting only a short time
9. lessening of a pain
10. proof that something has been received

ceiling
receipt
deceive
neither
field
achieve
belief
brief
relief
apiece

1. _____
2. _____
3. _____
4. _____
5. _____

6. _____
7. _____
8. _____
9. _____
10. _____

Word *Study*

EPONYMS   Did you know that the word *diesel* comes from Rudolf Diesel, the German inventor of the diesel engine? Words that come from people's names are called **eponyms.** Look at the words in the box. Write the word that came from the name of each person described.

saxophone	sideburns	boycott
Braille	bloomers	Melba toast

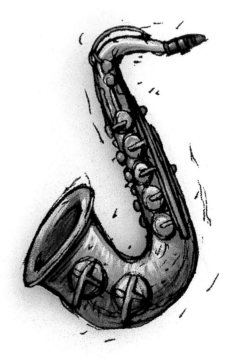

1. Charles Boycott tried to collect high rents from poor Irish tenant farmers and was silently ignored by them all.
2. Amelia Bloomer, an American feminist, was ridiculed for publicly wearing these baggy short pants instead of a dress.
3. Adolphe Sax invented this brass wind instrument.
4. Ambrose Burnside, a Union general in the Civil War, was famous for these whiskers he grew on the sides of his face.
5. Nellie Melba, an opera singer, decided she liked burnt toast, and this crisp toast was added to menus in her honor.
6. Louis Braille, a Frenchman who was blind, invented this system of writing with raised dots at the age of 15.

1. _____
2. _____
3. _____
4. _____
5. _____
6. _____

Vowel Sounds in *rule* and *view*

SPELLING FOCUS

The vowel sound /ü/ can be spelled **u-consonant-e, ew: reduce, sewer.** The vowel sound /yü/ can be spelled **iew, ue, u: review, value, United States.**

■ **STUDY** Say each word. Then read the sentence.

1. reduce — Wait until they **reduce** the price.
2. attitude — A good **attitude** will help you.
3. sewer — Rats lived in the city **sewer.**
4. New York — We went to the theater in **New York.**
5. review — Mr. Han helped us **review** the book.
6. value — This old vase has great **value.**
7. continue — Let's **continue** the game tomorrow.
8. humid — On hot, **humid** days, they swim.
9. United States — The **United States** is a democracy.
10. universe — Spacecraft explore the **universe.**

11. costume — Each actor wore a velvet **costume.**
12. absolutely — The movie is **absolutely** awful.
13. assume — We **assume** the map is correct.
14. renew — I need to **renew** my library book.
15. viewpoint — I agree with her **viewpoint.**
16. interview — The mayor's **interview** was on TV.
17. preview — The critic saw a **preview** of the movie.
18. rescue — Firefighters will **rescue** the man.
19. uniform — My soccer **uniform** is red this year.
20. reunion — The family **reunion** is June 12.

■ **PRACTICE** Sort the list words by writing
- five words that have a vowel sound spelled **u-consonant-e**
- seven words that have a vowel sound spelled **ew** or **iew**
- eight words that have a vowel sound spelled **u** or **ue**

■ **WRITE** Use two sentences in a paragraph about school.

1. _____
2. _____
3. _____
4. _____
5. _____
6. _____
7. _____
8. _____
9. _____
10. _____
11. _____
12. _____
13. _____
14. _____
15. _____
16. _____
17. _____
18. _____
19. _____
20. _____

CHALLENGE!

newcomer
aptitude
curlicue
ukulele
fugitive

ANTONYMS   Write the list word that completes each phrase.

1. not abandon, but ____
2. not worthlessness, but ____
3. not wait, but ____
4. not possibly, but ____
5. not increase, but ____
6. not know, but ____
7. not dry, but ____
8. not separation, but ____

CLASSIFYING   Write the word that belongs in each group.

9. New Jersey, Pennsylvania, ____
10. Mexico, Canada, ____
11. Milky Way, galaxies, ____
12. point of view, standpoint, ____
13. mask, actor, ____
14. conversation, interrogation, ____
15. drain, tunnel, ____
16. check out, return, ____
17. feeling, mood, ____
18. movie, feature, ____
19. study, memorize, ____
20. helmet, badge, ____

STRATEGIC SPELLING

Seeing Meaning Connections

Words with *new*
renew
newborn
newlywed
newscaster

Write words from the box that fit the definitions.

21. An infant recently born is a

_____.

22. A person recently married is a

_____.

23. To get something for a new period is to

_____ it.

24. A person reporting current events on TV is a

_____.

1. anistate
2.
3.
4.
5.
6.
7.
8.
9.
10.
11.
12.
13.
14.
15.
16.
17.
18.
19.
20.

Take a Hint
Remember to capitalize both words in place names such as *New York* and *United States*.

27

≡	Make a capital.
/	Make a small letter.
∧	Add something.
℮	Take out something.
⊙	Add a period.
¶	New paragraph

PROOFREAD FOR PUNCTUATION

Put quotation marks around direct quotations. For example:

> In an interview today, the mayor said, "I expect a large crowd for our summer festival."

Check for Quotation Marks Correct the punctuation in these sentences from the same article by writing the word and the quotation mark that should come before or after it.

> The mayor of New York explained, "We're absolutely delighted with the entertainment lineup. He told reporters, "The festival begins today and will continue through Sunday. He added, I plan to personally greet each visitor.

1. _____

2. _____

3. _____

4. _____

PROOFREAD A NEWS ITEM
Find the six misspelled words and write them correctly. Some may be words you learned before. Fix three incorrect uses of punctuation too.

> Margaret O'Brien was robbed on her way to a family reuion when a man grabed her purse, containing a ring and her driver's lisence. The ring had a valu of $100. The police chief said, We are trying to redouce crime in the area. In an interveiw, Mrs. O'Brien commented, "The police need to review their procedures.

Word List

renew	rescue
reduce	review
New York	humid
costume	uniform
assume	continue
attitude	interview
sewer	reunion
absolutely	preview
value	United States
viewpoint	universe

Personal Words

1. _____

2. _____

WRITE A NEWS ITEM
Write a short news item about a recent event. Use three spelling words and a personal word.

Review

DRAWING CONCLUSIONS
Write the list word that fits each clue.

reduce	value
attitude	continue
sewer	humid
New York	United States
review	universe

1. This country is sometimes called America.
2. This is a worthwhile activity before a test.
3. This can be done to fractions.
4. This describes weather that can be uncomfortable.
5. This city has the same name as a state.
6. This means "worth" and can increase or decrease.
7. This might depend on your mood.
8. This is part of a drainage and sanitary system.
9. This means "to keep on going."
10. This is absolutely everything.

1. _____
2. _____
3. _____
4. _____
5. _____
6. _____
7. _____
8. _____
9. _____
10. _____

Using a Dictionary

PARTS OF AN ENTRY
A dictionary is a quick resource for finding out about a word. Study the part of a dictionary page and the labels. Then answer the questions.

pronunciation —
54 assert | assure — guide words

entry word — **as sume** (ə süm′), **1** take for granted without proof; — definition
suppose: *He assumed that the train would be on time.* **2** take upon oneself; undertake: *She assumed the leadership of the project.* **3** take on; put on: *The* — illustrative sentence or phrase
problem has assumed a new form. v., **as sumed, as sum ing. —as sum′a ble,** *adj.* **—as sum′a bly,** *adv.* **—as sum′er,** *n.*

as sumed (ə sümd′), false; not real; pretended: *an assumed name. adj.* **—as sum ed ly** (ə süm′id lē),
part-of-speech — *adv.*
label
run-on entry —

pronunciation key —

a	hat	u̇	put
ā	age	ü	rule
ä	far, calm	ch	child
âr	care	ng	long
e	let	sh	she
ē	equal	th	thin
ėr	term	ŦH	then
i	it	zh	measure
ī	ice		
o	hot	**ə stands for**	
ō	open	a	in about
ȯ	saw	e	in taken
ô	order	i	in pencil
oi	oil	o	in lemon
ou	out	u	in circus
u	cup		

1. What part of an entry tells how to divide a word into syllables?
2. According to the guide words, which one of these words could also appear on the page: *assault, astonish,* or *assign?*
3. The **a** in *assume* is pronounced like the **i** in what word given in the pronunciation key?
4. In the sentence "I assume you are going," which definition of *assume* is being used?
5. What part of speech is *assume?*

1. _____   3. _____   5. _____

2. _____   4. _____

1. _____
2. _____
3. _____
4. _____
5. _____
6. _____
7. _____
8. _____
9. _____
10. _____
11. _____
12. _____
13. _____
14. _____
15. _____
16. _____
17. _____
18. _____
19. _____
20. _____

Adding -ed and -ing

SPELLING FOCUS

Here are five things to remember when adding **-ed** and **-ing**:

- The base word sometimes does not change: **answered, answering**.
- If the base word ends in **e**, drop the **e**: **decided, deciding**.
- If a two-syllable word ends with an accented syllable, often double the final consonant: **omitted, omitting**.
- If the base word ends in **y**, change the **y** to **i** before adding **-ed**: **satisfied**.
- If the base word ends in **y**, keep the **y** before adding **-ing**: **satisfying**.

■ **STUDY** Look at the words in each column. Notice if the word changes when different endings are added.

answer	1. answered	2. answering
decide	3. decided	4. deciding
include	5. included	6. including
omit	7. omitted	8. omitting
satisfy	9. satisfied	10. satisfying

delay	11. delayed	12. delaying
remember	13. remembered	14. remembering
exercise	15. exercised	16. exercising
interfere	17. interfered	18. interfering
occur	19. occurred	20. occurring

■ **PRACTICE** Sort the list words by writing
- seven words in which the base word was not changed when **-ed** or **-ing** was added
- one word in which the **y** was changed to **i**
- four words in which the final consonant was doubled
- eight words in which the final **e** was dropped

■ **WRITE** Choose ten words to write in sentences.

CHALLENGE!

staggered	staggering
patrolled	patrolling
dignified	dignifying

CONTEXT CLUES Write the list word that is a form of the word in parentheses below to complete each sentence.

1. Tony is (include) all his friends in his new plan.
2. Elena was (exercise) in the gym.
3. She noticed the time and (decide) to go home.
4. Duc dried his hands and (answer) the phone.
5. A cold drink is very (satisfy) on a hot day.
6. The accident (occur) last Tuesday night.
7. Erica started to leave and then (remember) her umbrella.
8. The band is (delay) the concert because of rain.
9. I am (omit) that question from the test.
10. My cousin often meddled and (interfere) with my plans.

ADDING ENDINGS Write the list words formed by adding **-ed** or **-ing.**

11. remember + ing
12. occur + ing
13. include + ed
14. satisfy + ed
15. delay + ed

16. interfere + ing
17. exercise + ed
18. answer + ing
19. omit + ed
20. decide + ing

STRATEGIC SPELLING

Building New Words

Add **-ed** and **-ing** to each of these words: *prefer, license, magnify, continue,* and *shield.* Remember what you learned.

Add -ed

21. _____
22. _____
23. _____
24. _____
25. _____

Add -ing

_____
_____
_____
_____
_____

1. _____
2. _____
3. _____
4. _____
5. _____
6. _____
7. _____
8. _____
9. _____
10. _____
11. _____
12. _____
13. _____
14. _____
15. _____
16. _____
17. _____
18. _____
19. _____
20. _____

Did You Know?
Answer comes from an Old English word that meant "to swear against." Can you guess which part of *answer* meant "swear"?

☰	Make a capital.
/	Make a small letter.
∧	Add something.
℮	Take out something.
⊙	Add a period.
¶	New paragraph

PROOFREAD FOR CARELESS ERRORS

When you proofread your writing, look for words you may have carelessly dropped or repeated. For example:

I am not satisfied with the quality $\overset{of}{\wedge}$ this machine.

Check for Dropped or Repeated Words For each sentence, write the word that was dropped or repeated by mistake.

1. I have decided to return it your company.
2. I am including a a self-addressed, stamped return envelope.
3. The problem has has been occurring for several weeks.
4. Please respond to my inquiry at this this address.
5. I look forward hearing from you.

1. _____
2. _____
3. _____
4. _____
5. _____

PROOFREAD A BUSINESS LETTER Find the six misspelled words in the body of this letter and write them correctly. Some may be words you learned before. Also fix three careless errors.

I returning this ansering machine for my money back. The problem first occured two two weeks ago. Wen my friend called, he heard a screeching noise and hung up. This problem has continued and is interfearing my social life! I have includeed my reciept.

Word List

answered	answering
delayed	delaying
remembered	remembering
decided	deciding
included	including
exercised	exercising
interfered	interfering
omitted	omitting
occurred	occurring
satisfied	satisfying

Personal Words

1. _____
2. _____

WRITE A BUSINESS LETTER Write to a company about a product you like or dislike. Use three spelling words and a personal word. Use correct business letter form. See page 245.

Review

SYNONYMS Write a list word that means the same as each word or phrase below.

1. left out
2. counted in
3. pleasing
4. responding
5. not having

6. ended a need or want
7. settled a question or dispute
8. making up one's mind
9. containing
10. spoke in return to a question

answered
answering
decided
deciding
included
including
omitted
omitting
satisfied
satisfying

1. _____
2. _____
3. _____
4. _____
5. _____

6. _____
7. _____
8. _____
9. _____
10. _____

Word *Study*

SIMILES Writers sometimes use similes to make their writing more vivid or humorous. A **simile** compares two unlike things using the word *like* or *as*. For example, instead of writing, "The ice cream was good," you could write, "The ice cream was as satisfying as a good laugh."

Work with a partner or group to complete these similes.

1. The alarm clock sounded like ___.
2. The student raised his hand as slowly as ___.
3. The students left the school building like ___.

1. _____
2. _____
3. _____

Write your own simile for each sentence below. Don't forget to use *like* or *as.*

1. Lindsay's bike is old.

_____

2. Gabe rode his skateboard quickly.

_____

33

Review

Lesson 1: Getting Letters in Correct Order
Lesson 2: Short Vowels
Lesson 3: Words with ei and ie

Lesson 4: Vowel Sounds in *rule* and *view*
Lesson 5: Adding *-ed* and *-ing*

REVIEW WORD LIST

1. adjusted	11. thirteen	21. method	31. niece	41. answering
2. beautiful	12. thousand	22. modern	32. absolutely	42. decided
3. building	13. through	23. property	33. assume	43. deciding
4. enemy	14. unusual	24. swimming	34. continue	44. exercising
5. instrument	15. admire	25. tissue	35. humid	45. included
6. judged	16. canyon	26. apiece	36. New York	46. including
7. neighborhood	17. comedy	27. brief	37. rescue	47. occurred
8. perform	18. distance	28. grief	38. review	48. omitted
9. pieces	19. dungeon	29. leisure	39. uniform	49. remembered
10. poetry	20. lemonade	30. neither	40. United States	50. remembering

■ PROOFREADING

Find the spelling errors in each passage and write the words correctly. All passages have seven errors except the last one, which has eight.

1. _____
2. _____
3. _____
4. _____
5. _____
6. _____
7. _____

PROOFREAD A NOTICE

Do you play an insterment? Do you like to preform? Do you want to make beutiful music? Tryouts for a niegborhood band are May 6 at Sherman Park at 7 P.M. in the arts biulding. You won't need a unifom, but you will need to play a few peices. We'll see you there!

PROOFREAD A POST CARD

July 18, 20__

Dear Luis,
The picture on the other side shows Piney Camp. So far, it has been hot and huemid here, so we get to go swiming twice a day. I hope this will continiew. We never have any liesure time. I guess they asume we will be homesick unless we are exercizing. Yesterday we hiked three miles. The food is absolutly great!
Your friend,
Alejandro

U.S.A.

Luis Escalona
4135 N. Oak St.
Rushville, IN 46173

1. _____
2. _____
3. _____
4. _____
5. _____
6. _____
7. _____

PROOFREAD A REPORT

National Parks

National parks contain many interesting sights. The oldest national park is Yellowstone. It has about three thousan geysers and many animals, includeding bear, bison, and moose. Arizona is the place to see the biggest canyon on the Colorado River. At Bryce, you will find enormous and unusal rock formations. The highest mountain in the Untied States is in Denali National Park in Alaska. You can idmire alligators in the Everglades, but only from a distanse.

1. _____
2. _____
3. _____
4. _____
5. _____
6. _____
7. _____

PROOFREAD A THANK-YOU NOTE

1. _____
2. _____
3. _____
4. _____
5. _____
6. _____
7. _____

April 3, 20__

Dear Aunt Julia,

Thank you for rememebering my birthday. I love the book of humorous peotry. Thanks also for decideing to send that great bracelet. I really like the madern design. It's hard to believe that I am thriteen. I haven't ajusted to being a teenager yet!

Love from your neice,

Jill

PROOFREAD A FRIENDLY LETTER

1. _____
2. _____
3. _____
4. _____
5. _____
6. _____
7. _____

August 9, 20__

Dear Mike,

How are you enjoying your vacation? I thought I ought to tell you why we aren't ansering the phone. A flood occured yesterday, and I rememberd that you were going to call. We have no water, no phone, and no lights! We deciede to move to a motel. We had to rescew Muggs from the porch roof and wade threw our praperty to a boat.

Your damp friend,

Darryl

PROOFREAD A LETTER TO THE EDITOR

Jefferson School Times, October 17, 20__   Page 5

Letters to the Editor

Dear Editor:

In your breif revue of the Jefferson School Craft Fair, you ommited the names of two entries: the beadwork belt by Shana Overton and the flowers made of tisshu and wire by Stacy McHenry. Although nether won a first prize, they should have been mentioned because the methid each person used was jugded to be extremely creative.

Sarah Walsh

PROOFREAD AN ADVERTISEMENT

Join us for a puppet show!

See "The Dreadful Disaster," a comidy about three daffy dogs trapped in a dark duengeon under the streets of new york.

They try to escape their enimy, but will they succeed or come to greif?

Tickets are a dollar apeice, and there's free lommanade encluded!

Time:
   Saturdays at 5 P.M.
Place:
   Barry Street Theater
   Chestnut and Willow

Creating Memory Tricks

DISCOVER THE STRATEGY We all have words that give us trouble. Try this next strategy with those troublesome words.

1. Ask yourself: Which part of the word gives me trouble? Then mark the letters that are problems for you.

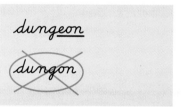

2. Find memory helpers—words or phrases you already can spell—that have the same letters.

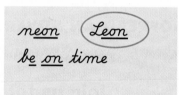

3. Create a memory trick by linking your word with a memory helper that helps you remember it.

Leon is in the dungeon.

Tips: If your trick can be pictured, **visualize** the scene as you say the trick to yourself. Also, don't think your trick has to be a serious phrase or sentence. It doesn't even have to make sense!

TRY IT OUT   Now practice this strategy with a partner.

Write a helper from the box to complete each memory trick.
Underline the matching letters.

field	omitted
Poe try	cannot

1. Trucks and trains are ___.
2. Did Mr. ___ writing poetry?
3. fire in the ___
4. I ___ shoot the cannon.

1. _____

2. _____

3. _____

4. _____

Remember this when you create memory tricks: Your helper
could be one word or more. Your trick could be a phrase **(glue
of great value)** or a sentence **(Sam and Sue used tissue).**

With a partner, create a memory trick for each item. Underline
the matching letters. Draw any tricks you can visualize.

5. neighborhood—eight _____

_____

6. lemonade—made _____

_____

7. swimming—masked monkeys _____

_____

LOOK AHEAD   Look ahead at the next five lessons for list
words that might give you problems. Create memory tricks for
two of them. Share your results with the class.

1. _____

2. _____

Homophones

A homophone is a word that sounds exactly like another word but has a different spelling and meaning: **their, there, they're.**

■ **STUDY** Say each word. Then read the sentence.

1. *their* ✳   We went to **their** house for dinner.
2. *there* ✳   The grocery store is over **there.**
3. *they're* ✳   He said **they're** coming on the train.
4. *wring*   I **wring** out water from the towel.
5. *ring*   She wore a sparkling ruby **ring.**
6. *chili*   This bowl of **chili** is too spicy!
7. *chilly*   A **chilly** wind blew the leaves.
8. *scent*   The **scent** of lilacs filled the air.
9. *sent*   Brian **sent** a post card from Paris.
10. *cent*   A **cent** is also called a penny.

11. *oversees*   The foreman **oversees** our work.
12. *overseas*   Some students study **overseas.**
13. *patients*   They are Dr. Smith's **patients.**
14. *patience*   Teaching children takes **patience.**
15. *cereal*   Kate eats wheat **cereal** for breakfast.
16. *serial*   The TV **serial** lasted six weeks.
17. *coarse*   Pretzels are coated with **coarse** salt.
18. *course*   The lost ship had got off **course.**
19. *counsel*   You need the **counsel** of a lawyer.
20. *council*   City **council** meetings are often noisy.

■ **PRACTICE** First write the homophone groups that are most confusing for you. Then write the rest of the homophones.

■ **WRITE** Choose two sentences to include in a paragraph.

1. _____
2. _____
3. _____
4. _____
5. _____
6. _____
7. _____
8. _____
9. _____
10. _____
11. _____
12. _____
13. _____
14. _____
15. _____
16. _____
17. _____
18. _____
19. _____
20. _____

CHALLENGE!

martial	marshal
bizarre	bazaar
discreet	discrete

✳ **WATCH OUT FOR FREQUENTLY MISSPELLED WORDS!**

HOMOPHONE SENTENCES   Write the homophone pair that completes each sentence.

The (1) sitting in the doctor's waiting room need lots of (2).

I only like to eat (3) when it is (4) outside.

The student (5) voted to create a committee of volunteers who could (6) new students.

The general (7) the troops that are stationed (8).

When she is nervous, Mona will either (9) her hands or twist and twirl the (10) on her finger.

WORD CHOICE   Write the correct list word for each sentence.

11. The bike-racing (course, coarse) is paved with asphalt.
12. A horse's mane is (course, coarse) and long.
13. Isabelle's favorite breakfast food is (serial, cereal).
14. Tonight Jesse plans to watch a (serial, cereal) drama on TV.
15. Mom would like (their, they're) phone numbers.
16. Are you sure (their, they're) going to be back for lunch?
17. Are the books over (their, there) yours or hers?
18. Marissa held the roses to breathe in their (sent, scent).
19. Harold (sent, scent) us a postcard while he was on vacation.
20. Reilly said his old hat wasn't even worth one (cent, sent), but he wouldn't sell it for a million dollars.

Strategic Spelling

Using the Memory Tricks Strategy

Use memory tricks to help you use homophones correctly. Create homophone sentences for each pair or triplet below.

21. serial—cereal _____

22. scent—sent—cent _____

23. course—coarse _____

1. _____
2. _____
3. _____
4. _____
5. _____
6. _____
7. _____
8. _____
9. _____
10. _____
11. _____
12. _____
13. _____
14. _____
15. _____
16. _____
17. _____
18. _____
19. _____
20. _____

FREQUENTLY MISSPELLED WORDS *FREQUENTLY MISSPELLED WORDS*

Students often get *there* and *their* mixed up. Remember *here* is in *there*, and think of this: I looked for it <u>here</u>, but it was over <u>there</u>.

≡	Make a capital.
/	Make a small letter.
∧	Add something.
ℓ	Take out something.
⊙	Add a period.
⫟	New paragraph

PROOFREAD FOR USAGE Two sentences shouldn't run together with only a comma or no punctuation between them. For example:

Crunchos is a crispy blend of corn and oats, it is delicious.

Check for Run-on Sentences Read each sentence. If a sentence is a run-on, write "RO." If a sentence is correct, write "Correct."

1.

2.

3.

4.

5.

1. It's a whole-grain cereal, you'll love the nutty taste.
2. People who are smart starters begin their day with Crunchos.
3. There are no artificial ingredients, this is a healthy cereal.
4. Kids will love the way it tastes and stays crispy in milk.
5. Crunchos provides vitamins fruit adds even more nutrition.

PROOFREAD AN ADVERTISEMENT Find the six misspelled words and write them correctly. Some may be words you learned before. Also fix three run-on sentences.

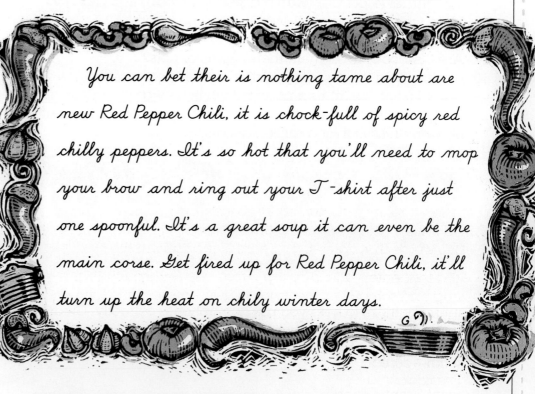

You can bet their is nothing tame about are new Red Pepper Chili, it is chock-full of spicy red chilly peppers. It's so hot that you'll need to mop your brow and ring out your T-shirt after just one spoonful. It's a great soup it can even be the main corse. Get fired up for Red Pepper Chili, it'll turn up the heat on chily winter days.

Word List

oversees	chili
overseas	chilly
wring	their
ring	there
patients	they're
patience	scent
cereal	sent
serial	cent
coarse	counsel
course	council

Personal Words

1.

2.

WRITE AN ADVERTISEMENT Plan and write an advertisement. Use three list words and a personal word.

Review

WORDS IN CONTEXT Complete each sentence with words from the box.

If you're looking for your books, I think (1) over (2).
Skunks are animals easily identified by (3) (4).
The (5) fall weather made me hungry for (6).
In the box of trinkets we found an antique wedding (7)
but not one single (8).
After the thunderstorm, all the campers were (9) to (10)
out the towels that had been left outside.

their	
there	
they're	
wring	
ring	
chili	
chilly	
scent	
sent	
cent	

1. _____   6. _____

2. _____   7. _____

3. _____   8. _____

4. _____   9. _____

5. _____   10. _____

Multicultural Connection

LANGUAGES There are many English words that come from **Spanish** words. Many of these words refer to foods, landforms, and farm implements commonly seen in the southwestern United States, which for a long time was part of Mexico. A few English words that come from Spanish are listed in the box.

chili	ranch
lariat	cafeteria

A word that enters one language from another can change spelling and sometimes meaning in the process. Write the English word from the box that each item refers to.

1. It comes from *la reata,* a Spanish word meaning "the rope." In English it means "a long, noosed rope used to catch livestock."
2. It comes from *rancho,* a Spanish word meaning "a group that eats together." In English it means "a large farm."
3. It comes from the Spanish word *chile,* a red pepper pod used in cooking for its spicy flavor.
4. In Spanish it means "coffee shop." In English it means "a restaurant where people serve themselves."

1. _____

2. _____

3. _____

4. _____

Unexpected Consonant Spellings

Sometimes two or three letters together stand for only one consonant sound: **dou_b_t**, **_sc_ience**, **autu_mn_**, **guilty**, **lea_gue_**.

■ **STUDY** Say each word. Then read the sentence.

1. doubt — I have a **doubt** about his honesty.
2. fascinate — Magicians' tricks **fascinate** people.
3. science — Use exact measures in **science**.
4. scenic — We picnicked by the **scenic** lake.
5. autumn — Leaves turn colors in **autumn**.
6. column — Add this **column** of numbers.
7. guilty — The jury believed he was **guilty**.
8. league — The voters formed a **league**.
9. guardian — Rob's uncle became his **guardian**.
10. disguise — The movie star wore a **disguise**.

11. subtle — The twins' differences are **subtle**.
12. debt — Mia repaid her **debt** of ten dollars.
13. reminiscent — Toys are **reminiscent** of childhood.
14. descend — Please **descend** the staircase slowly.
15. condemn — I **condemn** cruelty to animals.
16. solemn — The funeral ceremony was **solemn**.
17. guidance — We can do the job with **guidance**.
18. vague — Trees were **vague** shapes in the fog.
19. fatigue — After I ran four miles, **fatigue** set in.
20. intrigue — The spy movie was full of **intrigue**.

■ **PRACTICE** Sort the words by writing
- five words with **sc**
- three words with **bt**
- eight words with **gu** or **gue**
- four words with **mn**

■ **WRITE** Choose ten words to write in sentences.

1. _____
2. _____
3. _____
4. _____
5. _____
6. _____
7. _____
8. _____
9. _____
10. _____
11. _____
12. _____
13. _____
14. _____
15. _____
16. _____
17. _____
18. _____
19. _____
20. _____

CHALLENGE!

indebtedness
susceptible
discipline
misguided
monologue

ANTONYMS   Write the list word that completes each phrase.

1. not joking, but ___
2. not clear, but ___
3. not certainty, but ___
4. not forgive, but ___
5. not innocent, but ___
6. not obvious, but ___

ASSOCIATIONS   Write the list word that is associated with each word below.

7. mask
8. baseball
9. sleep
10. counselor
11. microscope
12. view
13. leaves

CLASSIFYING   Write the list word that belongs in each group.

14. plot, scheme, ___
15. pillar, post, ___
16. protector, keeper, ___
17. remember, memory, ___
18. bills, obligation, ___
19. charm, delight, ___
20. drop, sink, ___

Strategic Spelling

Seeing Meaning Connections

undoubtedly
doubter
doubtful

21. Write the list word that is related in spelling and meaning to the words in the box.

_____

Complete the sentences with words from the box.

If you were (22) of a fact you read in a newspaper article, then, (23), you would want to check other sources. If the other sources confirmed the fact stated in the article, you would stop being a (24).

22. _____

23. _____

24. _____

1. _____
2. _____
3. _____
4. _____
5. _____
6. _____
7. _____
8. _____
9. _____
10. _____
11. _____
12. _____
13. _____
14. _____
15. _____
16. _____
17. _____
18. _____
19. _____
20. _____

Take a Hint
In the word *columnist* you can hear the **n.** Think of *columnist* when spelling the word *column* and you won't forget the **n.**

	Make a capital.
/	Make a small letter.
∧	Add something.
ℓ	Take out something.
⊙	Add a period.
¶	New paragraph

PROOFREAD FOR PUNCTUATION

Use commas after greetings and closings and to set off a direct address.

Mrs. Twostar please bring your family.

Check Commas If a comma is missing, write the word after which a comma is needed. If an item is correct, write "Correct."

1. Dear Mrs. Twostar
2. I would like you to attend my barbecue Mrs. Twostar.
3. We will grill chicken, hot dogs, and hamburgers.
4. Very truly yours

1. _____

2. _____

3. _____

4. _____

PROOFREAD AN INVITATION

Find the four misspelled words in this invitation and write them correctly. These errors may be list words or words you learned before. Fix three comma errors.

October 18, 20__

Dear Faculty

You are invited too the autum masquerade party this Friday evening. Wear your best disgise. There is a prize for the most outrageous costum, so don't be subtle teachers!

Sincerely

The Party Committee

Word List

vague	solemn
fascinate	doubt
autumn	intrigue
league	descend
science	guardian
guidance	column
reminiscent	guilty
condemn	debt
fatigue	disguise
subtle	scenic

Personal Words

1. _____

2. _____

WRITE AN INVITATION

Plan and write an invitation to an upcoming event. Use three list words and a personal word.

Review

CLASSIFYING   Write the list word that belongs in each group.

1. math, history, ___
2. spring, summer, ___
3. question, suspect, ___
4. association, union, ___
5. mask, costume, ___

6. picturesque, pleasing, ___
7. pillar, row, ___
8. protector, defender, ___
9. chargeable, to blame, ___
10. delight, charm, ___

1. _____
2. _____
3. _____
4. _____
5. _____

6. _____
7. _____
8. _____
9. _____
10. _____

doubt
fascinate
science
scenic
autumn
column
guilty
league
guardian
disguise

Word *Study*

SYNONYMS   **Synonyms** are words with almost, but not quite, the same meaning. When you write, use the right synonym to say exactly what you want to say.

Write each of these synonyms under the list word where it belongs: **weariness, charm, exhaustion, grim, thrill, noble.**

fascinate	fatigue	solemn
1. _____	3. _____	5. _____
2. _____	4. _____	6. _____

Now choose the synonym for *fascinate, fatigue,* or *solemn* that you think best fits each sentence.

This true story about an adventurer will **(7) fascinate** you. She tells of her **(8) fatigue** while climbing the world's highest mountains and the exhilaration she feels when reaching their **(9) solemn** peaks. She is **(10) solemn** when she shares her exploration team's struggle for survival in the Antarctic. Her spirit will **(11) fascinate** you, and her unending energy will either bring on **(12) fatigue** or get you revved up for an adventure of your own.

7. _____
8. _____
9. _____
10. _____
11. _____
12. _____

One Consonant or Two?

SPELLING FOCUS

Many words have double consonants that stand for only one sound: **college, address.**

■ **STUDY**   Say each word. Then read the sentence.

1.	*connect*	The two lakes **connect** at the dam.
2.	*command*	I can **command** my dog to sit.
3.	*mirror*	A **mirror** reflects your image.
4.	*accomplish*	I hope to **accomplish** my goals.
5.	*according*	Dress **according** to the weather.
6.	*allowance*	Try to save half your **allowance.**
7.	*college* ✳	Dee attends a community **college.**
8.	*address*	Put your name and **address** here.
9.	*Mississippi*	St. Louis is on the **Mississippi** River.
10.	*recess*	We played kickball during **recess.**

11.	*committee*	A **committee** studied the problem.
12.	*immediate*	His **immediate** answer was "Yes!"
13.	*barricade*	A police **barricade** stopped traffic.
14.	*interrupt*	Don't let us **interrupt** your game.
15.	*broccoli*	The vegetable today is **broccoli.**
16.	*collect*	Troop 75 will **collect** canned food.
17.	*afford*	I can't **afford** that brand of shoes.
18.	*possess*	The Millers **possess** a sense of pride.
19.	*Tennessee*	Eastern **Tennessee** is quite hilly.
20.	*announce*	They **announce** the winner today.

■ **PRACTICE**   Sort the words by writing
- five words with two or three sets of double consonants
- five other words with double **s, m,** or **n**
- ten words with double **c, r, l,** or **f**

■ **WRITE**   Choose two sentences to write rhymes.

CHALLENGE!

dilemma
embarrassment
compassionately
unnecessarily
accompaniment

1.
2.
3.
4.
5.
6.
7.
8.
9.
10.
11.
12.
13.
14.
15.
16.
17.
18.
19.
20.

✳ **WATCH OUT FOR FREQUENTLY MISSPELLED WORDS!**

ANALOGIES Write list words to complete the analogies.

1. Fruit is to apple as vegetable is to ___.
2. Creation is to create as accomplishment is to ___.
3. Ocean is to Atlantic as river is to ___.
4. Disappear is to appear as disconnect is to ___.
5. City is to Memphis as state is to ___.
6. Jobs are to salary as chores are to ___.
7. Request is to ask as order is to ___.
8. Rent is to borrow as own is to ___.
9. Customers are to restaurant as students are to ___.
10. Cafeteria is to lunch as playground is to ___.
11. Opening up is to passageway as closing off is to ___.
12. Later is to eventual as now is to ___.
13. Car is to license plate as house is to ___.
14. Lovingly is to loving as accordingly is to ___.

1. _____
2. _____
3. _____
4. _____
5. _____
6. _____
7. _____
8. _____
9. _____
10. _____
11. _____
12. _____
13. _____
14. _____

CROSSWORD PUZZLE Use the clues to help you fill in the puzzle with list words.

ACROSS
15. proclaim or report
16. a deciding group
17. able to pay

DOWN
18. looking glass
19. talk out of turn
20. gather

Strategic Spelling

Using the Memory Tricks Strategy

Use memory tricks to help you spell. Choose two list words that are difficult for you. Identify the parts of these words that give you problems. Then create memory tricks for those words. Underline the matching letters in the list words and helpers.

21. _____

22. _____

Memphis 64 MI

Make a capital.	≡
Make a small letter.	/
Add something.	∧
Take out something.	ℓ
Add a period.	⊙
New paragraph	⨏

1. _____

2. _____

3. _____

4. _____

5. _____

PROOFREAD FOR CAPITALIZATION

Capitalize nouns that name cities, states, and street and highway names. For example:

> You will bypass rockford, illinois, if you
>
> take U.S. route 20.

Check Proper Nouns Read each sentence. Correctly write words that should be capitalized. If a sentence is correct, write "Correct."

1. Follow U.S. Highway Route 20 to the city of stockton.
2. Keep going through Elizabeth, illinois.
3. Continue on until you get to Galena, Illinois.
4. Detour at the construction barricade west of galena.
5. The address is 641 Heller drive, Frentress, Illinois.

PROOFREAD DIRECTIONS
Find the eight misspelled words in these directions and write them correctly. Some may be words you learned before. Three errors are capitalization errors.

> To get to Rhodes College in memphis, Tennesse, from coldwater, Mississipi, take Interstate 55 north into tennessee intill it connects with Interstate 240. Interstate 240 will conect with U. S. Route 70. Follow Route 70 east to the collage.

Word List

barricade	accomplish
mirror	according
interrupt	broccoli
Mississippi	allowance
recess	collect
possess	college
address	immediate
Tennessee	command
announce	committee
connect	afford

Personal Words

1. _____

2. _____

WRITE DIRECTIONS
Think about some place you would like to visit, and then plan and write directions from your home to that place. Try to use three spelling words and a personal word.

Review

MEANING CLUES   Write the list word that answers each question.

1. Which word names a school of higher learning?
2. What is another word for *looking glass?*
3. What is 1600 Pennsylvania Avenue?
4. Which word names both a state and a river?
5. Which word means "join"?
6. Which word might involve a payment of money?
7. Which word is a synonym of *order?*
8. Which word names something that takes place in elementary schools and courts of law?
9. Which word means almost the same as *achieve?*
10. Which word is usually followed by "to" and means "in agreement with"?

connect	
command	
mirror	
accomplish	
according	
allowance	
college	
address	
Mississippi	
recess	

1. _____
2. _____
3. _____
4. _____
5. _____

6. _____
7. _____
8. _____
9. _____
10. _____

Word *Study*

LATIN ROOTS: MOVEMENT WORDS   The list word *recess* and the rest of the words in the box come from the Latin root **cess**, sometimes spelled **ced**. Each of these words has something to do with movement, because **cess** and **ced** mean "to move."

recess	antecedent
process	concede
exceed	secede

Write the word that comes from

1. the Latin *sēcēdere,* "to withdraw"
2. the Latin *excēdere,* "to go beyond"
3. the Latin *concēdere,* "to yield"

Write the word that means

4. "a set of actions that proceed in a certain order"
5. "a stopping from usual work or study"
6. "going before" (the prefix **ante-** means "before")

1. _____
2. _____
3. _____
4. _____
5. _____
6. _____

Using Apostrophes

SPELLING FOCUS

An apostrophe takes the place of omitted letters in contractions: **we'd.** An apostrophe is used in forming possessives: **coach's, coaches', men's.**

■ **STUDY** Say each word. Then read the sentence.

1. *it's* ✳   **It's** not too late to join the club.
2. *let's* ✳   **Let's** invite them to the party.
3. *that's* ✳   **That's** an excellent idea.
4. *we'd*   **We'd** already finished dinner.
5. *don't* ✳   Dogs **don't** forget their owners.
6. *there's* ✳   **There's** no reason to yell.
7. *coach's*   The **coach's** outlook is cheerful.
8. *coaches'*   Two **coaches'** shirts are included.
9. *man's*   A **man's** shoes would fit him.
10. *men's*   The **men's** baseball game is today.

11. *you're* ✳   **You're** welcome to join us.
12. *she'd*   I thought **she'd** never stop the car.
13. *mustn't*   Children **mustn't** play with fire.
14. *o'clock*   At two **o'clock** the bell will ring.
15. *guide's*   The **guide's** speech was great.
16. *guides'*   All **guides'** tours end by the gate.
17. *director's*   A **director's** chair is comfortable.
18. *directors'*   Both **directors'** movies are respected.
19. *city's*   This **city's** roads need repair.
20. *cities'*   The **cities'** mayors met to consult.

■ **PRACTICE** Sort the words by writing
- six contractions ending in **'s** or **'d**
- four other listed contractions
- five singular possessive nouns
- five plural possessive nouns

■ **WRITE** Choose two sentences to include in a dialogue.

1. _____
2. _____
3. _____
4. _____
5. _____
6. _____
7. _____
8. _____
9. _____
10. _____
11. _____
12. _____
13. _____
14. _____
15. _____
16. _____
17. _____
18. _____
19. _____
20. _____

CHALLENGE!

millionaire's
millionaires'
roommate's
roommates'
New Year's Eve

✳ **WATCH OUT FOR FREQUENTLY MISSPELLED WORDS!**

CONTRACTIONS Write the contractions for the underlined words in the sentences.

1. When <u>it is</u> finished, the house will look great.
2. If you try your best, <u>that is</u> all you can do.
3. She shouted, "Before it starts raining, <u>let us</u> run to the car."
4. If we <u>had</u> only listened to the radio, we could have won.
5. When <u>you are</u> ready, ask Vivian to drive you home.
6. Yesterday <u>she would</u> have been able to work for me.
7. If <u>there is</u> anything Diego can do, he would be glad to help.
8. I <u>do not</u> enter my sister's room when her door is closed.
9. Malcolm <u>must not</u> want to go to the zoo.
10. Will you be ready at six <u>of the clock</u>?

POSSESSIVES Write the correct possessive form of each noun in parentheses to complete each sentence.

11. The tour (guides) bright uniforms helped us spot them easily.
12. The oldest (guide) knowledge of the trails amazed me.
13. The team met to hear the assistant (coach) pep talk.
14. Both (coaches) decision was to have Sumi play shortstop.
15. That (man) garden is full of vegetables and herbs.
16. Next week the (men) bowling tournament begins.
17. The twin (cities) parades were held on the same day.
18. They finally expanded our (city) main highway.
19. The choir (director) suggestion was to sing loudly and smile.
20. Several (directors) movies were shown at the festival.

Building New Words

| 1. _____ |
| 2. _____ |
| 3. _____ |
| 4. _____ |
| 5. _____ |
| 6. _____ |
| 7. _____ |
| 8. _____ |
| 9. _____ |
| 10. _____ |
| 11. _____ |
| 12. _____ |
| 13. _____ |
| 14. _____ |
| 15. _____ |
| 16. _____ |
| 17. _____ |
| 18. _____ |
| 19. _____ |
| 20. _____ |

Add the contraction for *had* or *would* to the base words. Remember what you learned.

Base Word   **Contraction with -'d**

21. I   _____

22. you   _____

23. he   _____

24. they   _____

FREQUENTLY MISSPELLED WORDS ✳ FREQUENTLY MISSPELLED WORDS ✳

Don't confuse *your* and *you're*. If you can substitute "you are" in the sentence, then use "you're." If not, use "your."

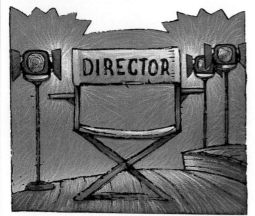

PROOFREAD FOR USAGE *Good* is an adjective and *well* is an adverb. Don't use one in place of the other.

> The actors were good. They played their parts well.

Check Adjectives and Adverbs Read each sentence. Write "Incorrect" if *good* or *well* is used incorrectly. Write "Correct" if *good* or *well* is used correctly.

1. It's a play that was written good.
2. There's good humor and suspense at the same time.
3. The woman who plays Ms. Constance acts good.
4. The suspense really picks up good after the first act.
5. The director's brief appearance in the play went well too.

1. _____
2. _____
3. _____
4. _____
5. _____

PROOFREAD A REVIEW Find the five misspelled words in the rest of the review. These errors may be list words or words you learned before. Also fix three errors with *good* or *well*.

> It's a good play, but I didnt like everything about it that good. The dead man's name is never revealed, and thats confusing. Also, the mens' locker room is a strange place for a murder. Lets just say I had a few complaints. I liked the play's plot really good, and the actors performed good. All in all, the play went well.

Word List

don't	coach's
mustn't	coaches'
it's	city's
let's	cities'
that's	director's
there's	directors'
she'd	guide's
we'd	guides'
you're	man's
o'clock	men's

Personal Words

1. _____

2. _____

WRITE A REVIEW Write a review of a movie or TV show you've seen. Try to use three list words and a personal word.

Review

WORDS IN CONTEXT   Write the list word that is missing from each person's statement.

1. Football fan: "That quarterback is a ___ dream."
2. Babysitter: "Why ___ we go inside now?"
3. Magician: "Now ___ see how many rabbits are in this hat."
4. Commissioner: "Four ___ contracts will expire this season."
5. Consumer: "I think ___ better ask about the warranty."
6. Club attendant: "The ___ locker room is straight ahead."
7. Hotel guest: "We've looked everywhere and ___ positively no soap."
8. Vendor: "One ___ junk is another person's treasure."
9. Painter: "Please don't go near that wall until ___ dry."
10. Judge: "It's the law and ___ all there is to it."

1. _____
2. _____
3. _____
4. _____
5. _____
6. _____
7. _____
8. _____
9. _____
10. _____

Word *Study*

INITIALS AND ACRONYMS   Nine o'clock in the morning is nine A.M. The initials *A.M.* stand for <u>ante meridiem</u>, which means "before noon." The initials *P.M.* stand for *post meridiem*, which means "after noon." In English there are many other **initials** and **acronyms**, or words formed from the first letters or syllables of other words. Some of these are listed below.

VIP	**R.S.V.P.**	**scuba**	**FYI**	**sonar**
BLT	**A.S.A.P.**	**radar**	**a.k.a.**	**P.S.**

Read these notes a boss wrote to her executive assistant. Write the initials and acronyms in the list above that stand for the underlined words. Use the Spelling Dictionary if you need help.

1. Distribute yesterday's meeting notes <u>as soon as possible</u>.
2. Ms. Grey, a <u>very important person</u> from our corporate headquarters, will be at tomorrow's meeting.
3. Mr. Conrad, <u>also known as</u> "The Terminator," will be there too, so be prepared!
4. Read up on <u>sound navigation ranging</u> for the meeting.
5. Make copies of the article on <u>radio detecting and ranging</u>.
6. <u>Répondez s'il vous plaît</u> to Mr. Diaz.
7. Order <u>bacon, lettuce, and tomato</u> sandwiches for our lunch.
8. <u>For your information</u>: I'll be on vacation next week.
9. Please call the sporting goods store to see if my <u>self-contained underwater breathing apparatus</u> gear is ready.
10. <u>Postscript</u>: Try to have a relaxing day!

1. _____
2. _____
3. _____
4. _____
5. _____
6. _____
7. _____
8. _____
9. _____
10. _____

Compound Words 1

Some compounds are written as one word: **myself.** Others are written as two words: **tape recorder.**

■ **STUDY** Say each word. Then read the sentence.

1. myself ✻   I like to spend time by **myself.**
2. themselves ✻   They think of **themselves** as lucky.
3. hallway   Walk single file in the **hallway.**
4. homeroom   I have Ms. Hill for **homeroom.**
5. everything ✻   We have **everything** we need.
6. ice cream   Is that **ice cream** or frozen yogurt?
7. locker room   Towels are in the **locker room.**
8. tape recorder   The reporter held a **tape recorder.**
9. root beer   He had hot dogs and **root beer.**
10. dead end   Our school's street is a **dead end.**

11. teenage   It's a new **teenage** hair style.
12. teammate   The pitcher thanked each **teammate.**
13. skateboard   Lori does tricks on her **skateboard.**
14. everybody ✻   I gave **everybody** in class a book.
15. doughnut   I ate a chocolate **doughnut.**
16. air conditioner   The **air conditioner** cooled us off.
17. polka dot   His tie had one green **polka dot.**
18. roller coaster   They love riding on a **roller coaster.**
19. ice pack   Use an **ice pack** on the swelling.
20. solar system   Our **solar system** has nine planets.

■ **PRACTICE** Sort the words by writing
- the ten closed compounds in alphabetical order
- the ten open compounds in alphabetical order

■ **WRITE** Choose two sentences to include in a paragraph.

CHALLENGE!

turtleneck
sweatshirt
brokenhearted
money order
health food

1. tape-recorder
2. them-selves
3. every-thing
4. every-body
5. ice-cream
6. ice-pack
7.
8.
9.
10.
11.
12.
13.
14.
15.
16.
17.
18.
19.
20.

   ✻ **WATCH OUT FOR FREQUENTLY MISSPELLED WORDS!**

DRAWING CONCLUSIONS Write the list word that answers each question.

1. What carnival ride has many ups and downs?
2. What includes the sun and all the planets?
3. What do you call someone who plays on your squad?
4. What can cool a room on a hot summer day?
5. What can reproduce sounds and voices?
6. What kind of soda pop has a lot of foam when it's poured?
7. What is a round spot that is repeated to form a pattern?

JOINING WORDS Find two words in each sentence that can be joined to make a list word. Write the word.

8. Can you find your way down the hall?
9. The whipped cream was as cold as ice.
10. At the end of the path you will see a dead oak tree.
11. I like to put a nut on top of the muffin dough before baking.
12. Alma's favorite room at home is the kitchen.
13. One thing we enjoy every year is the class picnic.
14. Tell them that the plural of *self* is *selves*.
15. You can skate until you see the sign on the board that says "No Skating."
16. Is the room with only one locker yours?
17. Did you pack the soft drinks in the cooler with plenty of ice?
18. Her father's body shop has every auto part you'd ever need.
19. In my opinion, he's not like his former self.
20. The latest teen hairstyles are even popular with kids your little sister's age.

Seeing Meaning Connections

1. _____
2. _____
3. _____
4. _____
5. _____
6. _____
7. _____
8. _____
9. _____
10. _____
11. _____
12. _____
13. _____
14. _____
15. _____
16. _____
17. _____
18. _____
19. _____
20. _____

Write the words from the box that fit the clues.

Words with *air*
air conditioner
air bag
air mattress

21. floats on water _____

22. safety device in car _____

23. regulates air temperature

_____

Everybody and *everything* are often misspelled. Remember to include the second **e**, even though you don't hear it.

FREQUENTLY MISSPELLED WORDS ✱ FREQUENTLY MISSPELLED WORDS ✱ FREQUENTLY MISSPELLED WORDS

PROOFREAD FOR CARELESS ERRORS

Be careful not to add or drop letters from words.

If your need us, the phon number is on the message board.

Check for Added or Dropped Letters For each sentence, write correctly words with added or dropped letters.

1. Both of the boys have fed themselves super already.
2. Please read a story to the boys at beddtime.
3. Help youself to a doughnut or any other snacks.
4. We won't be home any latter than 11:00.

1. _____

2. _____

3. _____

4. _____

PROOFREAD A NOTE

Find the eight misspelled words in this note and write them correctly. These errors may be list words or words you learned before. Three of them are careless errors.

> Norio,
>
> As your can see, everbody is gon. We'll be home in a few hours. Help yourself to the rootbear and vanilla icecream in the refrigerator. Feel free to use your cousin's skatboard or just watch teevee. Turn on the air conditioner if it get too hot.
>
> Aunt Reiko

Word List

hallway	ice cream
teenage	air conditioner
teammate	locker room
everybody	polka dot
everything	roller coaster
skateboard	tape recorder
homeroom	ice pack
doughnut	solar system
myself	root beer
themselves	dead end

Personal Words

1. _____

2. _____

WRITE A NOTE
Write a note to a friend or family member. Use three list words and a personal word.

Review

PARAGRAPH COMPLETION   Complete the diary entry.

Today was awful, but I have only (1) to blame. At school I was walking down the (2) toward my (3). Right in front of the boys' (4), I dropped (5) I was carrying. That included the (6) I needed to use for sound effects with my science project. It broke.

After school, I stopped for a big scoop of (7). Two four-year-olds were sitting by (8) near the door. One spilled (9) all over my shoes.

Then I took a shortcut home and wouldn't you know the street I chose was a (10)!

myself
themselves
hallway
homeroom
everything
ice cream
locker room
tape recorder
root beer
dead end

1. _____   6. _____

2. _____   7. _____

3. _____   8. _____

4. _____   9. _____

5. _____   10. _____

Word *Study*

IDIOMS   An idiom is an expression whose meaning can't be understood from the ordinary meanings of the words that form it. For example, the idiom *hold everything* doesn't mean "grab onto everything in sight." It means "stop what you are doing." The box has some more idioms you may have heard. To find their meanings, look up the underlined part in the Spelling Dictionary.

all **ears**	smell a **rat**	**life** of Riley	**silver**-tongued

Write the idiom that completes each sentence below.

1. I'm ready to listen, or you might say I'm ___.
2. Andrew's speech was great. He's certainly ___.
3. When we were at the beach, Mom said, "This is the ___."
4. I knew Haruo was suspicious when he said he could ___.

1. _____

2. _____

3. _____

4. _____

Review

Lesson 7: Homophones
Lesson 8: Unexpected Consonant Spellings
Lesson 9: One Consonant or Two?
Lesson 10: Using Apostrophes
Lesson 11: Compound Words 1

REVIEW WORD LIST

1. cent
2. cereal
3. chili
4. doubt
5. overseas
6. scent
7. sent
8. there
9. autumn
10. debt
11. descend
12. disguise
13. guidance
14. intrigue
15. league
16. reminiscent
17. scenic
18. science
19. solemn
20. accomplish
21. according
22. afford
23. allowance
24. barricade
25. broccoli
26. collect
27. college
28. mirror
29. coach's
30. don't
31. it's
32. man's
33. mustn't
34. o'clock
35. that's
36. there's
37. air conditioner
38. dead end
39. doughnut
40. everything
41. hallway
42. ice cream
43. ice pack
44. locker room
45. myself
46. roller coaster
47. root beer
48. solar system
49. tape recorder
50. teammate

■ PROOFREADING

Find the spelling errors in each passage and write the words correctly. All passages have seven errors except the last one, which has eight.

PROOFREAD A JOURNAL ENTRY

1. _____
2. _____
3. _____
4. _____
5. _____
6. _____
7. _____

Yesterday when I got my alowance, Marta and I went to buy chocolate yogurt after school. I had to pay off a det before I could spend one sent, however. Last week my brother loaned me some money to help pay for a taperecorder for Mom's birthday. I am now making a solem promise to my self not to buy what I can't aford.

PROOFREAD AN INTERVIEW

Reporter: *Last year you were part of a team that was tops in the Elmwood City leage. How do things look for the team this autum?*

Paul Jackson: The coachs' gidense this summer has really helped. He made us work on our passing. I think things look good.

Reporter: *Do you have any new players this season?*

Jackson: We have one new team mate, a kicker.

Reporter: *You had a knee injury last year. I noticed in the lockeroom that you had an icpack on that knee. Is it OK?*

Jackson: Yes it is. I just had a little soreness after practice, but the doctor says my knee is fine.

Reporter: *Thanks for talking to me. Good luck!*

1. _____
2. _____
3. _____
4. _____
5. _____
6. _____
7. _____

PROOFREAD A SCIENCE REPORT

A new radio telescope spread across 5,000 miles has ten antennas with which scientists hope to acomplish research never before possible. The system is called the Very Long Baseline Array (VLBA), and its antennas are scattered across North America. The antennas function as a single telescope. Several government agencies expect to colect data from VLBA. This data will be cent to a center in New Mexico and processed by a powerful computer. Radio telescopes can reach far beyond optical telescopes, and theres no dought that this one will make exciting discoveries. Perhaps it will even discover a new solrsystem, acording to one scientist.

1. _____
2. _____
3. _____
4. _____
5. _____
6. _____
7. _____

PROOFREAD A MENU

Pine Tree Patio
Great eating on senic Lake James

Open from June 15 to September 15
Light Breakfast and Lunch served daily from 9-3

Soups
cream of brocolli	$1.25
vegetarian chilly	$1.30
chicken noodle	$1.25

Breakfast
cold or hot serial	$ .75
dough nut	$ .95
bran muffin	$ .95

Salads
pasta salad	$4.95
spinach salad	$4.50
chicken salad	$5.50

Desserts
peach icecream	$1.50
blueberry pie	$1.75

Beverages
fruit juices	$1.25
rootbeer	$1.15
milk	$ .75

Sandwiches
grilled cheese	$3.95
sliced turkey	$4.95

PROOFREAD AN ADVERTISEMENT

The following items will be for sale at 5173 N. Kingston on September 11 beginning promptly at nine oclock. Almost every thing is like new. All items must go, and their will be bargains.

antiques	children's sience kit
mans' diamond ring	collage textbooks
porch swing	airconditioner
dining room furniture	outdoor grill
appliances	numerous small household items

PROOFREAD A BOOK REVIEW

The Mystery at Lockwood Hall is about a girl named Rachel who flies oversees to visit her grandmother in England. When Rachel gets to Lockwood Hall, a strange woman answers the door and says Rachel's grandmother is not there. Rachel follows the woman down a long hall way and into a sitting room. After the woman leaves, Rachel thinks she sees her grandmother reflected in a miror, but when she turns around, no one is there. There is a strong sent in the air, somewhat reminisent of dead roses. Can the strange woman be her grandmother in disgise? I can't reveal the ending, but if you like intrige, you will like this book.

1. _____
2. _____
3. _____
4. _____
5. _____
6. _____
7. _____

PROOFREAD A POEM

SKATEBOARD RIDE

Jump on.
Take a spin.
Then its over the curb
And do it again.
Next, desend the hill,
And round the curve.
Yes, thats hard.
It surely takes nerve.
Jump up.
Turn around.
Now I'm rolling, but
I'm homeward bound.

I must'nt hit
The baricade.
Easy now;
I've got it made.
I dont want to panic,
But I'm going faster.
I'm a rollercoaster
Heading for disaster.
Slow down now.
Take the bend.
Oh my goodness—
deadend!

1. _____
2. _____
3. _____
4. _____
5. _____
6. _____
7. _____
8. _____

Using Meaning Helpers

DISCOVER THE STRATEGY Word pairs like *allow* and *allowance* are related in spelling and meaning. You can use the shorter word as a **meaning helper**—a clue to help you spell the longer word. For example:

Longer Word	Helper	Clue
allowance	allow	allowance = allow + ance
universal	universe	universal = universe – e + al

TRY IT OUT Tell how the helper reminds you of how to spell the longer word. Be sure to note any spelling changes that take place between the two words.

Longer Word	Helper	Clue
1. lemonade	lemon	**lemon + ade**
2. descendant	descend	**descend + ant**
3. valuable	value	**value – e + able**
4. clumsily	clumsy	**clumsy – y + ily**
5. affordable	afford	**afford + able**
6. scientist	science	**science – ce + tist**
7. commandment	command	**command + ment**

Some meaning helpers give sound clues by reminding you how a certain sound is spelled in the longer word. For example:

Longer Word	Helper	Clue
admirable	admire	The **long i** in *admire* reminds me that *admirable* is spelled with an **i**.
recession	recess	The sound of **ss** at the end of *recess* reminds me that *recession* is spelled with an **ss**.

Work with a partner. Tell how the helper gives a sound clue for the longer word.

Longer Word	Helper	Clue
8. possession	possess	_____
9. interruption	interrupt	_____
10. composition	compose	_____

LOOK AHEAD Look ahead at the next five lessons for list words that you might use this strategy with. Find two words and write them down. Next to each one, write a meaning helper. Use this strategy when you study those words.

1. _____   _____

2. _____   _____

Words with ci and ti

■ **STUDY**   Say each word. Then read the sentence.

1.	*social*	Parties are **social** occasions.
2.	*precious*	Emeralds are **precious** stones.
3.	*commercial*	That TV **commercial** is funny.
4.	*especially* ✳	Dad **especially** likes apple pie.
5.	*national*	A band played the **national** anthem.
6.	*dictionary*	Look the word up in a **dictionary**.
7.	*motion*	The car's **motion** made us feel sick.
8.	*position*	The runners crouched in **position**.
9.	*population*	The town's **population** is growing.
10.	*question*	You have answered my **question**.

11.	*artificial*	The roses are real, not **artificial**.
12.	*financial*	A banker gave us **financial** advice.
13.	*gracious*	Be **gracious** to your guests.
14.	*glacier*	The ship struck the jagged **glacier**.
15.	*suggestion*	A longer lunch was my **suggestion**.
16.	*cautious*	Be **cautious** crossing the street.
17.	*mention*	Just **mention** this ad for a discount.
18.	*fraction*	I changed a percent to a **fraction**.
19.	*exhaustion*	Overwork leads to **exhaustion**.
20.	*digestion*	After we eat, **digestion** begins.

■ **PRACTICE**   Sort the list words by writing
- eight words with **ci**
- twelve words with **ti**

■ **WRITE**   Choose four sentences to rewrite as questions.

CHALLENGE!

malicious
precocious
sensational
vaccination
fictitious

1. _____
2. _____
3. _____
4. _____
5. _____
6. _____
7. _____
8. _____
9. _____
10. _____
11. _____
12. _____
13. _____
14. _____
15. _____
16. _____
17. _____
18. _____
19. _____
20. _____

✳ **WATCH OUT FOR FREQUENTLY MISSPELLED WORDS!**

SYNONYMS   Write the list word that means the same as each synonym below.

1. particularly
2. valuable
3. place
4. fatigue
5. courteous
6. people
7. fake
8. idea
9. query
10. advertisement
11. money matters

WORD SEARCH   12–20. Find the nine list words in the puzzle. They may be printed across or down. Write them.

```
d i c t i o n a r y m g
o s a e n g l a c i e r
f o h f r a c t i o n e
o c a u t i o u s i t b
x i r m o t i o n c i d
n a t i o n a l e j o l
e l d i g e s t i o n p
```

Strategic Spelling

Using the Meaning Helpers Strategy

A meaning helper—a shorter word related in spelling and meaning—can help you spell a longer word. For example, thinking of *suggest* will help you remember the **t** in *suggestion*. Write *gracious, exhaustion, digestion,* and *financial*. Write a meaning helper below each one and underline the matching letter that gives a sound clue.

21. _____

22. _____

23. _____

24. _____

1. _____
2. _____
3. _____
4. _____
5. _____
6. _____
7. _____
8. _____
9. _____
10. _____
11. _____
12. _____
13. _____
14. _____
15. _____
16. _____
17. _____
18. _____
19. _____
20. _____

FREQUENTLY MISSPELLED WORDS ✻ FREQUENTLY MISSPELLED WORDS ✻

Remember that the word *especially* has the word *special* in the middle of it.

≡	Make a capital.
/	Make a small letter.
∧	Add something.
ℓ	Take out something.
⊙	Add a period.
¶	New paragraph

PROOFREAD FOR USAGE Be careful to use the correct form of irregular verbs such as *eat, be,* and *have.* Also, don't write *of* when you mean *have.* For example:

I should ‸of told you my suggestion long ago.
                 have

Check Irregular Verbs Read these sentences. Correct any mistakes with verbs. If a sentence is correct, write "Correct."

1. I have ate broccoli for many years.
2. Did I mention that this vegetable have many benefits?
3. I should of told you that broccoli is a source of minerals.
4. It are especially rich in Vitamins A and C too.
5. It can be eaten every day.

1. _____

2. _____

3. _____

4. _____

5. _____

PROOFREAD A PERSUASIVE PARAGRAPH Find the six misspelled words and write them correctly. These errors may be list words or words you learned before. Fix three incorrect verbs.

I has a suggestion. We should have a nachenal campaign to get people to eat brocclii. This vegetable are rich in protien and is an important commertial crop in the Unite States. It can be ate raw or cooked, and it is espesially good in salads.

Word List

fraction	commercial
national	especially
social	cautious
exhaustion	financial
dictionary	mention
digestion	gracious
glacier	motion
artificial	precious
suggestion	position
question	population

Personal Words

1. _____

2. _____

WRITE A PERSUASIVE LETTER Write a letter to the President of the United States, with a suggestion for running the country. Use two spelling words and a personal word, and follow correct business letter form (see page 245). After proofreading your letter, copy it neatly on good paper and mail it to the White House, 1600 Pennsylvania Ave., N.W., Washington, D.C. 20500.

Review

ASSOCIATIONS   Write the list word that is associated with each pair of words below.

1. statement, answer
2. placement, ranking
3. friendly, companionable
4. movement, indication
5. citizenship, inhabitants
6. encyclopedia, thesaurus
7. particularly, chiefly
8. sponsored, advertisement
9. patriotic, countrywide
10. valuable, dear

social
precious
commercial
especially
national
dictionary
motion
position
population
question

1. _____
2. _____
3. _____
4. _____
5. _____

6. _____
7. _____
8. _____
9. _____
10. _____

Multicultural Connection

ENVIRONMENT   A glacier is a unique feature of cold environments. Every part of the world has natural features that affect how people live. The words in the box describe some features. Write the word that best completes each sentence. Use the Spelling Dictionary for help.

iceberg
arroyo
dunes
floodplain
rain forest

1. Farmers live along the low, flat ___ of the Huang He, or Yellow River, in China because of its rich soil, but they risk death and property damage each time the river floods.
2. Along the Amazon River in Brazil and Peru, heat and heavy rainfall produce the dense trees and plants of a tropical ___.
3. Oil rigs and tankers off the coast of Canada and Alaska are often at risk of being hit by an ___ floating in the ocean.
4. In the deserts of Arizona or New Mexico, it is wise not to walk in an ___ during a rainstorm, because the dry riverbed could suddenly fill with water.
5. In the Gran Desierto of Sonora, Mexico, the wind blows from many directions, stirring the sand into star-shaped ___.

1. _____
2. _____
3. _____
4. _____
5. _____

69

Easily Confused Words

SPELLING FOCUS

Some words are easily confused because they have similar pronunciations and spellings: **since, sense.**

■ **STUDY**   Say each word. Then read the sentence.

1.	*since* ✳	It has been raining **since** dawn.
2.	*sense*	Your explanation makes **sense.**
3.	*choose*	The people will **choose** a leader.
4.	*chose*	Leah **chose** a video yesterday.
5.	*finally* ✳	The snow has **finally** stopped.
6.	*finely*	Next add **finely** chopped celery.
7.	*except* ✳	Use any color **except** red.
8.	*accept*	Ted will **accept** the award for us.
9.	*beside*	A chair stood **beside** the bed.
10.	*besides*	No one has left **besides** you.

11.	*recent*	My jeans were a **recent** purchase.
12.	*resent*	Anyone would **resent** the insult.
13.	*access*	Water blocked our **access** to the park.
14.	*excess*	Later I regretted running to **excess.**
15.	*later*	The parade begins **later** today.
16.	*latter*	I prefer the **latter** to the former.
17.	*metal*	A **metal** pipe conducts heat well.
18.	*medal*	He received a **medal** for bravery.
19.	*personal*	Her **personal** mail is private.
20.	*personnel*	The firm hired more **personnel.**

■ **PRACTICE**   Write the word pairs that you use correctly. Then write the pairs that you aren't sure of. Underline the part of each word that is spelled differently from the other word in the pair.

■ **WRITE**   Choose two sentences to write rhymes or riddles.

1.
2.
3.
4.
5.
6.
7.
8.
9.
10.
11.
12.
13.
14.
15.
16.
17.
18.
19.
20.

CHALLENGE!

proceeding	preceding
envelope	envelop
immigrate	emigrate

✳ **WATCH OUT FOR FREQUENTLY MISSPELLED WORDS!**

WORD CHOICE   Write the correct list word for each sentence.

1. A cat's (since, sense) of smell is very sharp.
2. I have not seen her (since, sense) Monday.
3. No one is allowed (access, excess) to the building after dark.
4. We threw all (access, excess) cargo overboard.
5. You can't buy both hats; you have to (choose, chose) one.
6. Bill (choose, chose) the tape he liked best.
7. I hope you will (except, accept) my invitation.
8. Everyone is going (except, accept) you.
9. Two people were injured in a (recent, resent) accident.
10. I (recent, resent) that remark!
11. After many hours, Lupe (finally, finely) reached the shore.
12. The flour must be (finally, finely) ground in a mill.

CONTEXT CLUES   Write the list word that completes each sentence. Say each word carefully to help you spell it.

13. Kiko hopes to win the Olympic gold ____ in gymnastics.
14. The desk was made of wood and ____.
15. I'll write out a guest list now and buy the invitations ____.
16. Joe plays baseball and basketball, but he prefers the ____.
17. The students stood ____ their desks.
18. We have three goldfish, and we have two gerbils ____.
19. Your questions about my family are too ____.
20. All the ____ in this company are highly trained.

Strategic Spelling

Seeing Meaning Connections

Words with
accept
acceptance
acceptable
acceptably
unacceptable

Complete each sentence with a word from the box.

21. Student: I hope my paper is

_____.

22. Teacher: No, this messy work is

_____.

23. Student: How can I gain your _____?

24. Teacher: Turn in an _____ written paper.

1. _____

2. _____

3. _____

4. _____

5. _____

6. _____

7. _____

8. _____

9. _____

10. _____

11. _____

12. _____

13. _____

14. _____

15. _____

16. _____

17. _____

18. _____

19. _____

20. _____

Did You Know?
The words *resent* and *sense* both come from the
Latin word *sentire,* "to feel."

☰	Make a capital.
/	Make a small letter.
∧	Add something.
ℓ	Take out something.
⊙	Add a period.
¶	New paragraph

PROOFREAD FOR USAGE Do you see the mistake in this sentence?

I thought it was a good idea when my Dad suggests a party.

It should read "suggested." Don't switch verb tenses needlessly.

Check Verb Tenses Since Gina started with the past tense, she needs to stick with it. Correct five verbs in this passage.

I asked all my friends to my slumber party, and everyone comes except Amy. I was glad that Jessica brings her records. We all laughed when my younger brother starts singing one of his crazy songs. Dad serves us lemonade, and later we ate a pizza. We don't get to sleep until midnight.

1. _____

2. _____

3. _____

4. _____

5. _____

PROOFREAD A PERSONAL NARRATIVE Find the five misspelled words and write them correctly. Some may be words you learned before. Also fix three mistakes with verb tenses.

> On a recent weekend, I invited some friends over for the night. First, we desided to practice our dance steps. Than, we order a pizza and make a salad. Latter, we watched a video. Finely, we go to bed. Everyone had a good time accept my younger brother.

Word List

recent	except
resent	accept
choose	beside
chose	besides
access	since
excess	sense
finally	metal
finely	medal
later	personal
latter	personnel

Personal Words

1. _____

2. _____

WRITE A PERSONAL NARRATIVE Plan and write a paragraph about an important recent event in your life. Use three spelling words and a personal word.

Review

CROSSWORD PUZZLE Use the clues to fill in the puzzle with list words.

Across

3. from past time till now
6. select
7. feel
8. at last
10. leaving out

Down

1. next to
2. thinly
4. picked
5. in addition to
9. take what is given

| since |
| sense |
| choose |
| chose |
| finally |
| finely |
| except |
| accept |
| beside |
| besides |

Word *Study*

SYNONYMS Words that have the same or similar meanings are called **synonyms.** Use synonyms to make your writing more interesting and precise. When you realize you've used the same tired word over and over again, synonyms are especially useful. In the paragraph below, replace the word *fine* with one of the synonyms in the box.

| precious | beautiful | acceptable | healthy | pleasant | delicious |

Mom looked over my homework and said it was **(1) fine,** so I asked if I could go out. I had had a cold, but now I'm **(2) fine.** I walked by a jewelry store selling **(3) fine** gems. The necklaces in the window looked **(4) fine.** It was a **(5) fine** way to spend the day. I went home to a **(6) fine** dinner.

1. _____
2. _____
3. _____
4. _____
5. _____
6. _____

Using Just Enough Letters

SPELLING FOCUS

Pronouncing a word correctly and picturing how it looks can help you avoid writing too many letters.

■ **STUDY** Say each word. Then read the sentence.

1.	*similar*	The sisters had **similar** eyes.
2.	*doesn't* ✳	Mom **doesn't** like rap music.
3.	*experience*	They hire people with **experience.**
4.	*forward*	Traffic moved **forward** slowly.
5.	*exactly*	Cut the apple **exactly** in half.
6.	*partner*	Ben is her dance **partner.**
7.	*drawer*	Socks go in the first **drawer.**
8.	*expensive*	She wears **expensive** clothes.
9.	*develop*	Practice to **develop** your talent.
10.	*familiar*	It's good to see a **familiar** face.
11.	*pigeon*	A **pigeon** flew in the park.
12.	*tickling*	He was **tickling** my bare feet.
13.	*penalty*	The **penalty** was a year in jail.
14.	*frustrated*	We were **frustrated** by the delay.
15.	*athletic*	An **athletic** person enjoys sports.
16.	*celebration*	Come to a holiday **celebration.**
17.	*circling*	Vultures were **circling** the field.
18.	*helicopter*	A **helicopter** landed on the roof.
19.	*trembling*	They began **trembling** with cold.
20.	*sparkling*	Look at the ice **sparkling** in the sun.

■ **PRACTICE** First write the words that are easiest for you to spell correctly. Then write the words that are the most difficult for you to spell correctly. Underline the parts of any words that cause you problems.

■ **WRITE** Choose ten words to write in sentences.

1. _____
2. _____
3. _____
4. _____
5. _____
6. _____
7. _____
8. _____
9. _____
10. _____
11. _____
12. _____
13. _____
14. _____
15. _____
16. _____
17. _____
18. _____
19. _____
20. _____

CHALLENGE!

exquisite
mischievous
refrigerator
pastime
anxious

✳ **WATCH OUT FOR FREQUENTLY MISSPELLED WORDS!**

PRONUNCIATIONS Write the list word for each pronunciation below. Say each word carefully to yourself as you write it.

1. (ek spen′siv)
2. (tik′ling)
3. (ek spir′ē əns)
4. (trem′bling)
5. (hel′ə kop′tər)

6. (sim′ə lər)
7. (pen′l tē)
8. (di vel′əp)
9. (duz′nt)
10. (sel′ə brā′shən)

HIDDEN WORDS Each word below is hidden in a list word. Write the list word.

11. rust
12. park
13. let
14. liar
15. art

16. cling
17. for
18. raw
19. act
20. eon

Strategic Spelling

Using the Memory Tricks Strategy

Use memory tricks to help you spell. Create memory tricks using the list words and helpers below. Underline the matching letters.

21. pigeon—neon _____

_____

22. drawer—draw _____

_____

23. doesn't—doe _____

_____

24. forward—for _____

25. circling—cliff _____

_____

1. _____
2. _____
3. _____
4. _____
5. _____
6. _____
7. _____
8. _____
9. _____
10. _____
11. _____
12. _____
13. _____
14. _____
15. _____
16. _____
17. _____
18. _____
19. _____
20. _____

Did You Know?
The pigeon is one of the few birds that pairs for life. A young pigeon is called a squab.

 Make a capital.

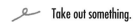 Make a small letter.

∧ Add something.

ℓ Take out something.

⊙ Add a period.

ℲℲ New paragraph

PROOFREAD FOR CARELESS ERRORS

What mistake do you see in this sentence?

Mary is sent to live with her rich Uncle.

"Uncle" should not be capitalized because it isn't a proper noun. Be sure a word really needs a capital letter before using one.

Check for Capital Letters Correct five words that are incorrectly capitalized in this passage from a summary of a novel.

Mary doesn't know what to do until she finds a forgotten Garden. Circling the garden is a tall, ivy-covered Wall. Mary is thrilled when a Robin shows her a Key that opens a door in the wall. Inside the secret garden, Mary and her cousin Colin begin to bring the Roses back to life.

PROOFREAD A SUMMARY

Find the five misspellings in this summary of a TV show and write them correctly. Some may be words you learned before. Also fix three careless errors.

1. _____

2. _____

3. _____

4. _____

5. _____

This real-life Drama was about a party. During the celerbration, a boy began trembling and collapsed. No one knew what to do untill someone called the Police. Finally a hellacopter appeared, circling overhead. It landed in a field and took the boy off to a Hospital. That must have been an exspensive ride!

Word List

pigeon	celebration
similar	partner
tickling	drawer
penalty	expensive
frustrated	develop
doesn't	circling
experience	helicopter
athletic	trembling
forward	sparkling
exactly	familiar

Personal Words

1. _____

2. _____

WRITE A SUMMARY

Write a summary of a recent TV show you have seen. Use three spelling words and a personal word.

Review

PARAGRAPH COMPLETION   Complete the book report.

One of my favorite authors (1) always turn out perfect stories. His last mystery was more than (2) to an earlier book; in fact, it was almost (3) like it.

The plots of both books (4) around a shared (5) of people in a resort hotel. Guests claim that (6) jewelry has been taken from a dresser (7). Then someone (8) with their routine is accused of the robbery.

The house detective and her (9) are not certain they have the right suspect until one of the guests comes (10) with an explanation.

similar	partner
doesn't	drawer
experience	expensive
forward	develop
exactly	familiar

1. _____
2. _____
3. _____
4. _____
5. _____
6. _____
7. _____
8. _____
9. _____
10. _____

Using a *Thesaurus*

PARTS OF AN ENTRY   A thesaurus is a helpful resource for finding precise words. Study the part of a thesaurus page and the labels. Then answer the questions.

Definition   Example Sentence

Entry Word — **Expensive** means costing a lot of money. *Luis decided not to buy those expensive sneakers.*

Part of Speech — (adjective)

Costly can mean expensive. *Dad gave Mom a bottle of costly perfume for her birthday.*

High can mean expensive. *Mr. and Mrs. Parks like the apartment, but the rent is too high for their budget.*

Overpriced means costing more than it is worth. *Gina says those tropical fish are really overpriced.*

Synonyms — **Steep** can mean very expensive. *The little grocery on the corner had steep prices compared to the supermarket.*

Sky-high can mean very expensive. *I can't believe anyone pays these sky-high rates for a motel room.*

Cost an arm and a leg is an idiom that means something is extremely expensive. *Marnie wants a computer with a color monitor, but they cost an arm and a leg.*

Cross-reference — SEE **valuable** for related words.

Antonyms — ANTONYMS: cheap, inexpensive

1. What part of speech is *expensive?*
2. What two words can mean "very expensive"?
3. What idiom means something is extremely expensive?
4. What are two antonyms for *expensive?*
5. Under what other entry could you look to find related words?

1. _____
2. _____
3. _____
4. _____
5. _____

Irregular Plurals

SPELLING FOCUS

Some plurals are formed by adding **-s** or **-es.** Sometimes the spelling of the singular form changes.

■ **STUDY**   Notice how each word becomes plural.

scarf	1.	*scarfs*
staff	2.	*staffs*
shelf	3.	*shelves*
wolf	4.	*wolves*
myself	5.	*ourselves*
solo	6.	*solos*
stereo	7.	*stereos*
volcano	8.	*volcanoes*
quiz	9.	*quizzes*
pants	10.	*pants*

sheriff	11.	*sheriffs*
reef	12.	*reefs*
chief	13.	*chiefs*
knife	14.	*knives*
thief	15.	*thieves*
studio	16.	*studios*
domino	17.	*dominoes*
buffalo	18.	*buffaloes*
scissors	19.	*scissors*
measles	20.	*measles*

■ **PRACTICE**   Sort the words by writing
- five plurals in which **f** is changed to **v** + **-es**
- four other plurals in which **-es** is added
- eight plurals in which just **-s** is added
- three plurals that don't change from the singular

■ **WRITE**   Choose ten words to write in sentences.

CHALLENGE!

bailiffs
wharves
flamingos
mosquitoes
desperadoes

1.
2.
3.
4.
5.
6.
7.
8.
9.
10.
11.
12.
13.
14.
15.
16.
17.
18.
19.
20.

CLASSIFYING   Write one or two list words that belong in each group.

1–2. foxes, coyotes, ____, ____
3–4. hats, shirts, ____, ____
5–6. saws, axes, scalpels, ____, ____
  7. marbles, checkers, ____
  8. tests, exams, ____
  9. chicken pox, mumps, ____
 10. yourselves, themselves, ____
 11. robbers, burglars, ____
 12. earthquakes, eruptions, ____

DRAWING CONCLUSIONS   Write the list word that matches each clue.

13. These can be used to hold books.
14. Only one person at a time can sing these.
15. These people arrest criminals and enforce the law.
16. Use these to listen to music.
17. Bosses need these groups of people to get the work done.
18. Other people follow these people's orders.
19. Boats have to watch out for these underwater ridges.
20. Painters and musicians do their work in these.

Strategic Spelling

Building New Words

Add either **-s** or **-es** to each word. If you're not sure how to spell the plural, look in your Spelling Dictionary.

belief

21. _____

cliff

22. _____

elf

23. _____

echo

24. _____

hero

25. _____

piano

26. _____

1. _____
2. _____
3. _____
4. _____
5. _____
6. _____
7. _____
8. _____
9. _____
10. _____
11. _____
12. _____
13. _____
14. _____
15. _____
16. _____
17. _____
18. _____
19. _____
20. _____

Did You Know?
The word *volcanoes* comes from *Vulcan,* the Roman god of fire. The Romans believed that Vulcan lived underneath a volcanic island off the coast of Italy.

 Make a capital.

 Make a small letter.

∧ Add something.

ℓ Take out something.

⊙ Add a period.

⌗ New paragraph

PROOFREAD FOR PUNCTUATION

Use an apostrophe with a contraction.

Don't forget—it's time for our fall sale.

The word *it's* is tricky; you know you need an apostrophe if you can replace *it's* with the two words *it is* in the sentence.

Check Contractions Read each sentence. Correct the mistakes with contractions. If a sentence is correct, write "Correct."

1. Thats right—all our scarfs and pants must go!
2. Isnt it time you checked out our selection of stereos?
3. We've filled our shelves with bargains.
4. Everythings in its original condition.

1. _____

2. _____

3. _____

4. _____

PROOFREAD AN ADVERTISEMENT Find eight misspelled words in this ad and write them correctly. Some may be words you learned before, and three are missing apostrophes.

Shop Smart Mart, were the sales never end! Youll find a wide selection of sterios and TVs on the second floor. Were offering scarfs and pantes on sale through Monday. Your invited to bring in your knifes and sisors, and we'll sharpen them for free in our cutlery department.

WRITE AN ADVERTISEMENT Write an ad for either (a) your special scarfs, or (b) pet buffaloes. Try to use two spelling words and a personal word.

Word List

knives	stereos
wolves	solos
shelves	studios
ourselves	volcanoes
thieves	dominoes
sheriffs	buffaloes
scarfs	quizzes
staffs	scissors
chiefs	pants
reefs	measles

Personal Words

1. _____

2. _____

Review

MAKING INFERENCES Write the list word that fits each clue.

scarfs	solos
staffs	stereos
shelves	volcanoes
wolves	quizzes
ourselves	pants

1. Dormant, or inactive, ___ might erupt again.
2. Ski ___ should be waterproof.
3. All the different White House ___ must have security clearance.
4. Paul had A's on all his current events ___.
5. There were two ___ and three duets listed on the program.
6. The preschool teacher helped tie ___ and pull on boots.
7. CD players have replaced phonographs and ___ in popularity.
8. My advice to my friends was "Let's just be ___."
9. It would be unusual to find ___ living in a desert.
10. The top ___ in the cupboard were too high to be useful.

1. _____

2. _____

3. _____

4. _____

5. _____

6. _____

7. _____

8. _____

9. _____

10. _____

Word *Study*

CONTEXT: DEFINITIONS AND EXPLANATIONS

Suppose you read in your science book: "Coral reefs look like ridges of rocks in the ocean. However, they are really the piled-up skeletons of tiny animals." If *reefs* were an unfamiliar word, you could still get its meaning from the **context,** or words around it.

Read the passages below. Then define each word listed, using information in the passage. Remember, the explanation of the word may not be in the same sentence as the word itself.

Researchers can explore the ocean floor in submersibles. Only two or three people at a time can travel in these tiny submarines. Diving into the darkest depths of the ocean, they have discovered organisms that are bioluminescent, creating their own light.

The sunlit upper layer of the ocean is home to plankton. These microscopic plants and animals are eaten by larger animals. Seaweeds use tough, rootlike bases called holdfasts to cling to the shore despite the pounding waves.

1. submersibles _____

2. bioluminescent _____

3. plankton _____

4. holdfasts _____

Related Words 1

Related words often have parts that are spelled the same but pronounced differently: **hum<u>a</u>n, hum<u>a</u>ne.**

■ **STUDY**   Say each word. Then read the sentence.

1.	*human*	It's only **human** to make mistakes.
2.	*humane*	Animals deserve **humane** treatment.
3.	*clean*	We **clean** house on Saturdays.
4.	*cleanse*	Use alcohol to **cleanse** the cut.
5.	*nature*	Forest rangers protect **nature.**
6.	*natural*	He is a **natural** athlete.
7.	*major*	She is a **major** writer of our time.
8.	*majority*	I won with a **majority** of the votes.
9.	*poem*	We like a **poem** that rhymes.
10.	*poetic*	The song's words are **poetic.**
11.	*equal*	Divide the pie into **equal** amounts.
12.	*equation*	Solve the **equation** for math class.
13.	*unite*	A common cause will **unite** us.
14.	*unity*	An experienced team has **unity.**
15.	*bomb*	The **bomb** exploded violently.
16.	*bombard*	Cannon will **bombard** the fort.
17.	*muscle*	Lifting can cause **muscle** pain.
18.	*muscular*	A weight lifter is **muscular.**
19.	*resign*	My boss said he will **resign.**
20.	*resignation*	We must accept his **resignation.**

■ **PRACTICE**   Sort the words by writing
- three pairs of words in which **g, c,** or **b** changes from silent to sounded
- seven pairs of words in which a vowel sound changes

■ **WRITE**   Choose two sentences to include in a paragraph.

1.   _____

2.   _____

3.   _____

4.   _____

5.   _____

6.   _____

7.   _____

8.   _____

9.   _____

10. _____

11. _____

12. _____

13. _____

14. _____

15. _____

16. _____

17. _____

18. _____

19. _____

20. _____

CHALLENGE!

haste	hasten
heir	inherit
harmony	harmonious

RELATED PAIRS   To complete each sentence below, write two list words that are related.

If we all (1) in this project, our (2) will give us strength.
The teacher asked us to write a (3) , but Judy couldn't think of any (4) words.
Scientists are working on methods to (5) the air of pollutants so that we can all breathe (6) air.
We believe in the (7) treatment of prisoners, since we are all (8) beings.
Although a few people disagreed, the (9) felt that our (10) goal was to build a playground.
This mathematical (11) shows that 4 × 5 is (12) to 20.
It is (13) to wish you were outdoors enjoying (14) on a beautiful sunny day.

EXACT MEANINGS   Write the list word that makes sense in each sentence below.

15. Your stomach is actually a large ____.
16. Working out on weight machines can make you more ____.
17. The president of the chess club decided to ____ his position.
18. We regretfully accepted the president's ____.
19. The explosion was caused by a ____.
20. Planes were sent in to ____ the area with missiles.

Strategic Spelling

Seeing Meaning Connections

Words related to *unite*
union
unify
unique
unison

Write the word from the box that completes each phrase. Use your Spelling Dictionary if you need help.

21. joined the labor _____

22. a _____ design

23. for us all to sing in _____

24. trying to _____ the students

1. _____
2. _____
3. _____
4. _____
5. _____
6. _____
7. _____
8. _____
9. _____
10. _____
11. _____
12. _____
13. _____
14. _____
15. _____
16. _____
17. _____
18. _____
19. _____
20. _____

Take a Hint
Do you see the <u>sign</u>
in *resign?*

☰	Make a capital.
/	Make a small letter.
∧	Add something.
ℓ	Take out something.
⊙	Add a period.
¶	New paragraph

ECOLOGY CLUB
JANUARY 26TH
2:00 P.M. MEETING CALLED
2:15- DR. CARMEN VEGA
SPOKE ON CLEAN AIR EFFORTS
3:30- MEETING ADJOURNED

1. _____
2. _____
3. _____
4. _____
5. _____

PROOFREAD FOR PUNCTUATION Use a colon between the hour and minute when writing the time, and don't forget the period in abbreviations and initials. For example:

Mr. T. Yu served refreshments at 3:15 P.M.

Check for Punctuation Read each sentence and correct the punctuation. If a sentence is correct, write "Correct."

1. Janine suggested we change our meeting time to 4.00.
2. Alvin said if we met at 4:00 PM he would resign.
3. Derrick suggested we meet at 120 N Green St. instead.
4. Mr Cole thought meeting at school would be better.
5. A majority voted to meet at 2:30 P.M. in the school.

PROOFREAD THE MINUTES OF A MEETING Find five misspelled words and write them correctly. Some may be words you learned before. Also fix three punctuation errors.

> The meeting of the Ecology Club was called to order at 2.00 P.M. A mojority of the club members where present. Sumiko J Numata read a peom celebrating the beauty of our natural world. At 2:15, Dr Carmen Vega spoke to us on resent efforts to clense the air of pollutants. The meeting adjourned at 3:30.

Word List

human	major
humane	majority
equal	poem
equation	poetic
clean	bomb
cleanse	bombard
unite	muscle
unity	muscular
nature	resign
natural	resignation

Personal Words

1. _____
2. _____

WRITE THE MINUTES OF A MEETING Plan and write the minutes for a fictional meeting of a club you'd like to belong to. Use three spelling words and a personal word.

Review

OPPOSITES   Write the list word that means the opposite.

1. artificial
2. cruel

3. minority
4. dirty

1. _____

2. _____

3. _____

4. _____

ASSOCIATIONS   Write the list word that is associated with each term below.

5. verse, rhyme
6. person, being
7. important, greater

8. wash, purify
9. lyrical, imaginative
10. earth, universe

5. _____

6. _____

7. _____

8. _____

9. _____

10. _____

human
humane
clean
cleanse
nature
natural
major
majority
poem
poetic

Word *Study*

GREEK AND LATIN WORD PARTS: NUMBERS   The words on page 83 related to *unite* all contain the word part **uni-**, which comes from a Latin word meaning "one." Some number word parts are shown below.

uni-	one	Latin *unus*
quadri-	four	Latin *quadri-*
octa-	eight	Greek *okta-*
deca-	ten	Greek *deka-*

decade
quadruplets
octopus
unicycle
decathlon
unilateral

Write the word from the red box that best fits each clue below. Use your Spelling Dictionary if you need help.

1. a sea creature with eight arms
2. ten years
3. a vehicle with only one wheel
4. one-sided
5. a physical contest with ten events
6. four siblings born at the same time

1. _____

2. _____

3. _____

4. _____

5. _____

6. _____

Review

Lesson 13: Words with ci and ti
Lesson 14: Easily Confused Words
Lesson 15: Using Just Enough Letters

Lesson 16: Irregular Plurals
Lesson 17: Related Words 1

REVIEW WORD LIST

1. cautious	11. suggestion	21. personnel	31. similar	41. thieves
2. commercial	12. accept	22. recent	32. tickling	42. volcanoes
3. especially	13. access	23. sense	33. trembling	43. wolves
4. exhaustion	14. beside	24. since	34. dominoes	44. clean
5. gracious	15. choose	25. athletic	35. knives	45. human
6. population	16. chose	26. celebration	36. ourselves	46. humane
7. position	17. except	27. exactly	37. quizzes	47. major
8. precious	18. excess	28. expensive	38. reefs	48. natural
9. question	19. finally	29. experience	39. scissors	49. nature
10. social	20. later	30. frustrated	40. shelves	50. poem

■ PROOFREADING

Find the spelling errors in each passage and write the words correctly. All passages have seven errors except the second one, which has eight.

1. _____

2. _____

3. _____

4. _____

5. _____

6. _____

7. _____

PROOFREAD A NOTICE

After 3 P.M. (accept on Saturdays) excess to the building will be through the Cactus Drive entrance only. All building personal must leave through that entrance as well. Anyone attending atheletic practice after 3 P.M. must have a building pass. Please be caucious in the parking lot. If you experiance any problems getting into the building, or if you have a quetion about this policy, please call the office.

PROOFREAD A POSTER

1. _____
2. _____
3. _____
4. _____
5. _____
6. _____
7. _____
8. _____

We're having a reading celerbration!

Our shelfs are full of resent books.

Do you want to read about natcher?

Would you like a book on coral reeves?

Are you interested in quizes?

Would you like to read a pome

or learn how to play domenos?

We've got it all!

Visit your school library.

PROOFREAD INSTRUCTIONS

1. _____
2. _____
3. _____
4. _____
5. _____
6. _____
7. _____

Here's a suggeshin for making sunflower gift wrap. Start with a clene paper bag. Use sisors to trim off the bottom and cut along the side of the bag so the paper lies flat. Cut off any access paper so you have neat edges. To decorate, postion a quarter on the paper and draw around it with a black marker. Fill in the circle. With an orange marker, draw petals around the circle. (You may chose to use watercolors instead.) Cover the paper with flowers. They need not be ecxactly the same size. Now you are ready to wrap!

PROOFREAD A REPORT

1. _____
2. _____
3. _____
4. _____
5. _____
6. _____
7. _____

Vesuvius is one of the most famous volcanos in the world. On August 24, A.D. 79, Vesuvius erupted and covered the city of Pompeii with twenty feet of ash. About ten percent of the populashin was killed. Those who escaped probably set out to sea or choose to take the roads leading into the countryside. Much latter, part of the lost city of Pompeii was uncovered. From the remains of the city and the many presish objects there, scientists have learned much about the artistic, socail, and commertial life of the city.

PROOFREAD A NEWS STORY

1. _____
2. _____
3. _____
4. _____
5. _____
6. _____
7. _____

January 25, 20__   Page 5

Davis School Doings

Two thiefs entered Mrs. McGowan's classroom through a screen last week, but they didn't have knifes. They used their teeth. They didn't steal anything exspensive, but they did steal a mager amount of bird food. In fact, the robbers weren't humen. Two squirrels, frusterated by an empty bird feeder, had the since to gnaw through a screen to attack a bag of birdseed on the windowsill. They escaped when Mrs. McGowan opened the classroom door Monday morning.

PROOFREAD A FABLE

A lion was asleep besid a tree one day when a mouse began tickeling him. The lion awoke and put his huge paw over the mouse, but the mouse begged for forgiveness. "Please," said the mouse, trembleling. "If you let me go, I may be able to help you some day." The lion laughed at this idea but was graceous enough to except an apology and release the mouse. Some time after, the lion was caught in a trap. Hunters tied him up and went to look for a wagon to carry him away. Just then the mouse passed by. Seeing that the lion was suffering from exhaustian, the mouse began to gnaw at the rope. The rope finely gave way. "You see that I was right," said the mouse.

Moral: Little friends may become great ones.

1. _____
2. _____
3. _____
4. _____
5. _____
6. _____
7. _____

PROOFREAD A FRIENDLY LETTER

October 7, 20__

Dear Matt,

    I am sending you a book about wolfs for your birthday. Your aunt and I read the book ourselfs and decided you would like it. It calls for human treatment of these beautiful creatures and for preservation of their naturale habitat. We think the photographs are especialy good. Sence you may already have this book, or a similiar one, you may return this if you wish, and we'll send you something else. Happy birthday!

        Sincerely,
        Uncle Jim

1. _____
2. _____
3. _____
4. _____
5. _____
6. _____
7. _____

STRATEGY WORKSHOP

Divide and Conquer

DISCOVER THE STRATEGY Here's another strategy for extra-hard words. If your word is longer than one syllable, try dividing it into smaller pieces. How do you divide it? That depends on the kind of word you're working with.

Compounds: divide between base words	Words with Affixes: divide between affix and base word	Other Words: divide between syllables
team/mate	beauti/ful	in/stru/ment
every/thing	mis/understand/ing	Mis/sis/sip/pi
dough/nut	un/usual	ar/ti/fi/cial

TRY IT OUT Now try this divide and conquer strategy.

Compounds Write these compounds:

> **themselves hallway homeroom everybody skateboard**

Draw a line between the two base words that make up each compound. *Note:* This will show you that two words have been put together with no letters lost.

1. _____   4. _____

2. _____   5. _____

3. _____

Affixes Write these words:

| unbuckle   athletic   business   celebration   exactly |

Draw lines between each base word and any prefixes or
suffixes. *Note:* This will show you the parts of the word and
whether adding a suffix changes the spelling of the base word.

Now look back at the words you wrote. Three base words
changed spelling when the suffix was added. Underline these
base words that changed spelling.

Syllables Write these words:

| experience   helicopter   broccoli   fascinate   accomplish |

Say each word. Listen carefully for the syllables and draw lines
between them. Check a dictionary for any words that you're not
sure of.

LOOK AHEAD Look ahead at the next five lessons. Write
six list words that you could use these strategies with. Say each
word to yourself and divide it into smaller pieces. Divide each
word the way that works best for you.

1. _____
2. _____
3. _____

4. _____
5. _____
6. _____

6. _____
7. _____
8. _____
9. _____
10. _____

11. _____
12. _____
13. _____
14. _____
15. _____

Vowels in Unstressed Syllables

SPELLING FOCUS

In some words the vowel sound you hear is a schwa sound /ə/. It gives no clue to its spelling: **diff_e_r_e_nt**.

■ **STUDY** Say each word. Then read the sentence.

1. different ✻ — Eat **different** kinds of food.
2. register — He can **register** for school today.
3. carnival — I saw clowns at the **carnival.**
4. variety — Choose from a **variety** of cereals.
5. atmosphere — Earth's **atmosphere** allows life.
6. favorite ✻ — I saw my **favorite** movie again.
7. pattern — Look for a **pattern** in the design.
8. understand — A teacher helps us **understand.**
9. sentence — End your **sentence** with a period.
10. instance — In this **instance** you are wrong.

11. elegant — The ladies wore **elegant** dresses.
12. aquarium — Goldfish swam in the **aquarium.**
13. communicate — We **communicate** by speaking.
14. gasoline — The car needs **gasoline.**
15. factory — Toys are made in a big **factory.**
16. definite — The answer was a **definite** no.
17. Chicago — **Chicago** is a city on a lake.
18. heavily — My backpack is **heavily** loaded.
19. garage — Aaron put his bike in the **garage.**
20. illustrate — Photos **illustrate** this story.

■ **PRACTICE** Sort the words by writing
- seven words that have two schwa sounds each
- six words in which this sound is spelled **e** or **i**
- three words in which this sound is spelled **a** or **u**
- four words in which it's spelled **o**

■ **WRITE** Choose two sentences to include in a paragraph.

CHALLENGE!

pessimism
prominent
controversy
suspicious
porpoise

1.
2.
3.
4.
5.
6.
7.
8.
9.
10.
11.
12.
13.
14.
15.
16.
17.
18.
19.
20.

✻ **WATCH OUT FOR FREQUENTLY MISSPELLED WORDS!**

DEFINITIONS   Write the list word that fits each definition.

1. air that surrounds the earth
2. building where things are made by machine or by hand
3. example, case
4. liked or favored more than all the others
5. fuel for engines in cars, boats, and lawn mowers
6. a number of different kinds
7. an arrangement of shapes or colors in a particular design
8. a glass tank for fish and other water plants and animals
9. with great weight
10. a large city in eastern Illinois
11. a group of words that expresses a statement
12. record or write in a list; sign up for

CLASSIFYING   Write the list word that belongs in each group.

13. draw, paint, ___
14. talk, chat, ___
15. shelter, car, ___
16. games, food, ___
17. clear, exact, ___
18. graceful, refined, ___
19. unusual, unique, ___
20. know, realize, ___

1. _____
2. _____
3. _____
4. _____
5. _____
6. _____
7. _____
8. _____
9. _____
10. _____
11. _____
12. _____
13. _____
14. _____
15. _____
16. _____
17. _____
18. _____
19. _____
20. _____

STRATEGIC SPELLING

Using the Divide and Conquer Strategy

Sometimes it helps to study long words piece by piece. Write four list words that are hard for you. Draw lines between the syllables. Then study the words syllable by syllable. Check the Spelling Dictionary if you need help.

21. _____   23. _____

22. _____   24. _____

Did You Know?
The word *gasoline* originated in the 1860s.
The first recorded shortening of the word to *gas*
was in 1905.

≡	Make a capital.
/	Make a small letter.
∧	Add something.
ℯ	Take out something.
⊙	Add a period.
¶	New paragraph.

PROOFREAD FOR USAGE *To leave* is to go away, and *to let* is to allow. People *sit* down, but they *set* something on the table. Be careful not to confuse these pairs of verbs.

Don't let anyone ~~set~~ ^sit at the buffet table.

1. _____

2. _____

3. _____

4. _____

5. _____

Check Verbs If the wrong verb from the verb pair is used, write the correct one. If a sentence is correct, write "Correct."

1. Always leave the guests serve themselves.
2. Direct the guests to set at the tables around the dance floor.
3. The wedding party will set at the head table.
4. Don't leave the wedding party serve themselves.
5. Tell the guests to sit their plates on the table.

PROOFREAD INSTRUCTIONS Find the five misspelled words and write them correctly. Some may be words you learned before. Also fix three errors with verbs.

> To create a festive party atmusphere, decorate using balloons in a veriety of colors, or choose one or two of your farvite colors. Attach streamers, and leave them float. For an elligant look, use a tablecloth with a pretty pattern. You can sit a vase with flowers on the table to. Leave the guest of honor select the music.

Word List

garage	heavily
elegant	favorite
pattern	gasoline
variety	illustrate
atmosphere	factory
definite	communicate
aquarium	understand
Chicago	sentence
carnival	different
instance	register

Personal Words

1. _____

2. _____

WRITE INSTRUCTIONS Plan and write instructions for something you do well. Use three list words and a personal word.

Review

MAKING INFERENCES   Write the list word that is missing from each person's statement.

different	favorite
register	pattern
carnival	understand
variety	sentence
atmosphere	instance

1. Teacher: "Please state your answer in a complete ___ ."
2. Student: "I don't ___ the question."
3. Driver: "I need to ___ my car and apply for a license."
4. Scientist: "Our study of the earth's ___ is ongoing."
5. Judge: "This is an ___ of irresponsible behavior."
6. Librarian: "This is one of my ___ books."
7. Tourist: "I'm sure the weather will be ___ tomorrow."
8. Salesperson: "We have a wide ___ of choices."
9. Detective: "We've discovered a ___ to these robberies."
10. Teenager: "I won this at the ___ ."

1. _____
2. _____
3. _____
4. _____
5. _____
6. _____
7. _____
8. _____
9. _____
10. _____

Multicultural *Connection*

CELEBRATIONS   People around the world celebrate important events with carnivals and festivals. A few celebrations are shown.

Santa Lucia Day

Festa del Grillo

Festival of the Autumn Moon

Carnival

Write the celebration shown above that each item describes.

1. On December 13, young girls in Sweden dress in white to play the Queen of Lights. This festival of light reminds everyone that spring and sunshine will return.
2. During this spring festival in Italy, children catch crickets. Italians say if the cricket, or *grillo,* sings, it brings good luck.
3. This festival takes place in September in China. Moon cakes are a traditional food at the celebration.
4. The most famous celebration in Brazil happens just before Lent in Rio de Janeiro. Thousands of people dress in colorful costumes and dance the samba in the streets.

1. _____
2. _____
3. _____
4. _____

Vowels in Final Syllables

■ **STUDY**   Say each word. Then read the sentence.

1.	*slogan*	The ad needs a catchy **slogan.**
2.	*citizen*	I am a U.S. **citizen.**
3.	*forgotten*	He had **forgotten** to buy milk.
4.	*propeller*	A pilot checked the **propeller.**
5.	*collector*	She is an eager stamp **collector.**
6.	*level*	The table surface must be **level.**
7.	*tunnel*	The train went into a **tunnel.**
8.	*double*	He ate a **double** cheeseburger.
9.	*single*	Not a **single** cookie was left.
10.	*example*	An **example** follows the meaning.
11.	*urban*	Traffic in **urban** areas is often heavy.
12.	*orphan*	The **orphan** puppy needs a home.
13.	*kindergarten*	School begins with **kindergarten.**
14.	*encounter*	The **encounter** surprised me.
15.	*conquer*	Research will **conquer** cancer.
16.	*appetizer*	We ordered an **appetizer** first.
17.	*dishonor*	That lie brought on **dishonor.**
18.	*tractor*	A red **tractor** crossed the field.
19.	*easel*	A painting rested on the **easel.**
20.	*recycle*	We **recycle** cans and paper.

■ **PRACTICE**   Sort the words by writing
- seven words ending in **er** or **or**
- seven words ending in **el** or **le**
- six words ending in **en** or **an**

■ **WRITE**   Choose two sentences to write rhymes or riddles.

1. _____
2. _____
3. _____
4. _____
5. _____
6. _____
7. _____
8. _____
9. _____
10. _____
11. _____
12. _____
13. _____
14. _____
15. _____
16. _____
17. _____
18. _____
19. _____
20. _____

CHALLENGE!

toboggan
enlighten
denominator
pummel
disentangle

ASSOCIATIONS Write the list word that is related to each item below.

1. airplane
2. snack
3. painter
4. farmer
5. preschooler
6. passageway
7. commercial

8. voting rights
9. widow
10. instance
11. reuse
12. meeting
13. baseball cards

ANTONYMS Write the list words that mean the **opposite** of the underlined words.

14. Anthony has always <u>remembered</u> my birthday.
15. Anna lives on a farm in a <u>rural</u> area.
16. I like to ride my bike on a <u>hilly</u> surface.
17. Mom and Louis always order a <u>single</u> order of fries.
18. Loyalty and <u>honor</u> are admirable qualities.
19. Yasuko plays <u>several</u> instruments well.
20. Did the bad guys in the movie <u>surrender to</u> the good guys?

STRATEGIC SPELLING

Seeing Meaning Connections

Words related to *cycle*

recycle
cyclical
tricycle
cyclone
cyclist

Write the words from the box that fit the definitions.

21. a violent wind storm or tornado
22. to process, to use again
23. rider of a bicycle, tricycle, or motorcycle
24. a three-wheeled vehicle
25. moving or occurring in cycles

1. _____
2. _____
3. _____
4. _____
5. _____
6. _____
7. _____
8. _____
9. _____
10. _____
11. _____
12. _____
13. _____
14. _____
15. _____
16. _____
17. _____
18. _____
19. _____
20. _____

21. _____
22. _____
23. _____

24. _____
25. _____

Did You Know?
The word *slogan* comes from a Scottish war cry. Maybe some advertisers still see a slogan as a war cry to their competitors.

≡	Make a capital.
/	Make a small letter.
∧	Add something.
ℓ	Take out something.
⊙	Add a period.
⌙	New paragraph

PROOFREAD FOR PUNCTUATION

When proofreading, make sure you haven't left out any end marks or used the wrong mark. Put end marks inside quotation marks.

"Will the neighborhood watch program make a difference?"

Check End Marks Correct five mistakes by writing the last word of each sentence with the correct punctuation.

Can we conquer urban crime. Police Chief Eugene Jones admits the police can't do it alone So far, the city's residents have embraced the crime-prevention campaign Throughout the neighborhoods people are asking, "What else can we do to help" Chief Jones says he's looking forward to the day he can exclaim, "We've won the battle."

1. _____

2. _____

3. _____

4. _____

5. _____

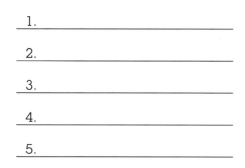

PROOFREAD AN EDITORIAL Find the five misspelled words in this editorial and write them correctly. Some may be words you learned before. Also fix three errors with end marks.

I would like to honor Harold Grey as citizin of the day for rescuing a young florida orphon The boy was exploring a cave with friends when he wandered into an old tunnle system. Grey, a city trash collecter, found the boy scared, but unharmed? Thanks for your good deed, Mr. Grey

Word List

citizen	level
easel	dishonor
slogan	double
tractor	conquer
single	kindergarten
encounter	tunnel
urban	appetizer
recycle	collector
propeller	orphan
forgotten	example

Personal Words

1. _____

2. _____

WRITE AN EDITORIAL Write an editorial that states your opinion about an issue. Use three list words and a personal word.

Review

slogan	level
citizen	tunnel
forgotten	double
propeller	single
collector	example

DEFINITIONS   Write the list word that matches each clue.

1. no longer remembered
2. something that shows what others are like
3. flat or even
4. someone who collects
5. someone who is a member of a nation
6. twice as much
7. one and no more
8. a revolving hub with blades
9. a word, phrase, or saying
10. an underground passage

1. _____
2. _____
3. _____
4. _____
5. _____
6. _____
7. _____
8. _____
9. _____
10. _____

Using a Dictionary

SYNONYM STUDIES   Some dictionary entries include synonym studies that explain the difference between words that are closely related in meaning. Illustrative sentences show each word used in context. Below is the synonym study that appears at the end of the entry for the word *single.*

> **Synonym Study** *adj.* **1 Single, sole, only** mean one alone. **Single** emphasizes one and no more: *She buys a single new dress each year.* **Sole** emphasizes being by itself, the only one there is: *My sole purpose is to help you.* **Only** emphasizes being one of a class of which it is the best or the single representative: *She is the only gymnast in the meet to win two events.*

Write the synonym that best completes each sentence below. Use the synonym study to help you decide which word works best.

1. Paula is now the ___ owner of the family business.
2. The ___ one from our school to qualify for the state speech and drama finals was Carl.
3. Juan hasn't watched a ___ television program all week.
4. Grandpa is the one and ___ senior citizen in his apartment building.
5. We had such a good time that not a ___ person complained about the rainy weather.

1. _____
2. _____
3. _____
4. _____
5. _____

Vowel Sounds with r

SPELLING FOCUS

The vowel sound /ôr/ can be spelled **or** and **ore**: re**port**, exp**lore**. The vowel sound /ėr/ can be spelled **er**, **ear**, **or**, **ur**: exp**er**t, res**ear**ch, w**or**th, dist**ur**b.

■ **STUDY** Say each word. Then read the sentence.

1.	*report*	The topic of Sue's **report** is Egypt.
2.	*order*	The books are in alphabetical **order.**
3.	*explore*	Climbers will **explore** the cave.
4.	*ignore*	I'll **ignore** that rude remark.
5.	*expert*	Jim is an **expert** auto mechanic.
6.	*service*	That restaurant has good **service.**
7.	*research*	Years of **research** led to a cure.
8.	*worth*	That baseball card is **worth** $25.
9.	*worst*	Our **worst** flood came in 1995.
10.	*disturb*	Don't let me **disturb** your nap.

11.	*sword*	A pirate waved his **sword.**
12.	*forty*	Dad will be **forty** years old on Friday.
13.	*enormous*	The whale's jaws were **enormous.**
14.	*therefore*	He lies and **therefore** can't be trusted.
15.	*determine*	Your genes **determine** your eye color.
16.	*permanent*	This hair dye isn't **permanent.**
17.	*earning*	I am **earning** money by walking dogs.
18.	*thorough*	Give the room a **thorough** cleaning.
19.	*attorney*	An **attorney** knows the law.
20.	*purchase*	Sara had to **purchase** poster board.

■ **PRACTICE** Sort the words by writing
- six words with /ėr/ spelled **or** or **ur**
- six words with /ėr/ spelled **er** or **ear**
- eight words with /ôr/ spelled **or** or **ore**

■ **WRITE** Choose ten words to write in sentences.

1.
2.
3.
4.
5.
6.
7.
8.
9.
10.
11.
12.
13.
14.
15.
16.
17.
18.
19.
20.

CHALLENGE!

informative
remorseful
trustworthy
observable
furthermore

BASE WORDS   Write the list word that is the base word of each word below.

1. reporting
2. undetermined
3. worthless
4. disorderly
5. explorer

6. disservice
7. ignorant
8. researcher
9. disturbing
10. thoroughly

ANALOGIES   Write the list word that completes each analogy.

11. Small is to tiny as big is to ___ .
12. But is to however as consequently is to ___ .
13. Soldier is to gun as knight is to ___ .
14. Doctor is to physician as lawyer is to ___ .
15. Short is to long as temporary is to ___ .
16. Most is to least as best is to ___ .
17. Two is to twenty as four is to ___ .
18. Get is to receive as buy is to ___ .
19. Sports is to playing as money is to ___ .
20. Young is to old as inexperienced is to ___ .

STRATEGIC SPELLING

Building New Words

Complete the chart by adding **-ed** and **-ing** to each of these words: *earn, determine, order, research, explore,* and *purchase.*

Add -ed

21. _____
22. _____
23. _____
24. _____
25. _____
26. _____

Add -ing

_____
_____
_____
_____
_____
_____

1. _____
2. _____
3. _____
4. _____
5. _____
6. _____
7. _____
8. _____
9. _____
10. _____
11. _____
12. _____
13. _____
14. _____
15. _____
16. _____
17. _____
18. _____
19. _____
20. _____

Take a Hint
You'll never miss the **w** in sword if you remember this: <u>*Sword*</u> is a very sharp <u>word</u>.

	Make a capital.
/	Make a small letter.
∧	Add something.
ℓ	Take out something.
⊙	Add a period.
¶	New paragraph

PROOFREAD FOR CARELESS ERRORS

When you proofread your writing, look for words you may have carelessly dropped or repeated. For example:

Do you like to t̶o̶ make people laugh?

Check for Dropped or Repeated Words Write the five words that were dropped or repeated in this help-wanted ad.

If you are worth a million laughs and would like explore an exciting career, this is is your dream job. We need two two high-schoolers to work part-time on on weekends and evenings as clowns children's birthday parties. For more information, call 555-FUNN.

1. _____
2. _____
3. _____
4. _____
5. _____

PROOFREAD A HELP-WANTED AD   Find six misspelled words and write them correctly. Some may be words you learned before. Also fix three careless errors.

An expurt paralegal is needed for permant employment. We need a person with five years of experience as a therough researcher. You must must be able work fourty hours a week and do reserch for a corporate aterney. Call 555-6592 to to request an application form.

Word List

attorney	expert
research	earning
thorough	report
purchase	explore
determine	order
worst	ignore
permanent	sword
disturb	enormous
service	therefore
worth	forty

Personal Words

1. _____
2. _____

WRITE A HELP-WANTED AD   Write an ad for a job you would like to have. Include the skills needed and responsibilities required for this job. Use three list words and a personal word.

Review

DRAWING CONCLUSIONS   Write the list word that fits each clue.

report	service
order	research
explore	worth
ignore	worst
expert	disturb

1. This is often conducted in a laboratory.
2. This is the opposite of *best.*
3. This is a person to consult for advice.
4. This can be presented orally or in writing.
5. This is what you place in a restaurant.
6. This is what you hope will be good in the restaurant.
7. This is the value of something.
8. This is what you'd do in the wilderness.
9. This means "pay no attention to."
10. This means "bother."

1. _____
2. _____
3. _____
4. _____
5. _____
6. _____
7. _____
8. _____
9. _____
10. _____

Word *Study*

HYPERBOLE   Sometimes in writing and speaking we use **hyperbole** (hī pèr′bə lē), or exaggeration, to make situations seem more extreme than they really are. Here is an example:

> The pizza we made was so enormous we needed a crane to lift it out of the oven.

Read the passage below. If a sentence is an example of hyperbole, write "Yes." If it is not, write "No."

> (1) It was a cold, but sunny, late November day. (2) The wind was so strong that it swept us up and carried us down to Miller's Lake in two seconds flat. (3) It was so cold, we could see our breath in the air. (4) Best of all, the ice on Miller's Lake was a million feet thick. (5) It was a good day for ice skating.

1. _____
2. _____
3. _____
4. _____
5. _____

Use the following starters to write your own hyperbole.

6. The batter hit the ball so hard _____

_____

7. I'm so strong I could _____

_____

Suffixes -ation, -ion, -tion

SPELLING FOCUS

When adding suffixes, some base words may change. A final **e** or **y** may be dropped. Some words have other changes.

■ **STUDY** Notice what happens to each base word.

relax + ation	=	1. *relaxation*
explore + ation	=	2. *exploration*
occupy + ation	=	3. *occupation*
destiny + ation	=	4. *destination*
infect + ion	=	5. *infection*
collect + ion	=	6. *collection*
react + ion	=	7. *reaction*
situate + ion	=	8. *situation*
televise + ion	=	9. *television*
convene + tion	=	10. *convention*

orient + ation	=	11. *orientation*
recommend + ation	=	12. *recommendation*
determine + ation	=	13. *determination*
generate + ion	=	14. *generation*
reflect + ion	=	15. *reflection*
destruct + ion	=	16. *destruction*
attend + tion	=	17. *attention*
deduce + tion	=	18. *deduction*
receive + tion	=	19. *reception*
solve + tion	=	20. *solution*

■ **PRACTICE** Sort the words by writing
- seven words with **-ation**
- five words with **-tion**
- eight words with **-ion**

■ **WRITE** Choose ten words to write in sentences.

1.
2.
3.
4.
5.
6.
7.
8.
9.
10.
11.
12.
13.
14.
15.
16.
17.
18.
19.
20.

CHALLENGE!

cancellation
administration
investigation
exhibition
prescription

DRAWING CONCLUSIONS   Write the list word that matches each clue.

1. You can watch sports, comedies, dramas, and news on this.
2. If you find the answer to a problem, you have found this.
3. This could happen to a sore if it isn't cleaned properly.
4. You see this when you look in a mirror.
5. This refers to all the people born at about the same time.
6. Many people experience this during a vacation.
7. Someone who firmly sticks to a plan has a great deal of this.
8. This is a gathering to receive or welcome people.
9. This is the work a person does to earn a living.
10. Traveling in little known areas in search of discovery is also called this.

CONTEXT CLUES   Add a suffix to each word in parentheses to form a list word to complete each sentence.

11. Please make a (recommend) about when the chess club should meet.
12. There will be a new-student (orient) next week.
13. Calvin's (collect) of baseball cards is impressive.
14. What was Elena's (react) when she came in second?
15. What is the (destiny) for the class trip this year?
16. There is a (convene) for middle school athletes this summer.
17. My boss made a (deduce) of five dollars from my paycheck for the dishes I broke last month.
18. When I baby-sit, I give the children a lot of (attend).
19. Jakob handled a difficult (situate) very well.
20. The (destruct) of the old building was ordered for safety reasons.

1. _____
2. _____
3. _____
4. _____
5. _____
6. _____
7. _____
8. _____
9. _____
10. _____
11. _____
12. _____
13. _____
14. _____
15. _____
16. _____
17. _____
18. _____
19. _____
20. _____

STRATEGIC SPELLING

Building New Words

Add the suffix **-tion** to the following base words: *deceive, reduce, resolve, assume.* Use your Spelling Dictionary if you need help.

21. _____   23. _____

22. _____   24. _____

Did You Know?
Television is considered a young word, having been around for less than a hundred years. The accepted abbreviation for *television* is *TV.*

Words from Many Cultures

SPELLING FOCUS

Many words in English come from other languages and may have unexpected spellings: **picnic**.

■ **STUDY** Say each word. Then read the sentence.

1. moose — We saw **moose** in the woods.
2. cobra — The **cobra** is a hooded snake.
3. alligator — An **alligator** is a large reptile.
4. vanilla — I'll have **vanilla** ice cream.
5. banana — The monkey stole a **banana.**
6. tomato — A **tomato** is red when ripe.
7. mustard — The yellow stain is **mustard.**
8. hula — Hawaiian women **hula** gracefully.
9. picnic — We always overeat at the **picnic.**
10. barbecue — Dad knows how to **barbecue** ribs.

11. crocodile — They saw a **crocodile** in the river.
12. coyote — A **coyote** is bigger than a fox.
13. koala — The Australian **koala** is not a bear.
14. macaroni — Dan cooked **macaroni** and cheese.
15. catsup — I prefer **catsup** on my hot dog.
16. polka — Dancing the **polka** made me dizzy.
17. ballet — A **ballet** dancer must be strong.
18. waltz — They circled as they danced a **waltz.**
19. banquet — We ate at the awards **banquet.**
20. buffet — The **buffet** lunch offers many foods.

■ **PRACTICE** Sort the words by writing
- six words that name animals
- six words that name things we eat
- eight words that name dances, meals, or feasts

■ **WRITE** Choose two sentences to write slogans or sayings.

1. _____
2. _____
3. _____
4. _____
5. _____
6. _____
7. _____
8. _____
9. _____
10. _____
11. _____
12. _____
13. _____
14. _____
15. _____
16. _____
17. _____
18. _____
19. _____
20. _____

CHALLENGE!

succotash
artichoke
sauerkraut
won ton
chutney

WORD HISTORIES   Write a list word for each description.

1. The Chinese probably named this popular tomato sauce.
2. The Aztec people of Mexico called this animal a *coyotl.*
3. The name of this yellow fruit comes from Africa.
4. The Algonquins named this large, antlered mammal.
5. This furry animal has kept its Australian name.
6. This dance was named after the Polish people who do it.
7. This word is Portuguese for "snake."
8. This is the Italian word for a well-known pasta.
9. This Hawaiian dance uses pantomime to tell a story.
10. The French named this dance done mostly on the toes.
11. The Aztecs of Mexico named this juicy red fruit a *tomatl.*
12. The name of this yellow seasoning comes from French.
13. This word for a feast or formal dinner comes from French.
14. This word for cooking over an open fire comes from Spanish.
15. The French call this outdoor meal a *piquenique.*
16. The Spanish named this popular flavor of ice cream.

COMPLETE A POEM   Write list words to complete the poem.

Arnold the (17)
Raids the refrigerator.
Cammie the (18)
Gets her snacks in the Nile.
My favorite way
Is strolling through a (19) .
I'd do a polka or a (20)
For a couple of chocolate malts.

STRATEGIC SPELLING

Using the Divide and Conquer Strategy

Write four list words that are hard for you. Draw lines between the syllables. Check the Spelling Dictionary if you need help. Then study the words syllable by syllable.

21. _____

22. _____

23. _____

24. _____

1. _____

2. _____

3. _____

4. _____

5. _____

6. _____

7. _____

8. _____

9. _____

10. _____

11. _____

12. _____

13. _____

14. _____

15. _____

16. _____

17. _____

18. _____

19. _____

20. _____

Did You Know?
Crocodiles' snouts come to a point in front while alligators' snouts are broader and more rounded. Also, crocodiles are much more active and aggressive than alligators.

109

═	Make a capital.
/	Make a small letter.
∧	Add something.
ℓ	Take out something.
⊙	Add a period.
¶	New paragraph

PROOFREAD FOR USAGE To decide what pronoun to use in a compound subject, say the sentence with just one subject. For example, "I planned the picnic" sounds better than "Me planned the picnic."

My mother and me planned the picnic.

Check Pronouns For each sentence, fix pronoun errors by writing the correct subject. Write "Correct" if all the pronouns are correct.

1. Her and I decided to make macaroni salad.
2. My father and I went shopping for the ingredients.
3. My brother and me had to go back for mustard.
4. Him and I weren't too happy about that.

PROOFREAD A DESCRIPTION Find six misspelled words and write them correctly. Fix three pronoun errors too.

1. _____

2. _____

3. _____

4. _____

Our family picknick was a big success. My mother and me brought the macaronie salad. Her and my sister also organized games for the children. My brothers Ted and Nick offered to barbaque hamburgers. Them and my father set up a table with catsup, pickles, musterd, and tomatoe slices. We even had vanila ice cream for dessert!

WRITE A DESCRIPTION Write a description of a recent family or neighborhood event. Try to use three spelling words and a personal word.

Word List

vanilla	hula
crocodile	banana
macaroni	catsup
ballet	moose
mustard	banquet
coyote	cobra
picnic	buffet
waltz	polka
barbecue	alligator
koala	tomato

Personal Words

1. _____

2. _____

RIDDLES Use the clues in the riddles to write the correct list word.

moose	tomato
cobra	mustard
alligator	hula
vanilla	picnic
banana	barbecue

1. I'm the companion to catsup on the condiments shelf.
2. I was discovered in Hawaii and go with grass skirts.
3. I'm usually celebrated outdoors and often draw ants.
4. I'm similar to a deer but not as graceful or pretty.
5. I'm really just a great big lizard—if you know Spanish.
6. I'm poisonous! Don't excite me.
7. I can be an outdoor meal or a sauce.
8. I'm green before I'm yellow and brown if kept too long.
9. I can be eaten fresh and red or fried and green.
10. I'm white as ice cream but brown as a flavoring.

1. _____
2. _____
3. _____
4. _____
5. _____
6. _____
7. _____
8. _____
9. _____
10. _____

Word *Study*

CONNOTATIONS Words sometimes have **connotations,** meanings that go beyond their exact dictionary definitions. A word's connotations may include feelings, images, and memories that the word suggests. For example, the dictionary defines *home* as "a place where a person lives," but the connotations of *home* can include love, comfort, security, and privacy.

healthy	exotic
dangerous	isolation
torture	wholesome

Under each word below, write two connotations from the box.

cobra

1. _____

2. _____

dungeon

3. _____

4. _____

natural

5. _____

6. _____

Many connotations are based on positive or negative feelings the words suggest. Read the pairs in the second box. For each pair, write one word under Positive and one under Negative.

| scent and stench |
| indecisive and cautious |
| communicate and chatter |

Positive

7. _____

8. _____

9. _____

Negative

10. _____

11. _____

12. _____

111

Review

Lesson 19: Vowels in Unstressed Syllables
Lesson 20: Vowels in Final Syllables
Lesson 21: Vowel Sounds with r
Lesson 22: Suffixes -ation, -ion, -tion
Lesson 23: Words from Many Cultures

REVIEW WORD LIST

1. aquarium
2. atmosphere
3. carnival
4. Chicago
5. communicate
6. different
7. garage
8. gasoline
9. sentence
10. understand
11. variety
12. collector
13. conquer
14. encounter
15. example
16. forgotten
17. level
18. orphan
19. single
20. slogan
21. tunnel
22. determine
23. enormous
24. expert
25. explore
26. purchase
27. research
28. sword
29. therefore
30. worth
31. attention
32. collection
33. convention
34. determination
35. exploration
36. occupation
37. reaction
38. reception
39. reflection
40. ballet
41. banquet
42. catsup
43. cobra
44. koala
45. macaroni
46. mustard
47. picnic
48. polka
49. vanilla
50. waltz

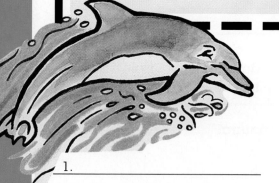

■ PROOFREADING

Find the spelling errors in each passage and write the words correctly. All passages have seven errors except the first one, which has eight.

PROOFREAD A JOURNAL ENTRY

1. _____
2. _____
3. _____
4. _____
5. _____
6. _____
7. _____
8. _____

> We visited the aquariam in chicago over the weekend and saw a lot of diffrent fish. I would like to have an ocupation where I could do reserch on marine animals or do underwater exploreation and become an expurt on underwater life. I might even learn more about how dolphins communcate. Maybe I'll look for a book about careers in marine biology.

PROOFREAD A TELEPHONE MESSAGE

Mom,

Aunt Louise called about the family picknick. We're supposed to take musterd, relish, and ketsup. She is making mackoroni salad, and Uncle Tyrone will make vanila ice cream, she hopes. Aunt Ruth will bring hot dogs and buns. Aunt Louise wants to know whether you can perchase paper plates and pick up Grandma. If not, she will under stand. You're supposed to call her back.

1. _____
2. _____
3. _____
4. _____
5. _____
6. _____
7. _____

PROOFREAD A TALE

Long ago there was fighting in Britain to determin who could conquor the most land and become king. One day, before a tournament, the citizens of London noticed an enourmous marble block into which a sord had been driven. A sign stated that whoever could pull the weapon from the stone would be king. When the tournament began, Sir Kay's weapon was missing. He asked the boy Arthur to get it. Unable to find it, Arthur ran to the courtyard, pulled the sword from the stone, and took it to Sir Kay. Sir Kay, in his determanition to be king, said that the throne was rightfully his. When the sword was put back in the stone, however, Sir Kay could not remove it. Arthur, therefor, was made king of Britain at a great bankwit.

1. _____
2. _____
3. _____
4. _____
5. _____
6. _____
7. _____

PROOFREAD A LETTER

1. _____
2. _____
3. _____
4. _____
5. _____
6. _____
7. _____

August 9, 20_ _

Dear Denise,

Last week I started to take lessons at a dancing school. We are learning the walzts, the poka, and other dances. Remember when we used to take balet lessons and had to watch the refleshion in the big mirror? I think I have forgotin most of what I learned then.

Every year the dance school holds a spring carnivel and a reseption for guests. I hope to be good enough to perform by that time! Let me know what you are doing this year.

Your friend,

Ursula

PROOFREAD A DESCRIPTIVE PARAGRAPH

1. _____
2. _____
3. _____
4. _____
5. _____
6. _____
7. _____

The atmusphere at the grage where Dad works is fine for someone who likes cars. The place smells of oil and gasaline. There is a colection of spare parts in one corner and a stack of tires in another. A convetion of sparrows twitters on the overhead lights. You may incounter Lube, a tired hound whose reacion to most customers is a big yawn. I have learned a lot about cars just hanging around this place.

PROOFREAD A BOOK REPORT

1. _____
2. _____
3. _____
4. _____
5. _____
6. _____
7. _____

My Life As a Vet is about Dr. Angela Sims, who works as a vet treating pets and zoo animals. When she was young, she rescued an orfen pup from a tunnle near her home. The pup was trapped when the water levle rose. She has treated a vriety of birds and animals, including a parrot who belonged to a bird collecter. She once treated a cobro who had swallowed a glass and a kuala who wandered away from the zoo.

PROOFREAD A NOTICE

1. _____
2. _____
3. _____
4. _____
5. _____
6. _____
7. _____

We're having a contest to choose a new slogen for Book Week at Brier School in October. For exampal:

"Brier kids read books."

"Borrow a book, find a friend."

"Let's explor the world of books."

Make your entry one sentince, something that will attract atenchen. Write or type it on a singal sheet of paper. Put your entry in the box in the library. First prize is a gift certificate werth $25.00, good at Main Street Bookstore.

STRATEGY WORKSHOP

Pronouncing for Spelling

I'm not sure about "ex-ac-ly." It sounds fine when I say it, but it doesn't look right. What's the problem?

There are exacly 5,280 feet in a mile.

DISCOVER THE STRATEGY Miranda wouldn't misspell the middle part of *exactly* if she didn't mispronounce it. She needs to use this correct pronunciation strategy:

1. Read the word aloud carefully and correctly. Listen to the sound of each letter.
2. Pronounce the word again as you write it.

TRY IT OUT Now practice this strategy. Pronounce the words in dark type slowly and correctly. As you do, listen carefully to the sounds of the underlined letters. Pronounce each word again as you write it.

1. **fav<u>o</u>rite** _____ (not "fav■rite")

2. **rem<u>em</u>bered** _____ (not "rem■bered")

3. **wol<u>ves</u>** _____ (not "wolfs")

4. **diff<u>e</u>rent** _____ (not "dif■rent")

5. **<u>per</u>form** _____ (not "pre■form")

6. **frust<u>r</u>ated** _____ (not "frus■ter■ated")

7. **spark<u>l</u>ing** _____ (not "spar■kel■ing")

"Ex-act-ly." That's better. But what about a word like "exhaustion"? I forget to include the "h" because it's silent, so how would pronouncing the word correctly help me?

It wouldn't—but making up a secret pronunciation might help.

- Go ahead and pronounce the silent letters to yourself. For example, say the sound of the **h** in *exhaustion*: "ex-**h**aus-tion."
- Or change the way you secretly say a tricky sound. For example, to remember the **ia** in *familiar,* in your mind say the end of the word like the word *liar:* "fami-**liar**." To remember the **i** in *carnival*, say it like the word **I**: "carn-**i**-val."

TRY IT OUT   Try using this secret pronunciation strategy on words that are not spelled as they're spoken. Make up secret pronunciations for these words. Concentrate on the underlined letters. Write each word as you say its secret pronunciation.

8. dou_b_t _____

9. alligator _____

10. tract_or_ _____

11. buff_e_t _____

12. pig_e_on _____

LOOK AHEAD   Look ahead at the next five lessons. Write four list words that you could use these strategies with. Mark the part of each word that you'll be paying special attention to when you pronounce it.

1. _____   3. _____

2. _____   4. _____

Including All the Letters

Some words have more letters than you expect. To spell these words, pronounce each syllable carefully or exaggerate the pronunciation of troublesome letters: **prob<u>a</u>bly, cab<u>i</u>net.**

■ **STUDY** Say each word. Then read the sentence.

1. probably ✳   It will **probably** rain tonight.
2. cabinet   Glasses are in a kitchen **cabinet.**
3. separate   The sisters want **separate** rooms.
4. wondering   The mystery has us **wondering.**
5. clothes ✳   Jeff folded the clean **clothes.**
6. temperature   Fever raises body **temperature.**
7. average   The **average** test score was 85.
8. beginning ✳   Read the **beginning** of the book.
9. restaurant   That's a good Chinese **restaurant.**
10. promise   Cam made a **promise** to practice.

11. aspirin   Take **aspirin** for your headache.
12. desperate   We are in **desperate** need of food.
13. awfully   The winner looks **awfully** happy.
14. fishhook   A worm wiggled on the **fishhook.**
15. twelfth   Paul had his **twelfth** birthday.
16. skiing   Downhill **skiing** is exciting.
17. unwritten   Learn the **unwritten** game rules first.
18. roughly   You can't handle china **roughly.**
19. schedule   Let's **schedule** the meeting today.
20. overrule   Mom can **overrule** my decision.

■ **PRACTICE** First write the words you use most in your writing. Then write the words you use least.

■ **WRITE** Choose two sentences to include in a paragraph.

1. _____
2. _____
3. _____
4. _____
5. _____
6. _____
7. _____
8. _____
9. _____
10. _____
11. _____
12. _____
13. _____
14. _____
15. _____
16. _____
17. _____
18. _____
19. _____
20. _____

CHALLENGE!

antidote
counterfeit
environmental
guarantee
sophomore

✳ **WATCH OUT FOR FREQUENTLY MISSPELLED WORDS!**

MAKING INFERENCES   Write the list word that matches each clue.

1. This is easily made and easily broken.
2. You're more likely to do this in Colorado than in Indiana.
3. You might reach for this if you have a headache.
4. You don't want yours to get higher than normal.
5. This is a popular place for people who don't want to cook.
6. You can store tools here.
7. You put these on in the morning.
8. This word is related to *despair.*
9. You'll need this if you plan to ride a train.

CONTEXT CLUES   Complete each sentence with a list word.

10. After I finished the book, I began reading it again from the ___.
11. The model airplane will break if it's handled too ___.
12. You'll need a bigger ___ if you expect to catch a salmon.
13. Tom said, "Let's ___ and meet back here later."
14. The class hoped the teacher wouldn't ___ their plan.
15. Hiro was so confused, he just sat there ___ what to do.
16. The children knew they must be quiet; it was an ___ rule.
17. Can you baby-sit on the ___ of June?
18. Your final grade will be based on the ___ of all your scores.
19. As Aaron worked on the puzzle, he said, "This is ___ hard to do!"
20. I'm not certain I can attend, but I ___ will be there.

STRATEGIC SPELLING

Pronouncing for Spelling

We sometimes spell words wrong because we say them wrong. Write *aspirin, cabinet, twelfth,* and *wondering.* Now say each word slowly and carefully. Be sure to pronounce the sounds of the underlined letters.

21. _____
22. _____
23. _____
24. _____

1. _____
2. _____
3. _____
4. _____
5. _____
6. _____
7. _____
8. _____
9. _____
10. _____
11. _____
12. _____
13. _____
14. _____
15. _____
16. _____
17. _____
18. _____
19. _____
20. _____

FREQUENTLY MISSPELLED WORDS

Don't forget that **cloth** is needed to make *clothes.*

Make a capital.	(double underline)
Make a small letter.	/
Add something.	/
Take out something.	e
Add a period.	⊙
New paragraph	¶

PROOFREAD FOR CAPITALIZATION

Capitalize the beginning of a sentence, the opening and closing of a letter, the pronoun **I**, and names of people and months.

Are you wondering where oscar and i went?

Check for Capitals Write five words that should be capitalized.

october 9, 20_ _

dear Enrique,

It's been months since i last wrote to you. how are you? For my birthday, my parents took me to a great restaurant.

sincerely,
Oscar

1. _____

2. _____

3. _____

4. _____

5. _____

PROOFREAD A LETTER   Find five misspelled words and write them correctly. Also fix three problems with capitalization.

December 3, 20__

dear Kelly,

I've had a busy scedual lately. I'm taking sking lessons! In the begining it was awfuly hard, but now i'm getting better. It's a good thing they have seperate classes for beginners!

yours,

Florence

Word List

probably	twelfth
average	clothes
separate	overrule
aspirin	skiing
desperate	beginning
wondering	fishhook
awfully	unwritten
temperature	roughly
restaurant	promise
cabinet	schedule

Personal Words

1. _____

2. _____

WRITE A LETTER   Write a letter to a friend. Use three list words and a personal word.

Review

ASSOCIATIONS   Write the word from the box that is
associated with the terms below.

1. humidity, barometer
2. pledge, oath
3. cupboard, hutch
4. apart, divided
5. garments, apparel
6. start, onset
7. likely, doubtlessly
8. considering, pondering
9. middle, usual
10. café, grill

probably
cabinet
separate
wondering
clothes
temperature
average
beginning
restaurant
promise

1. _____
2. _____
3. _____
4. _____
5. _____

6. _____
7. _____
8. _____
9. _____
10. _____

Using a *Thesaurus*

CHOOSING THE RIGHT SYNONYM   Writers use exact
words to make descriptive sentences interesting and clear. Write
the synonym that best fits the context of each sentence. Use your
Writer's Thesaurus if you need help.

1. The dramatic (beginning, opening) of the play startled
   everyone in the audience.
2. The (beginning, creation) of a voluntary clean-up crew
   saved our reputation as responsible campers.
3. During the (introduction, beginning) of her speech, the
   governor thanked her family and friends for their support.
4. Reputable business dealers will (promise, guarantee) their
   merchandise for a period of time.
5. Members of groups bond together when they (pledge, vouch
   for) allegiance to shared goals.

1. _____
2. _____
3. _____
4. _____
5. _____

Suffixes -ate, -ive, -ship

When adding suffixes **-ate, -ive,** or **-ship** to base words,
- do not change most base words: **origin, originate**
- drop the **e** in words ending in **e: create, creative**

■ **STUDY** Notice what happens to each base word.

origin + ate	=	1. *originate*
fortune + ate	=	2. *fortunate*
active + ate	=	3. *activate*
attract + ive	=	4. *attractive*
invent + ive	=	5. *inventive*
negate + ive	=	6. *negative*
create + ive	=	7. *creative*
friend + ship	=	8. *friendship*
champion + ship	=	9. *championship*
leader + ship	=	10. *leadership*

affection + ate	=	11. *affectionate*
consider + ate	=	12. *considerate*
oblige + ate	=	13. *obligate*
product + ive	=	14. *productive*
defect + ive	=	15. *defective*
construct + ive	=	16. *constructive*
owner + ship	=	17. *ownership*
member + ship	=	18. *membership*
hard + ship	=	19. *hardship*
relation + ship	=	20. *relationship*

■ **PRACTICE** Sort the list words by writing
- seven words with the suffix **-ship**
- seven words with the suffix **-ive**
- six words with the suffix **-ate**

■ **WRITE** Choose ten words to write in sentences.

1. _____
2. _____
3. _____
4. _____
5. _____
6. _____
7. _____
8. _____
9. _____
10. _____
11. _____
12. _____
13. _____
14. _____
15. _____
16. _____
17. _____
18. _____
19. _____
20. _____

CHALLENGE!

apprenticeship
comparative
appreciative
alienate
compassionate

ADDING SUFFIXES Add a suffix to each word in
parentheses to form a list word that completes the sentence.

1. (invent) An ____ person thinks of clever solutions.
2. (active) She turned a switch to ____ the laser beam.
3. (hard) Extreme cold is a ____ suffered by arctic explorers.
4. (product) Ted was ____ during the time he spent working.
5. (create) Iris is the most ___ student in the sculpture class.
6. (friend) The young boys developed a lasting ____.
7. (construct) We appreciated Ms. West's ____ criticism.
8. (oblige) Signing this form will ____ you to participate.
9. (attract) Do you think that bright colors are the most ___?
10. (negate) Joe's ____ attitude makes it hard to work with him.
11. (relation) "What is your ____ to the victim?" asked the officer.

WORDS THAT ADD UP Write the list word that completes
each equation given below.

12. flaw, blemish + -ive =
13. person belonging to a group + -ship =
14. luck + -ate =
15. first place winner + -ship =
16. love, tenderness + -ate =
17. one who owns + -ship =
18. source, starting point + -ate =
19. person who leads + -ship =
20. be thoughtful of others + -ate =

STRATEGIC SPELLING

Building New Words

To make new words, add one of the suffixes to each of these
base words: **partner, scholar, possess, select, citizen, effect.**

Add -ship

21. _____
22. _____
23. _____

Add -ive

24. _____
25. _____
26. _____

1. _____
2. _____
3. _____
4. _____
5. _____
6. _____
7. _____
8. _____
9. _____
10. _____
11. _____
12. _____
13. _____
14. _____
15. _____
16. _____
17. _____
18. _____
19. _____
20. _____

Take a Hint
A fr**ie**nd won't **lie**
and spoil a fr**ie**ndship.

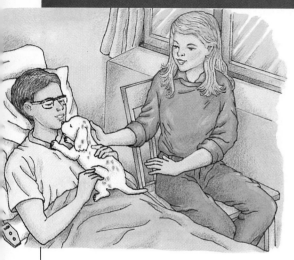

═	Make a capital.
/	Make a small letter.
/	Add something.
ℓ	Take out something.
⊙	Add a period.
¶	New paragraph

PROOFREAD FOR USAGE When you're proofreading, be sure the subject and verb fit together. For example:

The <u>relationship</u> between the two children <u>is</u> good.

Check Subjects and Verbs Correct five verbs in this passage.

The author of *The Pinballs* are Betsy Byars. The novel, one of my favorites, tell about three foster children. Carlie, one of the foster children, cheer up the others by telling jokes. Both Carlie and Harvey has had many hardships. Carlie, despite her problems, are still able to see the humor in life.

1. _____

2. _____

3. _____

4. _____

5. _____

PROOFREAD A CHARACTER DESCRIPTION Find the five misspelled words in this paragraph and write them correctly. Some may be words you learned before. Also fix three verbs.

> My favrit character in <u>The Pinballs</u> are Carlie. Even though she acts tough, she really is affectionit underneath. Her friendship with Harvey help him deal with the negitive things that are happening to him. At the end, she shows how consiterate she is wen she give Harvey a puppy as a birthday present.

Word List

affectionate	defective
considerate	constructive
fortunate	inventive
originate	ownership
obligate	membership
activate	friendship
creative	championship
productive	hardship
attractive	relationship
negative	leadership

Personal Words

1. _____

2. _____

WRITE A CHARACTER DESCRIPTION Describe a character in a story you've read recently. Use three list words and a personal word.

Review

originate	negative
fortunate	creative
activate	friendship
attractive	championship
inventive	leadership

CONTEXT CLUES Use the context in each sentence to help you write the correct list word.

1. Motion of any kind will ___ security lights.
2. The football ___ will be decided in today's game.
3. It's better to project positive, rather than ___, attitudes.
4. Thomas Edison was an ___ individual.
5. Walt Disney was a ___ person.
6. The models in the ad were all very ___.
7. Citizens look to the president for ___.
8. The trip will ___ in Dallas and end in San Diego.
9. The men's ___ had endured more than fifty years.
10. It was ___ that no one was hurt during the storm.

1. _____
2. _____
3. _____
4. _____
5. _____
6. _____
7. _____
8. _____
9. _____
10. _____

Multicultural *Connection*

FAMILY ORIGINS Unless you're an American Indian, your family didn't originate in the United States. You, your family, or your ancestors came from elsewhere to settle in this country. Today many people are interested in finding out about their family's origin.

Complete the sentences with words from the box. Use your Spelling Dictionary if you need help.

paternal	genealogy	ancestors	relationships
siblings	generation	maternal	

1. The study of family histories is called ___.
2. A family tree shows ___ among family members.
3. The people from whom you are descended are your ___.
4. Your ___ relatives are on your mother's side of the family.
5. The people on your father's side of the family are your ___ relatives.
6. You, your brothers, sisters, and cousins all belong to the same ___.
7. Your brothers and sisters are your ___.

1. _____
2. _____
3. _____
4. _____
5. _____
6. _____
7. _____

125

Opposite Prefixes

When adding prefixes **pre-**, **post-**, **over-**, **under-**, **in-**, and **ex-**, make no change in the base word.

■ **STUDY** Say each word. Then read the sentence.

1. pretrial   A jury avoids **pretrial** publicity.
2. prearrange   I will **prearrange** my entire trip.
3. postdate   Pay early and **postdate** the check.
4. postwar   The **postwar** jobs paid well.
5. overcook   Don't **overcook** the vegetables.
6. overlook   Those homes **overlook** the bay.
7. overflow   Someone let the tub **overflow.**
8. undercover   An **undercover** agent is a spy.
9. include   Your bill will **include** tax.
10. exclude   Don't **exclude** any of your friends.

11. premeditated   A practical joke is **premeditated.**
12. prehistoric   Some **prehistoric** art is crude.
13. precaution   A spare tire is a **precaution.**
14. postponement   The game **postponement** upset us.
15. postgraduate   A master's is a **postgraduate** degree.
16. overpopulated   A crowded city is **overpopulated.**
17. undernourished   The **undernourished** cat was weak.
18. underweight   The stray dog was **underweight.**
19. inhale   Never **inhale** poisonous chemicals.
20. exhale   Slowly **exhale** to the count of ten.

■ **PRACTICE** Sort the list words by writing
- seven words with the prefix **over-** or **under-**
- nine words with the prefix **pre-** or **post-**
- four words with the prefix **in-** or **ex-**

■ **WRITE** Choose four sentences to rewrite as questions.

1. _____
2. _____
3. _____
4. _____
5. _____
6. _____
7. _____
8. _____
9. _____
10. _____
11. _____
12. _____
13. _____
14. _____
15. _____
16. _____
17. _____
18. _____
19. _____
20. _____

CHALLENGE!

premonition
posthumous
overemphasize
underachiever
internally

DEFINITIONS Write the list word that fits each definition.

1. working in secret
2. breathe out
3. have a view of from above
4. leave out
5. belonging to times before histories were written
6. flood
7. contain
8. delay
9. breathe in
10. care taken beforehand

ADDING PREFIXES Write the list words that contain the base words below.

11. trial
12. arrange
13. cook
14. graduate
15. weight

16. war
17. meditated
18. date
19. populated
20. nourished

STRATEGIC SPELLING

Building New Words

Make new words by adding one of the prefixes to each of these base words: **ground, head, load, crowded, water, foot.** Add one word of your own to each column.

Add over-

21. _____
22. _____
23. _____
24. _____

Add under-

25. _____
26. _____
27. _____
28. _____

1. _____
2. _____
3. _____
4. _____
5. _____
6. _____
7. _____
8. _____
9. _____
10. _____
11. _____
12. _____
13. _____
14. _____
15. _____
16. _____
17. _____
18. _____
19. _____
20. _____

Did You Know?
Some paleontologists believe there are modern animals related to the prehistoric predator *Tyrannosaurus rex*. What animals are they? They're birds!

Make a capital.
Make a small letter.
Add something.
Take out something.
Add a period.
New paragraph

PROOFREAD FOR USAGE Use the indefinite article *a* before words that start with a consonant sound; use *an* before words that start with a vowel sound. For example:

As <u>a</u> precaution <u>an</u> officer asked for <u>a</u> uniform.

Check *A* and *An* Correct five articles in this news item by writing the correct article and the word that follows it.

Today a eighty-year-old woman received an postgraduate degree at Yale University. An audience of several thousand classmates cheered as Martha Tutt accepted an diploma. "This is quite a honor," she said. Ms. Tutt has completed research on an European tomb of a prehistoric family.

1. _____
2. _____
3. _____
4. _____
5. _____

PROOFREAD A NEWS ITEM Find the six misspelled words in this news item and write them correctly. Some may be words you learned before. Also fix three incorrect uses of *a* or *an*.

> In a pretrail hearing lasting a hour, the prosecuting atterney asked for an postponment of the trial for another month. The police said thay hope to include as evidence certain tape recordings made by a under cover officer that will prove the murder was premmeditated.

Word List

prehistoric	inhale
postwar	exhale
overcook	postdate
underweight	precaution
postponement	overlook
premeditated	include
postgraduate	exclude
prearrange	overflow
overpopulated	pretrial
undernourished	undercover

Personal Words

1. _____
2. _____

WRITE A NEWS ITEM Write a short news item about something that happened recently in your school. Try to use two or three spelling words and a personal word.

Review

MAKING INFERENCES Complete the statements with words from the box.

pretrial	overlook
prearrange	overflow
postdate	undercover
postwar	include
overcook	exclude

If a celebrity appears at a (1) hearing, you may expect an (2) crowd in the courtroom.

If you (3) certain friends from your plans, they may not (4) you in theirs.

If you (5) a check for payment, you may have to (6) credit to pay for other purchases.

If an (7) inspector ate at your restaurant, you wouldn't want to (8) her vegetables.

If you (9) reasons behind the countries' conflicts, you won't understand the (10) tensions.

1. _____
2. _____
3. _____
4. _____
5. _____
6. _____
7. _____
8. _____
9. _____
10. _____

Word *Study*

CONTEXT: SYNONYMS AND ANTONYMS When you come across an unfamiliar word, try using **context**—the words around the new word—to figure out its meaning. Synonyms or antonyms in the context may help you.

- Words such as *and, or, also,* and *as well* signal a synonym.

- Words such as *but, not, however,* and *instead of* signal an antonym.

For each sentence, write the synonym or antonym that explains the meaning of the underlined word. Write **S** after the words that are synonyms; write **A** after the antonyms.

1. The castle <u>commands</u>, or overlooks, the entire valley.
2. Rachel toured two <u>antebellum</u> mansions, but she wasn't interested in any postwar buildings.
3. The test will <u>encompass</u> math, science, and language arts. It may also include social studies.
4. The recent <u>inundation</u> destroyed their crops. The overflow damaged many homes as well.
5. The defendant's lawyer tried to prove that her client's actions were <u>impulsive</u>, not premeditated.

1. _____
2. _____
3. _____
4. _____
5. _____

Related Words 2

1. _____
2. _____
3. _____
4. _____
5. _____
6. _____
7. _____
8. _____
9. _____
10. _____
11. _____
12. _____
13. _____
14. _____
15. _____
16. _____
17. _____
18. _____
19. _____
20. _____

SPELLING FOCUS

Related words often have parts that are spelled the same but pronounced differently: **direct, direction; history, historical.**

■ **STUDY** Say each word. Then read the sentence.

1.	*direct*	Police sometimes **direct** traffic.
2.	*direction*	Our **direction** will be northeast.
3.	*history*	The mansion has quite a **history.**
4.	*historical*	We toured several **historical** homes.
5.	*fact*	That movie was based on **fact.**
6.	*factual*	Encyclopedias must be **factual.**
7.	*critic*	A food **critic** eats out often.
8.	*criticize*	Ty prefers to **criticize** and complain.
9.	*produce*	Our factories **produce** boxes.
10.	*production*	The **production** of cars increased.

11.	*magic*	The queen used a **magic** potion.
12.	*magician*	A **magician** made her disappear.
13.	*electric*	Plug in the **electric** blanket.
14.	*electrician*	An **electrician** wires new houses.
15.	*distract*	Toys **distract** fussy babies.
16.	*distraction*	TV is a **distraction** from studying.
17.	*remedy*	Aspirin is a **remedy** for headaches.
18.	*remedial*	My leg needs **remedial** exercise.
19.	*origin*	A word's **origin** is its history.
20.	*original*	Inventors have **original** ideas.

■ **PRACTICE** Sort the list words by writing
- four word pairs in which the sound of **c** changes
- three word pairs in which the sound of **t** changes
- three word pairs in which a vowel sound changes

■ **WRITE** Choose two sentences to include in a paragraph.

CHALLENGE!

intercept	interception
individual	individuality
cooperate	cooperation

RELATED PAIRS To complete each sentence below, write two list words that are related.

The dairy will increase its __(1)__ of cheese if its cows __(2)__ more milk.

Lorena is reading about the __(3)__ of Mexico because she plans to visit many __(4)__ sites when she travels there.

My older brother hopes that a class in __(5)__ algebra will __(6)__ his poor grades.

Her sister's radio was such a __(7)__ that Kara shouted, "Please don't __(8)__ me with that awful noise!"

The __(9)__ of the matter is, I don't think Nolan gave a __(10)__ description of what happened.

WORD RELATIONSHIPS First write the list word that is the base word of each word below. Then write another list word that is related to both words.

11–12. electricity
13–14. director
15–16. magical
17–18. originate
19–20. criticism

STRATEGIC SPELLING

Seeing Meaning Connections

1. _____
2. _____
3. _____
4. _____
5. _____
6. _____
7. _____
8. _____
9. _____
10. _____
11. _____
12. _____
13. _____
14. _____
15. _____
16. _____
17. _____
18. _____
19. _____
20. _____

Words related to produce
product
producer
unproductive

Complete the paragraph with words from the box.

The motion-picture __(21)__ was upset. He had watched the movie crew spend an __(22)__ day trying to shoot an important scene. No one was pleased with the finished __(23)__ . The entire scene would have to be reshot tomorrow.

21. _____
22. _____
23. _____

Did You Know?
A magician uses *misdirection* to fool the audience. To hide what one hand is doing, the magician cleverly draws people's attention to the other hand.

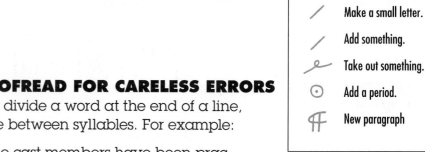

≡	Make a capital.
/	Make a small letter.
/	Add something.
ℓ	Take out something.
⊙	Add a period.
¶	New paragraph

PROOFREAD FOR CARELESS ERRORS

If you divide a word at the end of a line, divide between syllables. For example:

> The cast members have been prac-
> ticing the play for many weeks.

1. _____

2. _____

3. _____

Check Hyphenation Write the three words that are incorrectly divided and draw lines to show where the hyphen could be.

> Alvin Jones will play the part of Tom, and Tia Walker is perf-
> orming the part of Becky Thatcher. The play includes addit-
> ional roles for ten actors. Mrs. Perkins is assisting with cos-
> tumes and makeup. Mike Lomas and Alicia Ortiz will rese-
> arch the historical aspects of the play.

PROOFREAD A PRESS RELEASE
Find the five misspelled words and write them correctly. Some may be words you learned before. Also fix three incorrectly hyphenated words.

> Saturday night a producsion of <u>Tom Sawyer</u> will be performed by the West Middle School stude-nts. The play, wich is under the direction of Eleanor Sato, is based on the origonal book by Ma-rk Twain. This humorous story from the 1800s i-ncludes historicol details about life along the Mis-sissippi. You can perchase tickets at the door.

Word List

magic	origin
magician	original
fact	critic
factual	criticize
direct	history
direction	historical
remedy	produce
remedial	production
electric	distract
electrician	distraction

Personal Words

1. _____

2. _____

WRITE A PRESS RELEASE
Write a press release for a school event. Use three spelling words and a personal word.

 Review

MAKING CONNECTIONS Write a word from the box to complete each question.

direct	direction
history	historical
fact	factual
critic	criticize
produce	production

1. Can you ___ proof of ownership?
2. Does the movie ___ prefer to be called a reviewer?
3. Do you like ___ better than science?
4. Which state leads in the ___ of soy beans?
5. Is that a statement of fiction or ___?
6. Do you prefer biographies or ___ fiction?
7. Why did so many people ___ the judge's decision?
8. Do you have a good sense of ___?
9. Can you identify ___ and indirect objects?
10. Is that a ___ report or an editorial?

1. _____
2. _____
3. _____
4. _____
5. _____
6. _____
7. _____
8. _____
9. _____
10. _____

Word *Study*

LATIN ROOTS: *duc* The list words *produce* and *production* and the words in the Strategic Spelling activity on page 131 all have the root **duc**, which comes from the Latin word *ducere,* "to bring" or "to lead."

deduct	abduction
introduce	duct
conductor	

Complete the word web with the words in the box. Use your Spelling Dictionary if you need help.

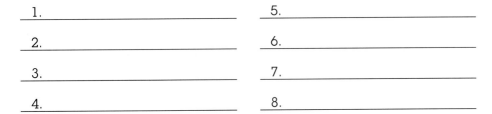

"tube for carrying liquid, air, and so on"
1. _____

"bring into use; acquaint with"
2. _____

ducere **"to bring, to lead"**

"a carrying off of someone by force"
5. _____

"leader or guide"
3. _____

"take away; subtract"
4. _____

One Word or Two?

SPELLING FOCUS

Some words that are often used together are never written as one word: **a lot, want to.** For other words you must think about their meanings to decide whether to write one word or two: **all ways, always.**

STUDY Say each word. Then read the sentence.

1.	a lot ✳	Sue peeled **a lot** of potatoes.
2.	want to	All the teams **want to** do well.
3.	all ways	Try **all ways** possible to succeed.
4.	always ✳	I **always** go to bed early.
5.	away	He moved **away** last summer.
6.	a way	I know **a way** to earn money.
7.	a little	Tim ate just **a little** goat cheese.
8.	below	A subway runs **below** the street.
9.	because ✳	Wear a coat **because** it's cold.
10.	together	They always sit **together** at lunch.

11.	forget	Don't **forget** to write me.
12.	around	The team jogged **around** the track.
13.	a while	This job could take **a while.**
14.	awhile ✳	Wait **awhile** and see who comes.
15.	forever	The sun won't last **forever.**
16.	again ✳	I saw my favorite movie **again.**
17.	tonight	The comet will be visible **tonight.**
18.	tomorrow	We can't go until **tomorrow** morning.
19.	become	Ona wants to **become** a doctor.
20.	going to	Mike is **going to** bake cookies.

PRACTICE Sort the list words by writing
- those that are one word
- those that are two words

WRITE Choose two sentences to write rhymes or riddles.

1.
2.
3.
4.
5.
6.
7.
8.
9.
10.
11.
12.
13.
14.
15.
16.
17.
18.
19.
20.

CHALLENGE!
sometimes
some times
backwards
pocketful
underneath

✳ **WATCH OUT FOR FREQUENTLY MISSPELLED WORDS!**

CONTEXT CLUES   Write the list word or words to complete each sentence. Choose from the words in parentheses.

In   (1)   Derrick is a great cook. He   (2)   prepares dinner for his family on Sunday. (always, all ways)

If Carla wants to find   (3)   to improve her grades, she shouldn't put her books   (4)   so soon. (away, a way)

We studied   (5)   and then went out to play. We played outside for quite   (6)   that evening. (awhile, a while)

(Hint: use *awhile* if you need an adverb; use *a while* if you need a noun.)

DEFINITIONS   Write the list word or words that mean the same as the underlined words in each sentence.

7. It looks as if it's <u>about to</u> rain.
8. Kenji plans to go to sleep early <u>this evening</u>.
9. We prefer an apartment <u>under</u> the third floor.
10. Add <u>a small amount of</u> salt.
11. George stayed at home <u>since</u> it was raining.
12. The day seemed to go on and on <u>without ending</u>.
13. If we all work <u>with each other</u>, we can get the job done.
14. What do you <u>wish to</u> do?
15. The car cost <u>a great deal</u> of money.
16. We have a test <u>the day after today</u>.
17. We'll go back <u>once more</u> next week.
18. Don't <u>fail to remember</u> to call me.
19. Pat has <u>grown to be</u> a very skillful pianist.
20. The dog turned <u>in a circle</u> three times.

1. _____
2. _____
3. _____
4. _____
5. _____
6. _____
7. _____
8. _____
9. _____
10. _____
11. _____
12. _____
13. _____
14. _____
15. _____
16. _____
17. _____
18. _____
19. _____
20. _____

STRATEGIC SPELLING

Seeing Meaning Connections

Write the word that fits each definition.

Words with *night*
tonight
nightingale
nightmare
nightly

21. happening every night: _____

22. bird that sings at night: _____

23. this night: _____

24. a scary dream: _____

≡	Make a capital.
/	Make a small letter.
⁄	Add something.
ℓ	Take out something.
⊙	Add a period.
¶	New paragraph

PROOFREAD FOR USAGE Avoid sentence **fragments.** Make sure each sentence has a subject and a verb.

We should meet. ⁄ Around six o'clock.

Check for Sentence Fragments Read each item below. If it is a fragment, write "F." If it is a complete sentence, write "Correct."

1. I can't talk to you tonight.
2. Because I'm visiting my grandparents.
3. Who live in Garland.
4. What are you going to do this weekend?
5. Baby-sitting again?

1. _____

2. _____

3. _____

4. _____

5. _____

PROOFREAD A NOTE Lisa slipped this note to Ana after school. Find the five misspelled words in the note. Some may be words you learned before. Also correct three sentence fragments.

> Ana, do you wanna get to-gether sometime soon? Maybe we could go roller-skating. Or ride our bikes. That would be alot of fun! I can't see you tomorrow. Because I'm gonna baby-sit. My usual job with the Murphys. I'll call you later to night.
>
> Lisa

Word List

always	tonight
all ways	together
away	tomorrow
a way	become
awhile	below
a while	because
a little	forget
a lot	forever
around	going to
again	want to

Personal Words

1. _____

2. _____

WRITE A NOTE Write a note to a friend suggesting an activity you both might like to do. Use three list words and a personal word.

Review

MAKING CONNECTIONS   Write the word from the box that fits each clue.

a lot
want to
all ways
always
a way
away
a little
below
because
together

1. This preposition is the opposite of *above.*
2. This is a conjunction, in a class with *and* and *since.*
3. This means "forever and ever."
4. This begins with a homophone for *two.*
5. This refers to a small amount.
6. This refers to a large quantity.
7. This expresses a desire for something.
8. This indicates a direction opposite of moving "toward."
9. The second of these words is a homophone for *weigh.*
10. The first of these words rhymes with *tall.*

1. _____   5. _____   9. _____

2. _____   6. _____   10. _____

3. _____   7. _____

4. _____   8. _____

Word *Study*

USING EXACT WORDS   Words such as *a lot* are vague. Can you think of more specific words for *a lot?* For example, instead of "I play basketball *a lot,*" you could say "I play basketball *frequently.*" Exact words help you express ideas more precisely.

In the first draft of her story, Sara used the word *suddenly* too often. Write a word from the box to replace each underlined word in the paragraph below. Use your Spelling Dictionary if you need help.

abruptly	unexpectedly	hastily	immediately	instantaneously

A letter arrived (1) <u>suddenly</u> at Dr. Tanaka's door. Dr. Tanaka ripped open the letter (2) <u>suddenly,</u> dropping the envelope to the floor. After reading its contents, he (3) <u>suddenly</u> ran out the door and jumped into his car. Driving at breakneck speed, he raced through the night. When the dirt road ended (4) <u>suddenly</u>, Dr. Tanaka slammed on the brakes. The car stopped (5) <u>suddenly</u>.

1. _____

2. _____

3. _____

4. _____

5. _____

Review

Lesson 25: Including All the Letters

Lesson 26: Suffixes -ate, -ive, -ship

Lesson 27: Opposite Prefixes

Lesson 28: Related Words 2

Lesson 29: One Word or Two?

REVIEW WORD LIST

1. average
2. awfully
3. beginning
4. cabinet
5. clothes
6. desperate
7. probably
8. restaurant
9. roughly
10. twelfth
11. wondering
12. affectionate
13. championship
14. constructive
15. creative
16. defective
17. inventive
18. productive
19. relationship
20. include
21. overflow
22. overlook
23. overpopulated
24. prehistoric
25. undercover
26. undernourished
27. underweight
28. critic
29. direction
30. distract
31. distraction
32. electric
33. historical
34. magic
35. magician
36. origin
37. original
38. produce
39. remedy
40. a lot
41. always
42. around
43. a way
44. away
45. because
46. become
47. below
48. going to
49. together
50. want to

■ PROOFREADING

Find the spelling errors in each passage and write the words correctly. All passages have seven errors except the last one, which has eight.

PROOFREAD A NOTICE

1. _____
2. _____
3. _____
4. _____
5. _____
6. _____
7. _____

Lost Kitten

We lost our white kitten who answers to the name Boots. She is all ways affectionit, and she won't run a way if you try to pick her up. She has black paws and is awfly small for her age, which is ruffly four months. She was under nourished and underwait when we found her. If you see her, please call 555-7211.

PROOFREAD AN ADVERTISEMENT

Amaze Your Friends!
You can learn majic tricks to astonish
your friends. In just ten lessons you will learn
to be a real magishen, and you will
be able to
- produse a rabbit out of a hat
  - destract an audience
  - becom expert at making
    objects vanish
- unlock a cabnet without a key
- discover away to make people disappear
Call or write now for a free brochure!

1. _____
2. _____
3. _____
4. _____
5. _____
6. _____
7. _____

PROOFREAD AN INTERVIEW

Interviewer: Congratulations on winning the city junior tennis championchip yesterday. How long have you been playing tennis?

Tennis Star: I was nine when my father gave me my first tennis lesson.

I.: Is your father a good coach?

T.S.: Yes, we have a good relashunship, and he's a good critick. His comments are really cunstructive.

I.: Are you headed for bigger competition now?

T.S.: Well, I don't want to over look educational opportunities. Practicing tennis takes a lot of time.

I.: There was an over flow crowd yesterday. Do spectators bother you when you play?

T.S.: No, I don't let any destraction spoil my concentration. It's just something I've learned to do.

1. _____
2. _____
3. _____
4. _____
5. _____
6. _____
7. _____

PROOFREAD A COMPLAINT

1. _____
2. _____
3. _____
4. _____
5. _____
6. _____
7. _____

March 12, 20_ _

Dear Sir or Madam:

The mystery jigsaw puzzle that I ordered is difective becaus it does not enclude all the pieces. Six or eight pieces are missing. My mother and I put the puzzle together right after it arrived, and the mystery is very origonal and crative. We enjoyed it alot. I am wondring whether you could send us another puzzle to replace this one. It is called "The Hidden Key" and is number J431.

Sincerely,

PROOFREAD A MYSTERY

1. _____
2. _____
3. _____
4. _____
5. _____
6. _____
7. _____

The resturant owner was desprate. "Get me an under cover agent! Get me a detective!" he cried. "Someone stole my fruits, my vegetables, and half my banana cream pie!"

Detective Hastings examined the kitchen from every drection. "The thief is a monkey," he said. "I found several red wool threads, black animal hairs, and a remady for indigestion. I asked myself, what kind of animal would steal vegetables and wear cloths? Not a dog. A dog would have stolen meat. But a trained monkey might wear a red coat."

"But why is the pie only half-eaten, and what about the medicine for indigestion?" asked the owner.

"Ah, my friend, I think you have a very bright monkey and only an averge cook," the detective replied.

140

PROOFREAD A FRIENDLY LETTER

November 5, 20__

Dear Manuel,

    When you come to visit at
Thanksgiving, we're gonna do something
great. Dad says he'll take us to the
eletric train show. We went last year,
and it was really fun. It has all kinds
of trains. Some of them run a round
historicol villages. Some run through
miniature tunnels, over bridges, and be
low real waterfalls. I know you'll wanna
see the show, and it'll be fun going to
gether. I just wanted to let you know
ahead of time!

Your cousin,

Diego

1. _____
2. _____
3. _____
4. _____
5. _____
6. _____
7. _____

PROOFREAD A REPORT

    In prehistoreic times, a people we call the Anasazi lived in the Southwest. *Anasazi* is a Navajo term meaning "ancient ones." The origan of these people is unknown. In the begining, they were hunters and gatherers, but about 2,000 years ago they settled in villages and began to farm. They were enventive in farming methods and in crafts, particularly pottery making. They were extremely productuve in the twelveth century. They built cliff dwellings such as the ones at Mesa Verde. By the mid-thirteenth century, their settlements became over populated. Perhaps for this reason, or perhaps because of invaders, the people left the cliff dwellings. They were probly the ancestors of many American Indian people living in New Mexico and Arizona today.

1. _____
2. _____
3. _____
4. _____
5. _____
6. _____
7. _____
8. _____

STRATEGY WORKSHOP

Choosing the Best Strategy

DISCOVER THE STRATEGY Use these **Steps for Spelling** to study new words:

> 1. Look at the word and say it. 2. Spell it aloud. 3. Think about it. 4. Picture it. 5. Look and write. 6. Cover, write, and check it.

Try these strategies for words that give you problems. For each hard word, choose the one that works best for you.

Strategies	How to Use Them
Developing Spelling Consciousness	Don't overlook familiar words wen you proofread your writing. (Did you catch the mistake in that last sentence?)
Creating Memory Tricks	Link your word with a memory helper that has the same problem letters: **(Leon is in the dungeon.)**
Using Meaning Helpers	Pair your word with a shorter, related word: **allowance—allow** **recession—recess**
Divide and Conquer	Divide your word into smaller parts: **team/mate** **beauti/ful** **ar/ti/fi/cial**
Pronouncing for Spelling	Pronounce the word correctly **("ex-act-ly")** or make up a secret pronunciation **("carn-i-val").**

TRY IT OUT Read each spelling problem. With a partner, decide which strategy would work best to help solve the problem.

1. The word *especially* is especially hard for me. It's so long!
2. How can I stop myself from misspelling itty-bitty words like *when* and *until*—words I really do know how to spell?
3. I keep leaving the **n** out of *autumn* because I don't hear it when I say the word.
4. How can I remember that *broccoli* has two **c**'s?
5. I have trouble learning new spelling words. I just sit and look at the word list and don't seem to get anywhere.
6. I keep spelling *collection* with a **ch** instead of a **t.**
7. I keep misspelling *possession* this way: **posseshion.**
8. *Communicate* has too many letters for me to remember.
9. How can I remember the part of *measles* I always misspell, the **eas?**
10. I keep leaving out the silent **i** in *business.*

1. _____
2. _____
3. _____
4. _____
5. _____
6. _____
7. _____
8. _____
9. _____
10. _____

LOOK AHEAD Look ahead at the next five lessons for list words that might give you problems. Write five of them. Then decide which strategy you will use to help remember each word, and write it next to the word.

Problem Word   **Strategy**

1. _____   _____
2. _____   _____
3. _____   _____
4. _____   _____
5. _____   _____

Words with No Sound Clues

SPELLING FOCUS

Some words have letters for sounds that you don't hear: **business.** In some words the vowel sound you hear gives no clue to its spelling: **opposite.**

■ **STUDY**   Say each word. Then read the sentence.

1.	*interested*	I am **interested** in her proposal.
2.	*usually* ✳	We **usually** go to bed by ten.
3.	*American*	I am proud to be an **American.**
4.	*toward*	Turn **toward** the flag and salute.
5.	*business* ✳	Stan owns a tire sales **business.**
6.	*vegetable*	Corn is her favorite **vegetable.**
7.	*really* ✳	That comedian is **really** funny.
8.	*opposite*	They went in **opposite** directions.
9.	*difficult*	This problem is **difficult** to solve.
10.	*Christmas* ✳	I love the lights at **Christmas.**

11.	*magazine*	Nita writes for a health **magazine.**
12.	*apologize*	I **apologize** for my rudeness.
13.	*multiply*	Rabbits **multiply** rapidly.
14.	*jealousy*	Fear or envy can lead to **jealousy.**
15.	*elementary* ✳	First take **elementary** French.
16.	*oxygen*	People need **oxygen** to breathe.
17.	*Maryland*	**Maryland** is a historic state.
18.	*sensitive*	My sunburn is **sensitive** and sore.
19.	*laughter*	Hearing **laughter** makes me smile.
20.	*disease*	A **disease** killed most of the elm trees.

1. _____
2. _____
3. _____
4. _____
5. _____
6. _____
7. _____
8. _____
9. _____
10. _____
11. _____
12. _____
13. _____
14. _____
15. _____
16. _____
17. _____
18. _____
19. _____
20. _____

■ **PRACTICE**   First write the words that are most difficult for you to spell. Then write the rest of the words. Underline any letters that cause you problems.

■ **WRITE**   Choose two sentences to include in a paragraph.

CHALLENGE!

temperamental
archaeology
parliament
nuisance
cantaloupe

✳ **WATCH OUT FOR FREQUENTLY MISSPELLED WORDS!**

ANTONYMS   Write the list word that completes each phrase.

1. not health, but ___
2. not unfeeling, but ___
3. not easy, but ___
4. not away from, but ___
5. not the same as, but the ___ of
6. not tears, but ___
7. not bored, but ___

CLASSIFYING   Write the list word that belongs in each group.

8. book, newspaper, ___
9. nitrogen, hydrogen, ___
10. Pennsylvania, Virginia, ___
11. Chinese, Mexican, ___
12. Thanksgiving, New Year's, ___
13. job, profession, ___
14. ask forgiveness, say you're sorry, ___
15. high school, middle school, ___ school
16. grain, fruit, ___
17. envy, resentment, ___
18. add, subtract, ___
19. generally, normally, ___
20. very, truly, ___

STRATEGIC SPELLING

Choosing the Best Strategy

Write two list words that you find hard to spell. Which strategy could help you spell each word? Name the strategy and tell why you chose it. Then compare choices with a partner. For a list of strategies, see page 142.

21. _____

_____

22. _____

_____

1. _____
2. _____
3. _____
4. _____
5. _____
6. _____
7. _____
8. _____
9. _____
10. _____
11. _____
12. _____
13. _____
14. _____
15. _____
16. _____
17. _____
18. _____
19. _____
20. _____

FREQUENTLY MISSPELLED WORDS

Use this sentence to help you remember to include the **i** in *business:* When **I** say **I** will do something, **I** mean bus<u>i</u>ness.

| Make a capital. |
| Make a small letter. |
| ∧ Add something. |
| Take out something. |
| ⊙ Add a period. |
| ¶ New paragraph |

PROOFREAD FOR USAGE Some nouns are made plural by adding either **-s** or **-es.** Others change in unusual ways (see Lesson 16). Don't use apostrophes to form plurals.

Many American's enjoy peachs, strawberrys, and potatos.

Check Plurals Correct the mistakes in this passage by writing the five misspelled plurals correctly.

Before starting your garden, buy supplys, such as a hoe, a shovel, and a rake. Remove weeds and dead leafs, and dig up the soil to a depth of eight to twelve inchs. You can grow some variety's of tomatoes on stake's for support.

1. _____

2. _____

3. _____

4. _____

5. _____

PROOFREAD A REPORT Find the nine misspelled words in this report and write them correctly. Some may be words you learned before. Three of the misspellings are incorrect plurals.

Planting a vegtable garden is a popular Amarican hobby. It's not realy that difficult. A gardening magizine or book can help you get started. Your plant's will need alot of sunshine. Weeding will help prevent desease. The most popular vegetables for home gardens are beans, lettuce, radishs, onions, and tomatos.

Word List

magazine	toward
apologize	usually
multiply	Maryland
jealousy	opposite
elementary	business
interested	laughter
oxygen	really
American	difficult
vegetable	Christmas
sensitive	disease

Personal Words

1. _____

2. _____

WRITE A REPORT Plan and write a report on a favorite hobby. Use three spelling words and a personal word.

Review

CROSSWORD PUZZLE
Use the clues to help you fill in the puzzle with list words.

interested	vegetable
usually	really
American	opposite
toward	difficult
business	Christmas

Across
1. as different as can be
3. in the direction of
4. December 25
5. commonly
8. plant used for food
9. hard to do or understand
10. work or occupation

Down
2. showing interest
6. of or in the United States
7. actually; truly

Multicultural Connection

LANGUAGES Arabic is spoken by more than 120 million people in Arabia, Iran, Syria, Jordan, Lebanon, and North Africa. Trade between these countries and Europe helped bring words such as *magazine* from Arabic into the English language. Here are some examples:

| magazine | hazard | tuna | massage | carafe | admiral |

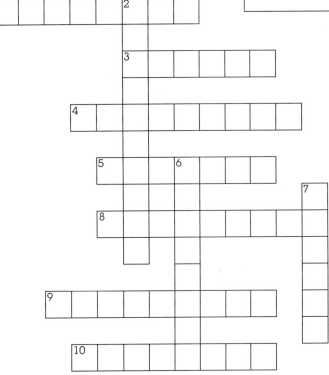

When a word comes into another language, it usually changes spelling, but often resembles the spelling of the word it came from. Write the word from the box that comes from each Arabic word.

1. *gharrāf*
2. *az-zahr*
3. *tun*
4. *massa*
5. *makhzan*
6. *amīral*

1. _____
2. _____
3. _____
4. _____
5. _____
6. _____

147

Negative Prefixes

When adding prefixes **il-**, **in-**, **im-**, and **ir-**, make no change in the base word. All of these prefixes mean "not."

■ **STUDY** Notice how each prefix is spelled in relation to the base word.

il + legal	=	1.	*illegal*
in + expensive	=	2.	*inexpensive*
in + accurate	=	3.	*inaccurate*
in + direct	=	4.	*indirect*
in + formal	=	5.	*informal*
im + polite	=	6.	*impolite*
im + proper	=	7.	*improper*
im + perfect	=	8.	*imperfect*
ir + responsible	=	9.	*irresponsible*
ir + regular	=	10.	*irregular*

il + logical	=	11.	*illogical*
il + legible	=	12.	*illegible*
in + capable	=	13.	*incapable*
in + credible	=	14.	*incredible*
im + patient	=	15.	*impatient*
im + balance	=	16.	*imbalance*
im + mature	=	17.	*immature*
ir + rational	=	18.	*irrational*
ir + resistible	=	19.	*irresistible*
ir + replaceable	=	20.	*irreplaceable*

■ **PRACTICE** Alphabetize the three words with **il-**, the six words with **in-**, the six words with **im-**, and the five words with **ir-**.

■ **WRITE** Choose three words to write a paragraph about shopping.

1.
2.
3.
4.
5.
6.
7.
8.
9.
10.
11.
12.
13.
14.
15.
16.
17.
18.
19.
20.

CHALLENGE!

illiterate
inconsiderate
inequality
immeasurable
irrelevant

HIDDEN WORDS

Each word below is hidden in a list word. Write the list word.

1. place
2. rate
3. edible
4. pens
5. form
6. lance
7. prop
8. mat
9. ration

SYNONYMS IN CONTEXT

Write a list word that means about the same as the underlined word or words in each sentence.

10. It's <u>unlawful</u> to park next to a fire hydrant.
11. The address on the envelope is <u>unreadable</u>.
12. The <u>slightly</u> <u>damaged</u> merchandise was quite a bargain, because it wasn't perfect.
13. In a <u>roundabout</u> way, she admitted to breaking the vase.
14. I love looking at the <u>tempting</u> desserts on the tray.
15. The customer was <u>rude</u> to the salesclerk.
16. His conclusions were <u>faulty</u> because he didn't use logic to support his argument.
17. Samantha was <u>unable</u> to run in the race because she had sprained her ankle.
18. Stuart gets <u>anxious</u> when he has to wait in line.
19. Mrs. Zorilla said she will fire <u>unreliable</u> employees.
20. There is an <u>abnormal</u> clicking sound in the car engine.

1. _____
2. _____
3. _____
4. _____
5. _____
6. _____
7. _____
8. _____
9. _____
10. _____
11. _____
12. _____
13. _____
14. _____
15. _____
16. _____
17. _____
18. _____
19. _____
20. _____

Building New Words

Make new words by adding one of the prefixes to each of these words: *active, practical, possible, personal, complete,* and *considerate.* Use your Spelling Dictionary if you need help.

Add *in-*

21. _____
22. _____
23. _____

Add *im-*

24. _____
25. _____
26. _____

Did You Know?
In Hartford, Connecticut, it's illegal to cross a street while walking on your hands.
In Lawrence, Kansas, it's illegal to carry bees in your hat in the streets.

≡	Make a capital.
/	Make a small letter.
∧	Add something.
ℓ	Take out something.
⊙	Add a period.
¶	New paragraph

PROOFREAD FOR USAGE When you make comparisons using *good, bad, much,* or *little,* don't add **-er** or *more* to comparative forms or **-est** or *most* to superlative forms.

It is irresponsible to waste water during our ~~worstest~~ *worst* drought in history. It is ~~more~~ better to save water than to waste it.

1. _____

2. _____

3. _____

4. _____

Check Adjectives Correct mistakes with comparisons.

1. We have had the leastest rain in twenty years.
2. We need to make more better use of the water we have.
3. If it is illegal to water lawns, people will use lesser water.
4. This is the bestest way to conserve our irreplaceable water.

PROOFREAD A LETTER TO THE EDITOR Find the five misspelled words in the body of this letter and write them correctly. Also fix three incorrect comparative adjectives.

It's incredible how many people don't use there seat belts. Not only is this elegal, but it is irrational to. People who wear seat belts have lesser chance of being injured and a much more better chance of surviving a car accident. The worstest thing is iresponsible parents who don't strap babies in car seats.

Word List

illegal	imbalance
illogical	improper
illegible	imperfect
inexpensive	impolite
incapable	immature
inaccurate	irreplaceable
informal	irresponsible
incredible	irresistible
indirect	irregular
impatient	irrational

Personal Words

1. _____

2. _____

WRITE A LETTER TO THE EDITOR Write a letter to the editor of your local newspaper. Use three spelling words and a personal word. Use correct business letter form (see page 245).

Review

ANTONYMS Write the word from the box that means the opposite of each word below.

1. trustworthy
2. dressy
3. precise
4. mannerly
5. costly

6. usual
7. lawful
8. straightforward
9. flawless
10. appropriate

illegal
inexpensive
inaccurate
indirect
informal
impolite
improper
imperfect
irresponsible
irregular

1. _____
2. _____
3. _____
4. _____
5. _____

6. _____
7. _____
8. _____
9. _____
10. _____

Word *Study*

LATIN ROOTS: COMMUNICATION WORDS The list word *illegible* comes from the Latin root **leg,** meaning "to read." The chart shows this root, another Latin root that means "to speak," and some prefixes that are added to words to change their meanings.

illegible   dictate
lecture   predict
legend

Latin Root or Prefix	Meaning
leg, lect	to read
dict	to speak
il-	not
pre-	in advance

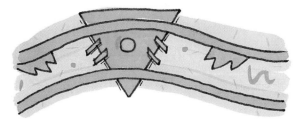

Look at the words in the red box. Write the word that best fits each meaning. Use the chart and Spelling Dictionary for help.

1. speak aloud as someone writes down the words
2. a story from the past that has been read for many years
3. read or give a speech on a chosen subject
4. not easy to read
5. tell beforehand

1. _____
2. _____
3. _____
4. _____
5. _____

Suffixes -ance, -ence, -ant, -ent

SPELLING FOCUS

When adding suffixes **-ance**, **-ence**, **-ant**, and **-ent**, there is no sound clue to help you decide whether to use an **a** or **e**.

■ **STUDY**   Say each word. Then read the sentence.

1. entrance — Banners mark the park **entrance.**
2. performance — Her **performance** was good.
3. appearance — His **appearance** is neat and clean.
4. clearance — Stores have **clearance** sales.
5. independence — Our country won its **independence.**
6. difference — I hear a **difference** in your tone.
7. excellence — This award is for **excellence** in art.
8. brilliant — The noonday sun was **brilliant.**
9. important — The next project is **important.**
10. intelligent — Dolphins are extremely **intelligent.**

11. insurance — Families need health **insurance.**
12. confidence — Coach has **confidence** in our team.
13. coincidence — We kept meeting by **coincidence.**
14. pollutant — Fertilizer can be a **pollutant.**
15. ignorant — A fool is **ignorant** of the law.
16. hesitant — Ike was **hesitant** to ask for a raise.
17. apparent — The artist's talent was **apparent.**
18. persistent — Her **persistent** efforts paid off.
19. convenient — Call me when it's **convenient.**
20. consistent — He gives us **consistent** support.

■ **PRACTICE**   Sort the list words by writing
- five words with the suffix **-ance**
- five words with the suffix **-ence**
- five words with the suffix **-ant**
- five words with the suffix **-ent**

■ **WRITE**   Choose ten words to write in sentences.

CHALLENGE!

significance
incompetence
disinfectant
disobedient
concurrent

1. _____
2. _____
3. _____
4. _____
5. _____
6. _____
7. _____
8. _____
9. _____
10. _____
11. _____
12. _____
13. _____
14. _____
15. _____
16. _____
17. _____
18. _____
19. _____
20. _____

ADDING SUFFIXES Add a suffix to each word in parentheses to form a list word that completes the sentence.

1. (clear) We hope to find some bargains at the ____ sale.
2. (pollute) It's illegal to dump a ____ into a river.
3. (confide) If you have ____ in yourself, you'll succeed.
4. (perform) The soloist was nervous before the ____.
5. (persist) The Parks were annoyed by the ____ salesman.
6. (appear) Father's tired ____ worried our family.
7. (coincide) It was a ____ that we took the same flight.
8. (differ) There's a big ____ in the prices of these two shirts.
9. (ignore) The tourists were ____ of Chinese customs.
10. (insure) Lack of health ____ is a serious problem.

DEFINITIONS Write the list word that fits each definition.

11. plain to see
12. door
13. quick to learn
14. superiority
15. sparkling

16. undecided
17. within easy reach
18. having value
19. steady; unchanged
20. freedom

STRATEGIC SPELLING

Building New Words

Add the suffix **-ence** or **-ance** to each base word to make a new word. Check the Spelling Dictionary if you need help.

Base Word	New Word
21. exist	
22. inherit	
23. refer	
24. attend	

1. _____
2. _____
3. _____
4. _____
5. _____
6. _____
7. _____
8. _____
9. _____
10. _____
11. _____
12. _____
13. _____
14. _____
15. _____
16. _____
17. _____
18. _____
19. _____
20. _____

Take a Hint
To spell *difference* correctly, be sure to clearly pronounce the second syllable: **dif-fer-ence.**

	Make a capital.
/	Make a small letter.
∧	Add something.
ℓ	Take out something.
⊙	Add a period.
⨍	New paragraph

PROOFREAD FOR PUNCTUATION

Use a comma before the conjunction in a compound sentence. For example:

> I worked and practiced all month, but I was still nervous when we got on stage.

Check for Commas If a comma is missing, write the word the comma should **follow.** If a sentence is correct, write "Correct."

1. I was reluctant to join the band and perform onstage.
2. I had no confidence in myself but Kika believed in me.
3. We had some problems but we still entertained the crowd.
4. We impressed our friends and we had fun too!

1. _____

2. _____

3. _____

4. _____

PROOFREAD A HUMOROUS PARAGRAPH

Find five misspelled words and write them correctly. Some are words you learned before. Also fix three missing commas.

> I was hesitent to join the rock band but my freind Kika gave me the confidence to try. Our first preformance was Friday and it nearly was a disaster! First an amplifier quit working and then a string on my guitar broke just before our appearence on stage. Now I know why it's importent to be prepared for any emergency.

Word List

confidence	difference
clearance	consistent
apparent	brilliant
entrance	insurance
persistent	important
performance	excellence
intelligent	ignorant
pollutant	appearance
independence	coincidence
convenient	hesitant

Personal Words

1. _____

2. _____

WRITE A HUMOROUS PARAGRAPH

Write a paragraph about something funny that happened to you recently. Use three spelling words and a personal word.

Review

ASSOCIATIONS
Write the word from the box that is associated with each word below.

1. smart	6. removal
2. freedom	7. show
3. sparkling	8. superiority
4. looks	9. imbalance
5. doorway	10. special

entrance
performance
appearance
clearance
independence
difference
excellence
brilliant
important
intelligent

1. _____

2. _____

3. _____

4. _____

5. _____

6. _____

7. _____

8. _____

9. _____

10. _____

Using a *Dictionary*

FINDING THE RIGHT MEANING
An entry word in a dictionary can have more than one meaning. Read the meanings of *brilliant* below.

> **bril•liant** (bril′yənt), **1** shining brightly; sparkling: *brilliant jewels, brilliant sunshine.* **2** splendid; magnificent: *The singer gave a brilliant performance.* **3** having great ability: *a brilliant musician.* **4** diamond or other gem cut to sparkle brightly. 1–3 *adj.*, 4 *n.* —**bril′liant ly,** *adv.*

Many words can be used as more than one part of speech. The abbreviations at the end of the entry for *brilliant* tell you which definitions are adjectives and which are nouns.

1. Is the fourth definition of *brilliant* an adjective or a noun?
2. How many adjective definitions does *brilliant* have?

1. _____

2. _____

For each sentence below, write the number of the meaning of *brilliant* used and its part of speech.

3. Although he was young, he was a <u>brilliant</u> chess player.
4. This <u>brilliant</u> is worth a thousand dollars.
5. We gazed in wonder at the <u>brilliant</u> ruby.
6. We all agreed that the celebration was a <u>brilliant</u> event.

3. _____

4. _____

5. _____

6. _____

Compound Words 2

Keep all the letters when writing a closed compound. Hyphenate numbers from twenty-one to ninety-nine, compounds with **in-law** and **self,** and compounds made up of a noun and a verb.

■ **STUDY**   Say each word. Then read the sentence.

1.	*basketball* ✳	Leon dribbles the **basketball** well.
2.	*everywhere*	I looked **everywhere** for my keys.
3.	*outside* ✳	Gym class is **outside** on nice days.
4.	*summertime*	We swim often in the **summertime.**
5.	*something* ✳	She has **something** to say to you.
6.	*baby-sit*	He will **baby-sit** for his cousins.
7.	*roller-skating*	I was **roller-skating** around the rink.
8.	*drive-in*	The **drive-in** theater closes in the fall.
9.	*self-control*	Dieting requires **self-control.**
10.	*part-time*	Fay has a **part-time** job at a bank.

11.	*afterthought*	His remark was an **afterthought.**
12.	*cheerleader*	A **cheerleader** is also a gymnast.
13.	*quarterback*	The **quarterback** passed the football.
14.	*bookstore*	She bought a book at the **bookstore.**
15.	*courthouse*	The **courthouse** is the county seat.
16.	*ice-skated*	They **ice-skated** on the frozen lake.
17.	*ninety-five*	Grandma is **ninety-five** years old.
18.	*brother-in-law*	My sister and **brother-in-law** came.
19.	*water-skied*	I **water-skied** until my legs shook.
20.	*old-fashioned*	Some **old-fashioned** cars look odd.

■ **PRACTICE**   Write each of these groups in alphabetical order.
- the ten closed compounds
- the ten hyphenated compounds

■ **WRITE**   Choose two sentences to include in a paragraph.

1. _____
2. _____
3. _____
4. _____
5. _____
6. _____
7. _____
8. _____
9. _____
10. _____
11. _____
12. _____
13. _____
14. _____
15. _____
16. _____
17. _____
18. _____
19. _____
20. _____

CHALLENGE!

bookkeeper
headstrong
vice-president
great-grandfather
warm-blooded

✳ **WATCH OUT FOR FREQUENTLY MISSPELLED WORDS!**

DRAWING CONCLUSIONS   Write the list word that answers each question.

1. What would you call someone who is married to your sister?
2. What is less than ninety-six but more than ninety-four?
3. Where do you go to mow the lawn?
4. In what game do you throw a ball through a hoop?
5. What do you need when you're about to lose your temper?
6. Which player might throw a touchdown pass?
7. What would you be doing at a roller rink?
8. What time of year do you have a vacation from school?
9. Where could you see lawyers, judges, and criminals?
10. Where could you buy an atlas, a dictionary, or a thesaurus?
11. If you're at sea, where would you see water?

COMBINING WORDS   Combine each word in the first column with a word from the second column to make a list word. Hint: Don't forget to use hyphens when you need to.

12. baby	fashioned
13. some	thought
14. ice	skied
15. drive	in
16. after	sit
17. old	thing
18. water	leader
19. part	skated
20. cheer	time

Seeing Meaning Connections

Complete the passage with words from the box.

My cousin and I (21) on a lake Saturday. The house we rented was located on the (22) . Our boat got so (23) it almost sank in the rain.

Words with
water
water-skied
waterlogged
waterfront

21. _____

22. _____

23. _____

1.	_____
2.	_____
3.	_____
4.	_____
5.	_____
6.	_____
7.	_____
8.	_____
9.	_____
10.	_____
11.	_____
12.	_____
13.	_____
14.	_____
15.	_____
16.	_____
17.	_____
18.	_____
19.	_____
20.	_____

*FREQUENTLY MISSPELLED WORDS * FREQUENTLY MISSPELLED WORDS*

If you remember that *something* is made up of the words *some* and *thing*, it will help you include the silent **e** when you're spelling the word.

≡	Make a capital.
/	Make a small letter.
∧	Add something.
ℰ	Take out something.
⊙	Add a period.
¶	New paragraph

PROOFREAD FOR CAPITALIZATION

Be sure a word really needs a capital letter before you give it one.

> Do you have a book about the Lions' new Quarterback?

Check for Capital Letters Correct the words that are incorrectly capitalized in this comment written on a form at a bookstore.

> I like the comfortable Reading area and the Snacks you serve in the Bookstore. Why don't you stock more Children's Books?

PROOFREAD A FORM   Find the five misspelled words in Janine's handwritten comments and write them correctly. Some may be words you learned before. Also fix three words Janine wrote that shouldn't be capitalized.

1. _____
2. _____
3. _____
4. _____
5. _____

TERRIFIC ATHLETIC CENTER

Name _Janine Cole_   **Phone** _555-8329_

☑ **suggestion**   ❑ **problem**   ❑ **compliment**

I like playing basket ball outside on your Courts in the summer time, but why don't you open an oldfashion rollrskating rink indoors for the Winter? Many Children would be intrested in it!

Word List

basketball
afterthought
cheerleader
quarterback
outside
everywhere
bookstore
courthouse
summertime
something

ice-skated
roller-skating
baby-sit
brother-in-law
ninety-five
drive-in
self-control
water-skied
old-fashioned
part-time

Personal Words

1. _____
2. _____

WRITE A FORM   Think of a store, restaurant, or sports facility you go to. Write some comments about it for a comment card. Use three spelling words and a personal word.

basketball	baby-sit
everywhere	roller-skating
outside	drive-in
summertime	self-control
something	part-time

Review

MAKING CONNECTIONS   Write a list word from the box that fits each clue.

1. Before getting a full-time job, many people work on this schedule.
2. This team sport is played by amateurs and professionals.
3. During this part of the year, lakes should be warm enough for swimming.
4. This activity can be done outdoors or inside on a rink.
5. A teenager might be paid to do this.
6. If you walk here, you might feel the wind or the sun.
7. This kind of movie theater is not as popular as it once was.
8. After you've searched here, you can declare an item lost.
9. This is the opposite of nothing.
10. People trying to change certain behaviors need to exercise this.

1. _____

2. _____

3. _____

4. _____

5. _____

6. _____

7. _____

8. _____

9. _____

10. _____

Word *Study*

JARGON   Every sport has its own special language, or **jargon,** that is mostly known only by fans and players. Read this passage about football, paying special attention to the highlighted words.

> In the **huddle,** the Lions listened intently as their rookie quarterback, Jacobs, called the next play. From the **line of scrimmage,** the Lions' center snapped the ball to Jacobs, who **rifled** a picture-perfect pass to the tight end, Johnson. We were afraid he'd **fumble,** but Johnson held onto the **pigskin** and galloped all the way for the winning touchdown!

Write the highlighted word from the passage above that fits each definition. Use your Spelling Dictionary if you need help.

1. place on the field where the ball rests at the start of a play
2. a football
3. drop the football while running with it
4. a gathering of players to plan the next play
5. threw the ball hard

1. _____   4. _____

2. _____   5. _____

3. _____

Words from Greek and Latin

SPELLING FOCUS

The Greek word part **auto-** means "self" and **tele-** means "far off." The Latin root **port** means "to carry" and **phon** means "voice" or "sound."

■ **STUDY** Say each word. Then read the sentence.

1.	*automobile*	The **automobile** rules the roads.
2.	*autograph*	The pitcher gave us his **autograph.**
3.	*telescope*	Point the **telescope** at the moon.
4.	*telecast*	We missed the **telecast** of the game.
5.	*telephone*	I made a **telephone** call to Canada.
6.	*microphone*	The singer needed a **microphone.**
7.	*headphones*	We listened through **headphones.**
8.	*portable*	A laptop computer is so **portable.**
9.	*import*	We **import** many cars from Japan.
10.	*export*	We **export** wheat and corn to Asia.

11.	*automatic*	The alarm clock is **automatic.**
12.	*autobiography*	The TV star wrote an **autobiography.**
13.	*autopilot*	The airplane can fly on **autopilot.**
14.	*telegram*	She sent me a singing **telegram.**
15.	*telegraph*	A **telegraph** requires electricity.
16.	*symphony*	This Mozart **symphony** is lovely.
17.	*saxophone*	I played **saxophone** in a jazz band.
18.	*megaphone*	A **megaphone** increases sound.
19.	*transport*	Trucks **transport** many goods.
20.	*passport*	A **passport** identifies you.

■ **PRACTICE** Sort the words by writing
- a word from **tele-** and **phon**
- four more words from **tele-**
- five more words from **phon**
- five words from **port**
- five words from **auto-**

■ **WRITE** Use two sentences to write an advertisement.

1. _____
2. _____
3. _____
4. _____
5. _____
6. _____
7. _____
8. _____
9. _____
10. _____
11. _____
12. _____
13. _____
14. _____
15. _____
16. _____
17. _____
18. _____
19. _____
20. _____

CHALLENGE!

autonomy
telecommunication
xylophone
cacophony
deportation

WORD PARTS Write the list word that includes the underlined part of each word below.

1. head<u>ache</u>
2. <u>broad</u>cast
3. trans<u>form</u>
4. micro<u>scope</u>
5. im<u>mers</u>e
6. <u>pass</u>word
7. <u>gram</u>mar
8. <u>micro</u>film
9. suit<u>able</u>
10. <u>ex</u>change
11. <u>bio</u>logy
12. syste<u>matic</u>

CONTEXT Write the list word that completes each sentence.

13. The official used a large, funnel-shaped ___ so the crowd could hear him speak.
14. We sent a telegram using the ___ equipment.
15. My favorite woodwind instrument is the ___.
16. The airplane was flying on ___.
17. If you're going to be late, find a ___ and call to let me know.
18. Jan asked her favorite player to ___ a baseball she caught.
19. Uncle Pete takes the old car he restored to ___ shows.
20. Our class will take a field trip to listen to a ___ orchestra.

STRATEGIC SPELLING

Seeing Meaning Connections

21. Write a list word that is related to the words in the box. _____

Write the words from the box that fit the definitions below.

headlight
headstrong
headline
headband

22. hard to control or manage _____

23. cloth or ribbon worn around the head _____

24. a bright light at the front of a vehicle _____

25. words in heavy type at the top of an article

_____

1. _____
2. _____
3. _____
4. _____
5. _____
6. _____
7. _____
8. _____
9. _____
10. _____
11. _____
12. _____
13. _____
14. _____
15. _____
16. _____
17. _____
18. _____
19. _____
20. _____

> **Did You Know?**
> The word *autopilot* is a blend of *automatic* and *pilot*.

	Make a capital.
/	Make a small letter.
∧	Add something.
ℓ	Take out something.
⊙	Add a period.
¶	New paragraph

PROOFREAD FOR USAGE Use only one negative word when you mean "no" or "not."

I (<u>have</u>, haven't) never thought of being anything but an astronomer.

Check for Double Negatives Choose the correct word from the pair in parentheses.

1. There isn't (any, no) place more fun than the planetarium.
2. I don't (never, ever) want to be without my telescope.
3. I couldn't see (nothing, anything) like Saturn's rings without my telescope.
4. I have seen (any, none) of the planets so far this week.
5. There (aren't, are) any visible because the moon is too bright.

1. _____

2. _____

3. _____

4. _____

5. _____

PROOFREAD A PERSONAL NARRATIVE Find five misspelled words and write them correctly. Some may be words you learned before. Also fix three double negatives.

If I where to write my autobiagrophy, I'd write about my love of music. There isn't no one who likes playing the saxaphone better than I do. There isn't nothing I'd rather do than preform. I haven't told no one this, but I even hope to write a saxophone synphony someday.

Word List

telegram	automatic
microphone	passport
telephone	automobile
symphony	transport
telescope	autobiography
saxophone	import
telegraph	autopilot
headphones	export
telecast	autograph
megaphone	portable

Personal Words

1. _____

2. _____

WRITE A PERSONAL NARRATIVE Plan and write a paragraph about something that is important to you. Use three spelling words and a personal word.

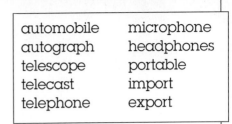

automobile	microphone
autograph	headphones
telescope	portable
telecast	import
telephone	export

Review

WORDS IN CONTEXT Write the word that is missing from each person's statement.

1. Pilot: "These ___ are too tight around my ears."
2. Celebrity: "I'd be happy to ___ your copy of my book."
3. Clerk: "Please write your ___ number on your check."
4. Car dealer: "This ___ will give you years of reliable service."
5. Singer: "Do you have a ___ I can clip to my shirt?"
6. Farmer: "I hope to ___ a lot of grain to Russia this year."
7. TV anchor: "This program is being ___ from the courthouse."
8. Camper: "I'm glad we brought along our ___ stove."
9. Astronomer: "The Hubble ___ has provided amazing information about outer space."
10. The President of the United States: "Our country will ___ millions of barrels of oil from Saudi Arabia this year."

1. _____
2. _____
3. _____
4. _____
5. _____
6. _____
7. _____
8. _____
9. _____
10. _____

Word *Study*

BLENDS AND CLIPS The list word *telecast* is a **blend** of *television* and *broadcast. Sax* is a **clip**, or shortened form, of the list word *saxophone.* For each blend below, write the two words it came from. Use your Spelling Dictionary if you need help.

1. brunch
2. camcorder
3. motel
4. cheeseburger
5. smog
6. infomercial

Write the long form of each underlined clip to complete the items below. If you need help, use your Spelling Dictionary.

7. At a <u>coed</u> school, males and females are educated together. State universities are ___ schools.
8. Ms. Kelly's favorite flower is the <u>mum</u>. She put a ___ plant on her desk to brighten up our classroom.
9. We visited the <u>zoo</u>. We saw baby pandas at the ___.
10. The first <u>movies</u> were short and simply made. Now, ___ are longer and expertly made.
11. The twins <u>gab</u> constantly. I hate listening to so much ___.
12. This is supposed to be a bad year for the <u>flu</u>. If you get ___, drink a lot of liquids and get plenty of rest.

1. _____
2. _____
3. _____
4. _____
5. _____
6. _____
7. _____
8. _____
9. _____
10. _____
11. _____
12. _____

Review

Lesson 31: Words with No Sound Clues
Lesson 32: Negative Prefixes
Lesson 33: Suffixes -ance, -ence, -ant, -ent
Lesson 34: Compound Words 2
Lesson 35: Words from Greek and Latin

REVIEW WORD LIST

1. American
2. Christmas
3. difficult
4. interested
5. jealousy
6. magazine
7. Maryland
8. really
9. sensitive
10. toward
11. illegal
12. illogical
13. impatient
14. improper
15. incapable
16. incredible
17. inexpensive
18. irrational
19. irresistible
20. irresponsible
21. apparent
22. appearance
23. brilliant
24. excellence
25. hesitant
26. ignorant
27. important
28. intelligent
29. performance
30. persistent
31. afterthought
32. brother-in-law
33. cheerleader
34. courthouse
35. drive-in
36. everywhere
37. old-fashioned
38. outside
39. roller-skating
40. summertime
41. automobile
42. autopilot
43. headphones
44. megaphone
45. quarterback
46. saxophone
47. symphony
48. telecast
49. telephone
50. telescope

■ PROOFREADING

Find the spelling errors in each passage and write the words correctly. All passages have seven errors except the last one, which has eight.

PROOFREAD A NARRATIVE PARAGRAPH

1. _____
2. _____
3. _____
4. _____
5. _____
6. _____
7. _____

When we were younger, my brother and I visited my grandparents in Indiana in the summer time. We spent the summer visiting the oldfashion ice cream parlor, exploring the court house in the middle of town, and rollrskating everwhere. Sometimes Granddad took us to the drive in theater, or we played games on the screened-in back porch when we couldn't play out side.

PROOFREAD A TALE

One day a young man saw three swans land, throw off their feathers, turn into maidens, and dive into the water. Then they returned to shore, put on their feathers, and flew away. He found one of the maidens iresistible, so his mother told him to go back to the place where he had seen this incredable sight. "If you are truly intrested," said she, "when the swans make their appearence, steal the feathers of the one you love." The young man was hesitent but soon decided that this would not be diffcult. The swans returned, repeated their preformence, and two of the maidens put on their feathers and flew away. He gave the third a cloak to wear and took her home. Seven years later, the husband showed his wife the feathers he had stolen. When she held them, however, she was changed into a swan, flew into the sky, and disappeared forever.

1. _____
2. _____
3. _____
4. _____
5. _____
6. _____
7. _____

PROOFREAD A SOCIAL STUDIES REPORT

Francis Scott Key, held by the British on a ship, watched as the British attacked Fort McHenry near Baltimore, Marilyn, on September 13, 1814. Although the British were persistant, it became apparant after twenty-five hours that they could not capture the Amarican fort. During the night, Key paced the ship, ignorent of the outcome of the battle. At dawn, he saw the U.S. flag still flying. Inspired, Key wrote a stanza of "The Star-Spangled Banner" as he looked from the ship tward shore. He finished the poem later that day and gave it to his brother in law, who had it printed and distributed.

1. _____
2. _____
3. _____
4. _____
5. _____
6. _____
7. _____

PROOFREAD A POEM

1. _____
2. _____
3. _____
4. _____
5. _____
6. _____
7. _____

Willful

My brillant dog, whose name is Will,
Is relly inexspensive,
But since my mom thinks otherwise,
He's grown to be quite sensative.
She's sure he's iresponsible,
And as an after thought,
She adds that he's incapible
Of ever being taught.

PROOFREAD A BUSINESS LETTER

1. _____
2. _____
3. _____
4. _____
5. _____
6. _____
7. _____

1501 Elm Street
Madison, WI 53707
October 8, 20_ _

CBS, Inc.
51 West 52nd Street
New York, NY 10019

Dear Sir or Madam:

    I was disappointed when I watched the telicast of the football game yesterday. My sister plays the saxofone in the Wisconsin band, but I saw about one minute of the band at halftime. Instead, after all the autamobile commercials, I watched a shot of a cher leader, a close-up of a megophone, and a discussion of an illigal play by a former quaterback. Perhaps you should poll your viewers about their preferences.

               Sincerely,
               Victor Delgado

PROOFREAD A JOURNAL ENTRY

Yesterday I took my first airplane ride. We flew all the way across Canada. After we took off, the pilot came back to talk to the passengers. (I hope the plane was on autapilot!) We had lunch and then watched a movie. After that, I could listen to a synphony, pop music, or several other kinds of music through the headfones. There was a telaphon in the back of the seat ahead of me, but I didn't make any calls. I read a magezine and looked out the window. I thought I would be inpatient to land, but I wasn't. This will probably be the most exciting chrismas I've ever had.

1. _____
2. _____
3. _____
4. _____
5. _____
6. _____
7. _____

PROOFREAD A SCIENCE REPORT

In the 1600s there was much jelousy and secretiveness among Dutch lens makers, some of whom made ilogical claims. Many people claimed to have invented the teloscope. We know that Galileo developed and improved this marvelous instrument, however. Many intellegent people had entirely different opinions about it. Some thought it inproper to examine the heavens. Others thought it irational to believe there were objects that could not be seen with the naked eye. There were many who marveled at the excellince of the instrument, however, and realized they were witnesses to an inportant scientific discovery.

1. _____
2. _____
3. _____
4. _____
5. _____
6. _____
7. _____
8. _____

Vocabulary, Writing, and Reference Resources

Cross-Curricular Lessons

Writer's Handbook

Dictionary Handbook

Spelling Dictionary

Writer's Thesaurus

English/Spanish Word List

21,000

21,000

42,000

Cross-Curricular Lessons

SOCIAL STUDIES

HEALTH

SCIENCE

READING

MATHEMATICS

historian
oral histories
documents
primary sources
secondary sources
archaeologist
site
prehistoric
artifacts
excavate

_____

_____

Gathering Facts About History

How do we learn about peoples and places of the past? The list words deal with the search for information about past events. Add more words to the list. Then do the activities. Use your Spelling Dictionary for help.

■ GETTING AT MEANING

Drawing Conclusions Use the chart to help you complete these paragraphs.

A person who studies and interprets the oral and written records of the past is called a **(1)** . Researchers of history use two kinds of sources for their work. They look at **(2)** , sources that give secondhand interpretations by people who were not present when the events occurred. They also look at **(3)** , which give direct, firsthand information about what people thought, wrote, or made.

Historians often make use of government records, diaries, letters, and other written **(4)** . For recent history, however, they can also talk to people about their memories. These **(5)** are especially valuable in finding out about the lives of ordinary people.

primary sources

● **documents**
diaries/old letters
government records
birth certificates

● **oral histories**
interviews
taped recordings
TV news programs

● **artifacts**
tools
paintings
pottery

Historian

secondary sources

history books
biographies
textbooks

1. _____   4. _____

2. _____   5. _____

3. _____

Dr. Frank Hibben (right) with an associate at an excavation site.

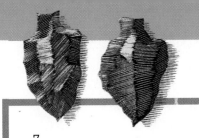

7. _____

flint knife

hand ax

bone fishhooks

Chart Use the paragraph below to help you complete the chart with list words.

In 1936, **archaeologist** Dr. Frank Hibben began to explore a new **site**, a cave in the Sandia Mountains of New Mexico. Soon after he began to dig, Dr. Hibben found the bones of an Ice Age ground sloth. As Hibben and his team continued to **excavate**, they discovered evidence of **prehistoric** people. The **artifacts** they found—scrapers, flint points for spears, and blades—may have been made by humans over eleven thousand years ago!

8. *tobrush*

to dig with shovels

to brush away dirt

to look for buried objects

9. *tomb*

cave

tomb

location

6. _____

thinks about the ancient past

studies ancient cultures

looks for objects made by prehistoric people

10. _____

long ago

before written history

when some people lived in caves

Making History Where You Live

What event has happened in your area recently that would make good history? Work with a partner or group to put together a record of the event. Plan to use both primary and secondary sources that will make your history more exciting. Share your completed "historical record" with your classmates.

Egyptians
Africa
pharaoh
Pyramids
mummy
artisans
sphinx
temple
tomb
hieroglyphics

_____

_____

Ancient Egyptian Culture

The list words deal with the culture of ancient Egypt. If you know other words related to ancient Egyptian culture, add them to the list. Then do the exercises. Use your Spelling Dictionary if you need help.

■ GETTING AT MEANING

Journal Entries Use the clues in the sentences to complete these journal entries with list words.

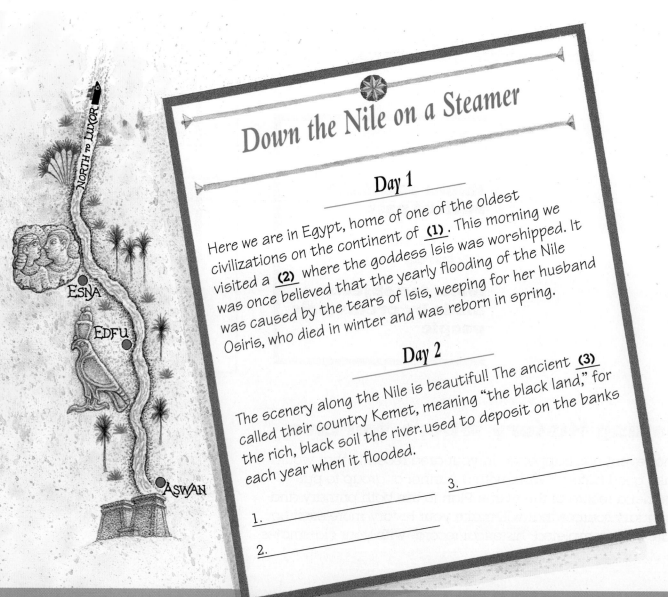

Down the Nile on a Steamer

Day 1

Here we are in Egypt, home of one of the oldest civilizations on the continent of __(1)__. This morning we visited a __(2)__ where the goddess Isis was worshipped. It was once believed that the yearly flooding of the Nile was caused by the tears of Isis, weeping for her husband Osiris, who died in winter and was reborn in spring.

Day 2

The scenery along the Nile is beautiful! The ancient __(3)__ called their country Kemet, meaning "the black land," for the rich, black soil the river used to deposit on the banks each year when it flooded.

1. _____

2. _____

3. _____

Down the Nile on a Steamer

Day 3

We docked at Luxor (Thebes). Then we took a ferry across to the west bank and drove to the Valley of the Kings! One highlight of this ancient cemetery is the __(4)__ in which Tutankhamen ("King Tut") was buried. The __(5)__ of King Tut, wrapped in bandages, had been lying inside a gilded wood coffin!

Days 4 & 5

We sailed on to Cairo, and then drove to Giza to see the great stone structures rising out of the desert sands— the __(6)__! These impressive monuments to the pharaohs were built by thousands of stone masons, sculptors, and other skilled __(7)__.

4. _____

5. _____   6. _____

                               7. _____

Word Association Write the list word that each group of words suggests. Use the definitions in the box for help.

---

pharaoh *a king or queen of ancient Egypt*

sphinx *statue of a lion's body with the head of a man, ram, or hawk*

hieroglyphics *a system of writing that uses pictures or symbols to stand for words or sounds*

---

8. emperor, sultan, president   _____

9. Morse code, sign language, alphabet _____

10. centaur, unicorn, mermaid   _____

Did You Know?

Ancient Egyptian work gangs were private citizens drafted to help build the Pyramids. One theory has it that workers used only log rollers, ramps, sledges, and ropes to build the massive tombs!

Greeks
myths
deities
philosophers
plays
amphitheater
Parthenon
columns
city-states
democracy

_____

_____

The Heritage of Ancient Greece

The list words name some of ancient Greece's contributions to Western civilization. If you can, add other words to the list. Then complete the activities. Use your Spelling Dictionary if you need help.

■ GETTING AT MEANING

Classifying Groups Use list words to classify each group.

1. _____

tragedies, comedies, live performances

2. _____

Zeus, Aphrodite,
other gods and goddesses of Mount Olympus

3. _____

*a story about the god Zeus throwing a thunderbolt,
a story in which Apollo drives the sun across the sky,
a story of how the goddess Athena was born*

4. _____

Corinthians, Athenians, Spartans,
other groups making up the population of Greece

5. _____

*form of government,
importance of individuals respected,
all citizens have the right to vote*

6. _____

Athens, Sparta,
other independent Greek cities

7. _____

Socrates, Plato,
other Greek writers and thinkers

Corinthian

The Parthenon

Using Pictures Use the pictures and captions on these pages to complete the sentences with list words.

8. Greek plays were performed in an ____, a huge structure with rows of seats that rose outward from the stage in the center.

9. Greek architects developed three kinds of ____: the simple Doric, the slightly decorated Ionic, and the very ornate Corinthian.

8. _____

9. _____

10. _____

An amphitheater

10. The ____, a temple built to house a huge gold-and-ivory statue of the goddess Athena, is regarded by many as one of the finest examples of Doric architecture in existence.

Design Your Own Temple

If you were to build a temple to house a very important object, what would that object be? What would your temple look like? Design your own temple and draw or build it out of any materials you'd like. Explain your temple to some of your classmates.

Ionic

Doric

Roman
patricians
plebeians
empire
forum
Senate
Colosseum
emperor
arena
gladiators

_____

_____

The People of Ancient Rome

The list words name people and places of ancient Rome. Add two more words to the list. Then complete the exercises. Use your Spelling Dictionary if you need help.

■ GETTING AT MEANING

Context Clues Use the context clues in the articles to help you fill in the blanks with list words. (Don't forget to capitalize the words that are parts of headlines.)

VENETIAN STAR

THE ROMAN TIMES

Augustus Is (1) During the Golden Age

Rome, A.D. 14. Caesar Augustus, our great ruler, died today, ending a reign of forty-one years of peace. Under Augustus, Romans enjoyed prosperity, new paved roads, more trade, and a strong army.

Borders of Roman (2) Stretch Far

A.D. 117. Lands under Roman rule now include Britain, Gaul, Judea, Egypt, and all other provinces bordering the Mediterranean Sea.

(3) Empire's Population Numbers Seventy Million!

A.D. 100. The latest government census tallies the empire's population at about seventy million. Nearly one million people live in Rome, about six million live in Italy, and the rest inhabit the provinces.

1. _____

2. _____

3. _____

Chariot Race Scheduled for This Saturday

Those wealthy patricians are at it again! The patricians have scheduled a chariot race for this Saturday, hoping once again to prove their superiority over Rome's common citizens, the plebeians. The race will begin in the center of town at the forum, as soon as the marketplace has closed for the day. It will end in the arena of the Colosseum.

The (4) Closes to Traffic

Rome's city officials have decreed that chariots can no longer be driven in the city's public square. Rome's center is too crowded with patrons of its shops and temples, as well as with many government workers, to allow wheeled vehicles.

Rich (5) Refuse to Share Power

Wealthy landowners don't want "ordinary" citizens to play a part in Rome's government. These wealthy men feel that they alone should have membership in the (6) and be able to pass laws and handle the government's finances.

(7) Gain Equal Rights

Rome, 287 B.C. After a 200-year struggle, Rome's common citizens have now won a voice in Roman government. Ordinary folk will take part in making and passing laws.

New Amphitheater to Be Named the (8)

Plans for Rome's new outdoor amphitheater call for about 45,100 seats. All seats have a clear view of the (9), so spectators can see their favorite (10) in combat.

The Colosseum

4. _____

5. _____

6. _____

7. _____

8. _____

9. _____

10. _____

Did You Know?

"All roads lead to Rome." At least, they did at the height of the Roman Empire. All the Roman provinces were connected to each other and to Rome by about a 50,000-mile paved road system! Some of these roads were built so well that they are still used today.

feudalism
fiefs
vassals
lord
knights
clergymen
serfs
manor
chivalry
tournament

_____

_____

Medieval Europe

These list words tell about society in western Europe during the medieval period, or Middle Ages, between the A.D. 400s and the 1500s. If you know other words related to this time period, add them to the list. Use the Spelling Dictionary for help with the activities.

■ GETTING AT MEANING

Who's the Boss? Read the passages. Then complete the chart.

In the Middle Ages, government in western Europe was based on a system of land ownership and loyalty called **feudalism.** At the top was the **lord,** who ruled the land he owned. Lords gave tracts of land called **fiefs** to their **vassals** in return for the vassals' promise of military support.

The soldiers who provided military service for the lords were **knights.** They developed a complex code of honor and bravery called **chivalry.** The knights often displayed their bravery in **tournaments.**

The people who farmed the land were **serfs.** They had to live and work on the estate, or **manor,** of a lord. By law, serfs were considered part of the lord's "property."

Who's the Boss?

Write the list word that names the people at each level of government in the Middle Ages.

↓

"I am the **(1)** who rules this land. My **(2)** owe me military service in exchange for the land I gave them."

↓

"We are the **(3)** who serve our lord in battle."

↓

"We are the **(4)** —treated like slaves, living and working on someone else's land."

1. _____   3. _____

2. _____   4. _____

Word Association Complete each set of words with the correct list word.

5. monks   priests   church   _____

6. estate   lands   property   _____

7. system   protection   land ownership   _____

8. joust   contest   lance   _____

9. courtesy   bravery   honesty   _____

10. protection   land   payment   _____

Design a Coat of Arms

During the Middle Ages, noble families and knights identified themselves by symbols on shields called coats of arms. Look under *Heraldry* in an encyclopedia to learn about the different shapes, designs, and colors used on coats of arms. Then design an emblem by which you and your family can be identified.

Renaissance
scholar
classic
patron
artist
masterpieces
anatomy
literature
architecture
philosophy

_____

_____

The European Renaissance

The list words tell of a time in European history when people took a renewed interest in learning. Add more words to the list. Then do the exercises. Use your Spelling Dictionary if you need help.

■ GETTING AT MEANING

Greek and Latin Roots Write the list words that "grew" from the Greek and Latin roots given.

1. _____

2. _____

3. _____

Greek

1. **ana**
   (up)
   $+$
   tomos
   (a cutting)

2. **archi**
   (chief)
   $+$
   tekton
   (builder)

3. **philos**
   (loving)
   $+$
   sophos
   (wise)

Latin

4. _____

5. _____

6. _____

7. _____

4. **ars, artista**
   (skill, craft)

5. **litteratura**
   (writing, learning)

6. **re**
   (again)
   $+$
   nasci
   (be born)

7. **schola**
   (school)

Word Portraits Finish each word portrait with a list word.

orenzo de' Medici supported artist Michelangelo during his early career. Medici's patronage of artists earned him the title " (8) of the arts."

8. _____

eonardo da Vinci is best known for his (9) , the *Mona Lisa* and *The Last Supper*.

9. _____

aldassare Castiglione wrote *The Book of the Courtier* about 1518. A guide that set the standards of conduct for royal court attendants, this book became a (10) of Renaissance literature.

10. _____

Did You Know?

Leonardo da Vinci liked to do mirror writing.

(It's easier if you are left-handed, as he was.)

Aztecs
calendar
causeways
chocolate
Incas
Mayas
potatoes
terraces
tomatoes
observatories

_____

_____

The Early Americas

The list words tell about three great Indian civilizations in the early Americas. If you know other words about the early Americas, add them to the list. Then do the activities. Use your Spelling Dictionary if you need help.

■ GETTING AT MEANING

Ingenious Inventions Use list words to complete the information about each culture's inventions or contributions.

1. _____

2. _____

3. _____

4. _____

5. _____

Mathematical Mayas By observing the positions of the sun, the moon, the planets,  and the stars from their __(1)__, the Mayas developed mathematical tables that predicted eclipses and the orbit of Venus. They also invented a __(2)__ of 365 days divided into 18 months of 20 days each, with 5 extra days at year's end.

Agricultural Aztecs Aztec farmers transported their crops over roadways called __(3)__, built to connect the capital city to the mainland.

Aztec farmers introduced Europeans to red, soft, juicy __(4)__, which are now enjoyed around the world. They also introduced Europeans to the cacao plant, whose beans make a dark brown sweet called __(5)__.

Ingenious Incas

The Incas were experts in making full use of growing space. They cut __(6)__ into the Andean mountainsides. These "shelves" with sloping sides gave the Incas much more farmland.

The Incas introduced Europeans to hard, starchy __(7)__ , now one of the world's most widely grown vegetables.

Book Reviews Complete each book review with one of the list words below.

Mayas   Aztecs   Incas

8. In the exciting historical novel *We, the ____* , readers learn how farmers managed to grow plants on the sides of mountains.

9. The history book *The Encounter of the ____ and the Europeans* describes the amazement of the Europeans when they first tasted tomatoes and delicious chocolate drinks.

10. The book *Ancient Astronomers* explains how the ____ predicted eclipses and learned about the stars.

6. _____

7. _____

8. _____

9. _____

10. _____

Your Pal, the Potato

The potato is one of nature's most nutritious foods—and one of its most versatile. There are over one hundred varieties of potatoes. Make a list of the ways you like to prepare or eat potatoes. Then work with a friend to develop a menu that offers a different potato dish with every meal, for as many meals as possible.

attitude
goal
relationship
self-control
stress
unique
strengths
weaknesses
counselor
realistic

_____

_____

1. _____

2. _____

3. _____

4. _____

5. _____

Learning About Yourself

A large part of being healthy includes thinking positively and feeling good about yourself. Add two other words to the list that tell about yourself and your health. Use your Spelling Dictionary if you need help with the activity.

■ GETTING AT MEANING

Descriptions Complete these descriptions of people with words from the list.

Jesse is strong in mathematics and science. She knows it is easy for her to get A's and B's in these subjects. On the other hand, she also knows she has to work extra hard to get C's in English. Jesse knows both her **(1)** and her **(2)** .

Jesse

Luz hopes to be an astronaut—after she writes a best-selling novel, that is. But first she wants to stop acid rain. Luz just can't stay focused on one **(3)** for her life.

Luz

Al's brother Mike does some very unusual things. He hang glides off mountains and canoes wild rivers. He studies in Europe and travels in India. Al thinks Mike is **(4)** .

Al

Mrs. Lee advises Leroy on his class schedule. She also helps him find information about different careers. Mrs. Lee is a good guidance **(5)** .

Mrs. Lee

"It's best if you..."

184

Ramón makes deliveries for his after-school job. He decides he has too many stops planned for one day, so he looks at his list and decides which ones he actually has time to make. Ramón is being **(6)** .

6. _____

7. _____

8. _____

9. _____

10. _____

One day **Jake** realized that he'd fallen into the bad habit of getting angry at people for no good reason. "I need to get a grip on myself," he said. "I need to gain more **(7)** ."

! Grrr !!

Paul waited impatiently for his friend Stu. Stu was always late, which made Paul anxious and put him under a great deal of **(8)** . He wondered if his **(9)** with Stu was worth the effort.

Sometimes **Bev** sees herself as positively brilliant. At other times she sees herself as not very smart at all. Bev's **(10)** about herself changes every day.

Create an Acrostic

In what ways do you think you are unique? Write an acrostic to show what's special about you. Write something that's unique about you for each letter of your name. For example:

Play**S** piano
C**O**llects autographs
Ow**N**s two cats
Just turned thirteen
H**A**s met Michael Jordan

fitness
cardiovascular
respiratory
body fat
calories
agility
coordination
therapist
exercise
energy

_____

_____

Being Physically Fit

Eating and exercise are keys to physical fitness. Look over the list and add other physical-fitness words. If you need help with the activities, use your Spelling Dictionary.

■ GETTING AT MEANING

Greek and Latin Roots The five list words below all have Greek and Latin origins. Complete each item with one of these five list words.

coordination therapist respiratory cardiovascular energy

1. _____

2. _____

3. _____

4. _____

5. _____

1. The Greek word *therapeuein* means "to treat or cure." A _____ helps sick or injured people get better.

2. The Greek word *kardio* means "heart" and the Latin word *vas* means "vessel." When we exercise the _____ system, we work the heart, blood, and blood vessels.

3. The Latin prefix **re** means "again" and the Latin word *spirare* means "to breathe." Our _____ system consists of the lungs and breathing passages.

4. The Greek *energes* means "active." When we have _____ we are able to work or play without tiring easily.

5. The Latin prefix **co** means "together" and the Latin word *ordinare* means "to regulate." We have good _____ when we can make our body parts work well together.

Paragraph Completion Complete the advertisement with the five list words below.

body fat   fitness   exercise   agility   calories

Forever Fit!

Workout Weekdays
with Jackie

6. _____

7. _____

8. _____

9. _____

10. _____

In her new video, Jackie Powell will show you how to (6) safely and effectively. She'll help you shed pounds and inches as you lose unwanted (7), especially in those problem areas. To improve your body movements, Jackie will help you work on your flexibility and (8). As an added bonus, she'll show you how to count (9) as you plan your daily meals. Jackie personally guarantees that her video will help you improve your overall physical (10) in just a few short weeks!

5 Times a Week!

Jackie Powell

On Sale Now

Burn Off Those Calories!

Find out more about how to burn off calories. Look in a health book or ask a nurse, a doctor, or a coach. Use what you learn to help you add up the calories in your next dinner. Then figure out how far you'd have to run to burn off those calories.

fiber
starch
fat
protein
vitamins
nutrients
processing
dietitian
additives
preservatives

_____

_____

Foods and Good Health

Eating the right foods goes a long way to keeping you healthy. Add two words about food and health to the list. Then do the activities. Use your Spelling Dictionary if you need help.

■ GETTING AT MEANING

Healthful Groups Use the passage to help you write a list word for each group in the chart.

Most Americans eat too much protein and not enough starch. Instead of a hamburger for lunch, try having a baked potato or spaghetti. Skip the milk shake too; fat is another thing we get too much of. Finally, start your day right and increase the fiber in your diet with wheat cereal or wheat toast for breakfast.

1. _____

2. _____

3. _____

4. _____

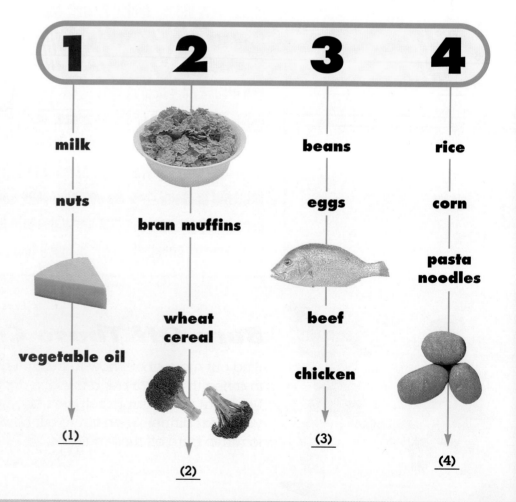

| 1 | 2 | 3 | 4 |

milk   beans   rice

nuts   eggs   corn

bran muffins   pasta
                      noodles

wheat   beef
cereal

vegetable oil   chicken

(1)   (2)   (3)   (4)

More Groups Write one of the words below to complete each sentence. Each sentence contains a related word to help you figure out the meaning.

> **vitamins**   **nutrients**   **processing**
> **dietitian**   **additives**   **preservatives**

5. Artificial flavoring and coloring added to foods are two examples of _____.

6. A, C, B_6, and E are examples of _____ that are vital for good health.

7. The procedures of heating, drying, and freezing are ways of _____ food.

8. Planning menus and counting calories for healthful diets are some things that a _____ does.

9. Vitamins, proteins, and starch are all kinds of _____ that are necessary for good nutrition.

10. Salt and other chemicals that preserve food from spoiling are called _____.

5. _____	8. _____
6. _____	9. _____
7. _____	10. _____

Good Nutrition Takes Planning!

Fruits and vegetables are high in fiber and rich in vitamins A and C. The American Cancer Society recommends eating five servings a day of fruits and vegetables. Of those, two to three servings a week should be from the cabbage family (vegetables like broccoli, brussels sprouts, cauliflower, and cabbage). Do you eat enough of these foods? Plan a one-week menu for yourself that follows these suggestions.

Make Your Own One-Week Menu

allergy
allergens
virus
antibodies
immunity
sinusitis
influenza
pneumonia
hypertension
bacteria

_____

_____

Diseases

These list words all have to do with diseases and their causes. Add two other words to the list. Then complete the activities. Use your Spelling Dictionary if you need help.

▊ GETTING AT MEANING

Word Parts Look at the words and word parts along the bottom of these two pages. Use them and the clues in the sentences to help you complete the sentences with list words.

1. _____

2. _____

3. _____

4. _____

1. A group of rod-shaped organisms called _____ cause many diseases.

2. _____ is a disease of the lungs.

3. If you have an inflammation in your nose and a bad headache, you probably have _____.

4. Another disease-causing agent might make you feel as if you've been poisoned; but really, you just have a _____.

ergon: action; effect

im: not; free from

pneumon: lung

gen: something that causes or produces

itis: inflammation

5. This agent can cause the flu, short for _____, a severe cold-like disease.

6. You can get shots to help keep you free from diseases—to help you develop an _____ to them.

7. Your white blood cells make substances that work against the disease. These substances are called _____.

8. If dust, hair, or a particular food has an unusual effect on your body, causing you to sneeze, cough, or break out in a rash, you probably have an _____.

9. Some substances in the air can cause coughing or sneezing. These substances are called _____.

10. Not all diseases are caused by germs. When people have more stress than normal, they may develop _____.

5. _____

6. _____

7. _____

8. _____

9. _____

10. _____

In Case of Emergency, Call...

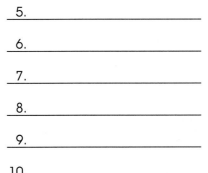

Did you know that if they are not treated quickly and properly, some allergies can be fatal? Would you know how to help someone who was having a serious allergic reaction? Get permission to interview a paramedic or a doctor about allergies and how to treat them. With your classmates, prepare a list of questions before the interview.

hyper: **more than is normal**

bakterion: **rod**

virus: **poison**

anti: **against**

flu: **severe disease**

Models of the Earth

equator
axis
grid
time zones
meridians
prime meridian
longitude
latitude
lines of latitude
International Date Line

_____

_____

You probably use maps and globes quite often. But do you know what all those lines mean? Add words about maps or globes to the list. Then do the activities. Use your Spelling Dictionary for help.

■ GETTING AT MEANING

Imaginary Lines Study Figures 1 and 2. Then write the list word that each item refers to.

1. These lines run north and south from pole to pole, but they're used to measure distance east and west.

2. This line, which is at 0 degrees, is the reference point for east-west locations. It runs through Greenwich, England.

3. These lines run east and west, but they're used to measure distance north and south.

4. This line, which is at 0 degrees, is the reference point for north-south locations. It runs through the nation of Ecuador.

5. We think of the earth as spinning around this line.

1._____   4._____

2._____   5._____

3._____

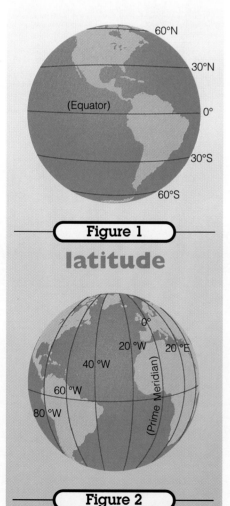

Figure 1

latitude

Figure 2

longitude

Space and Time Travel Use Figures 3 and 4 to help you complete each statement with a list word.

6. You can locate any place on earth by finding where the lines of latitude and longitude cross on a _____.

7. The approximate _____ of Phoenix, Arizona, is 33°N.

8. The approximate _____ of Phoenix is 112°W.

9. When it is 2 P.M. in Cairo, Egypt, it is 7 P.M. in Beijing, China. In other words, the two cities are in different _____.

10. You are on a ship in the Pacific Ocean, moving westward. It is 1 P.M. on June 21st. A moment later it is still 1 P.M., but now it's June 22nd. Your ship has just crossed the _____.

6. _____

7. _____

8. _____

9. _____

10. _____

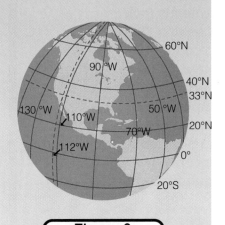

Figure 3

grid

Figure 4

International Date Line

Did You Know?

Christopher Columbus wasn't the first person to prove the earth is round. In the second century A.D., Ptolemy pointed out that during an eclipse, the shadow of the earth on the moon is round. He also observed that the mast of a ship approaching from the sea is the first part to appear over the horizon, which could only occur on a sphere and not on a flat surface.

igneous rock
basalt
granite
lava
sedimentary rock
limestone
sandstone
metamorphic rock
marble
quartzite

_____

_____

Rocks

Rocks can be classified into three main types, according to how they were formed. Add two more words about rocks to the list. Then do the activities.

■ GETTING AT MEANING

Classifying Rocks Complete the paragraph with list words from the chart.

Igneous rock forms from cooling of melted rock underground or from cooling of lava, melted rock on the earth's surface.

Metamorphic rock forms when rock is changed by intense heat, pressure, or chemical reactions.

Sedimentary rock forms when layers of pebbles, mud, sand, and other sediments are squeezed together; it often contains fossils.

On your way home from school, you pick up some rocks from an unpaved road. One rock has bands that look warped, as if they've been squeezed by awesome heat or pressure. It is probably a _(1)_. A second rock contains fossils such as shells. It is probably a _(2)_. A third rock has lots of shiny crystals in it. It formed from cooling _(3)_ on the earth's surface and is probably an _(4)_.

1. _____   3. _____

2. _____   4. _____

Building with Rocks A tour through an average city can provide examples of many rocks. Use the chart at the right to complete the tour guide's speech.

Granite can withstand weather well, so it is used for many outdoor structures.

Basalt is a hard, dark rock with small grains. It sometimes forms tall columns as it cools.

Sandstone feels like the sand it was formed from. It can be cut into large blocks for building.

Limestone is also used for building, but pollution can damage it.

Marble, a beautiful stone of white, or with colored markings, can be highly polished.

Quartzite is like marble but harder. It is sandstone that has been changed by heat and pressure.

"Here in the old post office, the stone floor is so polished, you can see yourself. It is made of (5) . The once-sharp corners of the museum across the street were dissolved and rounded by pollution. Its walls are made of (6) . The large stone blocks of that church on the corner are made of sand cemented together. They feel gritty; they are (7) . Even the oldest stone grave markers in the church cemetery look new. The weather has not damaged them; they are all (8) . Do you see those dark stone cliffs by the railroad yard that look like columns? They are (9) . And touch this fountain over here. It looks like marble, but is even harder. It is (10) ."

5. _____

6. _____

7. _____

8. _____

9. _____

10. _____

Rock Heads

Find an interesting rock the size of your hand or smaller. Observe it from all angles until you see a face in the rock. Use tempera paints to paint a face that makes use of the rock's natural features. Does the face look familiar to you?

evolved
woolly mammoth
preserved
sediment
tar pit
amber
petrified
mold
carbon imprint
fossils

_____

_____

Geologic History

The history of the earth and its living things can be interpreted from the earth's rocks. If you can, add two more words to the list. Then do the activities. Use your Spelling Dictionary if you need help.

■ GETTING AT MEANING

Words and Pictures Use the pictures and the captions to complete the sentences with list words.

1. The picture shows the remains of plants and animals. These remains are known as _____.

2. By studying these remains, we can see how living things have _____ from one form to another through time.

3. These remains are here for us to study because they have been _____ in various ways.

4. Some remains fell to the bottom of the ocean and were covered with mud, sand, and other tiny bits of _____, then dug up centuries later encased in rock.

5. Sometimes water passed through the rock, dissolving the remains encased in them and leaving a space called a _____.

6. Some remains were formed when their hydrogen and oxygen burned off, leaving a detailed _____.

1. _____   4. _____

2. _____   5. _____

3. _____   6. _____

fossil

mold

sediment

carbon imprint

196

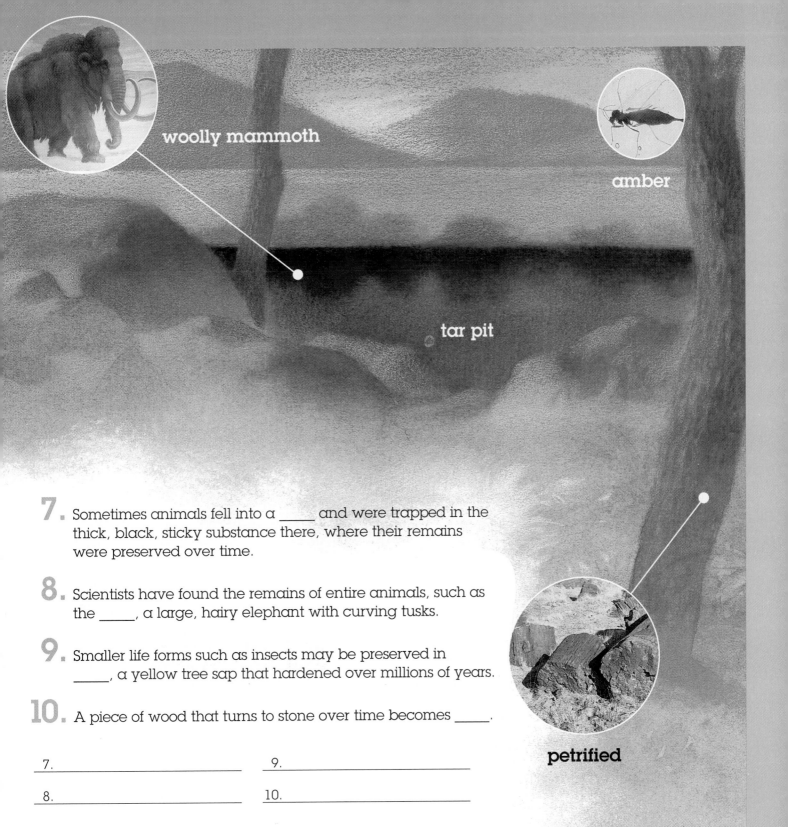

woolly mammoth

amber

tar pit

petrified

7. Sometimes animals fell into a _____ and were trapped in the thick, black, sticky substance there, where their remains were preserved over time.

8. Scientists have found the remains of entire animals, such as the _____, a large, hairy elephant with curving tusks.

9. Smaller life forms such as insects may be preserved in _____, a yellow tree sap that hardened over millions of years.

10. A piece of wood that turns to stone over time becomes _____.

7. _____   9. _____

8. _____   10. _____

Did You Know?

Scientists study dinosaur fossils with X-rays, CAT scans, and microscopes to find out what diseases the animals had. Dinosaurs are known to have had infections, bone spurs, and even arthritis!

plates
plate tectonic theory
trench
ridge
rift
crust
mantle
spreading boundary
colliding boundary
subducted plate

_____

_____

Plate Tectonics

For centuries, people have noticed that South America and Africa look like jigsaw puzzle pieces that fit together. Today, scientists think all the continents were once joined. Plate tectonics explains how the continents drifted apart. If you can, add more words to the list. Use your Spelling Dictionary if you need help doing the activities.

■ GETTING AT MEANING

Using a Diagram Use Diagram 1 to help you write a list word for each definition below.

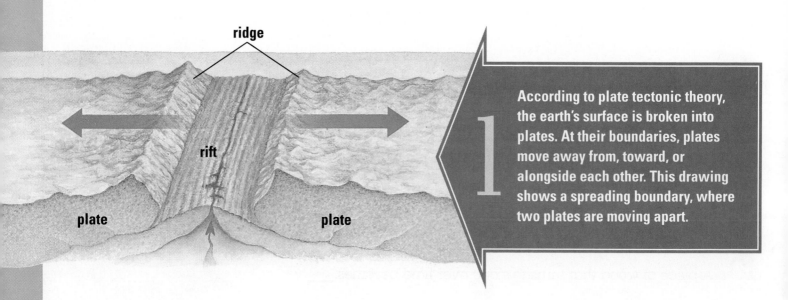

ridge

rift

plate

plate

According to plate tectonic theory, the earth's surface is broken into plates. At their boundaries, plates move away from, toward, or alongside each other. This drawing shows a spreading boundary, where two plates are moving apart.

1. _____

2. _____

3. _____

4. _____

5. _____

1. large sections of the earth's surface that move about, sometimes bumping into or spreading apart from each other

2. a long, narrow chain of hills or mountains

3. the center of a mid-ocean ridge, where the ridge appears to be torn apart

4. a region where two bordering plates are slowly moving away from each other

5. theory that says changes in the earth's crust are caused by movement of large, rigid sections of the earth called plates

Another Diagram Use Diagram 2 to help you write a list word for each definition below.

6. a long, narrow region on the ocean floor, where the water is extremely deep

7. a plate with an edge that has been pushed down under another plate

8. a region where two bordering plates are bumping into each other

9. a partially melted layer of the earth, beneath the earth's surface

10. the outer layer of rock covering the earth

6. _____

7. _____

8. _____

9. _____

10. _____

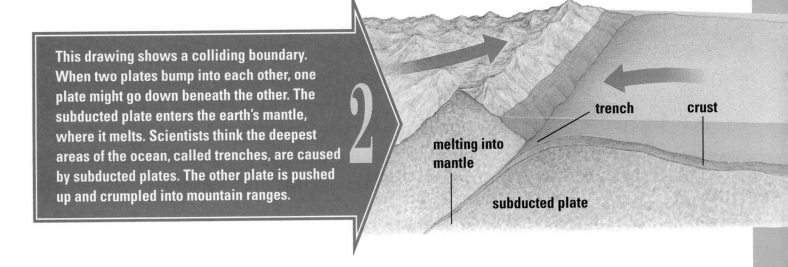

This drawing shows a colliding boundary. When two plates bump into each other, one plate might go down beneath the other. The subducted plate enters the earth's mantle, where it melts. Scientists think the deepest areas of the ocean, called trenches, are caused by subducted plates. The other plate is pushed up and crumpled into mountain ranges.

2

trench   crust

melting into mantle

subducted plate

Follow That Continent

Place a piece of tissue paper over a map of the world in your science or social studies book, a dictionary, or an atlas from the library. Trace each continent. Cut out the pieces. Try to fit them together like puzzle pieces. Then move the pieces to where you think they might be 250 million years from now. On separate paper, glue your puzzle pieces in those positions. Then write an explanation of your reasoning.

Richter scale
fault
seismic waves
tsunami
epicenter
aftershocks
seismograph
magnitude
seismologist
focus

_____

_____

Earthquakes

An earthquake is a shaking of the earth's crust. Most people think of California when they hear about earthquakes. What do you think of? Add two words to the list and then do the activities. Use your Spelling Dictionary for help.

▪ GETTING AT MEANING

Context Read the following article and think about the meaning of the highlighted words. Then do the activities that follow.

On March 27, 1964, an earthquake struck Anchorage, Alaska. Within minutes, seismic waves caused sections of the ground to suddenly jut up or fall away. Buildings collapsed, and people tumbled into chasms that opened beneath their feet, swallowing them. Most bodies were never found. Five hours later, a tsunami, a giant sea wave triggered by the quake, crashed into the coastal town of Valdez and utterly destroyed it. More than 10,000 aftershocks were felt in the region during the next eighteen months.

Analyzing the wavy lines recorded on their seismographs, scientists estimated that the quake measured 8.5 on the Richter scale. It was one of the most powerful quakes ever recorded. Its magnitude was so great that the entire earth vibrated!

Seismologists say the epicenter of the quake was somewhere in the wilderness between Anchorage and Valdez. The focus, where the shock originated, was at a shallow depth of twenty miles below the epicenter. The earthquake was probably caused by a sudden movement of the earth's crust along a giant crack, or fault, in the mountains.

Analogies Write the list word that completes each analogy.

1. Meteorologist is to weather as _____ is to earthquakes.

2. Electroencephalograph (EEG) is to brain waves as _____ is to seismic waves.

3. Decibel scale is to noise as _____ is to earthquakes.

4. Gentle wind is to hurricane as rippling water is to _____.

Definitions Write a list word for each definition below.

5. the point inside the earth where an earthquake starts

6. the point on the earth's surface directly above where an earthquake starts

7. the strength of an earthquake, or the total amount of energy it releases

8. a break in the earth's crust along which the rock moves, causing an earthquake

9. energy that moves through the earth or across the earth's surface in waves

10. small earthquakes or tremors that follow a major earthquake

1. _____

2. _____

3. _____

4. _____

5. _____

6. _____

7. _____

8. _____

9. _____

10. _____

A San Francisco Earthquake

Do you or members of your family remember the San Francisco earthquake of October 17, 1989? Many people saw its effects live on TV, including the horrifying collapse of a highway bridge during rush hour.

Which fault caused the earthquake?

troposphere
atmosphere
stratosphere
mesosphere
thermosphere
ionosphere
hydrogen
water vapor
nitrogen
ozone

_____

_____

Thermosphere (Ionosphere): 200 km	1112°F

Mesosphere: 80 km	-165°F

Stratosphere: 48 km	28°F

Troposphere: 16 km	-112°F

The Atmosphere

Without the air that surrounds us, we would not be able to survive. What words come to mind when you think of the atmosphere? Add them to the list and then do the activities. Use your Spelling Dictionary for help if you need it.

▊ GETTING AT MEANING

Using a Diagram Use the diagram to help you fill in the blanks with list words.

1. The entire mass of gases that surrounds the earth is called the ____.

2. The air is least dense in this layer of the atmosphere, yet it is the warmest. It is called by either of two names. One name, whose beginning means "heat" or "temperature," is ____.

3. This layer is also called the ____ because when the sun's energy forces electrons to go out of atoms, they are then called ions.

4. In this layer, the air gets colder with height. It is called the ____.

5. The air in the bottom layer of the atmosphere is always moving and changing. This layer, called the ____, is where our weather occurs.

6. This layer is still close to the earth, but the air here is calm and dry. Pilots prefer to fly in this layer, which is called the ____.

1._____   4._____

2._____   5._____

3._____   6._____

What Gas Is It? Answer the questions with these list words.

hydrogen   nitrogen   ozone   water vapor

7. Because this gas is decreasing in the atmosphere, people are more likely to get sunburned. There is even a "hole" in this layer of gas over Antarctica. What gas is it?

_____

8. Water turns into this when it evaporates. What gas is it?

_____

9. This gas is the H part of every water molecule H_2O. What gas is it?

_____

10. This gas passes from the air into the soil, where it is changed into nitrates that are used by green plants. What gas is it?

_____

Flights of Fancy

Interview a friend or family member who has been on an airplane flight recently. Ask the person to describe what he or she saw outside the plane window during the flight and how smooth the flight was. From the descriptions you get, try to infer which layers of the atmosphere the plane was flying in.

radar
high-pressure system
satellite
cold front
warm front
low-pressure system
barometer
tornado
hurricane
stationary front

_____

_____

Weather

Some amazing processes go on in the skies above us. These processes form the weather. Add two more weather words to the list. Then do the activity. Use your Spelling Dictionary if you need help.

■ GETTING AT MEANING

Definitions Read the following weather forecast. Replace the underlined definitions with the correct list words. Use the weather map and illustrations on these two pages to help you understand the words.

1. Lunchtime shoppers in Springfield got soaked today when the <u>instrument for measuring air pressure</u> dropped and a thunderstorm roared through around noon. Let's look at the map to see how that storm formed.

2. This blue line of triangles is a <u>boundary of a cold air mass pushing into a warm air mass</u>. The cold air wedged under the warm air and lifted it off the ground. Then the moisture in the warm air condensed and the storm occurred.

High Pressure

Stationary Front

Warm Front

Cold Front

Low Pressure

3. Farther away, a <u>boundary of a warm air mass pushing into a cold air mass</u>, shown by this red line with half-circles, will soon be moving through the northeast.

4. A <u>region where the pressure of the air is low</u> will develop, and towns in that area will be in for several days of steady rain.

5. The view from the <u>object circling earth</u> shows that our area was covered by clouds.

6. A <u>small but violent funnel-shaped cyclone</u> was sighted, in which winds were whirling at about 300 miles per hour.

7. Our <u>radio detecting and ranging</u> map shows that some areas of light rain are still being detected.

8. In the Atlantic, we'll have to watch this cyclone. It may move over the warm waters of the Caribbean and intensify into a <u>strong spiral-shaped storm that forms over warm oceans</u> that will cause much wind and water damage.

9. Meanwhile, a <u>boundary of two air masses that is not moving</u> remains over the southwest, causing rain to continue in that area.

10. Farther north, near the Canadian border, a <u>region where atmospheric pressure is high</u> has moved into the area, bringing sunny skies and fair weather. Now for tomorrow's forecast . . .

1. _____

2. _____

3. _____

4. _____

5. _____

6. _____

7. _____

8. _____

9. _____

10. _____

Did You Know?

A single lightning strike can have a temperature of 60,000° F, which is six times hotter than the sun!

60,000°

corona
sunspots
solar flare
solar eclipse
solar wind
constellation
light-years
absolute magnitude
apparent magnitude
asterism

_____

_____

Survey of the Stars

Some stars look like tiny dots of light in the night sky. However, our sun, a large yellow disk in the sky, is a star too. Add two more words about stars to the list. Then do the activities. Use your Spelling Dictionary for help if you need it.

■ GETTING AT MEANING

Speaking of the Sun Study the pictures of the sun. Then fill in the blanks with list words.

1. The moon's shadow blocking our view of the sun on earth is called a _____.

2. The sun's outer atmosphere, a faint crown of gas around the sun that we can see only during an eclipse, is called the _____.

3. Electrical storms on the sun, which look to us like dark spots on the sun's surface, are called _____.

4. An explosion on the sun, shooting gas particles and radiation into space, is a _____.

5. In early spacecraft missions, scientists discovered an invisible wind of solar gas, called the _____, that blows continuously out of the sun toward earth.

1. _____   4. _____

2. _____   5. _____

3. _____

solar eclipse

corona

solar flare

Star Gazing Use the definitions to complete the paragraphs with list words.

constellation group of stars named for an object, person, or animal

asterism a distinct star group that is part of a constellation

apparent magnitude a measure of how bright a star *appears* to an observer

absolute magnitude a measure of how bright a star really *is*

light-year the distance light travels in one year

Stars are so far away that by the time the light of a star reaches earth the star may be dead! It can take many **(6)** for the light of a star to reach the earth.

A star that gives off a lot of light will look dim to us if it is far from earth. The **(7)** of such a star tells us only how it looks to us. If we know the distance of the star from earth, we can also figure out the star's **(8)**, how bright it really is compared to other stars.

Stars often seem to form patterns. Each pattern, named for a figure or a shape, is called a **(9)**. A star group that is part of a larger constellation—as the Big Dipper is part of the constellation Ursa Major—is called an **(10)**.

6. ______________ 8. ______________

7. ______________ 9. ______________

10. ______________

Did You Know?

Pulsars are fast-moving stars that rotate up to 1,000 times per second!

competent
mourn
overcome
stereotypes
popularity
ridicules
humiliated
aspires
tone
conferences

_____

_____

Joys of the Real World

The words in this list are about the challenges and joys of everyday life. Add two more words to the list before you do the activity. Use your Spelling Dictionary if you need help.

■ GETTING AT MEANING

Plot Summaries Use list words to complete each book description. Then think about which book you would most enjoy reading.

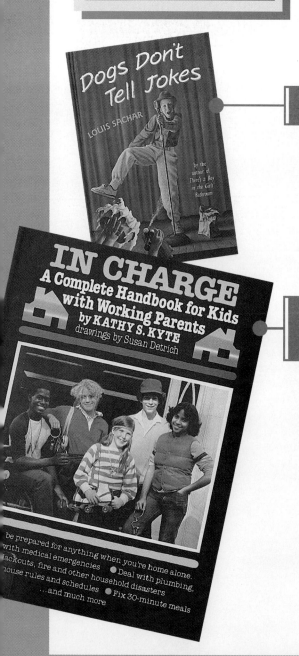

Dogs Don't Tell Jokes by Louis Sachar

Gary Boone has definite plans for the future. He **(1)** to be a stand-up comic, and the upcoming talent show fits right into his career plans. But joking can conceal loneliness, and being the class clown has not won Gary any **(2)** contests in seventh grade. This book is just as good as the author's hit novel, *There's a Boy in the Girls' Bathroom.*

In Charge: A Complete Handbook for Kids with Working Parents by Kathy S. Kyte

The tips in this book range from what to do in a fire to discussing schedules and chores during family **(3)** . There are even simple recipes for preparing meals. After reading this book you'll feel **(4)** to handle chores and emergencies when you're in charge at home.

1. _____   3. _____

2. _____   4. _____

Indian Summer by Barbara Girion

When Joni McCord spends a month on an Iroquois reservation, friendship seems impossible with her roommate, Sarah Birdsong. Joni tells Sarah she looks like Pocahontas, and Sarah laughingly **(5)** Joni's fear of swimming in the deep lake water. Slowly, the girls see that the **(6)** they have of each other are oversimplified and untrue, and they struggle to accept each other's differences.

The Gift-Giver by Joyce Hansen

Doris wants to fit in with her friends, and she feels **(7)** when her family won't allow her to do things her friends can do. Amir, the new boy in her Bronx neighborhood, doesn't seem to care what others think. His example helps Doris grow in self-confidence and **(8)** her insecurity.

Talking About Stepfamilies by Maxine B. Rosenberg

Children and adults discuss what it's like to be part of stepfamilies. Many describe feeling "odd" or "strange," and most still **(9)** the death of a parent or the losses that result from divorce. But the overall **(10)** is upbeat: over time, love and trust develop in stepfamilies, and the changes in their lives force stepchildren to become more flexible.

5. _____

6. _____

7. _____

8. _____

9. _____

10. _____

Author! Author!

What kind of book would you like to write? a humorous book about school? a romance? a how-to manual? Write a description of your book, make an outline for it, or draw a book cover that shows the kind of book you'd like to write.

agreement
communicate
creative
dispute
disputants
neutral
apologized
peer mediation
perspective
solution

_____

_____

Seeing the Other Side

The words in this unit all have to do with disagreeing and making peace. Add two words of your own to the list. If you need help with the activity, use your Spelling Dictionary.

■ GETTING AT MEANING

Interview Read the interview between Ruth, a writer for the school paper, and Marty, a student who leads a group that helps resolve arguments. Use list words to complete their statements.

1. _____

2. _____

3. _____

4. _____

Ruth: We heard you helped Jay and Tom find a _(1)_ to their problem.

Marty: Yes, they had a serious _(2)_ with each other. Each of the two _(3)_ thought he was right and the other was wrong.

Ruth: What was the problem?

Marty: Jay borrowed a jacket from Tom and got a ketchup stain on it. Jay _(4)_ and offered to give Tom his best sweater, but Tom wanted Jay to buy him a new jacket.

Ruth: Ouch! That sounds expensive!

Marty: Right, and Jay couldn't afford to do that. Both guys were so angry they could no longer _(5)_ with each other.

Ruth: Whose side did you take?

Marty: Neither! We can't take sides. We have to remain _(6)_ . Each guy had a totally opposite _(7)_ on the situation, so we had to find something in-between.

Ruth: Were you able to reach an _(8)_ ?

Marty: Yes. We got very inventive and came up with a truly _(9)_ solution. Jay would have Tom's jacket dry-cleaned.

Ruth: So you solved the problem through _(10)_ . Say, I have this neighbor who's always playing loud music. Do you think you could...?

5. _____

6. _____

7. _____

8. _____

9. _____

10. _____

perched
snickering
daydreams
quacking
fascinating
stadium
twittering
vanished
oompah
boring

_____

_____

A User's Guide to Imagination

If you have an active imagination you can make up any kind of story you want to. Do the list words suggest other words? Write two of them. Then do the activity. Use your Spelling Dictionary if you need help with any of the words.

■ GETTING AT MEANING

Context Use sentence context and the art to fill in each blank with a list word.

1. _____

2. _____

3. _____

4. _____

5. _____

6. _____

The TV show was unbearably (1), so I lost interest and began to have a series of (2).

They made no sense, but they were quite (3). In one, I was trying to give an important speech in a vast domed (4) as a trio of (5) ducks kept interrupting me.

Next, I was a magician reaching into a hat to pull out a rabbit, when the entire audience (6) into thin air!

AH!

Then I found myself (7) high in a tree. Suddenly I could understand the (8) of the birds. They were discussing cats and the weather.

Later, I was playing my tuba. After a while its (9) sounds made the house rise above the treetops!

Then I heard someone (10) , as if I'd done something funny. Finally, I realized the laughter was not in my dreams. I was actually laughing out loud to myself!

7. _____

8. _____

9. _____

10. _____

What's That Sound?

When a word sounds like the thing it names—such as *quack* for a duck's call—it is an example of onomatopoeia. But does a duck really say "quack," or is it more like "wock"? Does the dog that lives nearby say "bow-wow" or something else? Use your imagination and come up with new examples of onomatopoeia for the sounds of animals you're on speaking terms with!

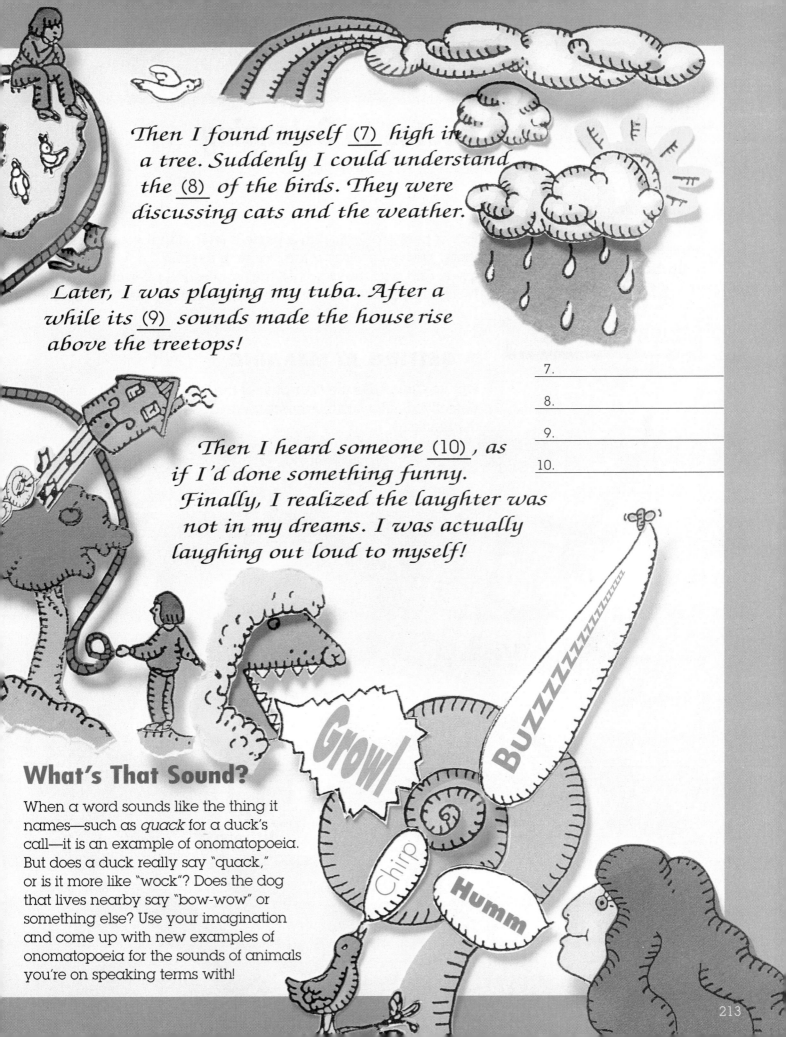

portico
reside
hallway
dining room
patio
balcony
family room
entranceway
garage
household

_____

_____

Routes to Belonging

Part of being "at home" in a place is feeling that you belong there. You are probably familiar with the place in which you live, inside and out. The words on the list describe parts of homes. Add two more words to the list. Then do the activity. Use your Spelling Dictionary if you need help.

■ GETTING AT MEANING

Picture Clues Use the floor plan of the Smith mansion to help Detective Shirley Holmes crack a case. Use list words to fill in the blanks.

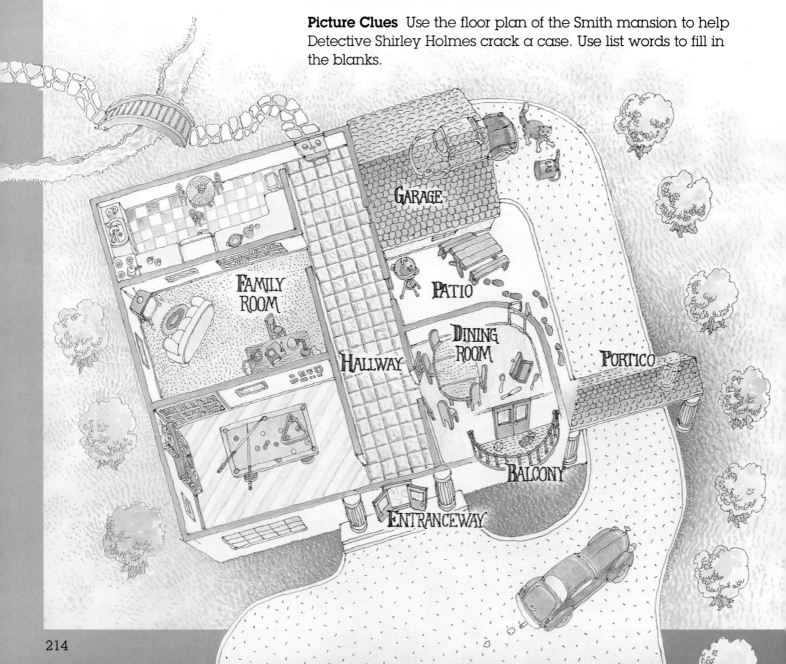

214

Detective Shirley Holmes rang the doorbell at the (1)_____ of the Smith mansion. "Come in," said Mr. Smith. "I'll take you to the (2)_____ , where we were sitting on the sofa watching a mystery when we heard the crash." The two walked down the long marble (3)_____ to the rest of the house.

"At first we thought it might have been a stray cat knocking over an empty gas can in the (4)_____ ," said Mr. Smith. "But then we heard running along the (5)_____ on the side of the house, and through a window we saw a shadow dart from pillar to pillar. When we searched the house we found a silverware chest lying open on the floor in the (6)_____ . All the silverware was missing."

"Luckily, your outside (7)_____ has not been swept lately," remarked Holmes. "I saw footprints near the picnic table. Those will be helpful clues. How many people (8)_____ here?"

"All the members of the (9)_____ were at home tonight— my wife, my daughter Maxine, and me. Oh, and of course my nephew Sam. He was upstairs on the (10)_____ at the time."

"Ah ha!" said Holmes. "Perhaps he saw something. . . ."

1. _____
2. _____
3. _____
4. _____
5. _____
6. _____
7. _____
8. _____
9. _____
10. _____

SOLVE THE CRIME

Who do you think did it? What does the nephew know? Write an ending to Holmes's case.

time machine
science fiction
technology
destination
extraterrestrial
robots
android
utopia
predict
dimensions

_____

_____

Passages Through Time

Traveling into the past or future is a common plot device in science fiction. The words in this list are all related to time travel. Add two more words to the list. Then do the activity. Use your Spelling Dictionary if you need help.

■ GETTING AT MEANING

Crossword Puzzle Use the clues on the next page to solve the crossword puzzle with list words.

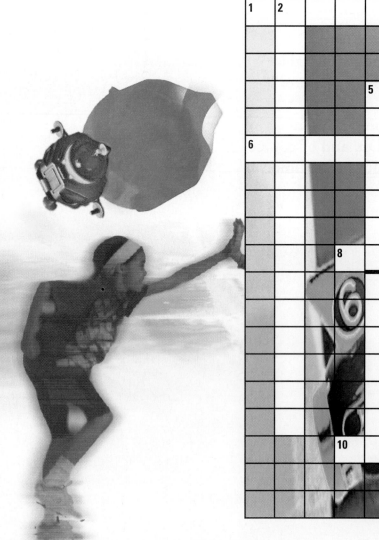
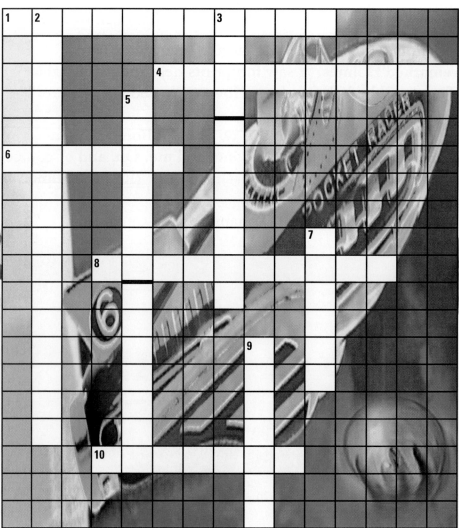

Across

1. This is where you'll be at journey's end when you step out of your time machine.
4. There are only three of these in space as we know it, but in some science fiction stories there are more.
6. a perfect place
8. The "science" in *science fiction* refers to this, as every "techie" will know.
10. This robot, which looks like a human being, is sometimes called a humanoid.

Down

2. not of this earth; other-worldly
3. A modern-day character in a science fiction story might use this to get to ancient Rome.
5. a story in which principles of science are applied to fantastic situations
7. In the future, these may do your work for you.
9. Science fiction writers do this when they describe the future.

Next Stop:???

Set the dial of your time machine for one of these three stops:

China, 551 B.C.

The United States, 1950

Italy, 1500

What would you see when you step out of your machine?
Find or draw pictures that illustrate the food, clothing, housing, or transportation you would find at the stop you chose.

courageously
reliable
determination
frantically
improvement
decisive
emergency
compassion
trembling
admiring

_____

_____

Talk About Leadership

Imagine that you find yourself in the middle of an emergency. What kind of person would you want as a leader? Write two other words related to leadership. Then do the activities. Use your Spelling Dictionary if you need help.

■ GETTING AT MEANING

Antonyms Write the list word that means the opposite of the boldfaced word or words in each sentence.

1. _____

2. _____

3. _____

4. _____

1. At first they all thought there was **no need for immediate action,** but as the wind picked up, the picnickers realized they were facing an ____.

2. When the storm hit, many people ____ ran around, but one person **calmly** took charge.

3. While others shouted **fearfully** as the water rose, Felicia ____ led them to high ground.

4. Most people were **unable to reach a decision** about what to do, but Felicia was ____ as she gave instructions.

218

5. She matched other people's **hesitation to carry out a plan** with her _____.

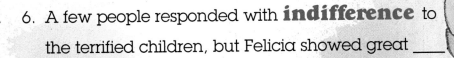

6. A few people responded with **indifference** to the terrified children, but Felicia showed great _____

7. With her **steady** manner, she calmed a _____ child.

8. The storm was no longer **getting worse,** and they began to see an _____.

5. _____

6. _____

7. _____

8. _____

9. _____

10. _____

9. People had always thought of Felicia as **irresponsible,** but now they recognized how _____ she was.

10. No one was **ridiculing** her now; they were all _____ her leadership.

Fearless Leader

In your opinion, what person or character would make a good leader? Why? Write a character sketch of that person or character that describes his or her leadership qualities.

Howdy, Pilgrim.

center
circumference
chord
diameter
radius
radii
central angle
degree
arc
compass

_____

_____

The Circle

The world is full of circles. They can be any size but only one shape. The list words deal with drawing and measuring circles. Add two more words to the list. Then do the activities. Use your Spelling Dictionary if you need help.

▇ GETTING AT MEANING

Circles in Real Life Study the drawing of a circle. Each phrase below deals with circles in real life. Write a list word for each phrase.

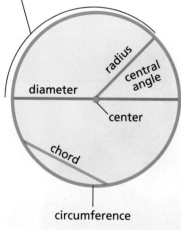

1. **the distance around a circular running track**

2. **a curve on a winding road**

3. **the line you make when you cut a pie in half**

4. **the wedge-shaped angle you make when you cut a piece of pie**

5. **the spot where the sharp point of the compass rests when you draw a circle with a compass**

6. **one spoke on a bicycle wheel**

7. **all the spokes on a bicycle wheel**

1. _____

2. _____

3. _____

4. _____

5. _____

6. _____

7. _____

Multiple Meanings Write the list word that each pair of phrases describes.

a tool for drawing circles

a tool for helping you find your way when you're lost

8. _____

a unit for measuring the angles and arcs of a circle

a unit for measuring temperature

9. _____

a line segment connecting two points on a circle

a combination of two or more musical notes sounded together

10. _____

Circles Around You

Look carefully at objects around your home. List all the objects you see that are circular in shape. Add any other circular objects you can think of.

congruent figures
similar figures
vertex
quadrilateral
parallelogram
trapezoid
rhombus
scalene triangle
isosceles triangle
equilateral triangle

_____

_____

Geometry

The list words deal with geometric figures. Can you think of others? Add them to the list and then do the activities. Use your Spelling Dictionary if you need help.

▪ GETTING AT MEANING

Quadrilaterals A quadrilateral is a four-sided polygon. Study the quadrilaterals and complete the sentences with list words.

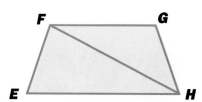

1. Figure *EFGH* has one pair of sides that are parallel (the same distance apart) but not congruent (equal), so *EFGH* is a _____.

2. A point that is the common endpoint of two rays that form an angle, such as point *E*, is called a _____.

Every rhombus is a parallelogram, but not every parallelogram is a rhombus. Use this information and the figures to complete items 3 and 4.

3. Any quadrilateral with opposite sides parallel and congruent is a _____.

4. A parallelogram with opposite sides parallel and four congruent sides is also a _____.

1. _____

2. _____

3. _____

4. _____

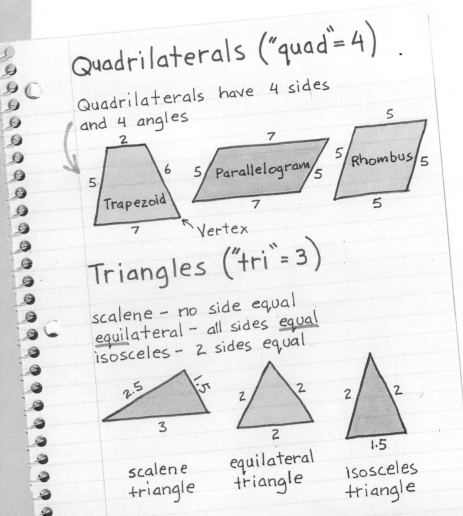

Quadrilaterals ("quad"= 4)

Quadrilaterals have 4 sides and 4 angles

2   7   5

5   6   5 Parallelogram 5   5 Rhombus 5

Trapezoid   7   5

7   ← Vertex

Triangles ("tri"= 3)

scalene – no side equal
equilateral – all sides equal
isosceles – 2 sides equal

2.5   1.5   2   2   2   2

3   2   1.5

scalene triangle   equilateral triangle   isosceles triangle

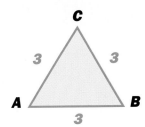

Triangles Use list words to complete the sentences.

5. Figure *ABC* has sides that are congruent (of equal length), so *ABC* is an _____.

6. Triangle *EFH* on page 222 has no congruent sides, so *EFH* is a _____.

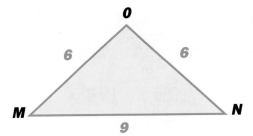

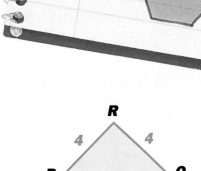

More Facts About Figures Study the figures and complete the sentences with list words.

7. Figures *MNO* and *PQR* have the same shape, but they are not the same size, so *MNO* and *PQR* are not exactly the same, but they are _____.

8. If figures *MNO* and *PQR* did have the same size and shape, they would be _____.

9. Figures *MNO* and *PQR* each have two congruent sides, so each figure is an _____.

10. Every three-sided polygon is a triangle. Every four-sided polygon is a _____.

5. _____

6. _____

7. _____

8. _____

9. _____

10. _____

Congruent Figures

same shape/ same size

Like two identical photos

Similar Figures

same shape/different sizes

Like a small photo and an enlarged photo

Do-It-Yourself

Geometry

Try making your own quadrilaterals with paper, a ruler, and scissors. Cut out and label a trapezoid, a parallelogram, and a rhombus. Then cut each of your quadrilaterals along one diagonal. What kinds of triangles have you made? Label those too.

prime
composite
prime factorization
exponent
factors
base
exponential form
greatest common factor
divisible
power

_____

_____

Number Theory

The words and phrases in the list are used in the study of number theory. Add more words to the list if you can. Then do the activities. Use your Spelling Dictionary for help.

■ GETTING AT MEANING

Number Talk If numbers could talk, what might they say? Read carefully as these numbers introduce themselves. Then complete the sentences with words from the list.

"Allow us to introduce ourselves."

1. In the problem 7 × 5 = 35, the numbers 7 and 5 are _____.

2. Six is the largest number that divides evenly into both 12 and 18, so six is their _____.

3. The number 45 has six factors: 1, 3, 5, 9, 15, and 45. Therefore, 45 is a _____ number.

1._____   2._____

3._____

*"I'm a **composite** number— a whole number with more than two **factors** (numbers that divide into me evenly). My factors are 1, 2, 4, 5, 8, 10, 20, and 40."*

*"I'm a composite number too. We share the factors 1, 2, 4, and 8. Our **greatest common factor** is 8."*

*"My **prime factorization** is 2 × 2 × 2 × 5. This can also be written as $2^3 \times 5$."*

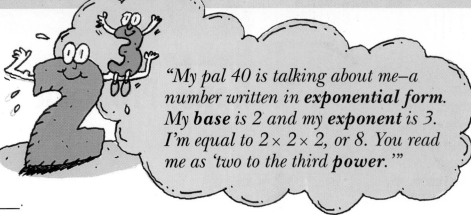

*"My pal 40 is talking about me—a number written in **exponential form**. My **base** is 2 and my **exponent** is 3. I'm equal to $2 \times 2 \times 2$, or 8. You read me as 'two to the third **power**.'"*

4. In 4^3, the 3 is called the _____.

5. If 5 is used as a factor three times, we could say "5 to the third _____."

6. When you write numbers using exponents, the numbers are said to be written in _____.

7. The _____ of 42 is $2 \times 3 \times 7$.

8. In 7^2, the 7 is called the _____.

9. A number is _____ by another number if the remainder is zero after dividing.

10. The number 11 is a _____ number because it has only two factors, 11 and 1.

*"Last but not least, there's me, a **prime** number. I'm **divisible** only by 1 and myself—without a remainder."*

4. _____

5. _____

6. _____

7. _____

8. _____

9. _____

10. _____

"I'm Special!"

Did You Know?

The number 1 is neither prime nor composite.

ratio
rate
term
proportion
cross-products
scale drawing
percent
sale price
discount
sales tax

_____

_____

Ratio, Proportion, and Percent

We use ratio, proportion, and percent almost every day as we travel, shop, and cook. Add two more words to the list. Then do the activities. Use your Spelling Dictionary if you need help.

▨ GETTING AT MEANING

Sentence Completion Study the pictures and information on these pages. Then fill in each blank with a list word.

Scale Drawing
Scale: **1** inch = **3** feet (One inch on the drawing equals 3 feet on the actual horse.)

Ratio

$\frac{1}{3}$ → first term
 → second term

The comparison of the size of the drawing to the actual size of the horse is shown as the **ratio** $\frac{1}{3}$ (1 inch to 3 feet).

Proportion

$$\frac{1}{3} = \frac{2}{6}$$

Two equal ratios form a **proportion.** One inch corresponds to 3 feet in the same way that 2 inches correspond to 6 feet.

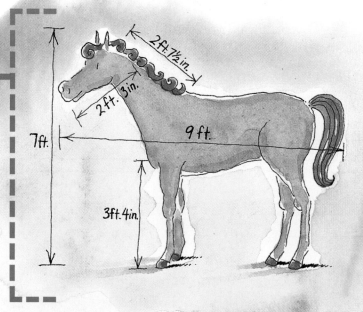

1. The diagram of a horse is an example of a ____.

2. The equation $\frac{3}{7} = \frac{9}{21}$ is also known as a ____.

3. In $\frac{5}{6}$, the first ____ is 5.

4. If a horse is 6 feet tall and 7 feet long, then the ____ of its height to its length is 6 to 7.

1. _____   3. _____

2. _____   4. _____

Is the rider correct? Use the information in the box to determine your answer.

$$\frac{3 \text{ mi.}}{1 \text{ hr.}} \stackrel{?}{=} \frac{6 \text{ mi.}}{2 \text{ hr.}}$$

$$3 \times 2 = 1 \times 6$$
$$6 = 6$$

In a proportion, the cross-products are equal.

5. If the rider rode her horse 6 miles in 2 hours, their traveling _____ would be 3 miles per hour.

6. In $\frac{2}{6} = \frac{8}{n}$ the _____ are 2 x n and 6 x 8.

5. _____

6. _____

Save 20% on Oats!	
Regular Price	**$9.00**
Discount (20%)	**- 1.80**
Sale Price	**$7.20**
Sales Tax (5%)	**+ .36**
Total Cost	**$7.56**

7. In the sale described above, a 20% _____ on a $9 bag of oats would be $1.80.

8. Therefore, the _____ of the oats is 80% of the regular price.

9. Getting a 20 _____ discount is the same as saving 20 cents out of every dollar.

10. In most areas, _____ is added to the price of an item.

7. _____

8. _____

9. _____

10. _____

Scaling Down

Make a scale drawing of your favorite animal. Measure its height, from the top of its head to the floor; its length, from the tip of its nose to the tip of its tail; and the length of its head, ears, legs, and body. Determine a scale and start drawing!

Probability

probability
outcome
likely
possible
choices
certain
impossible
predict
experiment
trials

_____

_____

Did you ever try to design your own board game? To make sure a game is fair to all players, the designer uses probability. The list words all deal with probability. Add two more of your own. Then do the activities. Use your Spelling Dictionary if you need help.

■ GETTING AT MEANING

Story Problems Read story A below. Then use it to help you complete story B with words from the list.

Story A

Sam and Sue are playing a game that uses a spinner. The spinner has 5 equal sections: 2 red, 2 blue, and 1 white. Sam and Sue want to know the **probability** of the spinner landing on the white section.

Sam says, "Let's do an **experiment**. I'll spin the spinner 20 times and keep track of every **outcome**. We know for **certain** that every spin will land on red, blue, or white—those are the only **choices**. We also know that it's **impossible** for the spinner to land on any other color. How **likely** is it that the spinner will land on white?"

Sue says, "There are 5 sections, so the number of **possible** outcomes is 5. There is only 1 white section, so I **predict** that the spinner will land on white only $\frac{1}{5}$ of the time—1 out of 5, or 4 out of 20, spins. The spinner is more likely to land on red or blue than on white."

After 20 **trials**, Sam's results show 7 red, 8 blue, and 5 white. Sue's prediction was close. The spinner landed on white just 1 more time than she had predicted.

Sam and Sue decide to toss a coin to see who has to wash dishes. Since a coin has two sides, "heads" or "tails," there are only two __(1)__, "heads" and "tails." Sue chooses "heads," and Sam chooses "tails." It is difficult to __(2)__ who will win the toss, since there are only two __(3)__ outcomes, and neither one is more __(4)__ than the other. Sam and Sue can be __(5)__ that only one of them will have to wash dishes because it is __(6)__ for both of them to win.

Sam flips the coin. The __(7)__ is "heads." Sue laughs and starts to leave the room, but Sam says, "Wait! Let's toss the coin four more times and make it the best of five __(8)__."

Sue thinks about this for a minute. "No," she says. "I don't have to do an __(9)__ to know that the __(10)__ of me winning is only one out of two. I'd better quit while I'm ahead!"

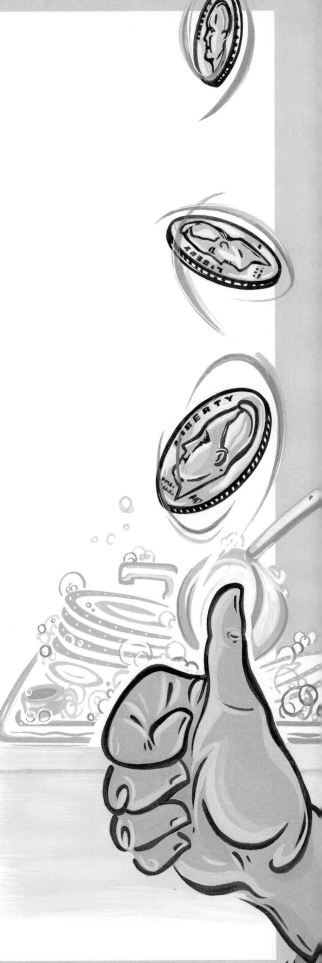

1. _____	6. _____
2. _____	7. _____
3. _____	8. _____
4. _____	9. _____
5. _____	10. _____

Probable **e**'s

The letter **e** occurs about one-eighth of the time in a typical English sentence. Use this fact to help you with the following activity:

1. Predict how many **e's** you would find in the first 80 letters of a newspaper or magazine article.

2. In a newspaper or magazine article of your choice, count the number of **e's** in the first 80 letters and write the result as a probability. Is the result close to your prediction? Do several more trials and average your results. Is the average close to 1 out of 8?

Writer's Handbook

INTRODUCTION

Spelling and punctuation help you communicate when you write, just as your hands and the tone of your voice help you communicate when you speak. If you spell and punctuate properly, your audience will more clearly understand what you write. This handbook will help you learn to become a more effective writer—and communicator.

CONTENTS

The Writing Process

Producing a polished piece of writing takes several steps: prewriting, drafting, revising, proofreading, and presenting. This section answers some of the questions you might have about these steps.

1. PREWRITING

What should I do before I begin writing?

Spend some time planning first. Skilled artists will tell you that before they begin creating a piece, they plan what it will look like, as well as the steps they will take to create it. Follow the suggestions below to plan and create your "masterpiece."

- **Select a topic** by brainstorming ideas; by looking through books, magazines, or newspapers; or by going through a journal in which you have recorded different thoughts, feelings, and observations.
- **Determine your purpose and audience.** What is your purpose for writing? Do you want to express certain feelings? describe or explain something? inform, persuade, or entertain? Who is your audience?
- **Narrow your topic.** To focus on an idea specific enough to deal with, you might write down questions, develop an outline, or group words or phrases related to your topic. You might also create a word web.
- **Gather information about your topic.** Depending on what you're writing about, you might proceed by taking notes; conducting interviews; listing points you want to make; arranging events on a time line; or noting how things look, sound, smell, taste, and feel.
- **Organize your information.** Think about what your purpose for writing is. Then choose time order, spatial order, or order of importance.

2. DRAFTING

How do I actually begin writing?

Gather your writing materials—including your prewriting notes and any resources you will need—and find a quiet, comfortable place to write. Plan on writing for at least twenty minutes. If you have trouble starting, try some of these strategies:

- **Set a goal.** Tell yourself you'll write a certain amount—then stick to it.
- **Tune out all distractions.** Turn off the TV and radio, for example. Don't sit down near the telephone.
- **Review** your notes to come up with an idea for a good opening line or paragraph.
- **Write away!** Don't worry about perfect spelling, punctuation, or capitalization. You'll have time to revise later. Just start with a sentence that is direct and interesting, and that states your main idea. Then let your ideas flow.

3. REVISING

How do I revise my writing?

Revising means rereading what you have written to make sure it communicates your ideas as clearly and effectively as possible. To begin revising, you might do the following:

- **Read your draft to yourself** to catch such errors as unclear or unnecessary sentences or ideas that are out of order.
- **Have a conference** with other classmates or your teacher. Read your draft aloud and ask for reactions. Did your listeners understand what you were trying to say? Can they suggest ways you could improve your draft?

What kinds of questions should I ask?

The questions you ask will depend on your purpose, audience, and type of writing. Here are some points to consider:

Ask yourself these questions!

- Does each paragraph have a topic sentence that sets up or summarizes the rest of the paragraph?
- Are all events, steps, or reasons in the right order?
- Can I take out extra words or replace inexact ones?
- Does any information need to be added or rearranged?
- Do I need to take out information that doesn't relate to the topic?
- Are all the facts and figures correct?
- Have I used language appropriate for my audience?
- Do I have a clear beginning, middle, and end?

What kinds of changes should I make?

You might do any or all of the following to clarify your writing:

- **Add or subtract** words or ideas.
- **Move** words, sentences, or paragraphs.
- **Substitute** words or ideas to improve your draft.

≡	Make a capital.
/	Make a small letter.
∧	Add something.
ℯ	Take out something.
⊙	Add a period.
¶	New paragraph

4. PROOFREADING

Why should I proofread, and when and how should I do it?

You should proofread to correct mistakes in grammar, punctuation, capitalization, and spelling. Proofread once after revising your first draft, to be sure you have included all corrections. Then proofread again after finishing your final draft.

Use proofreading symbols such as the ones above so that you can clearly see what corrections are needed.

What kinds of things should I look for when I proofread?

Use the following questions as a proofreading checklist:

- Did I capitalize all proper nouns and proper adjectives?
- Is each sentence correctly punctuated?
- Have I avoided fragments and run-on sentences?
- Did I keep the correct verb tense throughout?
- Do all subjects and verbs agree?
- Did I check the spelling of any unfamiliar words?
- Did I indent every paragraph?
- Is my handwriting clear and legible?

Check for these possible errors!

5. PRESENTING

How should I present my final work?

For regular assignments, these steps are often used:

- Copy your final draft neatly on one side of white, lined paper.
- If you are using a computer, make final corrections to your rough draft and print out a new, clean version.
- Put your name, the subject, and the date in the top right-hand corner.
- Skip a line and write the title of your piece. Center it on the line.
- Leave a one-inch margin on the sides and bottom of the paper.

Special ways to present your writing include displaying it on a bulletin board, binding it in an illustrated book or newspaper, sharing it in an author's conference, and sending it to a magazine for publication.

Taking Writing Tests

Do writing tests make you nervous? Taking these tests can be easier if you follow these tips.

GENERAL GUIDELINES FOR WRITING TESTS

- **Listen carefully to instructions.** Listen for how much time you have, whether to use a pen or a pencil, and when to begin and end.
- **Read the assignment and identify the key words.** Before you begin writing, make sure you understand the assignment. Here are some key words that often come up in test assignments:

Look for these key words!

Categorize or *Classify:* Sort ideas or facts into groups.
Compare and contrast: Point out similarities (compare) and differences (contrast).
Defend: Give evidence to show why a view is right.
Define: Tell what something is or means.
Describe: Create a word picture with details and examples.
Discuss: State your ideas about what something means.
Evaluate: Give your opinion, with support, on whether an idea is good or bad, right or wrong.
Explain: Make something clear by giving reasons, examples, or steps.
Summarize: State main points, or retell important parts of a story.

- **Plan how you'll use your time.** Take time at the beginning to plan what you will write. Also build in time at the end to reread and catch any errors.
- **Write a strong opening** to catch your readers' attention. Be sure it specifically addresses the topic of the assignment.
- **Use specific facts and details** to develop your ideas. The more specific information you can include, the stronger your writing will be.
- **Take time to wrap things up.** Don't just stop writing because your time is up. Write a conclusion that pulls things together.

WRITING A PERSONAL NARRATIVE

A personal narrative is a true story about something you have done, felt, or experienced.

KEY WORDS IN ASSIGNMENTS

- "What did you **do** when . . . ?"
- "Write how you **felt** when . . ."
- "Tell **what happened** when . . ."

SAMPLE ASSIGNMENTS

- "I was shaking in my boots!" Have you ever heard someone say that when describing a frightening moment? Think about a time when you were "shaking in your boots." What made you afraid? Write about what you were doing, thinking, and feeling during your experience.
- Did you ever start laughing in the wrong place and at the wrong time, and the harder you tried not to laugh, the harder you laughed? What were you laughing at, and where were you? Was anyone else laughing too? Write about your experience—and try not to laugh!

A PLAN OF ATTACK

- Before you begin writing, narrow down your topic to one particular scary or funny experience that you want to tell your readers about.
- Go through the whole story in your mind so you won't forget any parts of it. Then jot down words and phrases—even quotes—that explain exactly what you were doing, thinking, and feeling during your experience.
- Write a rough outline for your narrative that includes a beginning, a middle, and an end.
- When you write, imagine you are introducing yourself to your readers as you relate your story.

FOLLOW-UP CHECKLIST

- Does your narrative have a beginning, a middle, and an end?
- Does the beginning grab your readers' attention and tell them what you will be writing about?
- Did you "capture the moment" by using exact words and phrases to describe your thoughts and feelings?
- Will your readers know you better after reading your story?
- Is all capitalization, punctuation, and spelling correct?

WRITING AN EXPLANATION

In explanatory writing, writers explain something by stating a main idea and then giving reasons or examples to support or illustrate it.

KEY WORDS IN ASSIGNMENTS

- "Explain **why** . . ."
- "Tell **how** the . . ."
- "Explain **what** . . ."

SAMPLE ASSIGNMENTS

- A new student has arrived in your school. Explain one of the rules in your classroom, giving reasons why it is an important rule to follow.
- What is the most enjoyable thing you do in your free time? Explain what you do, and tell why it is enjoyable.

A PLAN OF ATTACK

- Before you begin writing, list reasons or examples that support your main idea. Review your list, and cross out any items that don't deal directly with your topic.
- Begin with a topic sentence that clearly states what you will explain.
- Organize your examples or reasons by **order of importance.** Make them build from least important (weakest) to most important (strongest) or from most important to least important.
- Use words and phrases that signal a new reason or example, such as *for this reason, for example, because, this is why, this proves.*

FOLLOW-UP CHECKLIST

- Have you stated your main idea in a topic sentence?
- Do all your supporting sentences keep to the main idea?
- Do they stick to the pattern of organization you've chosen?
- Have you used words and phrases that signal new reasons or examples?
- Is all your spelling, capitalization, and punctuation correct?

WRITING A DESCRIPTION

Descriptive writing helps writers share their observations about how things look, smell, taste, sound, or feel.

KEY WORDS IN ASSIGNMENTS
- "**Tell** what it **looks** (or **smells, tastes, sounds, feels) like** . . ."
- "**Describe** what you **see** (or **smell, taste, hear, feel)** . . ."

SAMPLE ASSIGNMENTS
- You have just opened a magical door and stepped into the perfect setting. Are you indoors or outdoors? What time of day or year is it? What is happening, and who is there? Describe what you see, hear, smell, feel, and/or taste in your perfect setting.
- Your pen pal has asked you to describe your favorite place in your neighborhood. Write about it, using exact words and colorful language to paint a clear picture for your pen pal.

A PLAN OF ATTACK
- Before you write, picture your perfect setting or favorite place in your mind. Jot down details that describe what things look, sound, smell, feel, and taste like there.
- Begin with a topic sentence that tells what you'll be describing.
- Use **spatial order** to organize your description. You might describe a place from left to right, from near to far, or from top to bottom.
- Use words and phrases that signal spatial order, such as *on the right, below, behind, at the top, next to, around, near.*
- Use figurative language and exact words to paint the best "word picture" possible for your readers.

FOLLOW-UP CHECKLIST
- Does your topic sentence clearly identify what you are describing?
- Do you stick to the spatial order you've chosen?
- Have you used words and phrases to signal that order?
- Do all your details focus on what you're describing?
- Is all your capitalization, punctuation, and spelling correct?

WRITING COMPARISON/CONTRAST

When you compare and contrast, you tell how people, places, ideas, or things are alike and different from each other.

KEY WORDS IN ASSIGNMENTS

- "Describe the **similarities and differences** between . . ."
- "Tell how these two things (or people, things, ideas, activities, stories, events, and so on) are **alike and different**."

SAMPLE ASSIGNMENTS

- Although watching a TV show and going to the movies are different experiences, they also have some similarities. Write a paragraph that compares and contrasts these two pastimes.
- Basketball and baseball are both popular American sports. Write about the two sports, describing how they are alike and different.

A PLAN OF ATTACK

- Before you write, make a comparison/contrast chart. On one side, list how the things are alike—for example: *both are popular American sports*. On the other side, list how the things are different—for example: *basketball is played on a court; baseball is played on a field.*
- Consider organizing your writing into two paragraphs, based on your chart. In the first paragraph, describe how the pastimes or sports are alike. In the second paragraph, describe how they are different.
- Begin each paragraph with a topic sentence that explains what you will be comparing or contrasting.
- Use words and phrases that help signal your comparisons and contrasts, such as *both, and, like, alike, similar;* and *although, while, each, unlike, different, on the other hand.*

FOLLOW-UP CHECKLIST

- Does each of your topic sentences clearly state what you are comparing or contrasting?
- For each point you make about one of the things you are comparing and contrasting, do you have a similar point about the other thing?
- Have you used appropriate words and phrases to signal comparisons and contrasts?
- Is all your capitalization, punctuation, and spelling correct?

WRITING A NEWS STORY

In a news story, a writer gives facts and information about a special event, issue, or person. The lead paragraph in a news story tells who, what, when, where, how, and why a thing happened.

KEY WORDS IN ASSIGNMENTS
- "Tell **who, what, when, where, how,** and **why** . . ."
- "Give the **facts and information** about . . ."

SAMPLE ASSIGNMENTS
- This year's edition of the *Guinness Book of Records* has just been published, and your school is in it! Write a news story that tells who was involved; what they did; and when, where, how, and why it happened.
- A huge storm hit your town last night, but it wasn't raindrops that fell from the sky—it was gumdrops! As the town's ace reporter, it's your job to write up the story. Give all the important facts and information about this most unusual storm.

A PLAN OF ATTACK
- Before you begin writing your news story, write *Who?, What?, When?, Where?, How?,* and *Why?* down or across a sheet of paper. Then write the answer to each question.
- Plan a lead paragraph that sums up the essential points of your story, telling who, what, when, where, how, and why.
- Organize the details of your news story by **order of importance.** Give the most important details first. Leave out any unnecessary or unrelated information.
- When you have finished your news story, give it a short, bold headline. Use a strong verb to grab your readers' attention.

FOLLOW-UP CHECKLIST
- Does your lead paragraph tell who, what, when, where, why, and how?
- Have you included only the important facts and information in your news story?
- Is your information organized from most important to least important?
- Does your headline grab readers' attention?
- Are your spelling, punctuation, and grammar correct?

WRITING A PERSUASIVE LETTER

When you write a persuasive letter, you are trying to convince someone to agree with your opinion or point of view on an issue.

KEY WORDS IN ASSIGNMENTS
- "Try to **persuade** others to . . . "
- "**Convince** others to agree with your opinion about . . . "

SAMPLE ASSIGNMENTS
- Your principal wants to start an after-school program for students whose parents work late. Some people think it's a great idea, but others disagree. What's your opinion? Write a letter to the editor of your school newspaper and try to persuade others to agree with you.
- All year long your school has been raising money for a field trip. Now your principal is asking for suggestions about where to go. Think about where you'd like to go and write your principal a letter. Try to convince him or her that your field trip suggestion is the best one.

A PLAN OF ATTACK
- Before you begin writing, decide what point of view you will take. Jot down several reasons that support your point of view.
- Look over your reasons and make sure they really do support your point of view. Cross out any reasons that don't.
- Begin with a topic sentence that clearly states your point of view.
- Organize your reasons or examples by **order of importance.** Make them build from least important (weakest) to most important (strongest) or from most important to least important.

FOLLOW-UP CHECKLIST
- Does your topic sentence clearly state your opinion or point of view?
- Do your reasons strongly support your opinion?
- Do they stick to the pattern of organization you've chosen?
- Have you included only information that is relevant to your argument?
- Are your spelling, punctuation, and grammar correct?

Rules, Guidelines, and Models

CAPITALIZATION

Capitalize the following in your writing:

Names, initials, titles, and abbreviations used with names:

> Gen. Ian Underwood, Jr.   Dr. Kathleen M. Pepitone

Proper adjectives:

> Spanish olives   Canadian bacon   Italian soccer team

The pronoun *I:*

> Michael and I are wearing the same kind of gym shoes.

Names of cities, states, countries, and continents:

> Santa Fe   Alaska   Ireland   Australia

Names of lakes, rivers, mountains, structures, and companies:

> Lake Ontario   Mississippi River   Taj Mahal
> Appalachian Mountains   Boswell Office Supplies

Names of streets and street abbreviations:

> Spruce St.   Gary Ave.   Habberton Rd.   South Owen

Days, months, holidays, and special events:

> Tuesday   Wed.   September   Dec.
> Thanksgiving   Super Bowl Sunday   World Series

First, last, and all important words in movie, book, story, play, and TV show titles:

> King Kong   The Phantom Tollbooth
> "The Gift of the Magi"

First word in the greeting and closing of a letter:

> Dear friend,   Sincerely yours,

First word in a sentence:

> What do you think of my costume?

First word inside quotation marks:

> Tricia said, "It looks very realistic!"

First word of each main topic and subtopic in an outline:

> I. Beginning a baby-sitting business
>   A. Advertising your services
>   B. Deciding what to charge

Both letters of the United States Postal Service state abbreviations:

AL (Alabama)	**LA** (Louisiana)	**OH** (Ohio)
AK (Alaska)	**ME** (Maine)	**OK** (Oklahoma)
AZ (Arizona)	**MD** (Maryland)	**OR** (Oregon)
AR (Arkansas)	**MA** (Massachusetts)	**PA** (Pennsylvania)
CA (California)	**MI** (Michigan)	**RI** (Rhode Island)
CO (Colorado)	**MN** (Minnesota)	**SC** (South Carolina)
CT (Connecticut)	**MS** (Mississippi)	**SD** (South Dakota)
DE (Delaware)	**MO** (Missouri)	**TN** (Tennessee)
FL (Florida)	**MT** (Montana)	**TX** (Texas)
GA (Georgia)	**NE** (Nebraska)	**UT** (Utah)
HI (Hawaii)	**NV** (Nevada)	**VT** (Vermont)
ID (Idaho)	**NH** (New Hampshire)	**VA** (Virginia)
IL (Illinois)	**NJ** (New Jersey)	**WA** (Washington)
IN (Indiana)	**NM** (New Mexico)	**WV** (West Virginia)
IA (Iowa)	**NY** (New York)	**WI** (Wisconsin)
KS (Kansas)	**NC** (North Carolina)	**WY** (Wyoming)
KY (Kentucky)	**ND** (North Dakota)	

PUNCTUATION

Use **periods**

- to end declarative sentences that tell something or imperative sentences that state commands or requests:

    Jack plays the violin.   Call me when you get home.

- after most abbreviations:

    Mrs. Sr. Rev. Dec. Wed. St. p.m.

Use **exclamation marks**

- after sentences that show strong feeling:

    I won the art contest!

Use **question marks**

- after interrogative sentences that ask a question:

    Are you going to the concert tomorrow?

Use **commas**

- between the day of the month and the year in a date:
    August 10, 1957

- between the day of the week and the month in a date:
    Saturday, January 23

- to set off a date in the middle of a sentence:
    October 18, 1993, is a day I will always remember.
    She was born on February 17, 1992, in the middle of a snowstorm.

- between the name of a city and state:
    Duluth, Minnesota

- to set off an address in the middle of a sentence:
    I will be at 5 Elm Street, Reno, Nevada, until Monday.

- after the greeting and closing of a letter:
    Dear Sally,   Best wishes,

- between a series of words in a sentence:
    We drove through Wisconsin, Illinois, and Indiana.
    The teacher asked Brad to collect the papers, put them in a folder, and leave them on her desk.

- before the word that joins a compound sentence:
    I am eating lunch, and Tara is taking a nap.
    Judy likes biking, but Maria prefers roller-skating.

- after introductory words or phrases:
    Yes, Kate will be coming with us.
    As usual, she will be taking her teddy bear.

- to set off interrupting words or phrases:
    Sam is going too, by the way, and he'll be driving.

- to set off a noun of address:
    Helen, I like your baseball cap.
    When is your birthday, Uncle Arnie?
    Are you listening, Lou, or do I have to tell you again?

- before quotation marks or inside end quotation marks:
    Jacqui said, "Saturday is the best day of the week."
    "It's my favorite day too," agreed Alec.

- to set off appositives (words or phrases that identify or explain nouns):

   Mr. Gordon, a terrific cook, has invited us to dinner.

   He will serve his specialty, pesto pasta.

- after mild interjections (words that express feeling):

   Oops, I spilled the juice.   Wow, that's some computer!

Use **quotation marks**

- around the exact words someone used when speaking:

   Arnetta said, "I'm getting hungry."

- around titles of stories, poems, songs, and articles:

   "The Tortoise and the Hare"   "Cats"   "Twist and Shout"

Underline titles of books and movies:

   Johnny Tremain   Father of the Bride

Use **apostrophes**

- to form the possessive of a noun:

   brother's   horses'   children's

- in contractions in place of dropped letters:

   we'll (we will)   didn't (did not)   you're (you are)

Use **colons**

- between hours and minutes to indicate time:

   12:15   6:30

- after the greeting in a business letter:

   Dear Ms. Allen: To whom it may concern:

BUSINESS LETTER FORM

A business letter is a letter that requests products or information; lodges complaints about products or services; or gives opinions and suggestions about products, services, or situations.

Since you usually write business letters to people you don't know, your tone should be rather formal, and you should be as brief and to-the-point as possible.

Study the business letter below. Notice the capitalization and punctuation used in each of the parts.

149 Cowper Street
Palo Alto, CA 94301
September 11, 20_ _

Heading

Family Fun Magazine
P.O. Box 929
Northampton, MA 01060–0929

Inside Address

Dear Family Fun:

Greeting

I received my first issue of Family Fun in the mail today, and I sat and read it from cover to cover! I've never seen a magazine with so many wonderful ideas for activities and projects that families can do together. I especially enjoyed the article you had entitled "Cool Toys That Teach." My daughter's sixth birthday is right around the corner, and you've given me some timely gift ideas.

Body

Keep up the good work! I'm looking forward to my next issue of Family Fun.

Sincerely,

Jody Ashton

Jody Ashton

Closing

Signature

Dictionary Handbook

Understanding and Using the Dictionary

Have you ever stopped while you were writing to wonder how to spell a word, or while you were reading to wonder what a certain word meant or how to pronounce it? You can find the answers to questions like these when you know how to use a dictionary. This handbook will help you to do this.

1. How do I look up a word quickly?

The **entry words** in a dictionary are arranged in alphabetical order. To find a word quickly, use the pairs of words at the top outside corner of each page—**guide words.** They tell you the first and last entry words on that page. If your word falls in-between these guide words, then you know it's somewhere on that page.

For example, if the guide words are **fly I fog,** you'll find *focus* on that page, but to find *fish* you'll have to turn back a few pages.

Exercise 1   Write two entry words that would appear on the same dictionary page as each set of guide words.

1. pit I prey	5. natural I nut
2. dark I dish	6. apart I atom
3. herb I hop	7. fable I family
4. burn I buy	8. change I chess

2. How do I look up a word I don't know how to spell?

The key is finding out how the word begins. For example, suppose you need to correct this misspelling: "He wanted to become a *sitizen*." How else might the word begin? Think about what letters could make the sound /s/ at the beginning of this word. You know that the letters **s** and **c** are common spellings of this sound, so you try them out.

1. _____

2. _____

3. _____

4. _____

5. _____

6. _____

7. _____

8. _____

First, you try *sitizen*. You look through the **guide words** until you find the page headed **sir | size,** but *sitizen* isn't there. So you try *citizen*, and there it is on the page headed **cistern | civilize.**

Exercise 2 Use your Spelling Dictionary to find out which one of each pair is spelled correctly. Write the correct spelling and the guide words from the dictionary page where each is found.

1. syclone—cyclone
2. foto—photo
3. chord—kord
4. calorie—kalorie
5. uspire—aspire
6. senic—scenic

3. What do I do if I still can't find the word?

Most dictionaries have a **spelling chart** that shows all possible spellings for each English sound. The part of the chart for the sound /k/ is shown.

k   **c**oat, **k**ind, ba**ck,** e**ch**o, a**ch**e, **q**uit, a**cc**ount, anti**que,**
        e**x**cite, a**cq**uire

Notice that there are ten possible spellings for this sound in English. Use the spelling chart if you still can't find a word after you've looked up every spelling you can think of.

Exercise 3 Use the spelling chart called "Spellings of English Sounds" at the beginning of your Spelling Dictionary to answer these questions.

1. How many ways can the sound /ü/ be spelled?
2. Which word in the chart has the sound /u/ spelled the same as in *blood?*
3. Which word in the chart has the sound /sh/ spelled the same as in *sugar?*
4. How many ways can the sound /n/ be spelled?
5. What are the four ways that the sound /f/ can be spelled?
6. What are the seven ways that the sound /ä/ can be spelled?

1. _____

2. _____

3. _____

4. _____

5. _____

6. _____

1. _____

2. _____

3. _____

4. _____

5. _____

6. _____

4. How do I know which definition fits my word?

Many words have more than one meaning. In fact, a word like *rest* has dozens of meanings. You can use the **context** of the word, the **parts of speech** labels, and the **illustrative phrases** and **sentences** provided to help you choose the proper **definition** of your word. What is the definition of the word *scratch* in this sentence: "Please scratch my name off the ballot."

> **scratch** (skrach), **1** break, mark, or cut slightly with something sharp or rough: *Your shoes have scratched the chair.* **2** mark made by scratching: *There are deep scratches on this desk.* **3** tear or dig with the nails or claws: *The cat scratched me.* **4** a very slight cut: *That scratch on your hand will soon be well.* **5** rub or scrape to relieve itching: *Don't scratch your mosquito bites.* **6** write in a hurry or carelessly. **7** withdraw (a horse, candidate, etc.) from a race or contest. 1,3,5,6,7 *v.,* 2,4 *n., pl.* **scratch es**

From the context of the sentence, you know that the definition you are looking for means "to withdraw or eliminate." Reading the definitions, you can see that the one you want is definition 7: withdraw from a race or contest.

Exercise 4   Write the number of the definition that fits the italicized words in these sentences. Use your Spelling Dictionary.

1. The judge *sentenced* him to five years in jail.
2. Wolves are said to have a keen *sense* of smell.
3. Do your work on a *flat* surface.
4. My native *tongue* is Spanish.
5. Write your *address* at the top of a business letter.

1. _____

2. _____

3. _____

4. _____

5. _____

5. How can I find out how to pronounce a word?

You can use the dictionary to help you pronounce words that may be unfamiliar to you. The entry word is broken into **syllables.** Right after it comes the pronunciation, enclosed in parentheses: **con·fide** (kən fīd′). The **accent mark** tells you which syllable to emphasize.

The **pronunciation key,** which appears once on each pair of facing pages in most dictionaries, shows how to sound out the pronunciations.

Some words can be said in more than one way. For example, two pronunciations are given in your Spelling Dictionary for *rodeo* (rō′dē ō *or* rō dā′ō). The pronunciation (rō′dē ō) is given first, not because it is more correct than (rō dā′ō), but because it is used by more people. If you say (rō dā′ō), you are just as correct as those people who say (rō′dē ō).

Exercise 5 Write the word that each pronunciation represents. Use the pronunciation key below to help you.

1. (hīr)
2. (mezh′ər)
3. (ri lij′ən)
4. (süp)
5. (sə lü′shən)
6. (mēk)
7. (gə räzh′ *or* gə räj′)
8. (dȯ′tər)
9. (hwāl)
10. (ku̇d)

a	hat	ī	ice	u̇	put	ə stands for		
ā	age	o	not	ü	rule	a	in about
ä	far, calm	ō	open	ch	child	e	in taken
âr	care	ȯ	saw	ng	long	i	in pencil
e	let	ô	order	sh	she	o	in lemon
ē	equal	oi	oil	th	thin	u	in circus
ėr	term	ou	out	ᴛʜ	then		
i	it	u	cup	zh	measure		

1. _____
2. _____
3. _____
4. _____
5. _____
6. _____
7. _____
8. _____
9. _____
10. _____

6. How do I find the correct spelling for a word that is not an entry word?

Sometimes when you add endings such as **-ed**, **-ing**, **-s**, and **-es** to words, the spelling changes. These are not listed as entry words. To find the correct spellings of these forms, look up the base word and find the **related forms** at the end of the entry.

Exercise 6 In your Spelling Dictionary, look up the base word of each misspelled related form. Write the related form correctly.

1. chillyer
2. shelfs
3. circld
4. pianoes
5. potatos
6. ignoreing

1. _____
2. _____
3. _____
4. _____
5. _____
6. _____

7. What if my dictionary lists two ways to spell a word?

Some words may be spelled in more than one way. Sometimes this is shown in a single entry, with the more common spelling first: **vi·ta·min** or **vi·ta·mine**. Other times, different spellings are listed as separate entries, and the definition is given under the more common spelling:

> **cat·a·log** (kat′l óg), list of items in some collection. *n.* Also, **catalogue.**
> **cat·a·logue** (kat′l óg), catalog. *n.*

Exercise 7 Look up these words in your Spelling Dictionary. Write the more common spelling for each word.

1. gasolene
2. monologue
3. teen-age
4. r.s.v.p.

1. _____
2. _____
3. _____
4. _____

8. How do I find out where a word in our language came from originally?

A dictionary also gives you information about how words came into our language. An explanation of a word's origin is called an **etymology.** A word's etymology is usually found at the end of the entry, enclosed in brackets. Read this entry for *kindergarten.*

> **kin·der·gar·ten** (kin′dər gärt′n), school or class for children from about 4 to 6 years old that educates them by games, toys, and pleasant occupations. *n. [Kindergarten* is from German *Kindergarten,* which comes from *Kinder,* meaning "children," and *Garten,* meaning "garden."]

From the etymology you learn that kindergarten came to our language from German and means a "garden for children."

Exercise 8 Use your Spelling Dictionary to find the etymologies of the following words. Write the language, languages, or other source each word came from.

1.	admiral	5.	saxophone
2.	corral	6.	safari
3.	koala	7.	iceberg
4.	aquarium	8.	decathlon

1. _____
2. _____
3. _____
4. _____
5. _____
6. _____
7. _____
8. _____

9. What else can I find in a dictionary entry?

Sometimes an entry is followed by a **synonym study.** These explain subtle differences between words that are closely related in meaning. Look at this entry for the word *burn:*

> **burn** (bėrn) **1** be on fire; be very hot: *The campfire burned all night.* **2** destroy or be destroyed by fire: *Please burn these old papers.* **3** injure or be injured by fire, heat, or acid: *The flame from the candle burned her finger.* **4** feel hot; give a feeling of heat to: *The child's forehead burned with fever. v.,* **burned** or **burnt, burn ing.**
> **Synonym Study Burn, scorch, sear** mean to injure or be injured by fire, heat, or acid. **Burn,** the general word, suggests any degree of damage from slight injury to destruction. **Scorch** means to burn the surface enough to discolor it, sometimes to damage the texture. **Sear** means to burn or scorch the surface by heat or acid enough to dry or harden it.

Exercise 9 Use **burn, scorch,** and **sear** each in a sentence to illustrate the differences in meaning.

1. _____
2. _____
3. _____

10. Why are there two different entries for some words?

These words are homographs. A **homograph** is a word that is spelled the same as another word but has a different origin and meaning. Look at the two entries for *rare*.

> **rare**[1] (râr), **1** seldom seen or found: *Storks and peacocks are rare birds in the United States.* **2** not happening often; unusual: *Snow is rare in Florida.* **3** unusually good or great: *Edison had rare powers as an inventor.* **4** thin; not dense: *The higher we go above the earth, the rarer the air is. adj.,* **rar er, rar est.** [*Rare*[1] comes from Latin *rarus.*] **—rare′ness,** *n.*
>
> **rare**[2] (râr), not cooked much: *a rare steak. adj.,* **rar er, rar est.** [*Rare*[2] comes from Old English *hrēr.*] **—rare′ness,** n.

If you look at the etymologies of the two words, you will see that *rare*[1] is originally from a Latin word and *rare*[2] is originally from an Old English word.

Exercise 10 Use a dictionary to look up these homographs. Explain the differences in their origins and meanings. (Note: You won't find these in your Spelling Dictionary.)

1. tear[1], tear[2]
2. fan[1], fan[2]
3. mail[1], mail[2]
4. arm[1], arm[2]
5. crow[1], crow[2]
6. scale[1], scale[2], scale[3]

1. _____

   _____

2. _____

   _____

3. _____

   _____

4. _____

   _____

5. _____

   _____

6. _____

   _____

Spelling Dictionary

Parts of a Dictionary Entry

1 ⟶ **tear²** (târ), **1** pull apart by force: *I tore the letter into tiny pieces.* **2** make by pulling apart: *She tore a hole in her jeans.* v., **tore, torn,**
5 ⟶
6
7 ⟶ **tear·ing.** [*Tear²* comes from the Old English word *teran*.] **—tear′a·ble,** *adj.*
9 ⟶
8

tear down, 1 pull down; raze; destroy: *to tear down an old building.* **2** bring about the wreck of; discredit; ruin: *tear down another's reputation.*
10

1 Entry word
2 Homograph number
3 Pronunciation
4 Definitions
5 Illustrative sentence or phrase
6 Part-of-speech label
7 Inflected forms
8 Etymology
9 Run-on entry
10 Idiom

Full Pronunciation Key

a	hat, cap	**i**	it, pin	**p**	paper, cup	**v**	very, save
ā	age, face	**ī**	ice, five	**r**	run, try	**w**	will, woman
ä	father, far			**s**	say, yes	**y**	young, yet
â	care, hair	**j**	jam, enjoy	**sh**	she, rush	**z**	zero, breeze
		k	kind, seek	**t**	tell, it	**zh**	measure,
b	bad, rob	**l**	land, coal	**th**	thin, both		seizure
ch	child, much	**m**	me, am	**ŦH**	then, smooth		
d	did, red	**n**	no, in			**ə**	represents:
		ng	long, bring	**u**	cup, cutter		a in about
e	let, best			**u̇**	full, put		e in taken
ē	equal, be	**o**	hot, rock	**ü**	rule, move		i in pencil
ėr	term, learn	**ō**	open, go				o in lemon
		ȯ	all, saw				u in circus
f	fat, if	**ô**	order, store				
g	go, bag	**oi**	oil, voice				
h	he, how	**ou**	house, out				

The contents of the dictionary entries in this book have been adapted from the *Scott, Foresman Intermediate Dictionary*, Copyright © 1997, 1993, 1988, 1979, 1974 by Scott, Foresman and Company or from the *Scott, Foresman Advanced Dictionary*, Copyright © 1997, 1993, 1988, 1983, 1979 by Scott, Foresman and Company.

Spellings of English Sounds*

Symbol	Spellings	Symbol	Spellings
a	at, plaid, half, laugh	**ng**	long, ink, handkerchief, tongue
ā	able, aid, say, age, eight, they, break, vein, gauge, crepe, beret	**o**	odd, honest
ä	father, ah, calm, heart, bazaar, yacht, sergeant	**ō**	open, oak, toe, own, home, oh, folk, though, bureau, sew, brooch, soul
âr	dare, aerial, fair, prayer, where, pear, their, they're	**ȯ**	all, author, awful, broad, bought, walk, taught, cough, Utah, Arkansas
b	bad, rabbit	**ô**	order, board, floor, tore
ch	child, watch, future, question	**oi**	oil, boy
d	did, add, filled	**ou**	out, owl, bough, hour
e	end, said, any, bread, says, heifer, leopard, friend, bury	**p**	pay, happy
		r	run, carry, wrong, rhythm
ē	equal, eat, eel, happy, cities, vehicle, ceiling, receive, key, these, believe, machine, liter, people	**s**	say, miss, cent, scent, dance, tense, sword, pizza, listen
		sh	she, machine, sure, ocean, special, tension, mission, nation
ėr	stern, earth, urge, first, word, journey	**t**	tell, button, two, Thomas, stopped, doubt, receipt, pizza
f	fat, effort, laugh, phrase		
g	go, egg, guest, ghost, league	**th**	thin
gz	example, exhaust	**ŦH**	then, breathe
h	he, who, jai alai, Gila monster	**u**	up, oven, trouble, does, flood
hw	wheat	**u̇**	full, good, wolf, should
i	it, England, ear, hymn, been, sieve, women, busy, build, weird	**ü**	food, junior, rule, blue, who, move, threw, soup, through, shoe, two, fruit, lieutenant
ī	I, ice, lie, sky, type, rye, eye, island, high, eider, aisle, height, buy, coyote	**v**	very, have, of, Stephen
		w	will, quick
		y	yes, opinion
j	jam, gem, exaggerate, schedule, badger, bridge, soldier, large, allegiance	**yü**	use, few, cue, view, vacuum
		z	zero, has, buzz, scissors, xylophone
k	coat, kind, back, echo, ache, quit, account, antique, excite, acquire	**zh**	measure, garage, division
		ə	alone, complete, moment, authority, bargain, April, cautious, circus, pageant, physician, oxygen, dungeon, tortoise
l	land, tell		
m	me, common, climb, solemn, palm		
n	no, manner, knife, gnaw, pneumonia		

*Not all English spellings of these sounds are included in this list.

A

ab·duc·tion (ab duk/shən), a kidnaping. *n.*

a·brupt (ə brupt/), showing sudden change; unexpected: *I made an abrupt turn to avoid another car.* *adj.* —**a·brupt/ly,** *adv.*

ab·so·lute·ly (ab/sə lüt/lē or ab/sə lüt/lē), without doubt; certainly: *She is absolutely the finest person I know.* *adv.*

ab·so·lute mag·ni·tude (ab/sə lüt mag/nə tüd), a measure of how bright a star is.

ac·cept (ak sept/), **1** take what is offered or given to one; consent to take: *She accepted the job.* **2** say yes to an invitation, offer, etc. *v.*

ac·cept·a·ble (ak sep/tə bəl), **1** likely to be well received; agreeable: *Flowers are an acceptable gift.* **2** good enough but not outstanding; satisfactory: *I received an acceptable mark on the test.* *adj.*

ac·cept·a·bly (ak sep/tə blē), in a way that pleases. *adv.*

ac·cept·ance (ak sep/təns), favorable reception; approval: *the acceptance of a story for publication.* *n.*

ac·cess (ak/ses), **1** right to approach, enter, or use; admittance: *All students have access to the library during the afternoon.* **2** approach to places, persons, or things; accessibility. 1,2 *n., pl.* **ac·cess·es.**

ac·com·pa·ni·ment (ə kum/pə nē mənt), anything that goes along with something else: *The rain was an unpleasant accompaniment to our ride.* *n.*

ac·com·plish (ə kom/plish), succeed in completing; carry out; finish: *Did you accomplish your purpose? She can accomplish more in a day than anyone else in class.* *v.*

ac·cord·ing (ə kôr/ding), **according to,** **1** in agreement with: *She came according to her promise.* **2** in proportion to; on the basis of: *You will be ranked according to the work you do.* **3** on the authority of: *According to this book, cats and tigers are related.* *adv.*

a·chieve (ə chēv/), reach by one's own efforts; get by effort: *achieve high grades in mathematics.* *v.,* **a·chieved, a·chiev·ing.**

ac·ro·nym (ak/rə nim), word formed from the first letters or syllables of other words. EXAMPLE: scuba (self-contained underwater breathing apparatus). *n., pl.* **ac·ro·nyms.** [Acronym comes from Greek *akros,* meaning "tip, outermost," and *onyma,* meaning "name." This word first appeared in English about 1943.]

ac·ti·vate (ak/tə vāt), make active; show movement. *v.,* **ac·ti·vat·ed, ac·ti·vat·ing.**

ad·di·tive (ad/ə tiv), substance added to another substance to preserve it, increase its effectiveness, etc. *n., pl.* **ad·di·tives.**

ad·dress (ə dres/; *also* ad/res *for 2*), **1** a speech, especially a formal one: *The President gave an address over television to the nation.* **2** the place to which one's mail is directed; place of residence or of business: *Write your name and address on this envelope.* **3** write on (a letter, package, etc.) where it is to be sent: *to address envelopes for greeting cards.* 1,2 *n., pl.* **ad·dress·es;** 3 *v.*

ad·e·quate (ad/ə kwit), as much as is needed for a particular purpose; sufficient; enough: *To be healthy one must have an adequate diet.* *adj.*

ad·just (ə just/), **1** change to make fit. **2** arrange satisfactorily; set right; settle: *The girls adjusted their difference of opinion and were friends again.* **3** accommodate oneself; get used: *Some wild animals never adjust to life in a zoo.* *v.,* **ad·just·ed, ad·just·ing.**

ad·min·is·tra·tion (ad min/ə strā/shən), **1** the managing of the affairs of a business, an office, etc.: *The administration of a big business requires skill in dealing with people.* **2** group of persons in charge. *n.*

ad·mir·a·ble (ad/mər ə bəl), worth admiring; very good; excellent: *She has an admirable character.* *adj.*

ad·mir·al (ad/mər əl), the commander of a navy or a fleet. [Admiral was borrowed from French *amiral,* and can be traced back to Arabic *amir al,* meaning "chief of the."]

abrupt
The rock appeared **abruptly** on the horizon.

ad·mire (ad mīr′), **1** regard with wonder, pleasure, or satisfaction. **2** think highly of; respect: *I admire your courage. v.*, **ad·mired, ad·mir·ing.**

af·fec·tion·ate (ə fek′shə nit), showing or having affection; loving and tender: *an affectionate letter, an affectionate farewell. adj.*

af·ford (ə fôrd′), **1** spare the money for. **2** manage to give, spare, or have: *A busy person cannot afford delay. He cannot afford to waste so much time. v.* —**af·ford′a·ble, adj.**

Af·ri·ca (af′rə kə), a continent that lies between the Atlantic Ocean and Indian Ocean, separated from Europe by the Mediterranean Sea. *n.*

af·ter·shock (af′tər shok), violent shake, blow, or crash; a small earthquake or tremor after the earthquake. *n., pl.* **af·ter·shocks.**

af·ter·thought (af′tər thȯt′), **1** thought that comes too late to be used. **2** a second or later thought or explanation. *n.*

a·gain (ə gen′), another time; once more. *adv.*

a·gil·i·ty (ə jil′ə tē), the ability to change the position of the body quickly and to control body movements. *n.*

a·gree·ment (ə grē′mənt), an understanding reached by two or more persons, groups of persons, or nations among themselves. *n.*

air bag (âr′ bag′), an inflatable bag that prevents automobile passengers from being thrown forward in the event of a collision. It is installed beneath the dashboard, and inflates instantly upon impact.

air con·di·tion·er (âr′ kən dish′ə nər), device used to air-condition a building, room, car, etc.

air mat·tress (âr′ mat′ris), pad that can be inflated to serve as a mattress on land or water.

a.k.a. or **aka,** also known as: *Jennifer Landon a.k.a. Jennie Lane.*

al·ien·ate (ā′lyə nāt), turn from affection to indifference, dislike, or hatred; make unfriendly: *The colonies were alienated from England by disputes over trade and taxation. v.*, **al·ien·at·ed, al·ien·at·ing.**

a lit·tle (ə lit′l), a small amount; a small number: *The young child ate a little bread.*

al·ler·gen (al′ər jen), a substance in the environment that causes an allergy. *n., pl.* **al·ler·gens.**

al·ler·gy (al′ər jē), an unusual reaction of body tissue to certain substances such as particular kinds of pollen, food, hair, or cloth. Hay fever, asthma, headaches, and hives are common signs of allergy. *n., pl.* **al·ler·gies.**

al·li·ga·tor (al′ə gā′tər), a large reptile with a rather thick skin, with a short, flat head. Alligators live in the rivers and marshes of the warm parts of America and China. *n.* [*Alligator* comes from Spanish *el lagarto,* meaning "the lizard."]

al·low (ə lou′), let (someone) do something; permit (something) to be done or happen: *They do not allow swimming at this beach. v.*

al·low·ance (ə lou′əns), a sum of money given or set aside for expenses: *a household allowance for groceries of $50 a week. My weekly allowance is $1. n.*

all ways (ȯl′ wāz), **1** all directions: *Look all ways before crossing the street.* **2** all methods; means: *I tried all ways, but the easiest way worked best.*

a lot (ə lot′), a great amount; a great deal: *The teenager ate a lot for lunch.*

al·ways (ȯl′wāz or ȯl′wiz), **1** at all times; every time: *Night always follows day.* **2** all the time; continually: *Home is always a cheerful place at holiday time. adv.*

air bag
testing an **air bag** in an automobile

allergen
This plant may be an **allergen.**

a	hat	ī	ice	u̇	put		**ə** stands for	
ā	age	o	not	ü	rule		a	in about
ä	far, calm	ō	open	ch	child		e	in taken
âr	care	ȯ	saw	ng	long		i	in pencil
e	let	ô	order	sh	she		o	in lemon
ē	equal	oi	oil	th	thin		u	in circus
ėr	term	ou	out	ᵺ	then			
i	it	u	cup	zh	measure			

amphitheater

an **amphitheater** in Arles, France

appetizer

Serve this delicious **appetizer** at any party.

am·ber (am′bər), a hard, yellow or yellowish-brown gum, used for jewelry, in making pipe stems, etc. Amber is the resin of fossil pine trees. *n.*

A·mer·i·can (ə mer′ə kən), **1** of or in the United States: *an American citizen.* **2** person born or living in the United States; citizen of the United States. *1 adj., 2 n.*

am·phi·the·a·ter or **am·phi·the·a·tre** (am′fə thē′ə tər), a circular or oval building with rows of seats around a central open space. Each row is higher than the one in front of it. *n.*

a·nal·o·gy (ə nal′ə jē), likeness in some ways between things that are otherwise unlike; similarity: *There is an analogy between the heart and a pump. n., pl.* **a·nal·o·gies.**

a·nat·o·my (ə nat′ə mē), **1** science of the structure of animals and plants. **2** the dissecting of animals or plants to study their structure. *n., pl.* **a·nat·o·mies.**

an·ces·tor (an′ses′tər), person from whom one is descended, such as one's great-grandparents: *Their ancestors came to America in 1812. n., pl.* **an·ces·tors.**

an·droid (an′droid), robot that resembles a human being. *n.* [*Android* comes from Greek *andros,* meaning "man," and *eidos,* meaning "form."]

an·nounce (ə nouns′), **1** give public or formal notice of: *The teacher announced that there would be no school tomorrow.* **2** introduce programs, read news, etc., on the radio or television. *v.,* **an·nounced, an·nounc·ing.**

an·swer (an′sər), **1** speak or write in return to a question: *I asked them a question, but they would not answer. He finally answered my question.* **2** act in return to a call, signal, etc.; respond: *I knocked on the door, but no one answered. She answered the doorbell. v.,* **an·swered, an·swer·ing.**

an·swer·ing ma·chine (an′sər ing mə shēn′), a telephone device that answers calls automatically by recording messages and playing them back for later listening.

an·te·bel·lum (an′ti bel′əm), before the war. *adj.*

an·te·ced·ent (an′tə sēd′nt), coming or happening before; previous: *Cave dwellers lived in a period of history antecedent to written records. adj.* [*Antecedent* comes from Latin *antecedentem,* meaning "going before."]

an·ti·bod·y (an′ti bod′ē), a protein substance produced in the blood or tissues that destroys or weakens bacteria or neutralizes poisons produced by them. *n., pl.* **an·ti·bod·ies.**

an·ti·dote (an′ti dōt), medicine or remedy that counteracts the harmful effects of a poison: *Milk is an antidote for some poisons. n.*

anx·ious (angk′shəs or ang′shəs), **1** uneasy because of thoughts or fears of what may happen; troubled; worried: *I felt anxious about my final exams.* **2** wishing very much; eager: *He was anxious for a bicycle. She was anxious to learn to play chess. adj.* [*Anxious* is from Latin *anxius,* which comes from *angere,* meaning "to choke, to cause distress."]

a·piece (ə pēs′), for each one; each: *These apples cost ten cents apiece. adv.*

a·pol·o·gize (ə pol′ə jīz), make an apology; say one is sorry; offer an excuse: *I apologized for being so late. v.,* **a·pol·o·gized, a·pol·o·giz·ing.**

ap·par·ent (ə par′ənt), appearing to be; seeming: *The apparent truth was really a lie. adj.* —**ap·par′ent·ly,** *adv.*

ap·par·ent mag·ni·tude (ə par′ent mag′nə tüd), a measure of how bright a star appears to be to someone.

ap·pear·ance (ə pir′əns), **1** act of coming in sight: *His sudden appearance in the doorway startled me.* **2** a coming before the public as a performer or author: *a singer's first appearance.* **3** outward look: *a pleasing appearance. n.*

ap·pe·tiz·er (ap′ə tī′zər), something that arouses the appetite, usually served before a meal. Spinach dip and crackers are appetizers. *n.*

ap·pre·ci·a·tive (ə prē′shə tiv or ə prē′shē ā′tiv), having or showing appreciation; recognizing the value: *The appreciative audience applauded the performer. adj.*

ap·pren·tice·ship (ə prenʹtis ship), condition of learning a trade or art. In return for instruction, the apprentice agrees to work for a certain time with little or no pay. *n.*

ap·ti·tude (apʹtə tüd *or* apʹtə tyüd), natural tendency or talent; ability; capacity. *n.*

a·quar·i·um (ə kwârʹē əm), **1** tank or glass bowl in which living fish or other water animals, and water plants are kept. **2** building used for showing collections of living fish, water animals, and water plants. *n., pl.* **a·quar·i·ums, a·quar·i·a** (ə kwerʹē ə). [*Aquarium* is from Latin *aquarium*, meaning "a watering place (for cattle)," which comes from *aqua*, meaning "water."]

aq·ue·duct (akʹwə dukt), an artificial channel or large pipe for bringing water from a distance. *n.*

Ar·a·bic nu·mer·als *or* **Arabic fig·ures** (arʹə bik nüʹmər əlz; arʹə bik figʹyərz), the figures 1, 2, 3, 4, 5, 6, 7, 8, 9, 0. They are called Arabic because they were introduced into western Europe by Arabian scholars, but probably were derived from India.

arc (ärk), **1** any part of the circumference of a circle. **2** any part of any curved line. *n.* [*Arc* came into English about 600 years ago from French *arc*, which is from Latin *arcus*, meaning "an arch, a bow, an arc."]

ar·chae·ol·o·gist (ärʹkē olʹə jist), a scientist who studies the people, customs, and life of ancient times. *n.*

ar·chae·ol·o·gy (ärʹkē olʹə jē), the scientific study of the people, customs, and life of ancient times. Archaeologists study buildings, tools, pottery, and weapons to find out how people lived in the past. *n.*

ar·chi·tec·ture (ärʹkə tekʹchər), the style or qualities that distinguish the buildings of a certain time, region, or group from other buildings. *n.*

a·re·na (ə rēʹnə), **1** space in an ancient Roman amphitheater in which contests or shows took place: *Gladiators fought with lions in the arena at Rome.* **2** a similar space, surrounded by seats, used today for contests or shows: *a boxing arena. n., pl.* **a·re·nas.**

a·round (ə roundʹ), **1** in a circle: *The top spun around.* **2** here and there; about: *We walked around to see the town* (*adv.*). *She leaves her books around the house* (*prep.*). **1** *adv.,* **2** *adv., prep.*

ar·roy·o (ə roiʹō), in southwestern United States: **1** the dry bed of a stream; gully. **2** a small river. *n., pl.* **ar·roy·os.** [*Arroyo* was borrowed from Spanish *arroyo.*]

ar·ti·choke (ärʹtə chōk), the flower bud of a thistlelike plant with large prickly leaves. Artichokes are a vegetable. *n.* [*Artichoke* comes from Italian *articiocco* and Arabic *al-kharshuf.*]

ar·ti·fact (ärʹtə fakt), anything made by human skill or work, especially a tool or weapon. *n., pl.* **ar·ti·facts.**

ar·ti·fi·cial (ärʹtə fishʹəl), made as a substitute or imitation; not real. *adj.*

ar·ti·san (ärʹtə zən), person skilled in some industry or trade; craftsman. Carpenters, masons, plumbers, and electricians are artisans. *n., pl.* **ar·ti·sans.**

art·ist (ärʹtist), person who is skilled in any of the fine arts, such as sculpture, music, or literature. *n.*

ASAP, as soon as possible.

as·pire (ə spīrʹ), have an ambition for something; desire earnestly; seek: *aspire to be captain of the team, aspire after knowledge. v.,* **as·pired, as·pir·ing.**

as·pir·in (asʹpər ən), drug used to relieve pain or fever, such as in headaches, colds, etc. *n.*

as·sas·sin (ə sasʹn), murderer; one who kills a well-known person, especially a political leader, by a sudden or secret attack. *n.*

aqueduct

an ancient Roman
aqueduct in Segovia,
Spain

artichoke

a	hat	**ī**	ice	**u̇**	put	**ə** *stands for*	
ā	age	**o**	not	**ü**	rule	**a**	in about
ä	far, calm	**ō**	open	**ch**	child	**e**	in taken
âr	care	**ȯ**	saw	**ng**	long	**i**	in pencil
e	let	**ô**	order	**sh**	she	**o**	in lemon
ē	equal	**oi**	oil	**th**	thin	**u**	in circus
ėr	term	**ou**	out	**ᴛʜ**	then		
i	it	**u**	cup	**zh**	measure		

as·sume (ə süm′), **1** take for granted without proof; suppose: *He assumed that the train would be on time.* **2** take upon oneself; undertake: *She assumed the leadership of the project.* **3** take on; put on: *The problem has assumed a new form. v.,* **as·sumed, as·sum·ing.** —**as·sum′a·ble,** *adj.* —**as·sum′a·bly,** *adv.* —**as·sum′er,** *n.*

as·sumed (ə sümd′), false; not real; pretended: *an assumed name. adj.* —**as·sum′ed·ly** (ə süm′id lē), *adv.*

as·sump·tion (ə sump′shən), an assuming: *The clerk bustled about with an assumption of authority. n.*

as·ter·ism (as′tə riz′əm), group of stars smaller than a constellation. *n.*

ath·let·ic (ath let′ik), **1** having to do with active games and sports: *an athletic association.* **2** strong and active: *an athletic girl. adj.*

at·mo·sphere (at′mə sfir), **1** air that surrounds the earth. **2** air in any given place. **3** general character or mood of one's surroundings; surrounding influence: *a religious atmosphere, an atmosphere of excitement. n.*

at·tend·ance (ə ten′dəns), number of people present; persons attending: *The attendance at the meeting last night was over 200. n.*

at·tend·ant (ə ten′dənt), person who waits on another, such as a servant or follower. *n.*

at·ten·tion (ə ten′shən), **1** power of attending; notice. **2** care and thought; consideration: *Your letter will receive early attention. n.*

at·ten·tive (ə ten′tiv), **1** paying attention; observant. **2** courteous; polite. *They were attentive to their guests. adj.*

at·ti·tude (at′ə tüd *or* at′ə tyüd), way of thinking, acting, or feeling. *n., pl.* **at·ti·tudes.**

at·tor·ney (ə tėr′nē), lawyer. *n., pl.* **at·tor·neys.**

at·trac·tive (ə trak′tiv), winning attention and liking; pleasing: *an attractive young couple. adj.*

au·to·bi·og·ra·phy (ȯ′tə bī og′ rə fē), story of a person's life written by that person. *n., pl.* **au·to·bi·og·ra·phies.**

au·to·graph (ȯ′tə graf), **1** a person's signature: *Many people collect the autographs of celebrities.* **2** write one's name on: *The star autographed my program.* 1 *n.,* 2 *v.*

avocado

an **avocado** cut in half

au·to·mat·ic (ȯ′tə mat′ik), moving or acting by itself: *Our building has an automatic elevator. adj.*

au·to·mo·bile (ȯ′tə mə bēl′), **1** a passenger vehicle, for use on roads and streets, that carries its own engine; car. **2** of or for automobiles: *an automobile mechanic.* 1 *n.,* 2 *adj.*

au·ton·o·my (ȯ ton′ə mē), self-government; independence: *Algeria achieved autonomy in 1962. n.*

au·to·pi·lot (ȯ′tə pī′lət), automatic pilot. *n.*

au·tumn (ȯ′təm), **1** season of the year between summer and winter; fall. **2** of autumn; coming in autumn: *autumn rains, autumn flowers.* 1 *n.,* 2 *adj.*

av·er·age (av′ər ij), **1** quantity found by dividing the sum of all the quantities by the number of quantities. The average of 3 and 5 and 10 is 6 (3 + 5 + 10 = 18; 18 ÷ 3 = 6). **2** obtained by averaging; being an average: *The average temperature for the week was 82°.* **3** usual; ordinary: *a person of average intelligence.* 1 *n.,* 2,3 *adj.*

av·o·ca·do (av′ə kä′dō), the dark-green, pear-shaped fruit of a tree that grows in warm regions; alligator pear. Avocados have a large seed surrounded by yellow-green pulp which is used in salads, dips, etc. *n., pl.* **av·o·ca·dos.** [*Avocado* is from Spanish *aguacate,* which came from Nahuatl *ahuacatl.*]

a way (ə wā′), a form of doing; a manner; style: *a way of wearing one's hair.*

a·way (ə wā′), **1** from a place; to a distance: *Stay away from the fire.* **2** at a distance; a way off: *The sailor was far away from home* (adv.). *His home is miles away.* (adj.). 1,2 *adv.,* 2 *adj.*

aw·ful·ly (ȯ′flē *or* ȯ′fə lē), **1** dreadfully; terribly: *The burn hurt awfully.* **2** INFORMAL. very: *I'm awfully sorry. adv.*

a while (ə hwīl), a time; a space of time: *She kept us waiting a while.*

a·while (ə hwīl′), for a short time: *Stay awhile. adv.*

ax·is (ak′sis), a straight line about which an object turns or seems to turn. The axis of the earth is an imaginary line through the North Pole and the South Pole. *n., pl.* **ax·es** (ak′sēz).

Az·tec (az′tek), member of an American Indian people of central Mexico. The Aztecs had a highly developed culture and ruled a large empire during the 1400s, which fell to the Spanish in 1521. *n., pl.* **Az·tec** or **Az·tecs.**

B

ba·by-sit (bā′bē sit′), take care of a child or children while the parents are away for a while. *v.,* **ba·by-sat** (bā′bē sat′), **ba·by-sit·ting.**

back·wards (bak′wərdz), backward; with the back first: *He tumbled backwards into the garden. adv.*

bac·te·ri·a (bak tir′ē ə), a group of organisms that can usually be seen only with a microscope. Some bacteria are harmful, causing disease and tooth decay. *n., sing.* **bac·te·ri·um** (bak tir′ē əm).

bail·iff (bā′lif), officer of a court of law who has charge of jurors and guards prisoners while they are in the courtroom. *n., pl.* **bail·iffs.**

bal·co·ny (bal′kə nē), an outside platform enclosed by a railing, that juts out from an upper floor of a building. *n., pl.* **bal·co·nies.**

bal·let (bal′ā or ba lā′), an elaborate dance by a group on a stage. A ballet tells a story through the movements of the dancing and is accompanied by music. *n.* [*Ballet* comes from French and Italian *balletto,* the diminutive of *ballo,* meaning "dance."]

ba·nan·a (bə nan′ə), a slightly curved, yellow or red tropical fruit with firm, creamy flesh. Bananas are five to eight inches long and grow in clusters two or three feet long. *n., pl.* **ba·nan·as.** [*Banana* was borrowed from Spanish or Portuguese *banana,* which came from a west African word.]
go bananas, SLANG. become very excited.

ban·quet (bang′kwit), **1** a large meal with many courses, prepared for a special occasion or for many people; feast: *a wedding banquet.* **2** a formal dinner with speeches. *n.* [*Banquet* comes from French and Italian *banchetto,* a diminutive of *banco,* meaning "bench."]

bar·be·cue (bär′bə kyü), **1** an outdoor meal in which meat is roasted over an open fire. **2** grill or open fireplace for cooking meat, usually over charcoal. *n., Also,* **barbeque.** [*Barbecue* was borrowed from Spanish *barbecue,* which comes from a Caribbean Indian word *barbacoa,* meaning "a framework of sticks." The sticks formed a primitive outdoor cooking device.]

ba·rom·e·ter (bə rom′ə tər), an instrument used to measure air pressure. *n.*

bar·ri·cade (bar′ə kād′ or bar′ə kād), any barrier or obstruction. *n.*

ba·salt (bə sôlt′), a hard, dark-colored rock of volcanic origin. It often occurs in a form resembling a group of columns. *n.*

base (bās), **1** the part on which anything stands or rests; bottom: *This big machine has a wide steel base.* **2** establish; found: *Their large business was based on good service.* **3** the number to be raised to a power: *In 4³, 4 is the base.* 1,3 *n.,* 2 *v.,* **based, bas·ing.**
off base, INFORMAL, incorrect; wrong.

bas·ket·ball (bas′kit bôl′), **1** game played with a large, round ball by two teams of five players each. The players try to toss the ball through a net. **2** ball used in this game. *n.*

ba·zaar or **ba·zar** (bə zär′), **1** street or streets full of small shops and booths in Oriental countries. **2** place for the sale of many kinds of goods. **3** sale of things contributed by various people, held for some charity. *n.* [*Bazaar* comes from Persian *bāzār.*]

ballet
a difficult movement
in **ballet**

basalt
a **basalt** rock

a	hat	**ī**	ice	**u̇**	put	**ə** stands for	
ā	age	**o**	not	**ü**	rule	**a**	in about
ä	far, calm	**ō**	open	**ch**	child	**e**	in taken
âr	care	**ȯ**	saw	**ng**	long	**i**	in pencil
e	let	**ô**	order	**sh**	she	**o**	in lemon
ē	equal	**oi**	oil	**th**	thin	**u**	in circus
ėr	term	**ou**	out	**ᴛʜ**	then		
i	it	**u**	cup	**zh**	measure		

bean·bag (bēn′bag′), a small bag partly filled with dried beans, used to toss back and forth in certain games. *n.*

bean·ball (bēn′bôl′), a baseball thrown deliberately by the pitcher near or at a batter's head. *n.*

beau·ti·ful (byü′tə fəl), very pleasing to see or hear; delighting the mind or senses. *adj.*

be·cause (bi kôz′), for the reason that; since. *conj.*

be·come (bi kum′), come to be; grow to be: *It is becoming colder. I became tired and fell asleep. v.*, **be·came** (bi kām′), **be·come, be·com·ing.**

be·gin·ning (bi gin′ing), **1** first part: *I enjoyed this book from beginning to end.* **2** source; origin: *The idea of the airplane had its beginning in the flight of birds. n.*

be·lief (bi lēf′), **1** what is held to be true or real; thing believed; opinion: *It was once a common belief that the earth is flat.* **2** acceptance as true or real: *His belief in ghosts makes him afraid of the dark. n., pl.* **be·liefs.**

be·low (bi lō), lower than; under. *prep.*

be·side (bi sīd′), by the side of; close to; near: *Grass grows beside the fence. prep.*

be·sides (bi sīdz′), **1** in addition to; over and above: *Others came to the school picnic besides our own class.* **2** other than; except: *They spoke of no one besides you. prep.*

bi·o·lu·mi·nes·cent (bī′ō lü′mə nes′nt), showing phosphorescence or other emission of light. *adj.*

bit (bit), the basic unit of information in an electronic computer. It is the same as a choice between two possibilities, such as "yes" or "no." *n.* [*Bit* is a blend of the words *bi(nary digi)t*].

bi·zarre (bə zär′), strikingly odd or queer in appearance or style; fantastic; grotesque: *The frost made bizarre figures on the windowpanes. adj.*

bloom·ers (blü′mərz), **1** loose trousers, gathered at the knee, formerly worn by women and girls for physical training. **2** underwear made like these. *n. pl.* [*Bloomers* were named for Amelia J. Bloomer, 1818–1894, an American magazine publisher who popularized the use of this type of trousers.]

Braille

using **Braille** to read

BLT, initials for a bacon, lettuce, and tomato sandwich.

bod·y fat (bod′ē fat), the amount of a person's weight that is fat.

bomb (bom), container filled with an explosive. A bomb is set off by a fuse, a timing device, or the force with which it hits something. *n.*

bom·bard (bom bärd′), attack with bombs or heavy fire of shot and shell from big guns. *v.*

book·keep·er (bůk′kē′pər), person who keeps a record of business accounts. *n.*

book·store (bůk′stôr′), store where books are sold. *n.*

bore (bôr), make weary by tiresome talk or by being dull: *This book bores me, so I shall not finish it. v.*, **bored, bor·ing.**

boy·cott (boi′kot), join together against and agree not to buy from, sell to, or associate with (a person, business, or nation) in order to force a change or to punish. *v.* [*Boycott* comes from Captain Charles Boycott, 1832–1897, an Irish estate manager whose tenants and neighbors boycotted him when he refused to lower rents.]

Braille or **braille** (brāl), system of writing and printing for blind people. The letters in Braille are represented by different arrangements of raised points and are read by touching them. *n.* [*Braille* comes from Louis Braille, 1809–1852, a French teacher of the blind who invented this system.]

brief (brēf), **1** lasting only a short time. **2** using few words. *adj.*

bril·liant (bril′yənt), **1** shining brightly; sparkling: *brilliant jewels, brilliant sunshine.* **2** splendid; magnificent: *The singer gave a brilliant performance.* **3** having great ability: *a brilliant musician.* **4** diamond or other gem cut to sparkle brightly. *1-3 adj., 4 n.* —**bril′liant·ly,** *adv.*

broc·co·li (brok′ə lē), vegetable with green branching stems and flower heads. It belongs to the same family as the cabbage. *n., pl.* **broc·co·li.** [*Broccoli* comes from Italian *broccoli,* meaning "sprouts."]

bro·ken·heart·ed (brō′kən här′tid), crushed by sorrow or grief; heartbroken: *The young boy was brokenhearted after losing the race. adj.*

bron·co (brong′kō), a wild or partly tamed horse of the western United States. *n., pl.* **bron·cos.** Also, **broncho.** [*Bronco* comes from Spanish *bronco,* meaning "rough, rude."]

broth·er-in-law (bruŦH′ər in lô′), **1** brother of one's husband or wife. **2** husband of one's sister. *n., pl.* **broth·ers-in-law.**

brunch (brunch), meal taken late in the morning and intended to combine breakfast and lunch. *n., pl.* **brunch·es.** [*Brunch* is a blend of *breakfast* and *lunch.*]

buf·fa·lo (buf′ə lō), **1** the bison of North America. **2** any of several kinds of oxen, such as the tame water buffalo of Asia and the Cape buffalo of Africa. *n., pl.* **buf·fa·loes, buf·fa·los,** or **buf·fa·lo.**

buf·fet (bu fā′ or bù fā′), meal at which guests serve themselves from food laid out on a table or sideboard. *n.* [*Buffet* comes from French, a diminutive of *buffe,* meaning "blow."]

build (bild), **1** make by putting materials together; construct: *People build houses, bridges, and machines. Birds build nests.* **2** form or produce gradually; develop: *build a business. The lawyer built her case on facts. v.,* **built** (bilt), **build·ing.**

build·ing (bil′ding), thing built. Barns, factories, stores, houses, and hotels are all buildings. *n.*

bull·pen (bùl′pen′), **1** a place outside the playing limits in which baseball relief pitchers warm up during a game. **2** any place in which people gather together for a definite purpose. *n.*

busi·ness (biz′nis), **1** thing that one is busy at; work; occupation: *A carpenter's business is building.* **2** of or having to do with business: *A business office usually has typewriters and other business machines.* **1** *n.,* **2** *adj.*

C

cab·i·net (kab′ə nit), piece of furniture with shelves or drawers, used to hold articles for use or display: *a medicine cabinet, a filing cabinet for letters. n.*

ca·coph·o·ny (kə kof′ə nē), succession of harsh, clashing sounds; dissonance; discord. *n.*

caf·e·ter·i·a (kaf′ə tir′ē ə), restaurant where people serve themselves. *n., pl.* **caf·e·ter·i·as.** [*Cafeteria* comes from Spanish *cafetería,* meaning "coffee shop".]

cal·en·dar (kal′ən dər), system by which the beginning, length, and divisions of the year are fixed: *The Julian calendar was established during Julius Caesar's reign. n.*

cal·or·ie (kal′ər ē), unit for measuring the amount of energy a food can produce in the body and the amount of energy the body uses during activity. *n., pl.* **cal·or·ies.**

cam·cor·der (kam′kôr′dər), a hand-held combination of a camera and a video recorder. *n.* [*Camcorder* is a blend of the word *camera* and the phrase *video recorder.*]

can·cel·la·tion (kan′sə lā′shən), a canceling or a being canceled: *cancellation of a baseball game because of rain. n.*

can·non (kan′ən), a big gun, especially one that is too large to be carried by hand and is fixed to the ground or mounted on wheels. The old-fashioned cannon was much used during the Civil War. *n., pl.* **can·nons** or **can·non.**

can·not (kan′ot or ka not′), can not. *v.*

can·ta·loupe or **can·ta·loup** (kan′tl ōp), kind of muskmelon with a hard, rough rind and sweet, juicy, orange-colored flesh. *My daughter's favorite melon is cantaloupe. n.*

camcorder

cannon
a breech-loading
cannon from the Civil
War years

a	hat	**ī**	ice	**ù**	put	**ə** stands for	
ā	age	**o**	not	**ü**	rule	**a**	in about
ä	far, calm	**ō**	open	**ch**	child	**e**	in taken
âr	care	**ò**	saw	**ng**	long	**i**	in pencil
e	let	**ô**	order	**sh**	she	**o**	in lemon
ē	equal	**oi**	oil	**th**	thin	**u**	in circus
ėr	term	**ou**	out	**ŦH**	then		
i	it	**u**	cup	**zh**	measure		

can·yon (kan′yən), a narrow valley with high, steep sides, usually with a stream at the bottom. n. Also, **cañon.**

ca·rafe (kə raf′), a glass bottle for holding water, wine, coffee, etc. n. [*Carafe* was borrowed from French, then Italian *caraffa,* and can be traced back to Spanish *garrafa,* and Arabic *gharraf,* meaning "drinking vessel."]

car·bon im·print (kär′bən im′print), an organic material that leaves an outline of the organism in carbon; a fossil.

car·di·o·vas·cu·lar (kär′dē ō vas′kyə lər), having to do with, or affecting both the heart and the blood vessels. adj.

car·ni·val (kär′nə vəl), place of amusement or a traveling show having merry-go-rounds, games, sideshows, etc. n.

car·ob (kar′əb), **1** an evergreen tree of the pea family, native to eastern Mediterranean regions and grown in other warm areas. **2** the edible pulp of its seed pod, used as a sweet flavoring especially in place of chocolate. n.

cat·sup (kech′əp, kach′əp, or kat′səp), sauce made to use with meat, fish, etc. Tomato catsup is made of tomatoes, onions, salt, sugar, and spices. n. Also, **catchup** or **ketchup.** [*Catsup* comes from Malay *kēchap,* meaning a "fish sauce," probably from a Chinese dialect *kētsiap,* meaning "brine of fish."]

cause·way (köz′wā′), a raised road or path, usually built across wet ground or shallow water: *A narrow causeway ran across the bog.* n., pl. **cause·ways.**

cau·tious (kö′shəs), very careful; taking care to be safe; not taking chances: *A cautious driver never drives too fast.* adj. —**cau′tious·ly,** adv.

ceil·ing (sē′ling), the inside, top covering of a room; surface opposite the floor. n.

cel·e·bra·tion (sel′ə brā′shən), special services or activities in honor of a particular person, act, time, or day: *A Fourth of July celebration often includes a display of fireworks.* n.

Cel·si·us (sel′sē əs), of, based on, or according to the Celsius scale; centigrade. adj.

Celsius scale, a scale for measuring temperature on which 0 degrees marks the freezing point of water and 100 degrees marks the boiling point. [This scale was named for Anders *Celsius,* 1701–1744, a Swedish astronomer who invented it in 1742.]

cent (sent), coin of the United States and Canada, usually an alloy of copper; penny. 100 cents make one dollar. n.

cen·ter (sen′tər), point within a circle or sphere equally distant from all points of the circumference or surface. n.

cen·tral an·gle (sen′trəl ang′gəl), an angle with its vertex at the center of a circle.

cer·e·al (sir′ē əl), food made from grain. Oatmeal and corn meal are cereals. n.

cer·tain (sert′n), without a doubt; sure: *It is certain that 2 and 3 do not make 6. I am certain that these are the facts.* adj.

cham·pi·on·ship (cham′pē ən ship), position of a champion; first place: *Our school won the championship in baseball.* n.

chaps (shaps or chaps), strong leather trousers without a back, worn over other trousers by cowhands. n. pl. [short for Spanish *chaparajos.*]

charm (chärm), **1** a pleasing quality or feature: *The book has many charms; the chief one is its delightful humor.* **2** please greatly; delight; fascinate; attract: *The children were charmed by the neighbor's pet raccoon.* 1 n., 2 v., **charmed, charm·ing.**

chau·vin·ism (shō′və niz′əm), **1** boastful, warlike patriotism. **2** an excessive enthusiasm for one's sex, race, or group: *no lack of female chauvinism.* n. [*Chauvinism* comes from French *chauvinisme,* which was named for Nicolas *Chauvin,* an early nineteenth-century soldier who was an enthusiastic admirer of Napoleon I.]

cheer·lead·er (chir′lē′dər), person who leads a group in organized cheering, especially at high school or college athletic events. n.

cheese·burg·er (chēz′bėr′gər), a hamburger sandwich with a slice of melted cheese on top of the meat. n. [*Cheeseburger* is a blend of the words *cheese* and *hamburger.*]

Chi·ca·go (shə kȯ′gō or shə kä′gō), city in NE Illinois, on Lake Michigan. *n.*

chief (chēf), head of a group; person highest in rank or authority; leader: *a police chief. n., pl.* **chiefs.**

chil·i (chil′ē), **1** a hot-tasting pod of red pepper, used for seasoning. **2** a highly seasoned Mexican dish of chopped meat cooked with red peppers and, usually, kidney beans. *n., pl.* **chil·ies.** Also, **chile** or **chilli.** [*Chili* is from Mexican Spanish *chile,* which came from Nahuatl *chilli.*]

chill·y (chil′ē), unpleasantly cool; rather cold. *adj.,* **chill·i·er, chill·i·est.**

chiv·al·ry (shiv′əl rē), the qualities of an ideal knight in the Middle Ages; bravery, honor, courtesy, protection of the weak, respect for women, and fairness to enemies. *n.*

choc·o·late (chȯk′lit or chȯk′ə lit), substance made by roasting and grinding cacao seeds. It has a strong, rich flavor and much value as food. *n.*

choice (chois), power or chance to choose: *I have my choice between a radio and a camera for my birthday. n., pl.* **choic·es.**

choose (chüz), pick out; select from a number: *to choose a book, to choose wisely. v.,* **chose, cho·sen** (chōz′n), **choos·ing.**

chord[1] (kôrd), combination of two or more musical notes sounded together in harmony. *n.*

chord[2] (kôrd), a straight line segment connecting two points on a curve. *n.*

chose (chōz), past tense of **choose.** *I chose the red shirt. v.*

Christ·mas (kris′məs), the yearly celebration of the birth of Christ; December 25. *n., pl.* **Christ·mas·es.**

chut·ney (chut′nē), a spicy sauce or relish made of fruits, herbs, pepper, etc. *n., pl.* **chut·neys.** [*Chutney* comes from Hindustani *chatnī.*]

cir·cle (sėr′kəl), **1** go around in a circle; revolve around: *The moon circles the earth. The airplane circled before it landed.* **2** form a circle around; surround; encircle: *A ring of trees circled the clearing. v.,* **cir·cled, cir·cling.**

cir·cum·fer·ence (sér kum′fər əns), **1** the boundary line of a circle or of certain other surfaces. Every point in the circumference of a circle is at the same distance from the center. **2** the distance around: *The circumference of the earth at the equator is almost 25,000 miles. n.*

cit·i·zen (sit′ə zən), **1** person who by birth or by choice is a member of a nation. A citizen owes loyalty to that nation and is given certain rights by it. **2** inhabitant of a city or town. *n.*

cit·i·zen·ship (sit′ə zən ship), the duties, rights, and privileges of a citizen. *n.*

cit·y (sit′ē), a large and important center of population and business activity: *The European cities' populations increased this year. Our city's school system is the largest in the midwest. n., pl.* **cit·ies.** [*City* came into English about 750 years ago from French *cite,* and can be traced back to Latin *civis,* meaning "citizen."]

cit·y-state (sit′ē stāt′), a city and its surrounding land, which acts like a nation. Athens and Sparta were two city-states in ancient Greece. *n., pl.* **cit·y-states.**

claim (klām), demand as one's own or one's right: *The settlers claimed the land beyond the river as theirs. Does anyone claim this pencil? v.* **stake a claim,** demand something for yourself.

clas·sic (klas′ik), work of literature or art of the highest rank or quality: *Louisa May Alcott's book "Little Women" is a classic. n.*

chili (def. 1)
red and green **chilies**

a	hat	**ī**	ice	**u̇**	put		**ə**	stands for
ā	age	**o**	not	**ü**	rule		a	in about
ä	far, calm	**ō**	open	**ch**	child		e	in taken
âr	care	**ȯ**	saw	**ng**	long		i	in pencil
e	let	**ô**	order	**sh**	she		o	in lemon
ē	equal	**oi**	oil	**th**	thin		u	in circus
ėr	term	**ou**	out	**ŦH**	then			
i	it	**u**	cup	**zh**	measure			

cliff

the white **cliffs** of
Dover, England

coach

The **coach** instructs a
young batter.

clean (klēn), **1** free from dirt or filth;
not soiled or stained. **2** make
clean: *clean a room. Washing
cleans clothes.* 1 *adj.,* 2 *v.*

cleanse (klenz), make clean: *cleanse
a wound before bandaging. v.,*
cleansed, cleans·ing.

clear·ance (klir′əns), sale of goods at
reduced prices. *n.*

cler·gy·man (klėr′jē mən), member of
the clergy; a minister, pastor,
priest, or rabbi. *n., pl.* **cler·gy·men.**

cli·ché (klē shā′), expression or idea
worn out by long use. *n., pl.*
cli·chés.

cliff (klif), a very steep slope of rock,
clay, etc. *n., pl.* **cliffs.**

clothes (klōz *or* klōᵺz), coverings for a
person's body: *I bought some new
clothes for my trip. n. pl.*

clum·si·ly (klum′zə lē), in a clumsy
manner; awkwardly. *adv.*

clum·sy (klum′zē), awkward in
moving; not graceful or skillful.
adj., **clum·si·er, clum·si·est.**

coach (kōch), person who teaches or
trains athletic teams, singers, etc.:
*a baseball coach, a swimming
coach's instructions, the drama
coaches' debate rules. n.*

coarse (kôrs), **1** made up of fairly
large parts; not fine: *coarse sand.*
2 heavy or rough in looks or
texture: *The old fisherman had
coarse, weathered features. adj.,*
coars·er, coars·est.

co·bra (kō′brə), a very poisonous
snake of Asia and Africa. When
excited, it flattens its neck so that
the head takes on the appearance
of a hood. *n., pl.* **co·bras.** [*Cobra*
comes from Portuguese *cobra (de
capello),* meaning "a snake (with a
hood)."]

co·coa (kō′kō), **1** powder made by
roasting and grinding the kernels
of cacao seeds, and removing
some of the fat. **2** drink made of
this powder with milk or water and
sugar. *n., pl.* **co·coas.** [*Cocoa* is a
different form of *cacao,* which was
borrowed from Spanish *cacao* and
Nahuatl *cacahuatl.*]

co·ed *or* **co-ed** (kō′ed′), INFORMAL. a
girl or woman student at a school
where both men and women
attend classes. *n.*

co·in·ci·dence (kō in′sə dəns), the
chance occurrence of two things at
the same time or place in such a
way as to seem remarkable, fitting,
etc. *n.*

cold front (kōld′ frunt′), the dividing
surfaces between two dissimilar air
masses, one being cold air.

col·lect (kə lekt′), bring or come
together; gather together. *v.* **col·
lect·ed, col·lect·ing.**

col·lec·tion (kə lek′shən), a bringing
together; coming together: *The
collection of these stamps took ten
years. n.*

col·lec·tor (kə lek′tər), person or thing
that collects. *n.*

col·lege (kol′ij), **1** school of higher
learning that gives degrees or
diplomas. A college is often a part
of a university. **2** school for special
training: *a business college. n.*

col·lid·ing bound·ar·y (kə lī′ding
boun′dər ē), an area where two
geological plates are moving
toward one another.

Col·os·se·um (kol′ə sē′əm), a large
amphitheater in Rome, completed
in A.D. 80. The Colosseum was used
for games and contests. *n.* Also,
Coliseum.

col·umn (kol′əm), **1** a slender, upright
structure; pillar. Columns are
usually made of stone, wood, or
metal, and are used as supports or
ornaments to a building. **2** a
narrow division of a page reading
from top to bottom, kept separate
by lines or by blank spaces. *n., pl.*
col·umns.

com·e·dy (kom′ə dē), an amusing
play or show having a happy
ending. *n., pl.* **com·e·dies.**

com·mand (kə mand′), **1** give an
order to; direct. **2** an order;
direction: *The admiral obeyed the
queen's command.* 1 *v.,* 2 *n.*

com·mand·ment (kə mand′mənt),
1 (in the Bible) one of the ten laws
that God gave to Moses; one of the
Ten Commandments. **2** any law or
command. *n.*

com·mer·cial (kə mėr′shəl), **1** having
to do with trade or business: *a store
or other commercial
establishment.* **2** made to be sold
for a profit: *Anything you can buy
in a store is a commercial product.*
3 an advertising message on radio
or television, broadcast between or
during programs. 1,2 *adj.,* 3 *n.*

com·mit·tee (kə mit′ē), group of
persons appointed or elected to do
some special thing, a deciding
group. *n.*

com·mu·ni·cate (kə myü′nə kāt),
give or exchange information or
news by speaking, writing, etc.;
send and receive messages. *v.*,
**com·mu·ni·cat·ed, com·mu·ni·
cat·ing.**

com·par·a·tive (kəm par′ə tiv),
1 measured by comparison with
something else; relative: *Screens
give us comparative freedom from
flies.* **2** the second of three degrees
of comparison of an adjective or
adverb. *Fairer is the comparative
of fair. More slowly is the
comparative of slowly.* **1** *adj.,* **2** *n.*

com·pass (kum′pəs), **1** instrument for
showing directions, especially one
consisting of a needle that points
to the North Magnetic Pole.
2 instrument consisting of two legs
hinged together at one end, used
for drawing circles and curved
lines and for measuring distances.
3 boundary; circumference: *within
the compass of four walls. n., pl.*
com·pass·es.

com·pas·sion (kəm pash′ən), feeling
for another's sorrow or hardship
that leads to help; sympathy; pity:
*Compassion for the earthquake
victims brought a flood of
contributions. n.*

com·pas·sion·ate (kəm pash′ə nit),
wishing to help those that suffer;
sympathetic; pitying. *adj.* —**com·
pas′sion·ate·ly,** *adv.*

com·pe·tent (kom′pə tənt), properly
qualified; able: *a competent
secretary. adj.*

com·pose (kəm pōz′), **1** make up;
form: *The ocean is composed of
salt water. Our party was
composed of three grown-ups and
four children.* **2** put together. *v.*,
com·posed, com·pos·ing.

com·pos·ite (kəm poz′it), a number
exactly divisible by some counting
number other than itself or one.
*4, 6, and 9 are composite numbers;
2, 3, 5, and 7 are prime numbers.
adj.*

com·po·si·tion (kom′pə zish′ən),
1 the makeup of anything; what is
in it: *The composition of this candy
includes sugar, chocolate, and
milk.* **2** a putting together of a
whole. *n.*

con·cede (kən sēd′), allow (a person)
to have; grant: *They conceded us
the right to use their driveway. v.*,
con·ced·ed, con·ced·ing. [*Concede*
comes from Latin *concedere,*
meaning "to yield."]

con·ceit·ed (kən sē′tid), having too
high an opinion of oneself or of
one's ability; vain. *adj.*

con·ceiv·a·ble (kən sē′və bəl), able
to be conceived or thought of;
imaginable: *We take every
conceivable precaution against
fire. adj.*

con·cur·rent (kən ker′ənt),
1 happening at the same time:
concurrent events. **2** agreeing;
harmonious: *concurrent ideas. adj.*

con·demn (kən dem′), express strong
disapproval of: *We condemn
cruelty to animals. v.*

con·du·cive (kən dü′siv or kən
dyü′siv), favorable; helpful:
*Exercise and proper eating habits
are conducive to good health. adj.*

con·duc·tor (kən duk′tər), person who
conducts; leader or guide: *the
conductor of a tour. n.*

con·fer·ence (kon′fər əns), meeting of
interested persons to discuss a
particular subject: *A conference
was called to discuss the fuel
shortage. n., pl.* **con·fer·en·ces.**

con·fi·dence (kon′fə dəns), **1** firm
belief or trust: *I have complete
confidence in his honesty.* **2** firm
belief in oneself; self-confidence:
*Years of experience at her
work have given her great
confidence. n.*

con·gru·ent fig·ures (kən grü′ənt
fig′yərz), two figures with the same
size and shape.

compass (def. 1)

using a **compass** to
show directions

a	hat	**ī**	ice	**u̇**	put		**ə** stands for	
ā	age	**o**	not	**ü**	rule		**a**	in about
ä	far, calm	**ō**	open	**ch**	child		**e**	in taken
âr	care	**ȯ**	saw	**ng**	long		**i**	in pencil
e	let	**ô**	order	**sh**	she		**o**	in lemon
ē	equal	**oi**	oil	**th**	thin		**u**	in circus
ėr	term	**ou**	out	**ᵺH**	then			
i	it	**u**	cup	**zh**	measure			

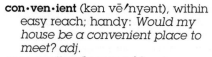

con·nect (kə nekt′), join one thing to another; link two things together; join: *connect a hose to a faucet. The telephone operator connected us. These two rooms connect. v.*

con·no·ta·tion (kon′ə tā′shən), what is suggested in addition to the simple or exact meaning. When Elaine is described in legends about King Arthur as "the lily maid," the connotation is that she was pale, delicate, and pure. *n.*

con·quer (kong′kər), **1** get by fighting; win in war: *The Romans conquered much of the ancient world.* **2** overcome by force; get the better of; defeat: *conquer an enemy, conquer a bad habit. v.*

con·sid·er·ate (kən sid′ər it), thoughtful of others and their feelings: *She is considerate enough to tell her parents where she is going and with whom. adj.*

con·sist·ent (kən sis′tənt), thinking or acting today in agreement with what you thought yesterday; keeping to the same habits. *adj.*

con·stant·ly (kon′stənt lē), often; again and again: *She has to be reminded constantly to clean her room. adv.*

con·stel·la·tion (kon′stə lā′shən), group of stars usually having a recognized shape. The Big Dipper is an easy constellation to locate. *n.*

con·struc·tive (kən struk′tiv), tending to be useful; helpful: *During the experiment the teacher gave some constructive suggestions that prevented accidents. adj.*

con·sume (kən süm′), eat or drink up: *We will each consume at least two sandwiches on our hike. v.,* **con·sumed, con·sum·ing.**

con·tin·ue (kən tin′yü), **1** keep up; keep on; go on; go on with: *The rain continued all day. The road continues for miles.* **2** go on after stopping; take up; carry on: *The story will be continued next week. The class begged the teacher to continue with the reading. v.,* **con·tin·ued, con·tin·u·ing.**

con·tra·dict (kon′trə dikt′), say that a statement is not true; deny. *v.*

con·tro·ver·sy (kon′trə vėr′sē), act of arguing a question about which differences of opinion exist; debate; dispute; argument: *The long controversy over slavery was one of the causes of the Civil War. n., pl.* **con·tro·ver·sies.**

constellation

constellations in the spring sky

con·ven·ient (kən vē′nyənt), within easy reach; handy: *Would my house be a convenient place to meet? adj.*

con·ven·tion (kən ven′shən), a meeting arranged for some particular purpose; gathering; assembly. *n.*

co·op·e·rate (kō op′ə rāt′), work together: *Everyone cooperated in helping to clean up after the class party. v.,* **co·op·e·rat·ed, co·op·e·rat·ing.**

co·op·e·ra·tion (kō op′ə rā′shən), a working together; united effort or labor: *Cooperation can accomplish many things which no individual could do alone. n.*

co·or·di·na·tion (kō ôrd′ n ā′shən), the ability to use the senses together with body parts or to use two or more body parts together. *n.*

co·ro·na (kə rō′nə), outermost part of the sun. *n., pl.* **co·ro·nas.**

cor·ral (kə ral′), **1** pen for horses, cattle, etc. **2** drive into or keep in such a pen: *The cowhands corralled the herd of wild ponies.* 1 *n.,* 2 *v.,* **cor·ralled, cor·ral·ling.** [*Corral* comes from the Spanish word *corral.*]

cos·tume (kos′tüm or kos′tyüm), dress belonging to another time or place, worn on the stage, at masquerades, etc. *n.*

coun·cil (koun′səl), **1** group of people called together to give advice and to discuss or settle questions. **2** group of persons elected to make laws or rules for and manage a city, town, or a school. *n.*

coun·sel (koun′səl), **1** advice. **2** give advice to; advise: *She counsels sophomores to help them choose their courses.* 1 *n.,* 2 *v.,* **coun·seled, coun·sel·ing** or **coun·selled, coun·sel·ling.**

coun·se·lor or **coun·sel·lor** (koun′sə lər), teacher appointed to advise students; adviser. *n.*

coun·ter·feit (koun′tər fit), **1** copy (money, handwriting, pictures, etc.) in order to deceive or defraud: *They were arrested for counterfeiting twenty-dollar bills.* **2** a copy made to deceive or defraud and passed as genuine: *This twenty-dollar bill looks genuine, but it is a counterfeit.* 1 *v.,* **coun·ter·feit·ed, coun·ter·feit·ing,** 2 *n.*

cou·ra·geous (kə rā′jəs), full of courage; brave; fearless. *adj.* —**cou·ra′geous·ly,** *adv.*

course (kôrs), **1** direction taken. **2** way, path, track, or channel. **3** part of a meal served at one time. *n.*

court·house (kôrt′hous′), **1** building in which courts of law are held. **2** building used for the government of a county. *n., pl.* **court·hous·es** (kôrt′hou′ziz).

cous·cous (küs′küs′), a North African dish consisting of coarsely ground hard wheat that has been soaked in water and steamed in broth. *n.*

coy·o·te (kī ō′tē *or* kī′ōt), a small wolflike mammal living on the prairies of western North America; prairie wolf. It is noted for loud howling at night. *n., pl.* **coy·o·tes** *or* **coy·o·te.** [*Coyote* is from Spanish, which came from Nahuatl *coyotl.*]

cre·a·tive (krē ā′tiv), having the power to create; inventive: *a creative person. adj.* —**cre·a′tive·ly,** *adv.*

crit·ic (krit′ik), person who makes judgments of the merits and faults of books, music, pictures, plays, acting, etc. *n.*

crit·i·cize (krit′ə sīz), find fault with; disapprove of; blame. *v.,* **crit·i·cized, crit·i·ciz·ing.**

croc·o·dile (krok′ə dīl), a large, lizardlike reptile with thick skin, a long narrow head, and webbed feet. Crocodiles live in the rivers and marshes of the warm parts of Africa, Asia, Australia, and America. *n.* [*Crocodile* comes from Latin *crocodilus* and Greek *krokodilos,* meaning "crocodile, lizard."]

cross-prod·uct (krós′ prod′əkt), (in a mathematical proportion) the product of the first number of one ratio and the second number of the other ratio. For ¾ and ⁹/₁₂, the cross-products are 3 × 12 and 9 × 4, both of which equal 36. *n., pl.* **cross-prod·ucts.**

crust (krust), the top layer of the earth. *n.*

curl·i·cue (kėr′lə kyü), a fancy twist, curl, or flourish: *Curlicues in handwriting often make it hard to read. n.*

cy·cli·cal (sī′klə kəl *or* sik′lə kəl), cyclic. *adj.*

cy·clist (sī′klist), rider of a bicycle, tricycle, or motorcycle. *n.*

cy·clone (sī′klōn), a very violent windstorm; tornado. *n.*

D

dam (dam), **1** wall built to hold back the water of a stream or any flowing water: *There was a flood when the dam burst.* **2** provide with a dam; hold back or block up with anything: *Beavers had dammed the stream.* **1** *n., pl.* **dams.** **2** *v.,* **dammed, dam·ming.**

day·dream (dā′drēm′), something imagined but not likely to come true. *n., pl.* **day·dreams.**

day·light-sav·ing time (dā′līt′sā′ving tīm′), time that is one hour ahead of standard time. It gives more daylight after working hours. Clocks are set ahead one hour.

dead end (ded′ end′), street, passage, etc., closed at one end.

debt (det), something owed to another. *n.*

dec·ade (dek′ād), period of ten years. Two decades ago means twenty years ago. *n.* [*Decade* came into English about 500 years ago from French *décade,* and can be traced back to Greek *deka,* meaning "ten."]

de·cath·lon (di kath′lon), an athletic contest with ten different parts, such as racing, jumping, throwing the javelin, etc. The person who scores the most points for all ten parts is the winner. *n.* [*Decathlon* comes from Greek *deka,* meaning "ten," and *athlon,* meaning "contest."]

courthouse (def. 1)
The Supreme Court meets in this **courthouse** in Washington, D.C.

a	hat	**ī**	ice	**u̇**	put	**ə** *stands for*	
ā	age	**o**	not	**ü**	rule	**a**	in about
ä	far, calm	**ō**	open	**ch**	child	**e**	in taken
âr	care	**ȯ**	saw	**ng**	long	**i**	in pencil
e	let	**ô**	order	**sh**	she	**o**	in lemon
ē	equal	**oi**	oil	**th**	thin	**u**	in circus
ėr	term	**ou**	out	**ŦH**	then		
i	it	**u**	cup	**zh**	measure		

democracy

The Declaration of Independence helped establish our country's **democracy.**

de·ceit·ful (di sēt′fəl), **1** ready or willing to deceive or lie: *a deceitful person.* **2** meant to deceive; deceiving; misleading: *She told a deceitful story to avoid punishment.* *adj.*

de·ceive (di sēv′), use deceit; lie. *v.,* **de·ceived, de·ceiv·ing.**

de·cep·tion (di sep′shən), trick meant to deceive; fraud; sham: *The scheme is all a deception. n.*

dec·i·bel (des′ə bel), unit for measuring the relative loudness of sounds. *n.* [*Decibel* comes from French *deci,* and can be traced back to Latin *decimus* meaning "tenth."]

de·cide (di sīd′), **1** settle (a question, dispute, etc.): *Fighting is not the best way to decide an argument.* **2** make up one's mind; resolve: *She decided to be a scientist. v.,* **de·cid·ed, de·cid·ing.**

de·ci·sive (di sī′siv), having or showing decision; resolute: *a decisive answer. adj.*

de·cor or **dé·cor** (dā kôr′), the overall arrangement of the decoration and furnishings of a room, house, store, office, etc. *n.*

dec·o·rate (dek′ə rāt′), make beautiful; adorn; trim. *v.,* **dec·o·rat·ed, dec·o·rat·ing.**

dec·o·ra·tive (dek′ər ə tiv or dek′ə rā′tiv), helping to adorn; ornamental; decorating. *adj.*

dec·o·ra·tor (dek′ə rā′tər), interior decorator. *n.*

de·duct (di dukt′), take away; subtract. *v.*

de·duc·tion (di duk′shən), amount deducted. *n.*

de·fec·tive (di fek′tiv), having a flaw or blemish; not perfect; not complete; faulty: *A watch with defective parts will not keep time. adj.*

de·fer·ment (di fėr′mənt), a putting off; delay. *n.*

def·i·nite (def′ə nit), clear or exact; not vague. *adj.*

de·gree (di grē′), **1** unit for measuring temperature: *The freezing point of water is 32 degrees (32 °) Fahrenheit, or 0 degrees (0 °) Celsius.* **2** unit for measuring an angle or an arc of a circle. *n.*

de·i·ty (dē′ə tē), a god or goddess worshiped by people. *n., pl.* **de·i·ties.**

desperado

desperadoes from a Jesse James movie

de·lay (di lā′), **1** putting off till a later time: *We are delaying the party for a week.* **2** make late; keep waiting; hinder the progress of: *The accident delayed the train for two hours. v.,* **de·layed, de·lay·ing.**

de·li·cious (di lish′əs), very pleasing or satisfying, especially to the taste or smell; delightful: *delicious cake. adj.*

de·mand (di mand′), **1** ask for as a right: *demand a trial by jury.* **2** call for; require; need: *Training a puppy demands patience. v.,* **de·mand·ed, de·mand·ing.**

de·moc·ra·cy (di mok′rə sē), a form of government run by the citizens who live under it. The people may rule directly, through meetings that all attend, or indirectly, through elected representatives. *n.*

de·nom·i·na·tor (di nom′ə nā′tər), the number below or to the right of the line in a fraction: *In ¾, 4 is the denominator, and 3 is the numerator. n.*

de·por·ta·tion (dē′pôr tā′shən), removal from a country by banishment or expulsion: *Deportation of criminals from England to Australia was once common. n.*

de·scend (di send′), go or come down from a higher to a lower place: *We descended the stairs to get to the basement. v.,* **de·scend·ed, de·scend·ing.**

de·scend·ant (di sen′dənt), **1** person born of a certain family or group: *a descendant of the Pilgrims.* **2** offspring; child, grandchild, great-grandchild, etc. *n.*

des·pe·ra·do (des′pə rä′dō), a bold, reckless criminal; dangerous outlaw. *A gang of desperadoes threatened the townspeople. n., pl.* **des·pe·ra·does** or **des·pe·ra·dos.**

des·per·ate (des′pər it), **1** showing recklessness caused by despair; violent: *Suicide is a desperate act.* **2** having little chance for hope or cure; very dangerous: *a desperate illness.* **3** extremely bad: *People in the slums live in desperate circumstances. adj.*

des·ti·na·tion (des′tə nā′shən), place to which a person or thing is going or is being sent. *n.*

de·struc·tion (di struk′shən), act or result of wrecking, ruining, or smashing something. *n.*

de·ter·mi·na·tion (di tèr/mə nā/shən), great firmness in carrying out a purpose; fixed purpose. *n.*

de·ter·mine (di tèr/mən), find out exactly: *The pilot determined how far she was from the airport. v.,* **de·ter·mined, de·ter·min·ing.**

de·ter·mined (di tèr/mənd), firm; resolute: *Her determined look showed that she had made up her mind. adj.*

de·vel·op (di vel/əp), come to have: *She developed an interest in collecting stamps. v.*

de·vour (di vour/), eat like an animal; eat very hungrily: *The hungry girl devoured her dinner. v.*

di·am·e·ter (dī am/ə tər), a line segment passing from one side through the center of a circle, sphere, etc., to the other side. *n.*

dic·tate (dik/tāt), say or read aloud to another person who writes down the words. *v.,* **dic·tat·ed, dic·tat·ing.**

dic·tion·ar·y (dik/shə ner/ē), book that explains the words of a language or of some special subject. It is arranged alphabetically. Find out the meaning, spelling, or pronunciation of a word in a dictionary. *n., pl.* **dic·tion·ar·ies.**

did·n't (did/nt), did not.

die·sel or **Die·sel** (dē/zəl), **1** equipped with or run by a diesel engine: *a diesel locomotive, a diesel tractor.* **2** of or for a diesel engine: *diesel fuel. adj.* [*Diesel* was named after Rudolf *Diesel,* 1858-1913, a German engineer, who invented this form of engine.]

di·e·ti·tian or **di·e·ti·cian** (dī/ə tish/ən), person trained to plan meals that have the right amount of various kinds of food. Many hospitals and schools employ dietitians. *n.*

dif·fer·ence (dif/ər əns), **1** a being different: *the difference between night and day.* **2** way of being different; point in which people or things are different. **3** amount by which one quantity is different from another; what is left after subtracting one number from another. *n.*

dif·fer·ent (dif/ər ənt), **1** not alike; not like: *We saw different kinds of animals at the zoo.* **2** not like others or most others; unusual. *adj.*

dif·fi·cult (dif/ə kult), hard to do or understand: *Cutting down the tree was difficult. Mathematics is difficult for some pupils. adj.*

di·ges·tion (də jes/chən or dī jes/chən), the digesting of food. *n.*

dig·ni·fied (dig/nə fīd), having dignity; noble; stately: *The queen has a dignified manner. adj.*

dig·ni·fy (dig/nə fī), give dignity to; make noble, worthwhile, or worthy: *The simple farmhouse was dignified by the great elms around it. v.,* **dig·ni·fied, dig·ni·fy·ing.**

di·lem·ma (də lem/ə), situation requiring a choice between two evils; difficult choice: *She was faced with the dilemma of either telling a lie or betraying a friend. n., pl.* **di·lem·mas.**

di·men·sion (də men/shən), measurement of length, breadth, or thickness. *n., pl.* **di·men·sions.**

din·ing room (din/ing rüm/), room in which dinner and other meals are served.

di·rect (də rekt/ or dī rekt/), order; command: *The policeman directed the traffic to stop. v.,* **di·rect·ed, di·rect·ing.**

di·rec·tion (də rek/shən or dī rek/shən), **1** a directing; managing or guiding: *the direction of a play or movie. The school is under the direction of the principal.* **2** any way in which one may face or point. *n.*

dining room
The family enjoys breakfast in the
dining room.

							ə stands for	
a	hat	ī	ice	u̇	put		ə stands for	
ā	age	o	not	ü	rule		a	in about
ä	far, calm	ō	open	ch	child		e	in taken
âr	care	ȯ	saw	ng	long		i	in pencil
e	let	ô	order	sh	she		o	in lemon
ē	equal	oi	oil	th	thin		u	in circus
ėr	term	ou	out	ᵺ	then			
i	it	u	cup	zh	measure			

di·rec·tor (də rek′tər *or* dī rek′tər), person who directs; manager. A person who directs the performance of a play, a motion picture, or a television or radio show is called a director: *one director's film; the directors' guild meetings.* n.

dis·ci·pline (dis′ə plin), **1** training, especially training of the mind or character: *Children who have had no discipline are often hard to teach.* **2** bring to a condition of order and obedience; bring under control; train: *The teacher was unable to discipline the unruly class.* 1 n., 2 v., **dis·ci·plined, dis·ci·plin·ing.**

dis·count (dis′kount), the amount taken off from a price: *We bought our new TV on sale at a 20 percent discount.* n.

dis·creet (dis krēt′), very careful in speech and action; having or showing good judgment; wisely cautious: *a discreet person, a discreet answer.* adj. —**dis·creet′ly,** adv.

dis·crete (dis krēt′), distinct from others; separate; individual: *An apple and a stone are discrete objects.* adj.

dis·cuss (dis kus′), consider from different points of view; talk over: *The class discussed several problems. Congress is discussing tax rates.* v.

dis·ease (də zēz′), **1** condition of poor health; sickness; illness: *People, animals, and plants are all liable to disease.* **2** any particular illness: *Measles and chicken pox are two diseases of children.* n.

dis·en·tan·gle (dis′en tang′gəl), free from tangles or complications; untangle: *disentangle a confusing story, disentangle a fishline.* v., **dis·en·tan·gled, dis·en·tan·gling.**

dis·guise (dis gīz′), **1** the use of changes in clothes or appearance so as to conceal identity or resemble someone else. **2** clothes, actions, etc., used in making such changes: *Glasses and a wig formed the spy's disguise.* **3** a false or misleading appearance; deception. n.

dis·hon·or (dis on′ər), loss of honor or reputation; shame; disgrace: *The robbers brought dishonor to their families.* n.

document

The diary was a

document of his

thoughts.

dis·in·fect·ant (dis′in fek′tənt), **1** substance used to destroy disease germs. **2** used to destroy disease germs: *a disinfectant soap.* 1 n., 2 adj.

dis·o·be·di·ent (dis′ə bē′dē ənt), refusing to obey; failing to obey: *The disobedient child would not do as she was told.* adj.

dis·pu·tant (dis′pyə tənt *or* dis pyüt′nt), person who takes part in a dispute or debate. n., pl. **dis·pu·tants.**

dis·pute (dis pyüt′), a quarrel: *The dispute between the two neighbors threatened their friendship.* n.

dis·tance (dis′təns), **1** space in between: *The distance from the farm to the town is five miles.* **2** a place far away: *He saw a light in the distance.* n.

dis·tract (dis trakt′), draw away (the mind, attention, etc.): *Noise distracts my attention from study.* v., **dis·tract·ed, dis·tract·ing.**

dis·trac·tion (dis trak′shən), **1** thing that draws away the mind, attention, etc.: *Noise is a distraction when you are trying to study.* **2** relief from continued thought, grief, or effort; amusement: *Movies and television are popular distractions.* n.

dis·turb (dis tėrb′), break in upon with noise or change: *Please don't disturb her while she's studying.* v., **dis·turbed, dis·turb·ing.**

di·vis·i·ble (də viz′ə bəl), able to be divided without leaving a remainder: *12 is divisible by 1, 2, 3, 4, 6, and 12.* adj.

doc·u·ment (dok′yə mənt), something written or printed that gives information or proof of some fact; any object used as evidence. Letters, diaries, government records, maps, and pictures are documents. n., pl. **doc·u·ments.**

does·n't (duz′nt), does not.

dom·i·no (dom′ə nō), game played with flat, oblong pieces of bone, wood, etc., that are either blank or marked with dots. Players try to match pieces having blanks or the same number of dots. n., pl. **dom·i·noes** *or* **dom·i·nos.**

don't (dōnt), do not.

dou·ble (dub′əl), twice as much, as many, as large, as strong, etc.: *She was given double pay for working on Sunday.* adj.

doubt (dout), **1** difficulty in believing: *Our faith helped overcome our doubt.* **2** an uncertain state of mind: *We were in doubt as to the right road.* *n.* —**doubt′er,** *n.*

doubt·ful (dout′fəl), full of doubt; not sure; uncertain: *We are doubtful about the weather for tomorrow.* *adj.* —**doubt′ful·ly,** *adv.*

dough·nut (dō′nut′), a small cake of sweetened dough cooked in deep fat. A doughnut is usually made in the shape of a ring. *n.*

drawer (drôr), box with handles built to slide in and out of a table, desk, or bureau: *He kept his shirts in the dresser drawer.* *n.*

drive-in (drīv′in′), **1** arranged and equipped so that customers may drive in and be served or entertained while remaining seated in their cars. **2** place so arranged and equipped. **1** *adj.,* **2** *n.*

duch·y (duch′ē), lands ruled by a duke or a duchess. *n., pl.* **duch·ies.**

duct (dukt), tube, pipe, or channel for carrying liquid, air, etc. *n.* [*Duct* is from Latin *ductus,* meaning "a leading," which comes from *ducere,* meaning "to lead."]

dune (dün or dyün), mound or ridge of loose sand heaped up by the wind. *n., pl.* **dunes.**

dun·geon (dun′jən), a dark underground room or cell to keep prisoners in. *n.*

E

ear (ir), part of the body by which people and animals hear. It consists of the external ear, the middle ear, and the inner ear. *n.* **all ears,** INFORMAL. listen eagerly; pay careful attention: *The children were all ears while their teacher read them the exciting story.*

earn (ėrn), get in return for work or service; be paid: *She earns 25 dollars a day.* *v.,* **earned, earn·ing.**

ea·sel (ē′zəl), a stand for holding a picture, chalkboard, etc. *n.*

ech·o (ek′ō), **1** a sounding again; repeating of a sound. You hear an echo when a sound you make bounces back from a distant hill or wall so that you hear it again. **2** sound again; repeat or be repeated in sound: *The gunshot echoed through the valley.* **1** *n., pl.* **ech·oes;** **2** *v.*

ef·fec·tive (ə fek′tiv), producing the desired effect; getting results: *Penicillin is an effective medicine in the treatment of many diseases.* *adj.*

E·gyp·tian (i jip′shən), **1** of Egypt or its people. **2** person born or living in Egypt. **1** *adj.,* **2** *n., pl.* **E·gyp·tians.**

e·lec·tric (i lek′trik), **1** of electricity: *an electric light, an electric current.* **2** run by electricity: *an electric stove.* *adj.*

e·lec·tri·cian (i lek′trish′ən), person whose work is installing or repairing electric wiring, lights, motors, etc. *n.*

el·e·gant (el′ə gənt), having or showing good taste; gracefully and richly refined; beautifully luxurious. *adj.* —**el′e·gant·ly,** *adv.*

el·e·men·tar·y (el′ə men′tər ē or el′ə men′trē), of or dealing with the simple, necessary parts or principles to be learned first; introductory: *Addition, subtraction, multiplication, and division are taught in elementary mathematics.* *adj.*

elf (elf), a tiny fairy that is full of mischief. *n., pl.* **elves.**

em·bar·rass·ment (em bar′əs mənt), condition of being embarrassed; uneasiness; shame: *He blushed in embarrassment at such a stupid mistake.* *n.*

e·mer·gen·cy (i mėr′jən sē), a sudden need for immediate action: *I keep tools in my car for use in emergencies.* *n., pl.* **e·mer·gen·cies.**

emergency

The paramedics quickly responded to the **emergency.**

a	hat	**ī**	ice	**u̇**	put	**ə**	stands for
ā	age	**o**	not	**ü**	rule	**a**	in about
ä	far, calm	**ō**	open	**ch**	child	**e**	in taken
âr	care	**ȯ**	saw	**ng**	long	**i**	in pencil
e	let	**ô**	order	**sh**	she	**o**	in lemon
ē	equal	**oi**	oil	**th**	thin	**u**	in circus
ėr	term	**ou**	out	**ŦH**	then		
i	it	**u**	cup	**zh**	measure		

em·i·grate (em′ə grāt), leave one's own country to settle in another: *My grandparents emigrated from Japan to the United States. v.,* **em·i·grat·ed, em·i·grat·ing.** [*Emigrate* comes from Latin *emigratum,* which comes from *ex-,* meaning "out," and *migrare,* meaning "to move."]

em·per·or (em′pər ər), man who is the ruler of an empire. *n.* [*Emperor* came into English about 700 years ago from French *empereor,* which came from Latin *imperator,* originally meaning "commander."]

em·pire (em′pīr), a group of lands or countries ruled by one leader or one government. *n.*

em·ploy·ee or **em·ploy·e** (em ploi′ē or em′ploi ē′), person who works for some person or firm for pay. *n., pl.* **em·ploy·ees.**

en·com·pass (en kum′ pəs), include; contain. *v.*

en·coun·ter (en koun′tər), meet unexpectedly: *What if we should encounter a bear? v.,* **en·coun·tered, en·coun·ter·ing.**

end run (end′ run′), (in football) a play in which the ball carrier tries to advance the ball by running between the defensive end and the sideline.

end zone (end′ zōn′), (in football) the part of the field between each goal line and the corresponding end of the field.

en·e·my (en′ə mē), 1 person or group that hates and tries to harm another. 2 anything harmful: *Drought is an enemy of farmers. n., pl.* **en·e·mies.**

en·er·gy (en′ər je), will to work; vigor: *The boy is so full of energy that he cannot keep still. n., pl.* **en·er·gies.**

en·light·en (en līt′n), give truth and knowledge to; inform; instruct: *The book enlightened me on the subject of medicine. v.*

e·nor·mous (i nôr′məs), extremely large; huge: *an enormous animal, an enormous appetite. adj.*

en·trance (en′trəns), place by which to enter; door, passageway, etc.: *The entrance to the hotel was blocked with baggage. n.*

en·trance·way (en′trəns wā), place by which to enter; passageway. *n.*

equator

Imagine the **equator** encircling our earth on this globe.

en·vel·op (en vel′əp), wrap, cover, or hide: *The baby was enveloped in blankets. v.* [*Envelop* came into English about 600 years ago from French *enveloper,* which is from *en-,* meaning "in," and *voloper,* meaning "to wrap."]

en·ve·lope (en′və lōp or än′və lōp), a paper cover in which a letter or anything flat can be mailed. It can usually be folded over and sealed by wetting a gummed edge. *n.*

en·vi·ron·men·tal (en vī′rən men′tl), having to do with the surrounding things, conditions of the air, water, soil, etc. *adj.*

ep·i·cen·ter (ep′ə sen′tər), point on the earth's surface directly above the true center of an earthquake. *n.*

e·qual (ē′kwəl), 1 the same in amount, size, number, value, or rank. 2 be the same as: *Four times five equals twenty.* 1 *adj.,* 2 *v.,* **e·qualed, e·qual·ing** or **e·qualled, e·qual·ling.** [*Equal* is from Latin *aequalis,* which comes from *aequus,* meaning "even, just."]

e·qua·tion (i kwā′zhən), 1 statement of the equality of two quantities. EXAMPLES: $(4 \times 8) + 12 = 44. C = 2\pi r.$ 2 act of equating or being equated. *n.*

e·qua·tor (i kwā′tər), an imaginary circle around the middle of the earth, halfway between the North Pole and the South Pole. The United States is north of the equator; Australia is south of it. *n.*

e·qui·lat·er·al tri·an·gle (ē′kwə lat′ər əl trī′ang′gəl), a triangle with three congruent sides.

es·pe·cial·ly (e spesh′ə lē), more than others; specially; particularly; principally; chiefly. *adv.*

e·ven (ē′vən), 1 having the same height everywhere; level; flat; smooth: *The countryside is even, with no hills or slopes.* 2 make level or equal; make even: *I evened the edges by trimming them.* 3 just: *She left even as you came.* 1 *adj.,* 2 *v.,* 3 *adv.*

eve·ry·bod·y (ev′rə bud′ē or ev′rē bod′ē), every person; everyone: *Everybody likes the new principal. pron.*

eve·ry·thing (ev′rē thing), every thing; all things: *She did everything she could to help her friend. pron.*

eve·ry·where (ev′rē hwâr), in every place; in all places: *A smile is understood everywhere. We looked everywhere for our lost dog.* *adv.*

e·volve (i volv′), develop gradually; unfold: *Buds evolve into flowers. The automobile evolved from the horse and buggy.* *v.,* **e·volved, e·volv·ing.**

ex·act·ly (eg zakt′lē), **1** accurately; precisely. **2** just so; quite right. *adv.*

ex·am·ple (eg zam′pəl), one thing taken to show what others are like; sample. *n.*

ex·ca·vate (ek′skə vāt), make by digging; dig, brush away dirt, look for ancient objects. *v.,* **ex·ca·vat·ed, ex·ca·vat·ing.**

ex·ceed (ek sēd′), do more than; go beyond: *Drivers are not supposed to exceed the speed limit.* *v.* [*Exceed* comes from Latin *excedere,* which comes from *ex-,* meaning "out" and *cedere,* meaning "go."]

ex·cel·lence (ek′sə ləns), unusually good quality; being better than others; superiority: *His teacher praised him for the excellence of his report.* *n.*

ex·cept (ek sept′), **1** leaving out; other than: *He works every day except Sunday.* **2** only; but. **1** *prep.,* **2** *conj.*

ex·cess (ek ses′ *for 1;* ek′ses *or* ek ses′ *for 2),* **1** part that is too much; more than enough. **2** beyond the usual amount; extra: *Passengers must pay for excess baggage taken on an airplane.* **1** *n., pl.* **ex·cess·es;** **2** *adj.*

ex·clude (ek sklüd′), shut out; keep out. *v.,* **ex·clud·ed, ex·clud·ing.**

ex·er·cise (ek′sər sīz), **1** active use; practicing: *Exercising of the body is good for the health.* **2** took exercise; went through exercises: *I exercised for ten minutes each morning last week.* **1** *n.,* **2** *v.,* **ex·er·cised, ex·er·cis·ing.**

ex·hale (eks hāl′), breathe out. *v.,* **ex·haled, ex·hal·ing.**

ex·haus·tion (eg zȯs′chən), **1** condition of being exhausted. **2** extreme fatigue. *n.*

ex·hi·bi·tion (ek′sə bish′ən), a showing; display; a public show: *Pushing and shoving in line is an exhibition of bad manners. The art school holds an exhibition every year.* *n.*

ex·ist·ence (eg zis′təns), **1** being: *When we are born, we come into existence.* **2** life: *Drivers of racing cars lead a dangerous existence.* *n.*

ex·pen·sive (ek spen′siv), costly; high-priced. *adj.*

ex·per·i·ence (ek spir′ē əns), **1** knowledge or skill gained by seeing, doing, or living through things; practice. **2** have happen to one; feel: *experience great pain.* **1** *n.,* **2** *v.,* **ex·per·i·enced, ex·per·i·enc·ing.**

ex·per·i·ment (ek sper′ə ment), try in order to find out; make trials or tests: *The painter is experimenting with different paints to get the color she wants.* *v.*

ex·pert (ek′spėrt′ *for 1;* ek spėrt′ *or* ek′spėrt′ *for 2),* **1** a very skillful person; person who knows a great deal about some special thing: *She is an expert at fishing.* **2** very skillful; knowing a great deal about some special thing. **1** *n.,* **2** *adj.*

ex·plo·ra·tion (ek′splə rā′shən), a traveling in little-known lands or seas for the purpose of discovery. *n.*

ex·plore (ek splôr′), **1** travel over little-known lands or seas for the purpose of discovery: *explore the ocean's depths.* **2** go over carefully; look into closely; examine. *v.,* **ex·plored, ex·plor·ing.**

ex·po·nent (ek spō′nənt), a number that tells how many times the base is to be used as a factor. In the following equation 3 is the exponent: $4^3 = 4 \times 4 \times 4.$ *n.*

ex·po·nen·tial form (ek′spō nen′shəl fôrm′), numbers using exponents.

excavate
an archaeologist
excavating a site

experiment
students
experimenting
in science class

a	hat	**ī**	ice	**u̇**	put	**ə** *stands for*	
ā	age	**o**	not	**ü**	rule	**a**	in about
ä	far, calm	**ō**	open	**ch**	child	**e**	in taken
âr	care	**ȯ**	saw	**ng**	long	**i**	in pencil
e	let	**ô**	order	**sh**	she	**o**	in lemon
ē	equal	**oi**	oil	**th**	thin	**u**	in circus
ėr	term	**ou**	out	**ŦH**	then		
i	it	**u**	cup	**zh**	measure		

ex·port (ek spôrt′ or ek′spôrt), send (goods) out of one country for sale and use in another: *The United States exports many kinds of machinery.* v.

ex·qui·site (ek′skwi zit or ek skwiz′it), **1** very lovely; delicate: *These violets are exquisite.* **2** sharp; intense: *A toothache causes exquisite pain.* adj.

ex·ten·sive (ek sten′siv), of great extent; far-reaching; large. adj. —**ex·ten′sive·ly,** adv.

ex·tra·ter·res·tri·al (ek′strə tə res′trē əl), beyond or outside the earth or its atmosphere. adj.

F

fact (fakt), **1** thing known to be true or to have really happened: *It is a fact that the Pilgrims sailed to America on the Mayflower in 1620.* **2** what is true; truth: *The fact of the matter is, I did want to go to the dance.* n. [*Fact* is from Latin *factum,* meaning "(a thing) done," which comes from *facere,* meaning "to make do."]

fac·tor (fak′tər), any of the numbers or expressions which, when multiplied together, form a product: *5, 3, and 4 are factors of 60.* n., pl. **fac·tors.**

fac·tor·y (fak′tər ē), building or group of buildings where things are made with machines, or by hand. n., pl. **fac·tor·ies.**

fac·tu·al (fak′chü əl), concerned with fact; consisting of facts. adj.

Fahr·en·heit (far′ən hīt), of, based on, or according to a scale for measuring temperature on which 32 degrees marks the freezing point of water and 212 degrees marks the boiling point. adj. [The *Fahrenheit* scale was named for Gabriel D. *Fahrenheit,* 1686–1736, a German physicist who introduced it.]

fa·mil·iar (fə mil′yər), well-known; common: *a familiar face.* adj.

fam·il·y room (fam′ə lē rüm′), a room in a home used for family activities, such as watching TV, listening to music, or reading.

factory
a **factory** for manufacturing automobiles

fan (fan), INFORMAL. person extremely interested in some sport, the movies, television, etc.: *A baseball fan would hate to miss the championship game.* n. [*Fan* was shortened from *fanatic.*]

fas·ci·nate (fas′n āt), **1** attract very strongly; enchant by charming qualities; charm. **2** hold motionless by strange power or by terror: *Snakes are said to fascinate small birds.* v., **fas·ci·nat·ed, fas·ci·nat·ing.**

fat (fat), a nutrient that provides energy and carries certain vitamins through the body. n.

fa·tigue (fə tēg′), **1** weariness caused by hard work or effort: *I felt extreme fatigue after studying for four hours.* **2** make weary or tired; cause fatigue in. 1 n., 2 v., **fa·tigued, fa·ti·guing.**

fault (fôlt), crack in the earth's crust along which rock layers move. n.

fa·vor·ite (fā′vər it), liked better than others. adj.

feu·dal·ism (fyü′dl iz′əm), the social, economic, and political system of western Europe in the Middle Ages, in which powerful nobles called lords controlled large areas of land. The lords divided their land among lesser nobles in return for military service and money. n.

fi·ber (fī′bər), any part of food, such as the cellulose in vegetables, that cannot be digested, and so stimulates the movement of food and waste products through the intestines. n.

fic·ti·tious (fik tish′əs), not real; imaginary: *a fictitious story.* adj.

fief (fēf), piece of land held on condition of giving military and other services to the feudal lord owning it, in return for his protection and the use of the land. n., pl. **fiefs.**

field (fēld), **1** land with few or no trees; open country. **2** piece of land used for crops or for pasture. **3** range of opportunity or interest; sphere of activity: *the field of politics, the field of art, the field of science.* **4** area where contests in jumping, throwing, etc., are held. **5** (in baseball, cricket, etc.) to stop or catch (a batted ball) and throw it in. 1-4 n., 5 v.

fi·nal·ly (fī'nl ē), at the end; at last. *adv.*

fi·nan·cial (fə nan'shəl *or* fī nan'shəl), having to do with money matters: *Their financial affairs are in bad condition. adj.*

fine (fīn), very small or thin: *Thread is finer than rope. Sand is finer than gravel. adj.,* **fin·er, fin·est.** [*Fine came into English about 700 years ago from French fin, meaning "perfected, finished," and can be traced back to Latin finis, meaning "end."*] **—fine'ly,** *adv.*

fish·hook (fish'huk'), hook with a barb used for catching fish. *n.*

fit·ness (fit'nis), a being fit. *n.*

fla·min·go (flə ming'gō), a tropical wading bird with very long legs and neck, and feathers that vary from pink to scarlet. *The flamingos enjoy the cool water in the wading pool. n., pl.* **fla·min·gos** *or* **fla·min·goes.**

flat (flat), **1** smooth and level; even: *flat land.* **2** a shallow box or basket: *I started the plants in flats, transplanting them in warm weather.* **3** exactly: *Her time for the race was two minutes flat.* 1,2 *adj.,* **flat·ter, flat·test;** 3 *adv.*

flood·plain (flud'plān'), plain bordering a river and made of soil deposited during floods. *n.*

Flo·ri·da (flôr'ə də), one of the southeastern states of the United States. *Abbreviation:* Fla. *or* FL *Capital:* Tallahassee. *n.*

flu (flü), influenza. *n.*

flur·ry (flèr'ē), a light fall of rain or snow. *n., pl.* **flur·ries.** [*Flurry is a blend of the words flutter and hurry.*]

fo·cus (fō'kəs), place where an earthquake begins inside the earth. *n.*

for·ev·er (fər ev'ər), without ever coming to an end; for always; for ever. *adv.*

for·get (fər get'), let go out of the mind; fail to remember. *v.,* **for·got** (fər got'), **for·got·ten** *or* **for·got, for·get·ting.**

for·got·ten (fər got'n), a past participle of **forget.** *He has forgotten what he has learned. v.*

for·tu·nate (fôr'chə nit), having good luck; lucky: *You are fortunate in having such a fine family. adj.*

for·ty (fôr'tē), four times ten; 40. *n., pl.* **for·ties;** *adj.*

fo·rum (fôr'əm), the public square or market place of an ancient Roman city. There business was done, and courts and public assemblies were held. *n.*

for·ward (fôr'wərd), toward the front; onward; ahead: *Forward, march! From this time forward we shall be good friends. adv.*

fos·sil (fos'əl), trace or remains of an organism that was once alive. *n., pl.* **fos·sils.**

frac·tion (frak'shən), one or more of the equal parts of a whole. ½, ⅓, and ¾ are fractions; so are ⅘ and ¹%. *n.*

fran·ti·cal·ly (fran'tik lē), in a frantic manner; with wild excitement. *adv.*

fre·quent·ly (frē'kwənt lē), often; repeatedly; every little while. *adv.*

friend (frend), person who knows and likes another. *n.*

friend·ship (frend'ship), condition of being friends. *n.*

frus·trate (frus'trāt), thwart; oppose: *The struggling artist was often frustrated in her ambition to paint. v.,* **frus·trat·ed, frus·trat·ing.**

fu·gi·tive (fyü'jə tiv), **1** person who is running away or who has run away: *The murderer became a fugitive from justice.* **2** running away; having run away: *a fugitive serf.* 1 *n.,* 2 *adj.*

fum·ble (fum'bəl), let (a ball) drop instead of catching and holding it: *The quarterback fumbled the ball, and the other team recovered it. v.,* **fum·bled, fum·bling.**

fur·ther·more (fèr'ŦHər môr), in addition; moreover; also; besides. *adv.*

FYI, for your information.

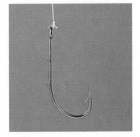

fishhook

fossil
a **fossil** of a crab

a	hat	**ī**	ice	**u̇**	put	**ə** stands for	
ā	age	**o**	not	**ü**	rule	**a**	in about
ä	far, calm	**ō**	open	**ch**	child	**e**	in taken
âr	care	**ȯ**	saw	**ng**	long	**i**	in pencil
e	let	**ô**	order	**sh**	she	**o**	in lemon
ē	equal	**oi**	oil	**th**	thin	**u**	in circus
èr	term	**ou**	out	**ŦH**	then		
i	it	**u**	cup	**zh**	measure		

G

gab (gab), INFORMAL. talk too much; chatter; gabble. *v.*, **gabbed, gab·bing.**

ga·rage (gə räzh′ or gə räj′), **1** place where motor vehicles are kept. **2** shop for repairing motor vehicles. *n.*

gas·o·line or **gas·o·lene** (gas′ə lēn′ or gas′ə lēn′), a colorless, liquid mixture of hydrocarbons which evaporates and burns very easily. It is made from petroleum or from gas formed in the earth. Gasoline is used chiefly as a fuel to run automobiles, airplanes, etc. *n.*

ge·ne·al·o·gy (jē′nē al′ə jē or jē′nē ol′ə jē), account of the descent of a person or family from an ancestor or ancestors. *n.*, *pl.* **ge·ne·al·o·gies.**

gen·e·ra·tion (jen′ə rā′shən), all the people born about the same time. Your parents and their friends belong to one generation; you and your friends belong to the next generation. *n.*

ger·ry·man·der (jer′ē man′dər or ger′ē man′dər), arrange the political divisions of (a state, county, etc.) to give one political party an unfair advantage in elections. *v.*, **ger·ry·man·dered, ger·ry·man·der·ing.** [*Gerrymander* comes from Elbridge *Gerry*, 1744–1814, an American politician, and the word *(sala)mander.* While Gerry was governor of Massachusetts from 1810 to 1812, his party redistricted the state, and Essex County was divided so that one district became shaped much like a salamander.]

gla·cier (glā′shər), a large mass of ice moving very slowly down a mountain or along a valley, or spreading slowly over a large area of land. Glaciers are formed over many years from snow on high ground. *n.*

glad·i·a·tor (glad′ē ā′tər), slave, captive, or paid fighter who fought at the public shows in the arenas in ancient Rome. *n.*, *pl.* **glad·i·a·tors.** [*Gladiator* was borrowed from Latin *gladiator*, which comes from *gladius*, meaning "sword."]

goal (gōl), something a person wants to do or achieve. *n.*

go·ing (gō′ing), a going away; leaving: *Her going was very sudden. n.*

going to, will; about to: *It is going to rain soon.*

gos·sip (gos′ip), **1** idle talk, not always true, about other people and their private affairs. **2** repeat what one knows or hears about other people and their private affairs. 1 *n.*, 2 *v.*, **gos·siped, gos·sip·ing.**

grab (grab), seize suddenly; snatch: *I grabbed the child before she fell.* *v.*, **grabbed, grab·bing.**

gra·cious (grā′shəs), pleasant and kindly; courteous. *adj.*

gran·ite (gran′it), a hard rock made of grains of other rocks, chiefly quartz and feldspar. It is an igneous rock, much used for buildings and monuments. *n.*

grate·ful (grāt′fəl), **1** feeling kindly because of a favor received; wanting to do a favor in return; thankful. **2** pleasing; welcome: *a grateful breeze on an extremely hot day. adj.*

great·est com·mon fac·tor (grā′tist kom′ən fak′tər), **1** The greatest number that is a factor of two or more numbers. **2** The greatest number that divides two or more numbers with no remainder.

great-grand·fa·ther (grāt′grand′ fä′thər), grandfather of one's father or mother. *n.*

Greek (grēk), **1** of Greece, its people, or their language. **2** native or inhabitant of Greece. **3** language of Greece. 1 *adj.*, 2,3 *n.*, *pl.* **Greeks.**

grid (grid), a pattern of evenly spaced vertical and horizontal lines. Grids are used on maps to locate places. *n.*

grief (grēf), **1** great sadness caused by trouble or loss; heavy sorrow. **2** cause of sadness or sorrow. *n.*

griev·ance (grē′vəns), a real or imagined wrong; reason for being angry or annoyed: *Report any grievances you may have to your supervisor. n.*

grim (grim), **1** without mercy; stern, harsh, or fierce: *grim, stormy weather.* **2** horrible; frightful; ghastly: *It was my grim task to tell them of their friend's death. adj.*, **grim·mer, grim·mest.**

glacier

granite
Granite is made of crystals and several different minerals.

guar·an·tee (gar′ən tē′), **1** a promise or pledge to replace or repair a purchased product, return the money paid, etc., if the product is not as represented: *We have a one-year guarantee on our new car.* **2** undertake to secure for another: *The landlady will guarantee us possession of the house by May.* **1** *n., pl.* **guar·an·tees; 2** *v.,* **guar·an·teed, guar·an·tee·ing.**

guard·i·an (gär′dē ən), **1** person who takes care of another or of some special thing. **2** person appointed by law to take care of the affairs of someone who is young or who cannot take care of his or her own affairs. *n.*

guid·ance (gīd′ns), a guiding; leadership; direction: *Under her mother's guidance, she learned how to swim. n.*

guide (gīd), person or thing that shows the way, leads, or directs: *The guide's talk was informative. The mountain guides' backpacks hold many supplies. n.*

guilt·y (gil′tē), having done wrong; deserving to be blamed and punished: *The jury pronounced the defendant guilty of theft. adj.,* **guilt·i·er, guilt·i·est.**

H

hai·ku (hī′kü), a poem of three lines and containing only 17 syllables. *n., pl.* **hai·ku.** [*Haiku* was borrowed from Japanese *haiku*, which comes from *hai*, meaning "sport, play," and *ku*, meaning "poem, verse."]

hall·way (hȯl′wā′), passage in a building; corridor; hall. *n.*

hal·vah (häl vä′ or häl′ vä), candy made from ground sesame seeds and honey. *n.*

hard·ship (härd′ship), something hard to bear; hard condition of living: *Hunger, cold, and sickness were among the hardships of pioneer life. n.*

har·mo·ni·ous (här mō′nē əs), agreeing in feelings, ideas, or actions; getting on well together: *harmonious neighbors. adj.*

har·mo·ny (här′mə nē), agreement of feeling, ideas, or actions; getting on well together: *The two brothers lived and worked in perfect harmony. n.*

haste (hāst), **1** a trying to be quick; hurrying: *All my haste was of no use; I missed the bus anyway.* **2** quickness without thought or care; rashness: *Haste makes waste. n.*

has·ten (hā′sn), cause to be quick; speed; hurry: *Sunshine and rest hastened his recovery. v.,* **has·tened, has·ten·ing.**

hast·i·ly (hā′stl ē), in a hurried manner. *adv.*

haz·ard (haz′erd), chance of harm; risk; danger; peril. *n.* [*Hazard* came into English about 650 years ago from French *hasard*, meaning "a game of dice," which came from Arabic *az-zahr*, meaning "the die."]

head·band (hed′band′), band worn around the head. *n.*

head·light (hed′līt′), a bright light at the front of an automobile, locomotive, etc. *n.*

head·line (hed′līn′), words printed in heavy type at the top of a newspaper article telling what it is about. *n.*

head·phone (hed′fōn′), earphone held against one or both ears by a band over the head. *n., pl.* **head·phones.**

head·strong (hed′strȯng′), rashly or foolishly determined to have one's own way; hard to control or manage; obstinate: *a headstrong person. adj.*

health food (helth′ füd′), food grown without chemicals or prepared without preservatives, selected for its nutritional value and believed to have health-giving properties. Yogurt, fresh fruit, and grains are excellent health foods.

headphone
Listen to audio tapes and CDs through these **headphones.**

a	hat	ī	ice	u̇	put	ə stands for	
ā	age	o	not	ü	rule	a	in about
ä	far, calm	ō	open	ch	child	e	in taken
âr	care	ȯ	saw	ng	long	i	in pencil
e	let	ô	order	sh	she	o	in lemon
ē	equal	oi	oil	th	thin	u	in circus
ėr	term	ou	out	ŦH	then		
i	it	u	cup	zh	measure		

health·y (hel′thē), having good health: *a healthy baby. adj.,* **health·i·er, health·i·est.**

heav·i·ly (hev′ə lē), in a heavy manner. *adv.*

he'd (hēd; *unstressed* ēd), **1** he had. **2** he would.

heir (âr), person who has the right to somebody's property or title after the death of its owner. *The prince's heir received the castle after the prince died. n.*

hel·i·cop·ter (hel′ə kop′tər), aircraft without wings that is lifted from the ground and kept in the air by horizontal propellers. *n.* [*Helicopter* is from French *hélicoptère,* which came from Greek *helikos,* meaning "a spiral," and *pteron,* meaning "wing."]

her·o (hir′ō), person admired for bravery, great deeds, or noble qualities: *Daniel Boone and Clara Barton are American heroes. n., pl.* **her·oes.**

hero

Clara Barton, an American **hero,** organized the American Red Cross in 1881.

hes·i·tant (hez′ə tənt), hesitating; doubtful; undecided: *I was hesitant about accepting the invitation. adj.*

hi·er·o·glyph·ic (hī′ər ə glif′ik), **1** picture, character, or symbol standing for a word, idea, or sound. The ancient Egyptians used hieroglyphics instead of an alphabet like ours. **2 hieroglyphics,** *pl.* writing that uses hieroglyphics. *n.* [*Hieroglyphic* can be traced back to Greek *hieros,* meaning "sacred," and *glyphein,* meaning "to carve."]

high-pres·sure sys·tem (hī′ presh′ər sis′təm), an area of air pressure greater than the surrounding air pressure.

his·to·ri·an (hi stôr′ē ən), person who writes about history; expert in history. *n.*

his·to·ri·cal (hi stôr′ə kəl), **1** of history: *historical documents.* **2** famous in history; historic: *a historical town. adj.*

his·tor·y (his′tər ē), **1** story or record of important past events connected with a person or a nation. **2** a known past: *This ship has a frightening history. n., pl.* **his·tor·ies.**

hold·fast (hōld′fast′), **1** thing used to hold something else in place, such as a catch, hook. **2** a rootlike base for a plant. *n., pl.* **hold·fasts.**

hieroglyphic (def. 1)

Egyptian **hieroglyphics**

home·room (hōm′rüm′ *or* hōm′rum′), classroom where members of a class meet to answer roll call, hear announcements, etc. *n.*

hon·es·ty (on′ə stē), honest behavior; honest nature; honest quality. *n.*

house·hold (hous′hōld), all the people living in a house; family; family and servants. *n.*

hud·dle (hud′l), a grouping of football players behind the line of scrimmage to receive signals, plan the next play, etc. *n.*

hu·la (hü′lə), a native Hawaiian dance. *n., pl.* **hu·las.** [*Hula* is of Hawaiian origin.]

hu·man (hyü′mən), **1** of persons; that people have: *Kindness is a human trait. To know all that will happen in the future is beyond human power.* **2** being a person or persons; having the form or qualities of people: *Men, women, and children are human beings.* **3** a human being; person. **1,2** *adj.,* **3** *n.*

hu·mane (hyü mān′), not cruel or brutal; kind; merciful: *We believe in the humane treatment of prisoners. adj.* **—hu·mane′ly,** *adv.*

hu·mid (hyü′mid), slightly wet; moist; damp. *adj.*

hu·mil·i·ate (hyü mil′ē āt), lower the pride, dignity, or self-respect of; make ashamed. *v.,* **hu·mil·i·at·ed, hu·mil·i·at·ing.**

hun·dredth (hun′drədth), next after the 99th; last in a series of 100. *adj., n.*

hur·ri·cane (hėr′ə kān), a large tropical storm that forms over warm oceans. *n.*

hus·band (huz′bənd), man who has a wife; a married man. *n.*

hy·dro·gen (hī′drə jən), a colorless, odorless gas that burns easily. Hydrogen is a chemical element that weighs less than any other element. *n.*

hy·per·bo·le (hī pėr′bə lē), an exaggerated statement used for effect and not meant to be taken literally. *n.* [*Hyperbole* can be traced back to Greek *hyper,* meaning "above, over, beyond," and *ballein,* meaning "to throw."]

hy·per·ten·sion (hī′pər ten′shən), an abnormally high blood pressure. *n.*

I

ice·berg (īs/bėrg/), a large mass of ice, detached from a glacier and floating in the sea. About 90 percent of its mass is below the surface of the water. *n.* [*Iceberg* comes from Dutch *ijsberg*, meaning "ice mountain."]

ice cream (īs/ krēm/), a smooth, frozen dessert made of cream or milk, sweetened and flavored.

ice pack (īs/ pak/), bag containing ice for application to the body.

ice-skate (īs/skāt/), skate on ice. *v.*, **ice-skat·ed, ice-skat·ing.**

I'd (īd), **1** I should. **2** I would. **3** I had.

id·i·om (id/ē əm), phrase or expression whose meaning cannot be understood from the ordinary meanings of the words in it. "Hold one's tongue" is an English idiom meaning "keep still." *n.*

ig·ne·ous rock (ig/nē əs rok/), formed by the cooling of melted rock material either within or on the surface of the earth. Granite is an igneous rock.

ig·nor·ant (ig/nər ənt), **1** knowing little or nothing; without knowledge. A person who has not had a chance to learn may be ignorant but not stupid. **2** uninformed; unaware: *He was ignorant of the fact that a sales tax had increased. adj.*

ig·nore (ig nôr/), pay no attention to; disregard. *v.*, **ig·nored, ig·nor·ing.**

il·le·gal (i lē/gəl), not lawful; against the law; forbidden by law. *adj.* —**il·le/gal·ly,** *adv.*

il·leg·i·ble (i lej/ə bəl), very hard or impossible to read; not plain enough to read. *adj.*

il·lit·er·ate (i lit/ər it), **1** not knowing how to read and write: *People who have never gone to school are usually illiterate.* **2** person who does not know how to read and write. 1 *adj.*, 2 *n.*

il·log·i·cal (i loj/ə kəl), **1** contrary to the principles of sound reasoning; not logical: *Your illogical behavior worries me.* **2** not reasonable; foolish: *an illogical fear of the dark. adj.*

il·lus·trate (il/ə strāt *or* i lus/trāt), provide with pictures, diagrams, maps, etc., that explain or decorate. *v.*, **il·lus·trat·ed, il·lus·trat·ing.**

im·bal·ance (im bal/əns), lack of balance. *n.*

im·ma·ture (im/ə chùr/, im/ə tùr/, or im/ə tyùr/), not mature; undeveloped. *adj.*

im·meas·ur·a·ble (i mezh/ər ə bəl), too large to be measured; very great; boundless: *the immeasurable vastness of the universe. She has immeasurable confidence in herself. adj.*

im·me·di·ate (i mē/dē it), coming at once; without delay: *Please send an immediate reply. adj.*

im·me·di·ate·ly (i mē/dē it lē), at once; without delay: *I answered his letter immediately. adv.*

im·mi·grant (im/ə grənt), person who comes into a country or region to live there: *Canada has many immigrants from Europe and Asia. n.*

im·mi·grate (im/ə grāt), come into a country or region to live there. *Rosalie will immigrate to France from Italy. v.*, **im·mi·grat·ed, im·mi·grat·ing.** [*Immigrate* comes from Latin *immigrate*, meaning "to remove", "go in."]

im·mi·gra·tion (im/ə grā/shən), a coming into a country or region to live there: *There has been immigration to America from many countries. n.*

im·mu·ni·ty (i myü/nə tē), resistance to disease, poison, etc.: *One attack of measles usually gives a person immunity to that disease. n., pl.* **im·mu·ni·ties.**

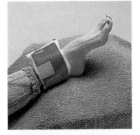

ice pack
using an **ice pack** on an injury

immigrant
immigrants arriving in the U.S., Ellis Island, 1912

a	hat	**ī**	ice	**ù**	put	**ə** stands for	
ā	age	**o**	not	**ü**	rule	**a**	in about
ä	far, calm	**ō**	open	**ch**	child	**e**	in taken
âr	care	**ȯ**	saw	**ng**	long	**i**	in pencil
e	let	**ô**	order	**sh**	she	**o**	in lemon
ē	equal	**oi**	oil	**th**	thin	**u**	in circus
ėr	term	**ou**	out	**ᴛʜ**	then		
i	it	**u**	cup	**zh**	measure		

im·pa·tient (im pā′shənt), uneasy and eager; restless: *The horses are impatient to start the race. adj.* —**im·pa′tient·ly,** *adv.*

im·per·fect (im pėr′fikt), not perfect; having some defect or fault: *A crack in the cup made it imperfect. adj.*

im·per·son·al (im pėr′sə nəl), **1** not referring to any one person in particular; not personal: *History is usually written from an impersonal point of view.* **2** having no existence as a person: *Electricity is an impersonal force. adj.*

inactive
inactive sea lions

im·po·lite (im′pə līt′), not polite; having or showing bad manners; rude; discourteous. *adj.*

im·port (im pôrt′ or im′pôrt), bring in from a foreign country for sale or use: *The United States imports coffee from Brazil. v.*

im·por·tant (im pôrt′nt), meaning or mattering much; worth noticing or considering; having value or significance: *important business, an important occasion. adj.*

im·pos·si·ble (im pos′ə bəl), **1** not capable of being, being done, or happening; not possible: *It is impossible for two and two to be six.* **2** not possible to use; not to be done: *He proposed an impossible plan. adj.*

im·prac·ti·cal (im prak′tə kəl), not practical; having to do with theory rather than actual practice; not useful. *adj.*

im·prop·er (im prop′ər), not correct; wrong: *"You is" is an improper usage. adj.*

im·prove·ment (im prüv′mənt), a making better or becoming better. *n.*

im·pul·sive (im pul′siv), acting or done upon impulse; with a sudden inclination or tendency to act. *adj.*

in·ac·cu·rate (in ak′yər it), not accurate; not exact; containing mistakes. *adj.*

in·ac·tive (in ak′tiv), not active; idle; slow: *Bears are inactive during the winter. adj.*

Inca
descendants of the **Incas**

In·ca (ing′kə), member of an ancient people of South America. The Inca had a highly developed culture, and ruled a large empire in Peru and other parts of South America, which fell to the Spaniards in the 1500s. *n., pl.* **In·ca** or **In·cas.**

in·ca·pa·ble (in kā′pə bəl), having very little ability; not capable; not efficient; not competent: *An employer cannot afford to hire incapable workers. adj.*
incapable of, without the ability, power, or fitness for: *I felt incapable of playing such difficult piano music.*

in·clude (in klüd′), **1** have within itself; contain; comprise: *Their farm includes land on both sides of the road.* **2** put in a total, a class, or the like; reckon in a count: *The price includes the land, house, and furniture. v.,* **in·clud·ed, in·clud·ing.**

in·com·pe·tence (in kom′pə təns), lack of ability, power, or fitness: *The worker was discharged for incompetence. n.*

in·com·plete (in′kəm plēt′), not complete; lacking some part; unfinished. *adj.*

in·con·sid·er·ate (in′kən sid′ər it), not thoughtful of others and their feelings; thoughtless. *adj.*

in·cred·i·ble (in kred′ə bəl), hard to believe; seeming too extraordinary to be possible; unbelievable: *The racing car rounded the curve with incredible speed. adj.*

in·debt·ed·ness (in det′id nis), money or gratitude owed; debts: *The father's indebtedness to his neighbor lasted a lifetime. n.*

in·de·pend·ence (in′di pen′dəns), condition of being independent; freedom from the control, influence, support, or help of others: *The American colonies won independence from England. n.*

in·di·rect (in′də rekt′), not straightforward and to the point: *She would not say yes or no but gave an indirect answer to my question. adj.*

in·di·vid·u·al (in′də vij′ü əl), **1** a single person, animal, or thing. **2** for or by one only; single; particular; separate: *Each student was given individual attention.* **1** *n.,* **2** *adj.*

in·di·vid·u·al·i·ty (in′də vij′ü al′ə tē), the character or sum of the qualities which distinguish one person or thing from another. *n.*

in·duct (in dukt′), **1** put formally in possession of an office; install: *She was inducted as treasurer.* **2** take into the armed forces. *v.*

in·e·qual·i·ty (in′i kwol′ə tē), **1** lack of equality; a being unequal in amount, size, value, rank, etc.: *There is a great inequality between the salaries of a bank president and a teller.* **2** a mathematical expression showing that two quantities are unequal. EXAMPLE: $a > b$ means a is greater than b; $a < c$ means a is less than b; $a \neq b$ means a and b are unequal. *n., pl.* **in·e·qual·i·ties.**

in·ex·pen·sive (in′ik spen′siv), not expensive; cheap; low-priced. *adj.*

in·fec·tion (in fek′shən), a causing of disease in people, animals, and plants by the introduction of germs or viruses. *n.*

in·flu·en·za (in′flü en′zə), contagious disease caused by a virus. Its symptoms sometimes resemble those of a very bad cold, but it is much more dangerous and exhausting; flu. *n.*

in·fo·mer·cial (in′fə mèr′shəl *or* in′fō mèr′shəl), a commercial that informs or instructs in an original and entertaining manner: *The infomercial for the portable grill was interesting. n.* [*Infomercial* is a blend of *information* and *commercial*.]

in·for·mal (in fôr′məl), **1** not formal; without ceremony: *an informal party.* **2** used in everyday, common talk, but not used in formal talking or writing. *adj.*

in·form·a·tive (in fôr′mə tiv), giving information; instructive: *The class trip to see how a newspaper is printed was very informative. adj.*

in·hale (in hāl′), draw (air, gas, fragrance, tobacco smoke, etc.) into the lungs; breathe in. *v.,* **in·haled, in·hal·ing.**

in·her·it (in her′it), **1** get or have after someone dies; receive as an heir: *After Grandfather's death, Mother inherited all of his property.* **2** receive (anything) by succession from one who came before: *I inherited this old pen from my grandfather. v.*

in·her·it·ance (in her′ə təns), **1** act or right of inheriting: *He obtained his house by inheritance from an aunt.* **2** anything inherited: *The house was her inheritance. n.*

in·jur·y (in′jər ē), hurt or loss caused to or endured by a person or thing; harm; damage: *She escaped without any injuries. n., pl.* **in·jur·ies.**

in·stance (in′stəns), **1** person or thing serving as an example; illustration; case. **2** give as an example; cite. **1** *n.,* **2** *v.,* **in·stanced, in·stanc·ing.**

in·stan·ta·ne·ous (in′stən tā′nē əs), coming or done in an instant; happening or made in an instant: *A flash of lightning is instantaneous. adj.* —**in·stan·ta·ne·ous·ly,** *adv.*

in·stru·ment (in′strə mənt), **1** a mechanical device that is portable, of simple construction, and usually operated by hand; tool: *a dentist's instruments.* **2** device for producing musical sounds. *n.*

in·su·la·tion (in′sə lā′shən), **1** an insulating: *The electrician checked the insulation of the wiring in the old house.* **2** material used in insulating. *n.*

in·sur·ance (in shür′əns), an insuring of property, person, or life. Fire insurance, burglary insurance, accident insurance, life insurance, and health insurance are some of the many kinds. *n.*

in·tel·li·gent (in tel′ə jənt), having or showing intelligence; able to learn and know; quick to understand. *adj.* [*Intelligent* is from Latin *intelligentem,* which comes from *inter-,* meaning "between," and *legere,* meaning "to choose."]

in·tend (in tend′), have in mind as a purpose; plan: *We intend to go home soon. v.* [*Intend* comes from Latin *intendere,* meaning "to stretch, strain, attend to." *In-* means "toward" and *tendere* means "to stretch."]

instrument (def. 2)
Violins are stringed **instruments.**

a	hat	**ī**	ice	**u̇**	put	**ə** stands for	
ā	age	**o**	not	**ü**	rule	**a**	in about
ä	far, calm	**ō**	open	**ch**	child	**e**	in taken
âr	care	**ȯ**	saw	**ng**	long	**i**	in pencil
e	let	**ô**	order	**sh**	she	**o**	in lemon
ē	equal	**oi**	oil	**th**	thin	**u**	in circus
ėr	term	**ou**	out	**ᵺ**	then		
i	it	**u**	cup	**zh**	measure		

in·tense (in tens′), **1** very much; very great; very strong; extreme: *intense happiness, intense pain, intense light.* **2** full of vigorous activity, strong feelings, etc. *adj.* [*Intense* comes from Latin *intensum* meaning "strained, stretched." *In-* means "toward" and *tendere* means "to stretch."]

in·tent (in tent′), **1** that which is intended; purpose; intention: *I'm sorry I hurt you; that wasn't my intent.* **2** meaning; significance: *What is the intent of that remark? n.* [*Intent* comes from Latin *intentum*, meaning "intense," a variant of *intensum.*] **—in·tent′ly,** *adv.*

in·ter·cept (in′tər sept′), take or seize on the way from one place to another: *intercept a letter. v.*

in·ter·cep·tion (in′tər sep′shən), an intercepting or a being intercepted. *n.*

in·ter·est·ed (in′tər ə stid or in′tə res′tid), **1** feeling or showing interest; with one's interest aroused: *an interested spectator.* **2** having an interest or share. *adj.*

in·ter·fere (in′tər fir′), **1** get in the way of each other; come into opposition; clash: *The two plans are interfering; one must be changed.* **2** mix in the affairs of others; meddle. *v.,* **in·ter·fered, in·ter·fer·ing.**

in·ter·nal·ly (in tėr′nl ē), **1** inside. **2** inside the body: *This ointment must not be taken internally. adv.*

In·ter·na·tion·al Date Line (in′tər nash′ə nəl dāt′ līn′), an imaginary line agreed upon as the place where each new calendar day begins. It runs north and south through the Pacific. When it is Sunday just east of the International Date Line, it is Monday just west of it.

in·ter·rupt (in′tə rupt′), break in upon (talk, work, rest, a person speaking, etc.); keep from going on; stop for a time; hinder. *v.*

in·ter·rup·tion (in′tə rup′shən), a being interrupted; a break; stopping: *The rain continued without interruption all day. n.*

in·ter·view (in′tər vyü), **1** a meeting, generally of persons face to face, to talk over something special: *My parents had an interview with the teacher about my work.* **2** a meeting between a reporter and a person from whom information is sought for publication or broadcast. *n.*

in·trigue (in trēg′ or in′trēg′), **1** secret scheming and plotting; crafty dealings. **2** a crafty plot; secret scheme. *n.*

in·tro·duce (in′trə düs′ or in′trə dyüs′), **1** bring into use, notice, knowledge, etc.: *Television and space travel are introducing many new words into our language.* **2** bring into acquaintance with; make known: *The principal introduced the speaker to the students. v.,* **in·tro·duced, in·tro·duc·ing.**

in·un·da·tion (in′un dā′ shən), an overflowing; flood. *n.*

in·ven·tive (in ven′tiv), good at inventing; quick to create things: *An inventive person thinks up ways to save time, money, and work. adj.*

in·ves·ti·ga·tion (in ves′tə gā′shən), a careful search; detailed or careful examination: *An investigation of the accident by the police put the blame on the drivers of both cars. n.*

i·on·o·sphere (ī on′ə sfir), region of ionized layers of air which extends from about 31 to 600 miles (50 to 965 kilometers) above the earth's surface. The ionosphere reflects certain radio waves, making transmission over long distances on earth possible. *n.*

ir·ra·tion·al (i rash′ə nəl), not rational; contrary to reason; unreasonable: *It is irrational to be afraid of the number 13. adj.*

ir·reg·u·lar (i reg′yə lər), not regular; not according to rule; out of the usual order or natural way. *adj.*

ir·rel·e·vant (i rel′ə vənt), not to the point; off the subject: *A question about mathematics is irrelevant in a French lesson. adj.*

ir·re·place·a·ble (ir′i plā′sə bəl), not replaceable; impossible to replace with another. *adj.*

ir·re·sist·i·ble (ir′i zis′tə bəl), not able to be resisted; too great to be withstood; overwhelming: *She had an irresistible desire for some ice cream. adj.*

ir·re·spon·si·ble (ir/i spon/sə bəl),
1 without a sense of responsibility;
untrustworthy; unreliable. 2 not
responsible; not able to be called to
account. *adj.*

i·sos·ce·les tri·an·gle (ī sos/ə lēz/
trī/ang/gel), triangle with two
congruent sides.

it's (its), 1 it is: *It's my turn.* 2 it has: *It's
been a beautiful day.*

J

jar·gon (jär/gən), language of a
special group, profession, etc.
Doctors, actors, and sailors have
jargons. *n.*

jeal·ous·y (jel/ə sē), dislike or fear of
rivals; jealous condition or feeling;
envy. *n., pl.* **jeal·ous·ies.**

judge (juj), 1 hear and decide (a case)
in a court of law. 2 settle a dispute;
decide who wins a race, contest,
etc. 3 form an opinion or estimate
about: *judge the merits of a book.*
v., **judged, judg·ing.**

K

kick·off (kik/òf/), kick that puts a
football in play at the beginning of
each half and after a score has
been made. *n.*

kin·der·gar·ten (kin/dər gärt/n),
school or class for children from
about 4 to 6 years old that
educates them by games, toys,
and pleasant occupations. *n.*
[*Kindergarten* is from German
Kindergarten, which comes from
Kinder, meaning "children," and
Garten, meaning "garden."]

knife (nīf), a thin, flat metal blade
fastened in a handle so that it can
be used to cut or spread. *n., pl.*
knives.

knight (nīt), (in the Middle Ages) a
warrior from the class of lesser
nobles. *n., pl.* **knights.**

knuck·le (nuk/əl), 1 a joint in a finger,
especially one of the joints
between a finger and the rest of
the hand. 2 put the knuckles on
the ground in playing marbles.
1 *n.,* 2 *v.,* **knuck·led, knuck·ling.**

ko·a·la (kō ä/lə), a gray, furry
mammal of Australia that looks
like a small bear and lives in trees.
The female koala carries her young
in a pouch. *n., pl.* **ko·a·las.** [*Koala*
is a native Australian name.]

L

lab (lab), INFORMAL. laboratory. *n.*

lar·i·at (lar/ē ət), a long rope with a
noose at the end, used for catching
horses and cattle; lasso. *n.* [*Lariat*
comes from Spanish *la reata,*
meaning "the rope."]

la·ser (lā/zər), device that produces a
very narrow and intense beam of
light going in only one direction.
Laser beams are used to cut or melt
hard materials, remove diseased
body tissues, and transmit
television signals. *n.* [*Laser* comes
from the words *light amplification*
by *stimulated emission* of
radiation.]

late (lāt), 1 after the usual or proper
time: *We had a late dinner last
night.* (*adj.*). *He worked late* (*adv.*).
2 near the end: *She reached
success late in life* (*adj.*). *It rained
late in the afternoon* (*adv.*). **lat·er**
or **lat·ter, lat·est** or **last** (last).

lat·i·tude (lat/ə tüd), distance north or
south of the Equator. *n.*

lat·ter (lat/ər), the second of two:
*Canada and the United States are
in North America; the former lies
north of the latter. adj.,* one of the
comparative forms of **late.**

laugh·ter (laf/tər), sound of laughing:
Laughter filled the room. n.

la·va (lä/və or lav/ə), magma that
flows on the surface of the earth. *n.*

judge (def. 1)
judging a case in court

lava
lava from a volcano

a	hat	**ī**	ice	**u̇**	put	**ə** stands for	
ā	age	**o**	not	**ü**	rule	**a**	in about
ä	far, calm	**ō**	open	**ch**	child	**e**	in taken
âr	care	**ȯ**	saw	**ng**	long	**i**	in pencil
e	let	**ô**	order	**sh**	she	**o**	in lemon
ē	equal	**oi**	oil	**th**	thin	**u**	in circus
ėr	term	**ou**	out	**ᵺ**	then		
i	it	**u**	cup	**zh**	measure		

lead·er·ship (lē′dər ship), **1** condition of being a leader. **2** ability to lead: *Leadership is a great asset to an officer. n.*

league (lēg), association of sports clubs or teams: *a baseball league. n.* [*League* came into English about 500 years ago from French *ligue*, and can be traced back to Latin *ligare*, meaning "to bind, tie."]

lec·ture (lek′chər), a planned talk on a chosen subject; such a talk written down or printed; speech. *n.*

left field (left′ fēld′), (in baseball) the section of the outfield beyond third base.

left·o·ver (left′ō′vər), thing that is left. Scraps of food from a meal are leftovers. *n.*

leg·end (lej′ənd), story coming down from the past, which may be based on actual people and events but is not regarded as historically true: *The stories about King Arthur are legends. n.*

lei·sure (lē′zhər), **1** time free from required work in which you may rest, amuse yourself, and do the things you like to do. **2** free; not busy: *leisure hours.* 1 *n.,* 2 *adj.*

lem·on (lem′ən), **1** a sour, light-yellow citrus fruit that grows on a thorny tree in warm climates. **2** pale-yellow. 1 *n.,* 2 *adj.*

lem·on·ade (lem′ə nād′), a drink made of lemon juice, sugar, and water. *n.*

let's (lets), let us.

lev·ee (lev′ē), a bank built to keep a river from overflowing: *There are levees in places along the lower Mississippi River. n., pl.* **lev·ees.**

lev·el (lev′əl), **1** having the same height everywhere; flat; even: *a level floor.* **2** something that is level; level or flat surface, tract of land, etc. 1 *adj.,* 2 *n.*

li·cense (lī′sns), **1** paper, card, plate, etc., showing permission given by law to do something. **2** give a license to; permit by law: *A doctor is licensed to practice medicine.* 1 *n.,* 2 *v.,* **li·censed, li·cens·ing.**

life (līf), quality or condition of living or being alive; the form of existence that people, animals, plants, and all living organisms have and that rocks, dirt, and metals lack. *n., pl.* **lives** (līvz). **life of Riley,** carefree and enjoyable way of living.

limestone

literature
Little Women is a classic novel of children's **literature.**

light-year (līt′yir′), unit of length used to measure astronomical distances. It is equal to the distance that light travels in one year, about six trillion (6,000,000,000,000) miles (ten trillion kilometers). *n., pl.* **light-years.**

like·ly (līk′lē), probable. *adj.,* **like·li·er, like·li·est.**

lime·stone (līm′stōn′), rock made mostly of calcium carbonate, used for building and for making lime. Marble is a kind of limestone. *n.*

lim·o (lim′ō), INFORMAL. a large car or small bus used to take passengers to or from an airport, railroad, or bus station. *The family enjoys taking the limo to the airport. n., pl.* **lim·os.** [*Limo* is short for *limousine*]

line of scrim·mage (līn′ əv skrim′ij), (in football) an imaginary line running across the field at any point where the ball is placed: scrimmage line.

lines of lat·i·tude (līnz′ əv lat′ə tüd), an imaginary series of lines that run around the earth parallel to the equator.

lit·er·a·ture (lit′ər ə chùr *or* lit′ər ə chər), **1** writings of a period or of a country, especially those kept alive by their beauty of style or thought: *Shakespeare is a great name in English literature.* **2** all the books and articles on a subject: *the literature of stamp collecting. n.*

lock·er room (lok′ər rüm′), room with lockers near a gymnasium, in a clubhouse, etc., for dressing and storing sports equipment.

lon·gi·tude (lon′jə tüd *or* lon′jə tyüd), distance east or west on the earth's surface, measured in degrees from a certain meridian, usually the one through Greenwich, England. *n.*

lord (lôrd), **1** ruler, master, or chief; person who has the power; ruler of the land. **2** rule proudly or absolutely. **3** a feudal superior. *n.* [*Lord* is from Old English *hlāford*, originally meaning "one who guards the loaf of bread" or "master of the house," which comes from *hlāf*, meaning "loaf," and *weard*, meaning "keeper, guard."]

low-pres·sure sys·tem (lō′presh′ər sis′təm), an area of air pressure less than the surrounding air pressure.

M

mac·a·ro·ni (mak′ə rō′nē), flour paste that has been dried, usually in the form of hollow tubes, to be cooked for food. *n.* [*Macaroni* was borrowed from Italian *maccaroni*.]

mag·a·zine (mag′ə zēn′ or mag′ə zēn′), **1** a publication issued at regular intervals, especially weekly or monthly, which contains stories, articles, photographs. **2** room in a fort or warship for storing gunpowder and other explosives. **3** place in a repeating or automatic gun from which cartridges are fed into the firing chamber. *n.* [*Magazine* came into English about 400 years ago from French *magazine*, and can be traced back to Arabic *makhzan*, meaning "storehouse."]

mag·ic (maj′ik), done by magic or as if by magic. *n.* [*Magic* is from Latin *magice*, which came from Greek *magikē technē*, meaning "magical art."]

ma·gi·cian (mə jish′ən), **1** person skilled in the use of magic: *The wicked magician cast a spell over the princess.* **2** person who entertains by magic tricks. *n.*

mag·nan·i·mous (mag nan′ə məs), noble in soul or mind; generous in forgiving; free from mean feelings or acts. *adj.*

mag·nate (mag′nāt), an important, powerful, or prominent person. *n.*

mag·nif·i·cent (mag nif′ə sənt), richly colored or decorated; splendid; grand; stately. *adj.* —**mag·nif′i·cent·ly,** *adv.*

mag·ni·fy (mag′nə fī), **1** cause to look larger than the real size; increase the apparent size of an object. **2** make too much of; go beyond the truth in telling: *Was the fish really that big, or are you magnifying its size? v.,* **mag·ni·fied, mag·ni·fy·ing.**

mag·ni·tude (mag′nə tüd or mag′nə tyüd), greatness of size or importance. *n.*

ma·jor (mā′jər), more important; larger; greater: *Take the major share of the profits. adj.*

ma·jor·i·ty (mə jôr′ə tē), **1** the larger number or part; more than half. **2** the number by which the votes on one side are more than those on the other. *n., pl.* **ma·jor·i·ties.**

ma·li·cious (mə lish′əs), showing ill will; wishing to hurt or make suffer; spiteful: *That story is malicious gossip. adj.* —**ma·li′cious·ly,** *adv.*

man (man), an adult male person. When a boy grows up, he becomes a man: *The man's haircut was too short. n., pl.* **men** (men). [*Man* comes from Old English *mann*, meaning "human being, adult male."]

man·or (man′ər), (in the Middle Ages) a feudal estate, part of which was set aside for the lord and the rest divided among the peasants, who paid the owner rent in goods, services, or money. If the lord sold the manor, the peasants or serfs were sold with it. *n.* [*Manor* came into English about 700 years ago from French *manoir*, meaning "a dwelling," and can be traced back to Latin *manere*, meaning "to stay."]

man·tle (man′tl), **1** anything that covers like a mantle: *The ground had a mantle of snow.* **2** the part of the earth beneath the crust and above the core. *n.*

mar·ble (mär′bəl), a hard rock formed from limestone by heat and pressure. It may be white or colored and can be polished. Marble is used for statues and in buildings. *n.*

mar·shal (mär′shəl), **1** officer of various kinds, especially a police officer. **2** chief of police or head of the fire department in some cities. **3** a high officer in an army. **4** person who arranges the order of march in a parade. *n.*

magazine (def. 1)
different kinds of
magazines

manor
a **manor** in England

						ə *stands for*	
a	hat	ī	ice	u̇	put		
ā	age	o	not	ü	rule	a	in about
ä	far, calm	ō	open	ch	child	e	in taken
âr	care	ȯ	saw	ng	long	i	in pencil
e	let	ô	order	sh	she	o	in lemon
ē	equal	oi	oil	th	thin	u	in circus
ėr	term	ou	out	ᵺH	then		
i	it	u	cup	zh	measure		

Maya

a **Maya** temple

megaphone

Use **megaphones** for cheering at football games.

mar·tial (mär′shəl), **1** of war; suitable for war: *martial music.* **2** fond of fighting; warlike: *a martial nation. adj.*

Mar·y·land (mer′ə lənd), one of the southeastern states of the United States. *Abbreviation:* Md. or MD *Capital:* Annapolis. *n.*

mas·sage (mə säzh′), a rubbing and kneading of the muscles and joints to increase the circulation of blood. *n.* [*Massage* was borrowed from French *massage,* and can be traced back to Arabic *massa,* meaning "to touch, handle."]

mas·ter·piece (mas′tər pēs′), a person's greatest piece of work. *n., pl.* **mas·ter·pieces.**

ma·ter·nal (mə tėr′nl), **1** of or like a mother; motherly. **2** related on the mother's side of the family. *adj.*

Ma·ya (mī′ə), member of an ancient people of Central America and Mexico. The Mayas had a highly developed culture from about A.D. 350 to about A.D. 800. *n., pl.* **Ma·ya** or **Ma·yas.** —**Ma′yan,** *adj., n.*

mea·sles (mē′zəlz), a contagious disease caused by a virus, characterized by the symptoms of a bad cold, fever, and red spots on the skin. Measles is more common in children than in adults. *n. sing. or pl.*

med·al (med′l), piece of metal like a coin, with a figure or inscription stamped on it. *n.*

me·di·o·cre (mē′dē ō′kər or mē′dē ō′kər), neither good nor bad; of average or lower than average quality; ordinary: *a mediocre book, a mediocre poet. adj.*

meg·a·phone (meg′ə fōn), a large, funnel-shaped horn used to increase the loudness of the voice or the distance at which it can be heard. *n.*

Mel·ba toast (mel′bə tōst′), a very thin, crisp toast. [*Melba toast* was named after Dame Nellie *Melba,* 1861–1931, an Australian soprano.]

mem·ber·ship (mem′bər ship), number of members of a group: *Our club has a large membership of men and women. n.*

men (men), plural of **man.** *The men's golf outings were canceled. n. pl.*

men·tion (men′shən), speak about; refer to: *I mentioned your idea to the planning committee. v.*

me·rid·i·an (mə rid′ē ən), an imaginary circle passing through any place on the earth's surface and through the North and South Poles. *n., pl.* **me·rid·i·ans.** [*Meridian* comes from Latin *meridianus,* meaning "of noon," and can be traced back to *medius,* meaning "middle," and *dies,* meaning "day."]

mes·mer·ize (mez′mə rīz′ or mes′mə rīz′), hypnotize. *v.,* **mes·mer·ized, mes·mer·iz·ing.** [*Mesmerize* comes from Franz A. *Mesmer,* 1734–1815, an Austrian physician.]

mes·o·sphere (mes′ə sfir), region of the atmosphere between the stratosphere and the ionosphere, which extends from about 10 to 50 miles (16 to 80 kilometers) above the earth's surface. Most of the ozone in the atmosphere is created in the mesosphere. *n.*

me·squite (me skēt′), tree or shrub, common in the southwestern United States and Mexico. Its pods furnish a valuable food for cattle. *n.* [*Mesquite* is from Spanish *mezquite,* which came from Nahuatl *mizquitl.*]

met·al (met′l), **1** any of a group of chemical elements which usually have a shiny surface, are good conductors of heat and electricity, and can be melted or fused, hammered into thin sheets, or drawn out into wires. Some metals are iron, gold, copper, lead, tin, and aluminum. **2** made of metal: *a metal container.* **1** *n.,* **2** *adj.*

met·a·mor·phic rock (met′ə môr′fik rok′), changed in structure by heat, moisture, and pressure. Slate is a metamorphic rock that is formed from shale, a sedimentary rock. *adj.*

meth·od (meth′əd), **1** way of doing something: *a method of teaching music.* **2** order or system in getting things done or in thinking. *n.*

mi·cro·phone (mī′krə fōn), instrument for magnifying or transmitting sounds by changing sound waves into an electric current. *n.*

mi·grate (mī′grāt), go from one region to another with the change in the seasons. *v.,* **mi·grat·ed, mi·grat·ing.** [*Migrate* comes from Latin *migratum,* meaning "moved."]

mi·gra·to·ry (mī′grə tôr′ē), **1** moving from one place or region to another; migrating: *migratory laborers, migratory birds.* **2** of or about migration: *the migratory pattern of elephants. adj.*

mil·lion·aire (mil′yə nâr′), person whose wealth amounts to a million or more dollars, pounds, francs, etc. *After the wedding, she became the millionaire's wife. The millionaires' club held a special dinner. n.*

mir·ror (mir′ər), a piece of glass that reflects images; looking glass. It is coated on one side with silver or aluminum. *n.*

mis·chie·vous (mis′chə vəs), **1** harmful: *mischievous gossip.* **2** full of pranks and teasing fun: *mischievous children. adj.*
—**mis′chie·vous·ly**, *adv.*

mis·guid·ed (mis gī′did), led into mistakes or wrongdoing; misled: *a misguided person, misguided plans. adj.*

Mis·sis·sip·pi (mis′ə sip′ē), **1** large river in the United States. It flows south from N Minnesota to the Gulf of Mexico. **2** one of the south central states of the United States. *Abbreviation:* Miss. or MS *Capital:* Jackson. *n.*

mis·un·der·stand·ing (mis′un′dər stan′ding), **1** wrong understanding; failure to understand; mistake as to meaning. **2** disagreement. *n.*

mob (mob), a lawless crowd, easily moved to act without thinking. *n.*

mo·dem (mō′dem), an electronic device that enables a computer to send or receive information or instructions by telephone lines. *n.* [*Modem* is a blend of the word *mod(ulator)* and *dem(odulator).*]

mod·ern (mod′ərn), **1** of the present time; of times not long past: *Color television is a modern invention.* **2** up-to-date; not old-fashioned: *modern views. adj.*

mo·hair (mō′hâr), cloth made from the long, silky hair of the Angora goat; angora. *n.*

mold (mōld), a fossil that is an imprint of an organism or its trace. *n.*

mon·ey or·der (mun′ē ôr′dər), order for the payment of a certain sum of money. You can buy a money order at a post office, bank, etc., and send it to a person in another city, who can cash it there.

mon·o·logue or **mon·o·log** (mon′l òg), **1** a long speech by one person in a group. **2** entertainment by a single speaker: *a host's monologue.* **3** part of a play in which a single actor speaks alone. *n.*

moose (müs), a large mammal found in wooded areas of Canada and the northern United States. The male has a large head and broad antlers. It is related to the deer. *n., pl.* **moose.** [*Moose* is of Algonquian origin.]

mosque (mosk), a Muslim place of worship. *n.*

mo·squi·to (mə skē′tō), any of various small, slender insects with two wings. The female's bite causes itching. One kind of mosquito transmits malaria; another transmits yellow fever. *n., pl.* **mo·squi·toes** or **mo·squi·tos.** [*Mosquito* is from Spanish *mosquito,* meaning "little fly," which came from Latin *musca,* meaning "fly."]

mo·tel (mō tel′), roadside hotel or group of furnished cottages or cabins providing overnight lodging and parking for motorists. *n.* [*Motel* is a blend of *motor* and *hotel.*]

moose

mo·tion (mō′shən), change of position or place; movement; moving. Anything is in motion which is not at rest. *n.*

mourn (môrn), feel or show grief over: *mourn a lost dog. v.*

mov·ie (mü′vē), moving picture. *n., pl.* **mov·ies.**

mul·ti·ply (mul′tə plī), add (a number) a given number of times: *To multiply 16 by 3 means to add 16 three times, making 48. v.,* **mul·ti·plied, mul·ti·ply·ing.**

a	hat	**ī**	ice	**u̇**	put		**ə** *stands for*
ā	age	**o**	not	**ü**	rule	**a**	in about
ä	far, calm	**ō**	open	**ch**	child	**e**	in taken
âr	care	**ȯ**	saw	**ng**	long	**i**	in pencil
e	let	**ô**	order	**sh**	she	**o**	in lemon
ē	equal	**oi**	oil	**th**	thin	**u**	in circus
ėr	term	**ou**	out	**ᴛʜ**	then		
i	it	**u**	cup	**zh**	measure		

NASA

Dr. Ellen Ochoa is an astronaut with **NASA.**

mul·ti·tude (mul′tə tüd or mul′tə tyüd), a great many; crowd: *a multitude of difficulties, a multitude of enemies. n.*

mum (mum), INFORMAL. chrysanthemum. *n.*

mum·my (mum′ē), a dead body preserved from decay. Egyptian mummies have lasted more than 3000 years. *n., pl.* **mum·mies.** [*Mummy* comes from a medieval Latin word *mumia,* and can be traced back to Persian *mūm,* meaning "wax." Wax was used in the embalming of the dead.]

mus·cle (mus′əl), **1** a body tissue composed of fibers. The fibers can tighten or loosen to move parts of the body. **2** a special bundle of such tissue which moves some particular bone or part. The biceps muscle bends the arm. *n.*

mus·cu·lar (mus′kyə lər), **1** having well-developed muscles; strong: *a muscular arm.* **2** consisting of muscle. *adj.*

mus·tard (mus′tərd), a yellow powder or paste made from the seeds of a mustard plant, used as seasoning. *n.* [*Mustard* comes from French *moustarde* from Latin *mustrum,* meaning "fresh wine."]

must·n't (mus′nt), must not.

my·self (mī self′), form used instead of *me* or *I* in cases like: *I can cook for myself. I hurt myself. pron.*

myth (mith), legend or story, usually one that attempts to account for something in nature: *The myth of Proserpina is the ancient Roman explanation of summer and winter. n., pl.* **myths.** [*Myth* comes from Greek *mythos,* meaning "word, story."]

N

NASA (nas′ə), National Aeronautics and Space Administration (an agency of the United States government set up to direct and aid civilian research and development in aeronautics and aerospace technology). *n.*

na·tion·al (nash′ə nəl), **1** of a nation; belonging to a whole nation: *national laws, a national disaster.* **2** citizen of a nation. **1** *adj.* **2** *n.*

newscaster

Newscasters broadcast the latest news several times a day.

nat·ur·al (nach′ər əl), **1** produced by nature; coming or occurring in the ordinary course of events: *natural feelings and actions, a natural death.* **2** instinctively felt to be right and fair: *natural rights. adj.*

na·ture (nā′chər), **1** the world; all things except those made by human beings: *the wonders of nature.* **2** Also, **Nature.** all the forces at work throughout the world: *the laws of nature. n.*

neg·a·tive (neg′ə tiv), not positive: *Her negative suggestions are not helpful. adj.*

neigh·bor·hood (nā′bər hùd), **1** place or district. **2** people living near one another; people of a place: *The neighborhood came to the party.* **3** of a neighborhood: *a neighborhood park.* 1,2 *n.,* 3 *adj.*

nei·ther (nē′ᴛʜər or nī′ᴛʜər), not either: *Neither you nor I will go* (conj.). *Neither statement is true* (adj.). *Neither of the statements is true* (pron.)

neu·tral (nü′trəl or nyü′trəl), on neither side in a quarrel or war: *neutral territory. adj.*

neu·tral·i·ty (nü tral′ə tē or nyü tral′ə tē), the attitude or policy of a nation that does not take part directly or indirectly in a war between other nations. *n.*

new·born (nü′bôrn′ or nyü′bôrn′), a newborn infant. *n., pl.* **new·born, new·borns.**

new·com·er (nü′kum′ər or nyü′kum′ər), person who has just come or who came not long ago: *newcomer to the street. n.*

new·ly·wed (nü′lē wed′ or nyü′lē wed′), person who has recently become married. *n.*

news·cast (nüz′kast′ or nyüz′kast′), a television or radio broadcast devoted to current events and news bulletins. *n.* [*Newscast* is a blend of the word *news* and *broadcast.*]

news·cast·er (nüz′kas′tər or nyüz′kas′tər), person who gives the news on a newscast. *n.*

New Year's Eve, the eve of New Year's Day, on December 31.

New York, 1 Often, **New York State.** one of the northeastern states of the United States. *Abbreviation:* N.Y. or NY *Capital:* Albany. **2** Often, **New York City.** seaport in SE New York State, at the mouth of the Hudson River.

nib·ble (nib′əl), **1** eat away with quick, small bites, as a rabbit or mouse does. **2** bite gently or lightly: *nibbled at the cheese. v.,* **nib·bled, nib·bling.**

niece (nēs), daughter of one's brother or sister; daughter of one's brother-in-law or sister-in-law. *n.*

night·in·gale (nīt′n gāl), a small, reddish-brown bird of Europe. The male sings sweetly at night as well as in the daytime. *n.*

night·ly (nīt′lē), **1** done, happening, or appearing every night. **2** every night: *Performances are given nightly except on Sunday.* **1** *adj.,* **2** *adv.*

night·mare (nīt′mâr′), a very distressing dream. *n.*

nine·ty-five (nīn′tē-fīv), nine times ten and one more than four; 95. *n., adj.*

ni·tro·gen (nī′trə jən), a mineral that plants need for growth. *n.*

no·ble (nō′bəl), **1** person high and great by birth, rank, or title. **2** excellent; fine; splendid; magnificent: *Niagara Falls is a noble sight. adj.,* **no·bler, no·blest.**

nose (nōz), **1** the part of the face or head just above the mouth which contains the nostrils and serves as the organ of smell. **2** the sense of smell: *a dog with a good nose. n.* **under one's nose,** in plain sight; very easy to notice.
win by a nose, 1 win a horse race by no more than the length of a horse's nose. **2** win by a small margin.

nui·sance (nü′sns or nyü′sns), thing or person that annoys, troubles, offends, or is disagreeable; annoyance: *Flies are a nuisance. n.*

nu·mer·ous (nü′mər əs or nyü′mər əs), very many: *The child asked numerous questions. adj.*

nu·tri·ent (nü′trē ənt or nyü′trē ənt), a substance found in food that your body needs to stay healthy. *n., pl.* **nu·tri·ents.**

o

ob·li·gate (ob′lə gāt), bind morally or legally; pledge: *A witness in court is obligated to tell the truth. v.,* **ob·li·gat·ed, ob·li·gat·ing.**

ob·serv·a·ble (əb zėr′və bəl), able to be noticed; noticeable; easily seen: *That star is observable on a dark night. adj.*

ob·serv·a·to·ry (əb zėr′və tôr′ē), place or building equipped with a telescope for observing the stars and other heavenly bodies. *n., pl.* **ob·serv·a·to·ries.**

ob·tain (əb tān′), get through effort; come to have; accept: *obtain a job one applies for, obtain knowledge through study. v.,* **ob·tained, ob·tain·ing.**

oc·cu·pa·tion (ok′yə pā′shən), work a person does regularly or to earn a living; business; employment; trade. *n.*

oc·cur (ə kėr′), take place; happen: *Storms often occur in winter. v.,* **oc·curred, oc·cur·ring.** [*Occur* is from Latin *occurrere,* which comes from *ob-,* meaning "in the way of," and *currere,* meaning "run."]

o'clock (ə klok′), of the clock; by the clock: *It is one o'clock. adv.*

oc·tet or **oc·tette** (ok tet′), piece of music for eight voices or instruments. *n.*

oc·to·pus (ok′tə pəs), a sea animal having a soft body and eight arms with suckers on them; devilfish. It is a mollusk. *n., pl.* **oc·to·pus·es, oc·to·pi** (ok′tə pī). [*Octopus* is from New Latin and Greek *oktōpous,* from *oktō* meaning "eight" and *pous* meaning "foot."]

off (óf), **1** from the usual or correct position, condition, etc.: *I took off my hat.* **2** from; away from: *I jumped off the step. We are miles off the main road.* **3** not on; not connected: *A button is off his coat* (prep.). *The electricity is off* (adj.). **1** *adv.,* **2,3** *prep.,* **3** *adj.*

nutrient

Fruits provide several **nutrients** important in a healthy diet.

observatory

a view of the telescope in the dome of an **observatory**

a	hat	**ī**	ice	**u̇**	put	**ə** stands for	
ā	age	**o**	not	**ü**	rule	**a**	in about
ä	far, calm	**ō**	open	**ch**	child	**e**	in taken
âr	care	**ȯ**	saw	**ng**	long	**i**	in pencil
e	let	**ô**	order	**sh**	she	**o**	in lemon
ē	equal	**oi**	oil	**th**	thin	**u**	in circus
ėr	term	**ou**	out	**ᴛʜ**	then		
i	it	**u**	cup	**zh**	measure		

old-fash·ioned (ōld′fash′ənd), out of date in style, construction, etc.; of or typical of an old style or time: *an old-fashioned dress. adj.*

o·mit (ō mit′), leave out: *omit a letter in a word. v.,* **o·mit·ted, o·mit·ting.**

on·ly (ōn′lē), by itself or themselves; one and no more; sole or single: *an only child. This is the only road to the cabin. adj.*

oom·pah (üm′pä or u̇m′pä), a continuous bass sound in music, usually provided by brass instruments. *adj.*

op·po·site (op′ə zit), **1** placed against; as different in direction as can be; face to face; back to back: *The house straight across the street is opposite to ours.* **2** as different as can be. *adj.*

o·ral his·tor·y (ôr′əl his′tər ē), passing of facts or presenting a story orally; description of an event. *n., pl.* **o·ral his·tor·ies.**

or·der (ôr′dər), **1** the way one thing follows another: *in order of size, in alphabetical order, to copy them in order.* **2** tell what to do; give an order **1** *n.,* **2** *v.* **or·dered, or·der·ing.**

o·ri·en·ta·tion (ôr′ē en tā′shən), a bringing into the right relationship with surroundings; adjustment to a new situation. *n.*

o·ri·gin (ôr′ə jin), **1** thing from which anything comes; starting point; source; beginning. **2** parentage, ancestry, or birth: *He is of Mexican origin. n.*

o·rig·i·nal (ə rij′ə nəl), **1** of the beginning; first; earliest: *They were the original owners of that house. The hat has been marked down from its original price.* **2** new; fresh; novel: *It is hard to plan original games for a party.* **3** able to do, make, or think something new; inventive: *a very original writer. adj.*

o·rig·i·nate (ə rij′ə nāt), cause to be; invent: *originate a new style of painting. v.,* **o·rig·i·nat·ed, o·rig·i·nat·ing.**

or·phan (ôr′fən), **1** child whose parents are dead; child whose father or mother is dead. **2** without a father or mother or both. **1** *n.,* **2** *adj.*

old-fashioned

an **old-fashioned** drugstore

our (our), of us; belonging to us. *adj.*

our·selves (our selvz′), form of *we* or *us* used to make a statement stronger: *We ourselves will do the work. pron.pl.*

out·come (out′kum′), a possible result in a probability experiment. *n.*

out-of-bounds (out′əv boundz′), outside the boundary line; out of play: *an out-of-bounds ball (adj.). He kicked the ball out-of-bounds (adv.). adj., adv.*

out·side (out′sīd′), **1** on the outside of or nearer the outside: *the outside leaves.* **2** space that is beyond or not inside. **3** INFORMAL. with the exception (of): *Outside of him, none of us liked the play.* **4** out of; beyond the limits of: *Stay outside the house. That is outside my plans.* **1** *adv.,* **2** *n.,* **3,4** *prep.*

o·ver·come (ō′vər kum′), **1** get the better of; win the victory over; conquer; defeat: *overcome an enemy, overcome one's faults, overcome all difficulties.* **2** make weak or helpless: *overcome by weariness. v.,* **over·came** (ō′vər kām′), **over·come, o·ver·com·ing.**

o·ver·cook (ō′vər ku̇k′), cook too much or too long. *adj.*

o·ver·crowd (ō′vər kroud′), crowd too much; put in too much or too many: *The store was overcrowded with holiday shoppers. v.*

o·ver·em·pha·size (ō′vər em′fə sīz), give too much force or emphasis to; stress too much. *v.,* **o·ver·em·pha·sized, o·ver·em·pha·siz·ing.**

o·ver·flow (ō′vər flō′ or ō′vər flō′), **1** to cover or flood: *The river overflowed my garden.* **2** flow over the top of: *The milk overflowed the cup.* **3** be very abundant: *an overflowing harvest, overflowing kindness. v.,* **o·ver·flowed, o·ver·flown** (ō′vər flōn′), **o·ver·flow·ing.**

o·ver·head (ō′vər hed′ for **1**; ō′vər hed′ for **2**), **1** over the head; on high; above: *the stars overhead.* **2** placed above; placed high up: *overhead wires.* **1** *adv.,* **2** *adj.*

o·ver·load (ō′vər lōd′ for **1**; ō′vər lōd′ for **2**), **1** load too heavily: *overload a boat.* **2** too great a load: *The overload of electric current blew the fuse.* **1** *v.,* **2** *n.*

o·ver·look (ō′vər lùk′), **1** fail to see: *overlook a bill.* **2** have a view of from above; be higher than: *This high window overlooks half the city. v.*

o·ver·pop·u·late (ō′vər pop′yə lāt), fill with an extreme number of people, reducing various supplies and resources. *v.,* **o·ver·pop·u·lat·ed, o·ver·pop·u·lat·ing.**

o·ver·rule (ō′vər rül′), **1** rule or decide against (a plea, argument, objection, etc.); set aside: *The president overruled my plan.* **2** prevail over; be stronger than: *I was overruled by the majority. v.,* **o·ver·ruled, o·ver·rul·ing.**

o·ver·seas (ō′vər sēz′), **1** across the sea; beyond the sea; abroad: *travel overseas.* **2** of countries across the sea; foreign: *overseas trade.* **1** *adv.* **2** *adj.*

o·ver·see (ō′vər sē′), look after and direct (work or workers); supervise; manage: *oversees a factory. v.,* **o·ver·saw** (ō′vər sò′), **o·ver·seen** (ō′vər sēn′), **o·ver·see·ing.**

own·er·ship (ō′nər ship), condition of being an owner; the possessing (of something); right of possession: *He claimed ownership of the abandoned car. n.*

ox·y·gen (ok′sə jən), a colorless, odorless gas that forms about one fifth of the atmosphere. Oxygen is a chemical element found in water, carbon dioxide, iron ore, and many other substances. Animals and plants cannot live, and fire will not burn, without oxygen. *n.*

o·zone (ō′zōn), form of oxygen with a sharp, pungent odor, produced by electricity and present in the air, especially after a thunderstorm. *n.* [*Ozone* is from German *Ozon,* which came from Greek *ozein,* meaning "to smell."]

P

pants (pants), **1** trousers. **2** underpants. *n. pl.*

par·al·lel·o·gram (par′ə lel′ə gram), a four-sided plane figure whose opposite sides are parallel and equal. *n.*

par·lia·ment (pär′lə mənt), council or congress that is the highest lawmaking body in some countries. *n.*

Par·the·non (pär′thə non), temple of Athena on the Acropolis in Athens, regarded as the finest example of Doric architecture. *n.*

part·ner (pärt′nər), player on the same team or side in a game. *n.*

part·ner·ship (pärt′nər ship), a being a partner; joint interest; association: *a business partnership, the partnership of marriage. n.*

part-time (pärt′tīm′), for part of the usual time: *A part-time job helped her finish college. adj.*

pass·port (pas′pôrt), paper or book giving official permission to travel abroad, under the protection of one's own government. *n.* [*Passport* came into English about 500 years ago from French *passeport,* which comes from *passer,* meaning "to pass," and *port,* meaning "a harbor."]

pas·teur·ize (pas′chə rīz′), heat (milk, wine, beer, etc.) to a high enough temperature and for a long enough time to destroy harmful bacteria. *v.,* **pas·teur·ized, pas·teur·iz·ing.** [*Pasteurize* was named for Louis *Pasteur,* 1822–1895, a French chemist who invented a way of preventing rabies and of keeping milk from spoiling.]

pas·time (pas′tīm′), a pleasant way of passing time; amusement; recreation. Games and sports are pastimes. *n.*

pa·ter·nal (pə tėr′nl), related on the father's side of the family. *adj.*

Parthenon
the **Parthenon** in Greece

passport
A **passport** gives one official permission to travel in a foreign country.

a	hat	ī	ice	u̇	put	ə stands for	
ā	age	o	not	ü	rule	a	in about
ä	far, calm	ō	open	ch	child	e	in taken
âr	care	ȯ	saw	ng	long	i	in pencil
e	let	ô	order	sh	she	o	in lemon
ē	equal	oi	oil	th	thin	u	in circus
ėr	term	ou	out	ŦH	then		
i	it	u	cup	zh	measure		

performance (def. 2)

playing piano for an

important

performance

petrify

a piece of **petrified**

wood

pa·tience (pā/shəns), willingness to put up with waiting, pain, trouble, etc.; calm endurance of anything that annoys, troubles, or hurts. *n.*

pa·tient (pā/shənt), person who is being treated by a doctor. *n.*

pat·i·o (pat/ē ō), terrace for outdoor eating, lounging, etc. *n., pl.* **pat·i·os.**

pa·tri·cian (pə trish/ən), (in ancient Rome) a member of the Roman upper class. *n., pl.* **pa·tri·cians.**

pa·trol (pə trōl/), go around in an area watching and guarding in order to protect life and property: *The police patrolled once every hour. v.,* **pa·trolled, pa·trol·ling.**

pa·tron (pā/trən), person who gives approval and support to some person, art, cause, or undertaking: *a patron of artists. n.*

pat·tern (pat/ərn), arrangement of forms and colors; design. *n.*

peer me·di·a·tion (pir/ mē/dē ā/ shən), a mediating of equals; effecting an agreement; friendly intervention towards another.

pen·al·ty (pen/l tē), **1** punishment imposed by law: *The penalty for speeding is usually a fine.* **2** disadvantage imposed on a side or player for breaking the rules of some game or contest. *n., pl.* **pen·al·ties.**

per·cent (pər sent/), parts in each hundred; hundredths. 5 percent is 5 of each 100, or ⁵/₁₀₀ of the whole. *n.*

per·cep·tion (pər sep/shən), act of perceiving: *His perception of the change came in a flash. n.*

perch (pėrch), sit rather high: *I perched on a stool. v.,* **perched, perch·ing.**

per·form (pər fôrm/), act, play, sing, or do tricks in public. *v.*

per·form·ance (pər fôr/məns), **1** a carrying out; doing; performing: *in the performance of one's regular duties, the efficient performance of an automobile.* **2** the giving of a play, concert, circus, or other show: *The performance is at 8 o'clock. n.*

per·ma·nent (pėr/mə nənt), intended to last; not for a short time only; lasting. *adj.*

per·sist·ent (pər sis/tənt), not giving up, especially in the face of dislike, disapproval, or difficulties; persisting: *a persistent worker, a persistent salesperson. adj.*

per·son·al (pėr/sə nəl), of a person; individual; private: *a personal letter, a personal matter. adj.*

per·son·nel (pėr/sə nel/), persons employed in any work, business, or service. *n.*

per·spec·tive (pər spek/tiv), a view of things or facts in which they are in the right relations. *n.*

pes·si·mism (pes/ə miz/əm), tendency to look on the dark side of things or to see all the difficulties and disadvantages. *The parent's pessimism affected the child's outlook. n.*

pet·ri·fy (pet/rə fī), turn into stone; change (plant or animal matter) into a substance like stone. *v.,* **pet·ri·fied, pet·ri·fy·ing.**

phar·aoh (fer/ō), a king of ancient Egypt. Egyptians believed that each pharaoh was a living god on earth. *n.*

phi·los·o·pher (fə los/ə fər), a person who studies nature and human beings, searching for truths and principles. *n., pl.* **phi·los·o·phers.**

phi·los·o·phy (fə los/ə fē), a calm and reasonable attitude; accepting things as they are and making the best of them. *n., pl.* **phi·los·o·phies.**

pho·to (fō/tō), INFORMAL. a photograph. *n., pl.* **pho·tos.**

pi·an·o (pē an/ō), a large musical instrument whose tones come from many wires. The wires are sounded by hammers that are worked by striking keys on a keyboard. *n., pl.* **pi·an·os.**

pic·nic (pik/nik), a pleasure trip with a meal in the open air. *n.* [*Picnic* comes from French *piquenique.*]

piece (pēs), **1** one of the parts into which a thing is divided or broken; bit: *The cup broke in pieces.* **2** a single composition in an art: *a piece of music. n., pl.* **pieces.**

pig·eon (pij/ən), any of a family of birds with thick bodies, short tails, and usually short legs, comprising numerous species found throughout the world and including doves and domestic pigeons. *n.*

pig·skin (pig/skin/), **1** the skin of a pig. **2** leather made from it. **3** INFORMAL. a football. *n.*

pinch-hit (pinch/hit/), (in baseball) to bat for another player, especially when a hit is badly needed. *v.,* **pinch-hit, pinch-hit·ting.**

pink (pingk), **1** having this color. **2** the highest degree or condition: *The athlete was in the pink of health.* 1 *adj.,* 2 *n.*

pix·el (pik′səl), any one of the many tiny points, each able to be bright or dark, that make up an electronic image. *n.* [*Pixel* is a blend of the words *picture* and *element.*]

plank·ton (plangk′tən), the small animal and plant organisms that float or drift in water, especially at or near the surface. *n.* [*Plankton* comes from German *Plankton,* and can be traced back to Greek *plazesthai,* meaning "to wander, drift."]

plate (plāt), a large section of the earth's surface made up of the crust and upper mantle. *n., pl.* **plates.**

plate tec·ton·ic the·or·y (plāt′ tek ton′ik thē′ər ē *or* thir′ē), theory stating that the earth's surface is covered with moving plates.

play (plā), a story written for or presented as a dramatic performance; drama: *"Peter Pan" is a charming play. n., pl.* **plays.**

pleas·ant (plez′nt), that pleases; giving pleasure; agreeable: *a pleasant swim on a hot day. adj.*

ple·be·ian (pli bē′ən), (in ancient Rome) one of the ordinary people. *n., pl.* **ple·be·ians.**

pneu·mo·nia (nü mō′nyə *or* nyü mō′nyə), an infectious disease that causes inflammation of the lungs and often a high fever and a hard, dry cough. It often follows a bad cold or other disease. Pneumonia in both lungs is called **double pneumonia.** *n.*

pock·et·ful (pok′it fül), as much as a pocket will hold. *n., pl.* **pock·et·fuls.**

po·em (pō′əm), arrangement of words in lines having rhythm or a regularly repeated accent and, often, rhyme; composition in verse. *n.*

po·et·ic (pō et′ik), **1** suitable for poems or poets. *Alas, o'er,* and *blithe* are poetic words. **2** showing beautiful or noble language, imagery, or thought: *poetic fancies. adj.*

po·et·ry (pō′i trē), **1** poems: *a collection of poetry.* **2** art of writing poems: *Our class is studying the masters of English poetry. n.*

pol·ka (pōl′kə *or* pō′kə), **1** a kind of lively dance. **2** music for it. *n.* [*Polka* was borrowed from Czech *polka.*]

pol·ka dot (pō′kə dot′), dot or round spot repeated to form a pattern on cloth.

pol·lu·tant (pə lüt′nt), something that pollutes. *A Styrofoam cup is a pollutant to the environment. n.*

pop·u·lar·i·ty (pop′yə lar′ə tē), fact or condition of being liked by most people. *n.*

pop·u·la·tion (pop′yə lā′shən), **1** people of a city, country, or district. **2** part of the inhabitants distinguished in any way from the rest: *the urban population. n.*

por·poise (pôr′pəs), a sea mammal with a blunt, rounded snout. Porpoises are related to the whale, and live in groups in the northern Atlantic and Pacific. *n., pl.* **por·pois·es** *or* **por·poise.**

port·a·ble (pôr′tə bəl), capable of being carried; easily carried: *a portable typewriter, a portable radio. adj.*

por·ti·co (pôr′tə kō), roof supported by columns, forming a porch or a covered walk. *n., pl.* **por·ti·coes** *or* **por·ti·cos.**

po·si·tion (pə zish′ən), **1** place where a thing or person is. **2** way of being placed: *Sit in a more comfortable position. n.*

pos·sess (pə zes′), **1** have as belonging to one; own. **2** hold as property; hold; occupy. *v.*

pollutant

smokestacks emitting **pollutants** into the air

						ə stands for	
a	hat	**ī**	ice	**u̇**	put		
ā	age	**o**	not	**ü**	rule	**a**	in about
ä	far, calm	**ō**	open	**ch**	child	**e**	in taken
âr	care	**ȯ**	saw	**ng**	long	**i**	in pencil
e	let	**ô**	order	**sh**	she	**o**	in lemon
ē	equal	**oi**	oil	**th**	thin	**u**	in circus
ėr	term	**ou**	out	**ŦH**	then		
i	it	**u**	cup	**zh**	measure		

pos·ses·sion (pə zesh′ən), **1** a possessing; holding: *I have in my possession the books you thought you'd lost.* **2** ownership: *On her 21st birthday she came into possession of 50 thousand dollars.* *n.*

pos·ses·sive (pə zes′iv), showing possession. *My, your, his,* and *our* are in the possessive case because they indicate who possesses or owns. *adj.*

pos·si·ble (pos′ə bəl), capable of being, being done, or happening: *It is possible to cure tuberculosis. Space travel is now possible. adj.*

post·date (pōst′dāt′), **1** give a later date than the true date to (a letter, check, etc.) **2** follow in time. *v.,* **dat·ed, dat·ing.**

post·grad·u·ate (pōst graj′ü it), taking a course of study after graduation. *adj.*

post·hu·mous (pos′chə məs), happening after death: *posthumous fame. adj.* —**post′hu·mous·ly,** *adv.*

post·pone·ment (pōst pōn′mənt), a putting off till later; a putting off to a later time; delay. *n.*

post·war (pōst′wôr′), after the war. *adj.*

po·ta·to (pə tā′tō), a round or oval, hard, starchy vegetable with a thin skin; Irish potato; white potato. It is one of the most widely used vegetables. Potatoes grow underground. *n., pl.* **po·ta·toes.**

pow·er (pou′ər), operated by a motor; equipped with its own motor: *a power drill. adj.*

prair·ie (prer′ē), a large area of level or rolling land with grass but few or no trees. *n.*

pre·ar·range (prē′ə rānj′), arrange beforehand. *v.,* **pre·ar·ranged, pre·ar·rang·ing.**

pre·cau·tion (pri kȯ′shən), care taken beforehand; thing done beforehand to ward off evil or secure good results. *n.*

pre·cede (prē sēd′), go or come before: *A precedes B in the alphabet. The band preceded the floats in the parade. v.,* **pre·ced·ed, pre·ced·ing.**

pre·cious (presh′əs), having great value; worth much; valuable. Gold, platinum, and silver are often called the precious metals. Diamonds, rubies, and sapphires are precious stones. *adj.*

pre·co·cious (pri kō′shəs), developed earlier than usual in knowledge, skill, etc.: *This very precocious child could read well at the age of four. adj.*

pre·dict (pri dikt′), tell beforehand; prophesy; forecast: *The Weather Service predicts rain for tomorrow. v.*

pre·fer (pri fėr′), **1** like better; choose rather. *She prefers swimming to fishing.* **2** put forward or present, especially a charge against someone for consideration in a court of law: *The policeman preferred charges of speeding against the driver. v.,* **pre·ferred, pre·fer·ring.**

pre·his·to·ric (prē′hi stôr′ik), of or belonging to times before histories were written: *Prehistoric peoples used stone tools. adj.*

pre·lim·i·nar·y (pri lim′ə ner′ē), a preliminary step; something preparatory: *An examination is a preliminary to entering that school. n., pl.* **pre·lim·i·nar·ies.**

pre·med·i·tate (prē med′ə tāt), consider or plan beforehand. *v.,* **pre·med·i·tat·ed, pre·med·i·tat·ing.**

pre·mo·ni·tion (prē′mə nish′ən *or* prem′ə nish′ən), notification or warning of what is to come; forewarning: *a vague premonition of disaster. n.*

pre·scrip·tion (pri skrip′shən), a written direction or order for preparing and using a medicine: *a prescription for a cough. n.*

pre·serv·a·tive (pri zėr′və tiv), any substance that will prevent food from spoiling: *Salt is a preservative for meat. n., pl.* **pre·serv·a·tives.**

pre·serve (pri zėrv′), keep from harm or change; keep safe; protect. *v.,* **pre·served, pre·serv·ing.**

pre·tense (prē′tens *or* pri tens′), make-believe; pretending. *n.*

pre·tri·al (prē′trī′əl), **1** having to do with a meeting held by a judge or other legal professionals to clarify the issues so as to save time and costs at the trial. **2** occurring or existing before a trial: *Pretrial publicity had prejudiced the jury. adj.*

pre·view (prē′vyü′), an advance showing of a motion picture, play, television program. *n.*

prehistoric

prehistoric ceremonial spear points

pri·mar·y source (prī/mer/ē sôrs/), firsthand account of what occurred in history through experience, letters, diaries, photos, government documents, or autobiographies. *n.*, *pl.* **pri·mar·y sourc·es.**

prime (prīm), prime number; a whole number, greater than 1, that has exactly two factors: itself and 1. Prime numbers are 2, 3, 5, 7, and 11. *n.*

prime fac·tor·i·za·tion (prīm/ fak tər ə zā/shən), a number written as the product of prime numbers: $30 = 2 \times 3 \times 5$.

prime me·rid·i·an (prīm/ mə rid/ē ən), meridian from which the longitude east and west is measured. It passes through Greenwich, England, and its longitude is 0 degrees.

prob·a·bil·i·ty (prob/ə bil/ə tē), a number from 0 to 1 that tells how likely it is that a given event will occur. The closer to 1, the *more likely* the event is to occur. The closer to 0, the *less likely* it is to occur. *n.*

prob·a·bly (prob/ə blē), more likely than not. *adv.*

pro·ceed·ing (prə sē/ding), what is done; action; conduct. *n.*

proc·ess (pros/es *or* prō/ses), **1** set of actions or changes in a special order: *The processing of film is expensive. By what process is cloth made from wool?* **2** treating or preparing by some special method: *To make the cloth waterproof, he is processing it immediately.* 1 *n.*, *pl.* **proc·ess·es**; 2 *v.*, **proc·essed, proc·ess·ing.** [*Process comes from Latin processus, meaning "progress."*]

pro·duce (prə düs/ *or* prə dyüs/), **1** bring forth or yield offspring, crops, products, dividends, interest, etc. **2** bring forth; supply; create; yield: *Hens produce eggs.* **3** bring (a play, motion picture, etc.) before the public. *v.*, **pro·duced, pro·duc·ing.**

pro·duc·er (prə dü/sər *or* prə dyü/sər), person in charge of presenting a play, a motion picture, or a television or radio show. *n.*

prod·uct (prod/əkt), that which is produced; result of work or of growth: *factory products, farm products. n.*

pro·duc·tion (prə duk/shən), **1** act of producing; creation; manufacture: *the production of automobiles, production of grain.* **2** something produced: *the yearly production of a farm. n.*

pro·duc·tive (prə duk/tiv), producing much; fertile: *a productive farm, a productive writer. adj.*

prom·i·nent (prom/ə nənt), **1** well-known or important; distinguished: *a prominent citizen.* **2** easy to see: *I hung the picture in a prominent place in the living room. adj.*

prom·ise (prom/is), **1** words said or written, binding a person to do or not to do something: *You can count on her to keep her promise.* **2** give one's word; make a promise: *They promised to stay till we came.* 1 *n.*, 2 *v.*, **prom·ised, prom·is·ing.**

pro·pel·ler (prə pel/ər), device consisting of a revolving hub with blades, for propelling boats and aircraft. *n.*

prop·er·ty (prop/ər tē), thing or things owned; possession or possessions: *This house is that man's property. That book is my property; please return it to me. n.*, *pl.* **prop·er·ties.**

pro·por·tion (prə pôr/shən), statement of equality between two ratios. EXAMPLE: 4 is to 2 as 10 is to 5. *n.*

pro·tein (prō/tēn), one of the substances containing nitrogen which are a necessary part of the cells of animals and plants. Meat, milk, cheese, eggs, and beans contain protein. Proteins build, repair, and maintain body cells. *n.*

P.S., postscript.

propeller
airplane **propellers**

a	hat	**ī**	ice	**u̇**	put	**ə** stands for		
ā	age	**o**	not	**ü**	rule	**a**	in about	
ä	far, calm	**ō**	open	**ch**	child	**e**	in taken	
âr	care	**ȯ**	saw	**ng**	long	**i**	in pencil	
e	let	**ô**	order	**sh**	she	**o**	in lemon	
ē	equal	**oi**	oil	**th**	thin	**u**	in circus	
ėr	term	**ou**	out	**ʹH**	then			
i	it	**u**	cup	**zh**	measure			

pyramid (def. 2)
one of the **Pyramids**
in Egypt

pum·mel (pum′əl), strike or beat; beat with the fists. *v.*, **pum·meled** or **pum·melled, pum·mel·ing** *or* **pum·mel·ling.** Also, **pommel.**

punt (punt), **1** kick (a football) before it touches the ground after dropping it from the hands. **2** INFORMAL. delay; avoid committing oneself. *v.*

pur·chase (pér′chəs), **1** get by paying a price; buy: *We purchased a new car.* **2** a buying: *the purchase of a new car.* **1** *v.*, **pur·chased, pur·chas·ing; 2** *n.*

pyr·a·mid (pir′ə mid), **1** a solid figure having a polygon for a base and triangular sides which meet in a point. **2 Pyramids,** *pl.* the huge, massive stone pyramids, serving as royal tombs, built by the ancient Egyptians. *n.*

Q

quack (kwak), **1** the sound a duck makes. *The quacking of the ducks on the river woke me up.* **2** make such a sound. **1** *n.,* **2** *v.*

quad·ri·lat·er·al (kwäd′rə lat′ər əl), **1** having four sides and four angles. **2** a plane figure having four sides and four angles. **1** *adj.,* **2** *n.* [*Quadrilateral* comes from Latin *quadrilaterus, quadri-* meaning "four" and *latus* meaning "side."]

qua·dru·plet (kwä drü′plit), **1** one of four children born at the same time of the same mother. **2** any group or combination of four. *n., pl.* **qua·dru·plets.**

quar·ter·back (kwôr′tər bak′), an offensive back who stands directly behind the center in football. He begins each play by handing the ball to a running back, passing it to a teammate, or running with it himself. *n.*

quartz·ite (kwôrt′sīt), a granular rock consisting of compressed sandstone. *n.*

ques·tion (kwes′chən), thing asked in order to get information; inquiry: *The teacher answered the girl's question. n.* [*Question* came into English about 700 years ago from French *question,* and can be traced back to Latin *quaerere,* meaning "to ask, seek."] —**ques′tion·er,** *n.*

rain forest
a tropical **rain forest**

quiz (kwiz), a short or informal test: *Each week the teacher gives us a quiz in social studies. n., pl.* **quiz·zes.**

R

ra·dar (rā′där), instrument for determining the distance, direction, speed, etc., of unseen objects by the reflection of radio waves. *n.* [*Radar* comes from the words *radio detecting and ranging.*]

ra·di·us (rā′dē əs), a line segment going straight from the center to the outside of a circle or a sphere. Any spoke in a wheel is a radius. *n., pl.* **ra·di·i** (rā′dē ī), **ra·di·us·es.** [*Radius* comes from Latin *radius,* meaning "ray, spoke of a wheel."]

rain fo·rest (rān′ for′ist), a very dense forest in a region where rain is very heavy throughout the year. Rain forests are usually in tropical areas.

ranch (ranch), a large farm with grazing land, used for raising cattle, sheep, or horses. *n.* [*Ranch* comes from Spanish *rancho.*]

rat (rat), SLANG. turn informer against one's associates; squeal. *v.,* **rat·ted, rat·ting.**
smell a rat, suspect a trick or scheme.

rate (rāt), quantity, amount, or degree measured in proportion to something else: *The rate of interest is 6 cents on the dollar. The car was going at the rate of 40 miles an hour. n.*

ra·ti·o (rā′shē ō), quotient expressing this relation. The ratio between two quantities is the number of times one contains the other. The ratio of 10 to 3 is written as 10:3, 10/3, 10÷3, or $^{10}/_3$. The ratios of 3 to 5 and 6 to 10 are the same. *n., pl.* **ra·ti·os.**

re·ac·tion (rē ak′shən), action in response to some influence or force. *n.*

re·al·is·tic (rē′ə lis′tik), seeing things as they really are; practical. *adj.*

re·al·ly (rē′ə lē), **1** actually; truly; in fact: *Try to see things as they really are.* **2** indeed: *Oh, really? adv.*

re·ceipt (ri sēt′), a written statement that money, a package, a letter, etc., has been received. *n.*

re·ceive (ri sēv′), **1** take (something offered or sent); take into one's hands or possession: *receive gifts*. **2** take or let into the mind; accept *receive new ideas* **3** accept; mean to take what is given, offered, or delivered: *She received a gift from him, but did not accept it. v.,* **re·ceived, re·ceiv·ing.**
Synonym Study 1 **Receive, accept** mean to take what is given, offered, or delivered. **Receive** carries no suggestion of positive action or of activity of mind or will on the part of the receiver, and means nothing more than to take what is given or given out: *He received a prize.* **Accept** always suggests being willing to take what is offered, or giving one's consent: *She received a gift from him, but did not accept it.*

re·ceiv·er (ri sē′vər), **1** the part of a telephone held to the ear. **2** device that changes electromagnetic waves into sound or picture signals: *a radio or television receiver. n.*

re·cent (rē′snt), done or made not long ago: *recent events. adj.*

re·cep·tion (ri sep′shən), a gathering to receive and welcome people. *n.*

re·cess (rē′ses or ri ses′), time during which work stops. *n.*

re·ces·sion (ri sesh′ən), **1** a going backward; moving or sloping backward; withdrawal. **2** period of temporary business reduction. *n.*

rec·om·men·da·tion (rek′ə men dā′shən), **1** act of recommending. **2** words of advice or praise. *n.*

rec·on·cile (rek′ən sīl), make friends again: *The children had quarreled but were soon reconciled. v.,* **rec·on·ciled, rec·on·cil·ing.**

re·cy·cle (rē sī′kəl), to process or treat (something) in order that it may be used again. Paper, aluminum, and glass products are commonly recycled. *v.,* **re·cy·cled, re·cy·cling.**

re·dec·o·rate (rē dek′ə rāt′), decorate again or anew, especially by painting or papering a room, etc. *v.,* **re·dec·o·rat·ed, re·dec·o·rat·ing.**

re·duce (ri düs′ or ri dyüs′), make less; make smaller, decrease: *We have reduced expenses this year. She is trying to reduce her weight. v.,* **re·duced, re·duc·ing.**

re·duc·tion (ri duk′shən), **1** a reducing or a being reduced: *a reduction of ten pounds in weight.* **2** amount by which a thing is reduced: *The reduction in cost was $5.* **3** copy of something on a smaller scale. *n.*

reef (rēf), a narrow ridge of rocks, sand, or coral at or near the surface of the water: *The ship was wrecked on a hidden reef. n., pl.* **reefs.**

ref·er·ence (ref′ər əns), **1** a referring or a being referred. **2** direction of the attention: *The report contained many references to newspaper articles.* **3** statement referred to: *You will find that reference on page 16. n.*

re·flec·tion (ri flek′shən), likeness; image. *n.*

re·frig·e·ra·tor (ri frij′ə rā′tər), box, room, etc., that keeps foods and other items cool, usually by mechanical means. *Please put the produce into the refrigerator. n.*

reg·is·ter (rej′ə stər), have one's name written in a list or record: *Citizens must register before they can vote. v.*

re·la·tion·ship (ri lā′shən ship), **1** connection: *What is the relationship of clouds to rain?* **2** condition of belonging to the same family. *n., pl.* **re·la·tion·ships.**

re·lax·a·tion (rē′lak sā′shən), relief from work or effort; recreation; amusement. *n.*

re·li·a·ble (ri lī′ə bəl), worthy of trust; able to be depended on. *adj.*

a	hat	**ī**	ice	**u̇**	put	**ə**	*stands for*
ā	age	**o**	not	**ü**	rule	**a**	in about
ä	far, calm	**ō**	open	**ch**	child	**e**	in taken
âr	care	**ȯ**	saw	**ng**	long	**i**	in pencil
e	let	**ô**	order	**sh**	she	**o**	in lemon
ē	equal	**oi**	oil	**th**	thin	**u**	in circus
ėr	term	**ou**	out	**ᴛʜ**	then		
i	it	**u**	cup	**zh**	measure		

re·lief (ri lēf´), **1** the lessening of, or freeing from, a pain, burden, difficulty, etc.: *His relief came as the medicine began to work.* **2** something that makes a change or lessens strain. *n.*

re·luc·tant (ri luk´tənt), **1** unwilling; showing unwillingness: *The teacher led the reluctant student to the principal.* **2** slow to act because unwilling: *I am reluctant to go out in very cold weather.* *adj.*

re·me·di·al (ri mē´dē əl), remedying; curing; helping; relieving. *adj.*

rem·e·dy (rem´ə dē), **1** a means of removing or relieving diseases or any bad condition; cure: *Aspirin is used as a remedy for headaches.* **2** put right; make right; cure: *A nap remedied my weariness.* **1** *n.*, *pl.* **rem·e·dies;** **2** *v.*, **rem·e·died, rem·e·dy·ing.**

re·mem·ber (ri mem´bər), **1** call back to mind: *I can't remember that man's name.* **2** have (something) return to the mind: *Then I remembered where I was.* **3** keep in mind as deserving a reward, gift, etc.: *Uncle is remembering us in his will.* *v.*

rem·i·nis·cent (rem´ə nis´nt), **1** recalling past persons, events, etc.: *reminiscent talk.* **2** awakening memories of something else; suggestive: *a manner reminiscent of a statelier age.* *adj.*

re·mod·el (rē mod´l), make over; change or alter. *v.*, **re·mod·eled, re·mod·el·ing** or **re·mod·elled, re·mod·el·ling.**

re·morse·ful (ri môrs´fəl), feeling or expressing remorse. *adj.*

ren·ais·sance (ren´ə säns), a period of new or revived interest in something, such as art or learning. *The Renaissance began in Italy in the 1300s.* *n.*

re·new (ri nü´ *or* ri nyü´), begin again; get again; say, do, or give again. *v.*

re·port (ri pôrt´), an account of something seen, heard, read, done, or considered. *n.*

re·quest (ri kwest´), **1** ask for; ask as a favor: *She requested a loan from the bank.* **2** what is asked for: *He granted my request.* **1** *v.*, **re·quest·ed, re·quest·ing.** **2** *n.*

res·cue (res´kyü), save from danger, capture, harm, etc.; free; deliver: *rescue someone from drowning.* *v.*, **res·cued, res·cu·ing.**

re·search (ri sėrch´ *or* rē´sėrch´), **1** a careful hunting for facts or truth; inquiry; investigation: *cancer research.* **2** to hunt for facts or truth; inquire; investigate. **1** *n.*, *pl.* **re·search·es;** **2** *v.*, **re·searched, re·search·ing.**

re·sent (ri zent´), feel injured and angry at; feel indignation at: *I resented being called lazy.* *v.* **re·sent·ed, re·sent·ing.**

re·side (ri zīd´), live (in or at a place) for a long time; dwell. *This family has resided in our town for 100 years.* *v.*, **re·sid·ed, re·sid·ing.**

re·sign (ri zīn´), give up a job, position, etc.; renounce: *I resigned my position on the school paper.* *v.*, **re·signed, re·sign·ing.**

res·ig·na·tion (rez´ig nā´shən), **1** act of resigning: *There have been two resignations from the committee.* **2** a written statement giving notice that one resigns. *n.*

res·o·lu·tion (rez´ə lü´shən), thing decided on; thing determined: *We made a resolution to get up early.* *n.*

re·solve (ri zolv´), make up one's mind; determine; decide: *I resolved to do better work in the future.* *v.*, **re·solved, re·solv·ing.**

res·pir·a·to·ry (res´ pər ə tôr´ē), the body system that includes the nose, air passages, and lungs. This system helps bring oxygen to the body and removes carbon dioxide from the body. *adj.*

res·tau·rant (res´tər ənt *or* res´tə ränt´), place to buy and eat a meal. *n.* [*Restaurant* was borrowed from French *restaurant*, and can be traced back to Latin *restaurare*, meaning "restore."]

re·triev·al (ri trē´vəl), act of retrieving; recovery. *n.*

re·un·ion (rē yü´nyən), **1** a coming together again: *the reunion of parted friends.* **2** a social gathering of persons who have been separated or who have interests in common. *n.*

re·view (ri vyü´), **1** study again; look at again. **2** a looking back on; survey: *a review of recent events.* **1** *v.*, **2** *n.*

rhom·bus (rom´bəs), parallelogram with equal sides, usually having two obtuse angles and two acute angles. *n.*, *pl.* **rhom·bus·es, rhom·bi** (rom´bī).

Rich•ter scale (rik′tər skāl′), scale that is used to compare the strengths of earthquakes.

ridge (rij), a mountain area located on the ocean floor. *n., pl.* **rid•ges.**

rid•i•cule (rid′ə kyül), laugh at; make fun of: *My neighbor ridicules the design of my garden. v.,* **rid•i•culed, rid•i•cul•ing.**

ri•fle (rī′fəl), **1** gun with spiral grooves in its long barrel which spin or rotate the bullet as it is shot. A rifle is usually fired from the shoulder. **2** to propel (a ball) at high speed 1 *n.,* 2 *v.,* **ri•fled, ri•fling.**

rift (rift), a split; break; crack: *The sun shone through a rift in the clouds. n.*

ring (ring), a thin circle of metal or other material: *a napkin ring, a wedding ring, a key ring. n.*

ro•bot (rō′bot *or* rō′bət), machine with moving parts and sensing devices controlled by a computer. Computer programs enable a robot to carry out complex series of tasks repeatedly, without human supervision. *n., pl.* **ro•bots.** [*Robot* was borrowed from Czech *robot,* which comes from *robota,* meaning "work."]

ro•de•o (rō′dē ō *or* rō dā′ō), **1** a contest or exhibition of skill in roping cattle, riding horses and steers, etc. **2** (in the western United States) the driving of cattle together. *n., pl.* **ro•de•os.** [*Rodeo* was borrowed from Spanish *rodeo,* which comes from *rodear,* meaning "go around," and can be traced back to Latin *rota,* meaning "wheel."]

rol•ler coast•er (rō′lər kō′stər), an amusement park ride consisting of inclined tracks along which small cars roll and make sudden drops and turns.

roll•er-skate (rō′lər skāt′), move on roller skates. *v.,* **roll•er-skat•ed, roll•er-skat•ing.**

Ro•man (rō′mən), of ancient or modern Rome or its people. *adj.*

Ro•man nu•mer•als (rō′mən nü′mər əlz), numerals like XXIII, LVI, and MDCCLX, used by the ancient Romans in numbering. In this system I = 1, V = 5, X = 10, L = 50, C = 100, D = 500, and M = 1000.

rook•ie (ru̇k′ē), INFORMAL. **1** an inexperienced recruit. **2** beginner; novice. **3** a new player on an athletic team, especially a professional baseball player in his first season. *n., pl.* **rook•ies.**

room•mate (rüm′māt′ *or* ru̇m′māt′), person who shares a room with another or others: *I borrowed my roommate's math book. n.*

root beer (rüt′ bir′), a soft drink flavored with the juice of the roots of certain plants, such as sarsaparilla, sassafras, etc.

rope (rōp), a strong, thick line or cord made by twisting smaller cords together. *n.*
know the ropes, INFORMAL. know about a business or activity.
rope in, INFORMAL. get or lead in by tricking.

rough•ly (ruf′lē), **1** in a rough manner. **2** approximately: *From her house to mine is roughly two miles. adv.*

R.S.V.P. or **r.s.v.p.,** please answer. [*R.S.V.P.* stands for French *répondez s'il vous plaît.*]

robot

a **robot** doing one of his jobs

S

sa•fa•ri (sə fär′ē), **1** journey or hunting expedition in eastern Africa. **2** any long trip or expedition. *n., pl.* **sa•fa•ris.** [*Safari* was borrowed from Swahili *safari,* which came from Arabic *safar,* meaning "a journey."]

sale price (sāl′ prīs′), an amount lower than the usual price of an item.

sales tax (sālz′ taks′), tax based on the amount received for articles sold.

rodeo (def. 1)

a	hat	**ī**	ice	**u̇**	put	**ə stands for**	
ā	age	**o**	not	**ü**	rule	**a**	in about
ä	far, calm	**ō**	open	**ch**	child	**e**	in taken
âr	care	**ȯ**	saw	**ng**	long	**i**	in pencil
e	let	**ô**	order	**sh**	she	**o**	in lemon
ē	equal	**oi**	oil	**th**	thin	**u**	in circus
ėr	term	**ou**	out	**ŦH**	then		
i	it	**u**	cup	**zh**	measure		

sandstone

Sandstone is held together by a natural cement.

sand·stone (sand′stōn′), kind of rock formed mostly of sand and used in building. Sandstone is a sedimentary rock. *n.*

sat·el·lite (sat′l īt), an object that circles another object in space. *n.*

sat·is·fy (sat′i sfī), give enough to; fulfill (desires, hopes, demands, etc.); put an end to (needs, wants, etc.): *He satisfied his hunger with a sandwich and milk. v.,* **sat·is·fied, sat·is·fy·ing.**

sauer·kraut (sour′krout′), cabbage cut fine, salted, and allowed to sour. *n.* [*Sauerkraut* is from German *Sauerkraut,* which comes from *sauer,* meaning "sour," and *Kraut,* meaning "cabbage."]

sax·o·phone (sak′sə fōn), a woodwind instrument having a curved metal body with keys for the fingers and a mouthpiece with a single reed. *n.* [*Saxophone* was formed in French from the name of its Belgian inventor, Adolphe *Sax,* 1814–1894, and Greek *phōnē,* meaning "sound."]

scale draw·ing (skāl′ drò′ing), a drawing made so that distances in the drawing are proportional to actual distances.

sca·lene tri·an·gle (skā lēn′ trī′ang′gəl *or* skā′lēn′ trī′ang′gəl), triangle with no congruent sides.

scarf (skärf), a long, broad strip of silk, lace, etc., worn about the neck, shoulders, head, or waist. *n., pl.* **scarfs, scarves** (skärvz).

scen·ic (sē′nik *or* sen′ik), having much fine scenery: *a scenic highway. adj.*

scent (sent), a smell: *The scent of roses filled the air. n.*

sched·ule (skej′ül), **1** a written or printed statement of details; list: *A timetable is a schedule of the coming and going of trains.* **2** to plan or arrange (something) for a definite time or date: *Schedule the convention for the fall.* **1** *n.,* **2** *v.,* **sched·uled, sched·ul·ing.**

schol·ar (skol′ər), **1** a learned person; person having much knowledge: *The professor was a famous scholar.* **2** pupil at school; learner. *n.*

schol·ar·ship (skol′ər ship), money or other aid given to help a student continue his or her studies: *The college offered her a scholarship of one thousand dollars. n.*

scuba

portable breathing equipment for a **scuba** diver

sci·ence (sī′əns), knowledge based on observed facts and tested truths arranged in an orderly system: *the laws of science. n.* [*Science* came into English about 600 years ago from French *science,* which came from Latin *scientia,* meaning "knowledge."]

sci·ence fic·tion (fik′shən), story or novel that combines science and fantasy. Science fiction deals with life in the future, in other galaxies, etc., but makes much use of the latest discoveries of science and technology.

sci·en·tist (sī′ən tist), person who has expert knowledge of some branch of science. Persons specially trained in and familiar with the facts and laws of such fields of knowledge as biology, chemistry, mathematics, physics, geology, and astronomy are scientists. *n.*

scis·sors (siz′ərz), tool or instrument for cutting that has two sharp blades so fastened that their edges slide against each other. *n. pl. or sing.*

scraw·ny (skrò′nē), having little flesh; lean; thin; skinny: *Turkeys have scrawny necks. adj.,* **scraw·ni·er, scraw·ni·est.**

scu·ba (skü′bə), portable equipment for breathing underwater. It consists of one or more tanks of compressed air strapped to the diver's back, a hose and mouthpiece with valves to regulate the air, and a glass face mask. *n.,* [*Scuba* comes from the first letters of the words *self contained underwater breathing apparatus.*]

se·cede (si sēd′), withdraw formally from an organization. *v.,* **se·ced·ed, se·ced·ing.** [*Secede* is from Latin *secedere,* which comes from *se-,* meaning "apart," and *cedere,* meaning "to go."] —**se·ced′er,** *n.*

sec·ond·ar·y source (sek′ən der′ē sôrs′), retelling of an event by someone who was not present at the actual event; textbooks and biographies are examples. *n., pl.* **sec·ond·ar·y sourc·es.**

sed·i·ment (sed′ə mənt), (in geology) earth, stones, etc., deposited by water, wind, or ice: *When glaciers melt, they leave sediment. n.*

sed·i·men·tar·y rock (sed′ə men′tər ē rok′), rock that forms from cemented or pressed sediments.

seis·mic waves (sīz'mik wāvz'), waves caused by an earthquake.

seis·mo·graph (sīz'mə graf), instrument that records the strengths of earthquakes. *n.*

seis·mol·o·gy (sīz mol'ə jē), the scientific study of earthquakes and other movements of the earth's crust. *n.* —**seis·mol'o·gist,** *n.*

seize (sēz), **1** take hold of suddenly; clutch; grasp. **2** take prisoner; arrest; catch. *v.*, **seized, seiz·ing.**

se·lec·tive (si lek'tiv), having the power to choose; selecting. *adj.*

self-con·trol (self'kən trōl'), control of one's actions, feelings, etc. *n.*

Sen·ate (sen'it), a governing or lawmaking assembly. In the Roman Republic, the Senate was made up of members elected by wealthy landowners. *n.*

send (send), cause to be carried: *send a letter, send news. v.,* **sent, send·ing.**

sen·sa·tion·al (sen sā'shə nəl), arousing strong or excited feeling: *The outfielder's sensational catch made the crowd cheer wildly. adj.*

sense (sens), **1** power of an organism to know what happens outside itself. Sight, hearing, touch, taste, and smell are senses. **2** understanding; appreciation: *He has a delightful sense of humor. n.*

sen·si·tive (sen'sə tiv), **1** receiving impressions readily: *The eye is sensitive to light.* **2** easily hurt or offended: *to be sensitive about one's weight. adj.*

sent (sent), past tense and past participle of **send.** *They sent the trunks last week. She was sent on an errand. v.*

sen·tence (sen'təns), **1** group of words that is grammatically complete and expresses a statement, request, command, exclamation, etc. **2** pronounce punishment on: *The judge sentenced her to a year in prison.* **1** *n.,* **2** *v.,* **sen·tenced, sen·tenc·ing.**

sep·a·rate (sep'ə rāt' *for 1;* sep'ər it *for 2*), **1** keep apart; be between; divide: *The Atlantic Ocean separates America from Europe.* **2** divided; not joined: *separate seats, separate questions.* **1** *v.,* **sep·a·rat·ed, sep·a·rat·ing;** **2** *adj.*

serf (sėrf), (in the Middle Ages) one of the poorest peasants, who lived almost as a slave. *n., pl.* **serfs.**

ser·i·al (sir'ē əl), of a series; arranged in a series; making a series. *Place volumes 1 to 5 on the shelf in serial order. adj.*

serv·ice (sėr'vis), **1** manner of serving food or the food served: *The service in this restaurant is excellent.* **2** set of dishes, etc.: *a solid silver tea service. n.*

sew·er (sü'ər), an underground pipe or channel for carrying off waste water and refuse. *n.*

she'd (shēd; *unstressed* shid), **1** she had. **2** she would.

shelf (shelf), a thin, flat piece of wood, metal, stone, etc., fastened to a wall or frame to hold things, such as books, dishes, etc. *n., pl.* **shelves** (shelvz).

sher·iff (sher'if), the most important law-enforcing officer of a county. A sheriff appoints deputies who help to keep order in the county. *n., pl.* **sher·iffs.**

shield (shēld), **1** piece of armor carried on the arm to protect the body in battle. **2** be a shield to; protect; defend: *They shielded me from unjust punishment.* **1** *n.,* **2** *v.* **shield·ed, shield·ing.**

shrap·nel (shrap'nəl), shell filled with fragments of metal and powder, set to explode in midair and scatter the fragments over a wide area. *n.* [*Shrapnel* was named for Henry Shrapnel, 1761–1842, a British army officer who invented it.]

shut·out (shut'out'), the defeat of a team without allowing it to score. *n.*

sib·ling (sib'ling), brother or sister. An only child has no siblings. *n., pl.* **sib·lings.**

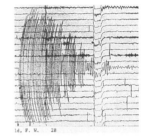

seismograph

a record made by a

seismograph

a	hat	**ī**	ice	**u̇**	put	**ə** *stands for*	
ā	age	**o**	not	**ü**	rule	**a**	in about
ä	far, calm	**ō**	open	**ch**	child	**e**	in taken
âr	care	**ȯ**	saw	**ng**	long	**i**	in pencil
e	let	**ô**	order	**sh**	she	**o**	in lemon
ē	equal	**oi**	oil	**th**	thin	**u**	in circus
ėr	term	**ou**	out	**ᵺ**	then		
i	it	**u**	cup	**zh**	measure		

skateboard

solar eclipse

side·burns (sīd/bėrnz/), whiskers in front of the ears, especially when the chin is shaved. *n. pl.* [*Sideburns* is a different form of *burnsides*, which were named for Ambrose E. Burnside, 1824–1881, a Union general in the Civil War, who wore such whiskers.]

side·line (sīd/līn/), **1** line that marks the limit of play on the side of the field in football, etc. **2** sidelines, *pl.* space just outside these lines: *watch a game from the sidelines. n., pl.* **side·lines.**

sig·nif·i·cance (sig nif/ə kəns), **1** importance; consequence: *The President wanted to see him on a matter of significance.* **2** meaning: *She did not understand the significance of my nod. n.*

sil·ver-tongued (sil/vər tungd/), eloquent. *adj.*

sim·i·lar (sim/ə lər), much the same; alike; like. *adj.* —**sim/i·lar·ly,** *adv.*

sim·i·lar fig·ures (sim/ə lər fig/yərz), figures with the same shape but not necessarily the same size.

sim·i·le (sim/ə lē/), a statement that one thing is like another. EXAMPLES: *a face like marble, as brave as a lion. n.*

since (sins), **1** from a past time till now. **2** after the time that; from the time when. **1** *prep.,* **2** *conj.*

sin·gle (sing/gəl), **1** one and no more; only one: *Please give me a single piece of paper.* **2** pick from among others: *The teacher singled us out for praise.* **3** in baseball: **a** a hit that allows the batter to reach first base only. **b** make such a hit. **1** *adj.,* **3a** *n.,* **2,3b** *v.,* **sin·gled, sin·gling.**

Synonym Study *adj.* **1** **Single, sole, only** mean one alone. **Single** emphasizes one and no more: *She buys a single new dress each year.* **Sole** emphasizes being by itself, the only one there is: *My sole purpose is to help you.* **Only** emphasizes being one of a class of which it is the best or the single representative: *She is the only gymnast in the meet to win two events.*

si·nus·i·tis (sī/nə sī/tis), a disease in which the sinus openings become blocked. *n.*

site (sīt), position or place (of anything); location: *The site for the new school has not yet been chosen. n.*

sit·u·a·tion (sich/ü ā/shən), circumstances; case; condition. *n.*

skate·board (skāt/bôrd/), a narrow board resembling a surfboard, with roller-skate wheels attached to each end, used for gliding or moving on any hard surface. *n.*

ski (skē), glide over the snow on skis. *v.,* **skied, ski·ing.** [*Ski* was borrowed from Norwegian *ski.*]

slen·der (slen/dər), long and thin; not big around; slim: *a slender child. adj.*

slo·gan (slō/gən), word or phrase used by a business, club, political party, etc., to advertise. *n.*

smog (smog), mixture of smoke and fog in the air: *Automobile exhaust fumes were blamed as one of the major causes of smog. n.* [*Smog* is a blend of *smoke* and *fog.*]

smooth (smüŦH), **1** having an even surface, like glass, silk, or still water; flat; level: *smooth stones.* **2** make smooth or smoother; make flat, even, or level: *Smooth this dress with a hot iron.* **3** in a smooth manner. **1** *adj.,* **2** *v.,* **3** *adv.*

snick·er (snik/ər), **1** a half-suppressed and often disrespectful laugh; sly or silly laugh; giggle. **2** laugh in this way. **1** *n.,* **2** *v.,* **snick·ered, snick·er·ing.**

so·cial (sō/shəl), **1** of or dealing with human beings in their relations to each other; having to do with the life of human beings in a community or society. **2** living, or liking to live, with others: *People are social beings.* **3** for companionship or friendliness; having to do with companionship or friendliness. *adj.* [*Social* is from Latin *socialis,* which comes from *socius,* meaning "companion."]

so·lar e·clipse (sō/lər i klips/), when the moon passes between the sun and the earth.

so·lar flare (sō/lər flâr/), powerful eruptions of very hot gases from the sun.

so·lar sys·tem (sō/lər sis/təm), the sun and all the planets, satellites, comets, etc., that revolve around it.

so·lar wind (sō/lər wind), the expanding corona.

sol·dier (sōl/jər), person who serves in an army. *n.*

sole (sōl), one and only; single: *He was the sole heir to the fortune when his aunt died. adj.*

sol·emn (sol′əm), **1** serious; grave; earnest. **2** causing serious or grave thoughts: *The organ played solemn music.* **3** done with form and ceremony: *a solemn procession.* **4** connected with religion; sacred. **5** gloomy; dark; somber in color. *adj.* —**sol′emn·ly,** *adv.*

so·lo (sō′lō), piece of music for one voice or instrument: *She sang three solos. n., pl.* **so·los.** [*Solo* comes from Italian *solo,* meaning "alone."]

so·lu·tion (sə lü′shən), **1** the solving of a problem. **2** explanation: *The police are seeking a solution of the crime.* **3** mixture formed by combining a solid, liquid, or gas with another solid, liquid, or gas: *Salt and water form a solution. n.*

some·thing (sum′thing), some thing; a particular thing not named or known: *have something on one's mind. n.*

some times (sum′ tīmz′), certain or particular times: *Some times are more fun than others.*

some·times (sum′tīmz), now and then; at times: *She comes to visit sometimes. adv.*

so·nar (sō′när), device for finding the depth of water or for detecting and locating underwater objects. Sonar sends sound waves into water, which return when they strike the bottom or any object. *n.* [*Sonar* comes from the words *sound navigation ranging.*]

soph·o·more (sof′ə môr), student in the second year of high school or college. *n.*

spar·kling (spär′kling), shining; glittering: *sparkling stars. adj.*

sphinx (sfingks), statue of a lion's body with the head of a man, ram, or hawk. There are many sphinxes in Egypt. The **Great Sphinx** is a huge statue near Cairo, with a man's head and a lion's body. *n., pl.* **sphinx·es.**

spread·ing bound·ar·y (spred′ing boun′dər ē), an area where two geological plates are moving away from one another.

sta·di·um (stā′dē əm), an oval, U-shaped, or round building, usually without a roof. Tiers of seats for spectators surround the playing field. *n.*

staff (staf), group assisting a chief; group of employees: *Our school has a staff of twenty teachers. n., pl.* **staffs.**

stag·ger (stag′ər), **1** sway or reel (from weakness, a heavy load, or drunkenness): *I staggered and fell while trying to carry too many books.* **2** a swaying or reeling: *The hunting dog was staggering after the chase.* **1** *v.,* **2** *n.*

starch (stärch), **1** a white, tasteless food substance. Potatoes, wheat, rice, and corn contain much starch. **2** stiffen (clothes, curtains, etc.) with starch: *starch curtains.* **1** *n.,* **2** *v.*

sta·tion·ar·y front (stā′shə ner′ē frunt′), boundary between the leading edges of a warm and a cold air mass, neither of which is moving.

steal (stēl), (in baseball) run to (second base, third base, or home plate) as the pitcher throws the ball to the catcher. *v.,* **stole** (stōl), **sto·len, steal·ing.**

ster·e·o (ster′ē ō or stir′ē ō), stereophonic equipment. *n., pl.* **ster·e·os.**

ster·e·o·type (ster′ē ə tīp′ or stir′ē ə tīp′), a fixed form, character, image, etc.; something stereotyped; conventional type. *n., pl.* **ster·e·o·types.**

straight (strāt), **1** without a bend or curve; not crooked or irregular: *a straight line, a straight path, a straight nose, straight hair.* **2** frankly; honestly; uprightly: *Live straight.* **1** *adj.,* **2** *adv.*

sphinx

a **sphinx** near an oasis

a	hat	ī	ice	u̇	put		ə *stands for*		
ā	age	o	not	ü	rule		a	in about
ä	far, calm	ō	open	ch	child		e	in taken
âr	care	ȯ	saw	ng	long		i	in pencil
e	let	ô	order	sh	she		o	in lemon
ē	equal	oi	oil	th	thin		u	in circus
ėr	term	ou	out	ᵺ	then			
i	it	u	cup	zh	measure			

strat·o·sphere (strat′ə sfir), region of the atmosphere between the troposphere and the mesosphere, which extends from about 5 to 40 miles (8 to 64 kilometers) above the earth's surface. *n.*

strength (strengkth), quality of being strong; power; force; vigor: *I do not have the strength to lift that heavy box. n., pl.* **strengths.**

stress (stres), the body's physical and mental reactions to demanding situations. *n.*

strict (strikt), harsh; severe: *a strict parent, strict discipline. adj.*

stub·born (stub′ərn), **1** fixed in purpose or opinion; not giving in to argument or requests: *The stubborn child refused to listen to reasons for not going out in the rain.* **2** hard to deal with or manage: *a stubborn cough. adj.*

stu·di·o (stü′dē ō *or* styü′dē ō), workroom of a painter, sculptor, photographer, etc. *n., pl.* **stu·di·os.**

sub·duct·ed plate (səb duk′tid plāt′), a portion of the earth's crust sliding under another portion of the earth's crust.

sub·mers·i·ble (səb mėr′sə bəl), a submarine. *n., pl.* **sub·mers·i·bles.**

sub·tle (sut′l), not obvious; delicate; fine: *a subtle odor of perfume. Subtle humor is often hard to understand. adj.,* **sub·tler, sub·tlest.**

suc·co·tash (suk′ə tash), kernels of sweet corn and beans, usually lima beans, cooked together. *n.* [*Succotash* comes from Narragansett Indian *msiquatash.*]

sug·ges·tion (səg jes′chən), thing suggested; proposal: *The picnic was an excellent suggestion. n.*

sum·mer·time (sum′ər tīm′), the summer season. *n.*

sun·spot (sun′spot′), dark region on the sun's surface. *n., pl.* **sun·spots.**

sur·plus (sėr′pləs *or* sėr′plus), amount over and above what is needed; extra quantity left over; excess: *The bank keeps a large surplus of money in reserve. n.*

sur·rep·ti·tious (sėr′əp tish′əs), secret and unauthorized. *adj.*

sus·cep·ti·ble (sə sep′tə bəl), easily influenced by feelings or emotions; very sensitive: *Poetry appealed to his susceptible nature. adj.*

studio

posing in a photo

studio

sus·pi·cious (sə spish′əs), causing one to suspect: *a suspicious manner. adj.*

SWAT *or* **S.W.A.T.** (swät), Special Weapons and Tactics (a specially trained section of police). *n.*

sweat·shirt (swet′shėrt′), a heavy pullover with long sleeves, sometimes with a fleece lining, worn especially by athletes to keep warm before and after exercise. *n.*

swim (swim), move along on or in the water by using arms, legs, fins, etc.: *Fish swim. Most boys and girls like to swim. v.,* **swam** (swam), **swum** (swum), **swim·ming.**

sword (sôrd), weapon, usually metal, with a long, sharp blade fixed in a handle or hilt. *n.*

sym·pho·ny (sim′fə nē), an elaborate musical composition for an orchestra. A symphony usually has three or more movements in different rhythms but related keys. *n., pl.* **sym·pho·nies.**

syn·o·nym (sin′ə nim), word that means the same or nearly the same as another word. "Keen" is a synonym of "sharp." *n., pl.* **syn·o·nyms.**

sys·tem (sis′təm), an orderly way of getting things done: *They work by a system, not by chance. n., pl.* **sys·tems.**

all systems go, everything is entirely ready to start working: *Everything at the space center signaled all systems go.*

T

tape re·cord·er (tāp′ ri kôr′dər), machine that records sound magnetically on plastic tape and plays the sound back after it is recorded.

tar pit (tär′ pit′), a hidden hole with a thick, black, sticky substance inside it. Remains can be preserved here over time.

team·mate (tēm′māt′), a fellow member of a team. *n.*

tech·nol·o·gy (tek nol′ə jē), science of the mechanical and industrial arts: *I studied engineering at a school of technology. n.*

teen·age *or* **teen-age** (tēn′āj′), of or for a teenager or teenagers: *a teenage club. adj.*

tel·e·cast (tel′ə kast′), a television broadcast. *n.*

tel·e·com·mu·ni·ca·tion (tel′ə kə myü′nə kā′shən), the electrical and electronic transmission of messages, as by radio, telephone, television, satellite, etc. *The telecommunication of the results of the election was received in Japan immediately.* *n.*

tel·e·gram (tel′ə gram), message sent by telegraph: *receive a telegram.* *n.*

tel·e·graph (tel′ə graf), device used for sending coded messages over wires by means of electrical impulses. *n.*

tel·e·phone (tel′ə fōn), 1 apparatus, system, or process for sending sound or speech to a distant point over wires by means of electrical impulses. 2 make a telephone call to. 1 *n.,* 2 *v.,* **tel·e·phoned, tel·e·phon·ing.**

tel·e·scope (tel′ə skōp), instrument for making distant objects appear nearer and larger. The stars are studied by means of telescopes. *n.* [*Telescope* comes from Greek *tēle,* meaning "far," and *skopein,* meaning "look at."]

tel·e·vi·sion (tel′ə vizh′ən), process of sending and receiving images and sounds over wires or through the air by means of electrical impulses. Waves of light and sound are changed into electrical waves and transmitted to a receiver where they are changed back into waves of light and sound to be seen and heard. *n.*

tem·per·a·men·tal (tem′pər ə men′tl), subject to moods and whims; easily irritated; sensitive: *A temperamental person can be hard to live with.* *adj.*

tem·per·a·ture (tem′pər ə chər), 1 degree of heat or cold. 2 a body temperature higher than normal (98.6 degrees Fahrenheit or 37.0 degrees Celsius); fever. *n.*

tem·ple (tem′pəl), building used for the service or worship of a god or gods. *n.*

Ten·nes·see (ten′ə sē′), one of the south central states of the United States. *Abbreviation:* Tenn. or TN *Capital:* Nashville. *n.*

tense (tens), 1 stretched tight; strained to stiffness: *a tense rope, a face tense with pain.* 2 stretch tight; stiffen: *She tensed her muscles for the leap.* 1 *adj.,* **tens·er, tens·est;** 2 *v.,* **tensed, tens·ing.** [*Tense* is from Latin *tensum,* which comes from *tendere,* meaning "to stretch."]

ten·sion (ten′shən), 1 a stretching. 2 a stretched condition: *The tension of the bow gives speed to the arrow.* 3 mental or nervous strain: *Overwork sometimes causes tension.* *n.* [*Tension* comes from Latin *tensionem,* which came in turn from *tendere,* meaning "to stretch."]

term (tėrm), numerator or denominator in a fraction. *n.*

ter·race (ter′is), a flat, raised level of land with vertical or sloping sides, especially one of a series of such levels placed one above the other. *n., pl.* **ter·races.**

that's (ᴛʜats), that is.

their (ᴛʜâr), of them; belonging to them: *I like their house and the colorful garden.* *adj.*

them·selves (ᴛʜem selvz′ or ᴛʜəm selvz′), form used instead of *them* in cases like: *They speak for themselves. They hurt themselves sledding down the hill.* *pron.*

then (ᴛʜen), at that time: *Father talked of his childhood, and recalled that prices were lower then.* *adv.*

ther·a·pist (ther′ə pist), person who specializes in some form of therapy. *n.*

there (ᴛʜâr; *unstressed* ᴛʜər), 1 in or at that place: *Sit there. Finish reading the page and stop there.* 2 that place: *We go to New York and from there to Boston.* *adv.*

there·fore (ᴛʜâr′fôr), for that reason; as a result of that. *adv.*

there's (ᴛʜârz), there is.

telescope
viewing through a
telescope

temperature (def. 1)
temperature on the
thermometer

a	hat	**ī**	ice	**u̇**	put	**ə** <u>stands for</u>	
ā	age	**o**	not	**ü**	rule	**a**	in about
ä	far, calm	**ō**	open	**ch**	child	**e**	in taken
âr	care	**ȯ**	saw	**ng**	long	**i**	in pencil
e	let	**ô**	order	**sh**	she	**o**	in lemon
ē	equal	**oi**	oil	**th**	thin	**u**	in circus
ėr	term	**ou**	out	**ᴛʜ**	then		
i	it	**u**	cup	**zh**	measure		

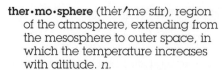

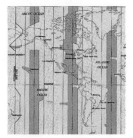

time zone

The United States has six

standard **time zones.**

ther·mo·sphere (ther′mə sfir), region of the atmosphere, extending from the mesosphere to outer space, in which the temperature increases with altitude. *n.*

the·sau·rus (thi sôr′əs), **1** dictionary in which synonyms, antonyms, and other related words are classified under certain headings. **2** any dictionary, encyclopedia, or other book of information. *n., pl.* **the·sau·rus·es, the·sau·ri** (thi sôr′ī).

they (ᴛʜā), the persons, animals, things, or ideas spoken about. *pron. pl.*

they'd (ᴛʜād), **1** they had. **2** they would.

they're (ᴛʜâr), they are.

thief (thēf), person who steals, especially one who steals secretly and usually without using force: *A thief stole my bicycle from the yard. n., pl.* **thieves** (thēvz).

thir·teen (ther′tēn′), three more than ten; 13. *n., adj.*

thor·ough (ther′ō), being all that is needed; complete: *Please make a thorough search for the lost money. adj.*

thou·sand (thou′znd), ten hundred; 1000. *n., adj.*

thrill (thril), **1** give a shivering, exciting feeling to: *Stories of adventure thrilled him.* **2** have a shivering, exciting feeling: *The children thrilled at the sight of their presents. v.*

through (thrü), **1** from end to end of; from side to side of; between the parts of; from beginning to end of: *march through a town, cut a tunnel through a mountain, drive through a snowstorm.* **2** having reached the end; finished: *I am almost through.* **1** *prep.,* **2** *adj.* Also, **thro, thro′,** or **thru.**

thun·der·storm (thun′dər stôrm′), storm with thunder and lightning. *n.*

tick·le (tik′əl), touch lightly, causing little thrills, shivers, or wriggles: *He tickled the baby's feet and made her laugh. v.,* **tick·led, tick·ling.**

time ma·chine (tīm′ mə shēn′), a fictional device that would convey one to the past or the future.

time zone (tīm′ zōn′), a geographical region within which the same standard time is used. The world is divided into 24 time zones, beginning and ending at the International Date Line.

tis·sue (tish′ü), **1** tissue paper. **2** a thin, soft paper that absorbs moisture easily. Tissue is used to wipe the face or the nose. *n.*

to (tü; *unstressed* tù *or* tə), **1** in the direction of. **2** as far as; until: *rotten to the core. prep.*

to·bog·gan (tə bog′ən), **1** a long, narrow, flat sled, without runners, with its front end curved upward. **2** slide downhill on such a sled. **1** *n.,* **2** *v.* [*Toboggan* comes from French Canadian *tabagane,* which is of Algonquian origin.]

to·geth·er (tə geᴛʜ′ər), with each other; in company. *adv.*

to·ma·to (tə mā′tō *or* tə mä′tō), a juicy, slightly acid, red or yellow fruit, eaten as a vegetable. Tomatoes grow on a spreading, strong-smelling plant with hairy leaves and stems and yellow flowers. *n., pl.* **to·ma·toes.** [*Tomato* is from Spanish *tomate,* which came from Nahuatl *tomatl.*]

tomb (tüm), grave, vault, mausoleum, etc., for a dead body, often above ground. *n.*

to·mor·row *or* **to-mor·row** (tə môr′ō), **1** the day after today. **2** on the day after today. **1** *n.,* **2** *adv.*

tone (tōn), manner of speaking or writing: *We disliked their disrespectful tone. n.*

tongue (tung), **1** the movable fleshy organ in the mouth. The tongue is used in tasting and, by people, for talking. **2** the language of a people: *the English tongue.* **3** something shaped or used like a tongue: *Tongues of flame leaped from the fire.* **4** the strip of leather under the laces of a shoe. *n.*

to·night *or* **to-night** (tə nīt′), **1** the night of this day; this night: *I am going to bed early tonight.* **2** on or during this night: *Do you think it will snow tonight?* **1** *n.,* **2** *adv.*

too (tü), **1** in addition; also; besides. **2** beyond what is desirable, proper, or right; more than enough. *adv.*

tor·na·do (tôr nā′dō), a violent, funnel-shaped cloud with extremely strong winds. *n.,* **tor·na·does** *or* **tor·na·dos.**

tour·na·ment (ter′nə mənt *or* tùr′nə mənt), a medieval contest between two groups of knights on horseback who fought for a prize. *n.*

to·ward (tôrd *or* tə wôrd′), in the direction of: *She walked toward the north. prep.*

toboggan (def. 1)

tow·el (tou′əl), piece of cloth or paper for wiping and drying something wet. *n.*
  throw in the towel, INFORMAL. admit defeat; surrender.

trac·tor (trak′tər), a heavy, motor-driven vehicle which moves on wheels or on two endless tracks, used for pulling wagons, plows, etc., along roads or over fields. *n.* [*Tractor* is from Latin *tractus,* meaning "drawn, pulled," which comes from *trahere,* meaning "to drag."]

tra·di·tion (trə dish′ən), the handing down of beliefs, opinions, customs, stories, etc., from parents to children. *n.*

tra·di·tion·al (trə dish′ə nəl), according to tradition: *traditional furniture. adj.*

trans·port (tran spôrt′), carry from one place to another: *Wheat is transported from the farms to the mills. v.*

trap·e·zoid (trap′ə zoid), a four-sided plane figure having two sides parallel and two sides not parallel. *n.*

trem·ble (trem′bəl), **1** shake because of fear, excitement, weakness, cold, etc. **2** move gently: *The leaves trembled in the breeze.* **3** a trembling: *There was a tremble in her voice as she began to recite.* 1,2 *v.,* **trem·bled, trem·bling;** 3 *n.*

tre·men·dous (tri men′dəs), **1** very severe; dreadful; awful: *The army suffered a tremendous defeat.* **2** INFORMAL. very great; enormous: *That is a tremendous house for a family of three. adj.*

trench (trench), a long, narrow depression in the ocean floor. *n., pl.* **trench·es.**

tri·al (trī′əl), attempts to do something; efforts. *n., pl.* **tri·als.**

tri·cy·cle (trī′sə kəl *or* trī′sik′əl), vehicle having three wheels, worked by pedals. *n.*

trop·o·sphere (trop′ə sfir), region of the atmosphere between the earth and the stratosphere, extending to about 13 miles (21 kilometers) above the earth's surface. Most cloud formations occur in the troposphere. *n.*

trust·wor·thy (trust′wėr′ᵺē), able to be depended on; reliable: *a trustworthy person. adj.*

tsu·na·mi (sü nä′mē *or* tsü nä′mē), an oceanic tidal wave caused by a submarine earthquake. *n.*

tu·na (tü′nə), a large sea fish closely related to the mackerel, having coarse, oily flesh that is widely used as food; tunny. *n., pl.* **tu·nas** *or* **tu·na.** [*Tuna* comes from Spanish *atún,* and can be traced back to Arabic *tūn.*]

tun·nel (tun′l), an underground passage: *Motor traffic passes under the river through a tunnel. n.*

tur·tle·neck (tėr′tl nek′), a round, high, closely fitting collar on a sweater, etc., usually worn turned down over itself: *My turtleneck will keep my stiff neck warm. n.*

TV, television.

twelfth (twelfth), next after the 11th; last in a series of 12. *adj., n.*

twit·ter (twit′ər), **1** sound made by birds; chirping. **2** make such a sound: *Birds begin to twitter just before sunrise.* 1 *n.,* 2 *v.,* **twit·tered, twit·ter·ing.**

towel
folded bath **towels**

U

u·ku·le·le (yü′kə lā′lē), a small guitar having four strings. *n.* [*Ukulele* comes from Hawaiian *ukulele,* which originally meant "leaping flea."]

un·ac·cept·a·ble (un′ak sep′tə bəl), not acceptable; not agreeable. *adj.*

un·buck·le (un buk′əl), unfasten the buckle or buckles of. *v.,* **un·buck·led, un·buck·ling.**

a	hat	**ī**	ice	**u̇**	put	**ə** stands for	
ā	age	**o**	not	**ü**	rule	**a**	in about
ä	far, calm	**ō**	open	**ch**	child	**e**	in taken
âr	care	**ȯ**	saw	**ng**	long	**i**	in pencil
e	let	**ô**	order	**sh**	she	**o**	in lemon
ē	equal	**oi**	oil	**th**	thin	**u**	in circus
ėr	term	**ou**	out	**ᵺ**	then		
i	it	**u**	cup	**zh**	measure		

un·der·a·chiev·er (un′dər ə chē′vər), a student who fails to work at his or her level of ability. *n.*

un·der·cov·er (un′dər kuv′ər), working or done in secret. *adj.*

un·der·foot (un′dər fut′), **1** under one's foot or feet; on the ground; underneath. **2** in the way: *The cat is always underfoot when I'm cooking a meal. adv.*

un·der·ground (un′dər ground′ for 1; un′dər ground′ for 2), **1** beneath the surface of the ground: *The mole burrowed underground.* **2** being, working, or used beneath the surface of the ground: *an underground passage.* 1 *adv.,* 2 *adj.*

un·der·neath (un′dər nēth′), beneath; below; under: *They sat underneath a tree* (prep.). *Someone was pushing underneath* (adv.). *prep., adv.*

un·der·nour·ished (un′dər nėr′isht), not sufficiently nourished or nurtured. *adj.*

un·der·stand (un′dər stand′), **1** get the meaning of: *Now I understand the teacher's question.* **2** get the meaning: *I have told her three times, but she still doesn't understand.* **3** know how to deal with; know well; know. *v.,* **un·der·stood** (un′dər stud′), **un·der·stand·ing.**

un·der·wa·ter (un′dər wô′tər or un′dər wot′ər), **1** below the surface of the water: *an underwater current* (adj.), *to swim underwater* (adv.). **2** made for use under the water: *A submarine is an underwater boat.* 1,2 *adj.,* 1 *adv.*

un·der·weight (un′dər wāt′), **1** having too little weight; below the normal or required weight. **2** weight that is not up to standard. 1 *adj.,* 2 *n.*

un·doubt·ed·ly (un dou′tid lē), beyond doubt; certainly. *adv.*

un·ex·pect·ed·ly (un′ek spek′tid lē), without being expected; in a way that is not expected; suddenly. *adv.*

u·ni·cy·cle (yü′nə sī′kəl), vehicle made up of a frame mounted on a single wheel, propelled by pedaling, used especially by acrobats, circus performers, etc. *n.*

u·ni·form (yü′nə fôrm), the distinctive clothes worn by members of a group when on duty, by which they may be recognized as belonging to that group. *n.*

uniform

police officers in **uniform** at attention

u·ni·fy (yü′nə fī), make or form into one; unite: *Several small states were unified into one nation. v.,* **u·ni·fied, u·ni·fy·ing.**

u·ni·lat·er·al (yü′nə lat′ər əl), of, on, or affecting one side only: *unilateral disarmament. adj.*

un·ion (yü′nyən), group of workers joined together to protect and promote their interests; labor union or trade union. *n.*

u·nique (yü nēk′), INFORMAL. very uncommon or unusual; rare; remarkable: *a rather unique idea. adj.* [*Unique* was borrowed from French *unique,* and can be traced back to Latin *unus,* meaning "one."]

u·ni·son (yü′nə sən), agreement in pitch of two or more tones, voices, etc.; a sounding together at the same pitch. *n.*

u·nite (yü nīt′), join together; make one; become one; combine: *The businesses united to form one company. v.,* **u·nit·ed, u·nit·ing.**

U·nit·ed States (yu nī′tid stāts′), country in North America composed of 50 states and the District of Columbia. It extends from the Atlantic to the Pacific and from the Gulf of Mexico to Canada. *Capital:* Washington, D.C.

u·ni·ty (yü′nə tē), **1** a being united; oneness: *The group's unity of purpose helped it get results.* **2** harmony: *work together in unity. n., pl.* **u·ni·ties.** [*Unity* came into English about 700 years ago from French *unité,* and can be traced back to Latin *unus,* meaning "one."]

u·ni·ver·sal (yü′nə vėr′səl), **1** of all; belonging to all; concerning all: *Food is a universal need.* **2** existing everywhere: *The law of gravity is universal. adj.*

u·ni·verse (yü′nə vėrs′), the whole of existing things; everything there is, including all space and matter; the cosmos. *Our world is but a small part of the universe. n.*

un·nec·es·sar·i·ly (un nes′ə ser′ə lē), in an unnecessary manner; needlessly: *The roses were unnecessarily cut by the gardener. adv.*

un·pro·duc·tive (un′prə duk′tiv), not producing much; not fertile: *an unproductive farm, an unproductive writer. adj.*

un·til (un til′), up to the time when: *We waited until dawn. conj.*

un·u·su·al (un yü′zhü əl), not usual; not ordinary; not in common use; uncommon; rare. *adj.*

un·wield·y (un wēl′dē), hard to handle or manage because of size, shape, or weight; bulky and clumsy: *a large, unwieldy package. adj.*

un·writ·ten (un rit′n), understood or customary, but not actually expressed in writing: *an unwritten law. adj.*

ur·ban (ėr′bən), **1** of cities or towns: *an urban district, urban planning.* **2** characteristic of cities: *urban life. adj.* [*Urban* is from Latin *urbanus,* which comes from *urbs,* meaning "city."]

u·su·al·ly (yü′zhü ə lē), according to what is usual; commonly; ordinarily; customarily: *We usually eat dinner at 6:00. adv.*

u·to·pi·a or **U·to·pi·a** (yü tō′pē ə), an ideal place or condition; a perfect place or way to live: *This island seems like a utopia. n.*

V

vac·ci·na·tion (vak′sə nā′shən), act or process of vaccinating: *Vaccination has made smallpox a very rare disease. n.*

vague (vāg), not definite; not clear; not distinct. *adj.,* **va·guer, va·guest.**

val·u·a·ble (val′yü ə bəl or val′yə bəl), having value; being worth something: *valuable information, a valuable friend. adj.*

val·ue (val′yü), the real worth; proper price. *n.*

va·nil·la (və nil′ə), a flavoring extract made from the bean of a tropical climbing plant. It is used in candy, ice cream, etc. *n.* [*Vanilla* comes from Spanish *vainilla,* meaning "little pod."]

van·ish (van′ish), disappear, especially suddenly: *The sun vanished behind a cloud. v.,* **van·ished, van·ish·ing.**

va·ri·e·ty (və rī′ə tē), number of different kinds. *This shop has a variety of toys. n., pl.* **va·ri·e·ties.**

vas·sal (vas′əl), (in the feudal system) a person who held land from a lord or superior, to whom in return he gave help in war or some other service. *n., pl.* **vas·sals.**

veg·e·ta·ble (vej′ə tə bəl), **1** plant whose fruit, seeds, leaves, roots, or other parts are used for food. Peas, corn, lettuce, and beets are vegetables. **2** of or like plants: *the vegetable kingdom, vegetable life.* **1** *n.,* **2** *adj.* [*Vegetable* is from Latin *vegetabilis,* meaning "refreshing," and can be traced back to *vegetus,* meaning "vigorous."]

ver·tex (vėr′teks), **1** point opposite the base of a triangle, pyramid, etc. **2** the point where the two sides of an angle meet. *n., pl.* **ver·tex·es, ver·ti·ces** (vėr′tə sēz).

vet (vet), INFORMAL. **1** veterinarian. **2** veteran. *n.*

vi·a·duct (vī′ə dukt), bridge for carrying a road or railroad over a valley, a part of a city, etc. *n.*

vice-pres·i·dent (vīs′prez′ə dənt), officer next in rank to the president, who takes the president's place when necessary. If the President of the U.S. dies or resigns, the Vice-President becomes President. *n.*

view·point (vyü′point′), attitude of mind. *n.*

VIP or **V.I.P.,** INFORMAL. very important person.

vi·rus (vī′rəs), any of a group of disease-producing substances composed of protein and nucleic acid. Viruses cause rabies, polio, chicken pox, the common cold, and many other diseases. They are so small that they cannot be seen through most microscopes. *n., pl.* **vi·rus·es.** [*Virus* comes from Latin *virus,* meaning "poison."]

vegetable (def. 1)
vegetables on display

a	hat	**ī**	ice	**u̇**	put		**ə** _stands for_	
ā	age	**o**	not	**ü**	rule		**a**	in about
ä	far, calm	**ō**	open	**ch**	child		**e**	in taken
âr	care	**ȯ**	saw	**ng**	long		**i**	in pencil
e	let	**ô**	order	**sh**	she		**o**	in lemon
ē	equal	**oi**	oil	**th**	thin		**u**	in circus
ėr	term	**ou**	out	**ᵀH**	then			
i	it	**u**	cup	**zh**	measure			

wharf

a **wharf** in Hong Kong

wolf

Wolves are related to the dog.

---

vi·ta·min (vī′tə mən), a group of nutrients needed in small amounts to keep the body working properly. *n., pl.* **vi·ta·mins.**

vol·ca·no (vol kā′nō), **1** an opening in the earth's crust through which steam, ashes, and lava are forced out in periods of activity. **2** a cone-shaped hill or mountain around this opening, built up of the material that is forced out. *n., pl.* **vol·ca·noes** or **vol·ca·nos.** [*Volcano* was borrowed from Italian *volcano,* which came from Latin *Vulcanus,* meaning "Vulcan."]

W

waltz (wȯlts), a smooth, even, gliding dance with three beats to a measure. *n., pl.* **waltz·es** [*Waltz* is from German *Walzer,* which comes from *walzen,* meaning "to roll, dance."]

want (wänt *or* wȯnt), wish for; wish: *I want to become an engineer. v.*

warm-blood·ed (wôrm′blud′id), having blood that stays about the same temperature regardless of the air or water around the animal. Birds and mammals are warm-blooded. *adj.*

warm front (wôrm′ frunt′), the advancing edge of a warm air mass as it passes over and displaces a cooler one.

wa·ter (wȯ′tər *or* wot′ər), the liquid that constitutes rain, oceans, rivers, lakes, and ponds. *n.*
    back water, 1 make a boat go backward. **2** retreat; withdraw.
    in deep water, in trouble, difficulty, or distress.

wa·ter·front (wȯ′tər frunt′ *or* wot′ər frunt′), land at the water's edge, especially the part of a city beside a river, lake, or harbor. *n.*

wa·ter·logged (wȯ′tər lȯgd′ *or* wot′ər lȯgd′), so full of water that it will barely float. *adj.*

wa·ter-ski (wȯ′tər skē *or* wot′ər skē′), glide over the water on water skis. *v.,* **wa·ter-skied, wa·ter-ski·ing.**

wa·ter va·por (wȯ′tər vā′pər), water in a gaseous state, especially when fairly diffused, as it is in the air, and below the boiling point, as distinguished from steam.

---

watt (wät), unit of electric power, equal to the flow of one ampere under the pressure of one volt: *My lamp uses 60 watts; my toaster uses 1000 watts. n.* [The *watt* was named for James *Watt,* 1736–1819, Scottish engineer and inventor who perfected the steam engine.]

weak·ness (wēk′nis), a weak point; slight fault: *Putting things off is her weakness. n., pl.* **weak·ness·es.**

wear·i·ness (wir′ē nis), weary condition; tired feeling: *After tramping all day the hikers were overcome with weariness. n.*

we'd (wēd), **1** we had. **2** we should. **3** we would.

were (wėr), form of the verb **be** used with *you, we, they* or any plural noun to indicate the past tense. *The officer's orders were obeyed. v.*

we're (wir), we are.

wharf (hwôrf), platform built on the shore or out from the shore, beside which ships can load and unload: *The waves washed upon the wharves at Atlantic City. n., pl.* **wharves** (hwôrvz), **wharfs.**

when (hwen), at the time that. *adv.*

where (hwâr), **1** in what place; at what place: *Where do you live? Where is he?* **2** in which; at which: *That is the house where I was born.* 1 *adv.,* 2 *conj.*

which (hwich), *Which* is used in connecting a group of words with some word in the sentence. *Read the book which you have (pron.). pron., adj.*

whole (hōl), full; entire. *adj.*

wolf (wu̇lf), a flesh-eating mammal related to the dog, with a long muzzle, high pointed ears, and a bushy tail. Wolves usually hunt in packs and sometimes kill livestock. *n., pl.* **wolves** (wu̇lvz).

won·der (wun′dər), **1** feel wonder: *We are wondering about the number of stars.* **2** be curious; be curious about; wish to know: *I wonder where she has gone. v.,* **won·dered, won·der·ing.**

won ton (won′ ton′), **1** a Chinese dumpling consisting of dough wrapped around minced vegetables mixed with meat or shrimp. **2** soup made with these dumplings. [*Won ton* comes from Chinese *wan t'an.*]

wool·ly mam·moth (wùl′ ē mam′əth), a very large, extinct kind of elephant with a hairy skin and long, curved tusks. It appeared in North America during the Ice Age.

worst (wèrst), in the worst manner or degree: *He acts worst when he's tired. adv.*

worth (wèrth), **1** value. *I got my money's worth out of this coat.* **2** equal in value to: *That book is worth $5.* 1 *n.,* 2 *adj.*

wring (ring), twist with force; squeeze hard. *v.,* **wrung** (rung), **wring·ing.**

X

xy·lo·phone (zī′lə fōn), a musical instrument consisting of two rows of wooden bars of varying lengths, which are sounded by striking with wooden hammers. *n.* [*Xylophone* comes from Greek *xylon,* meaning "wood," and *phōnē,* meaning "a sound."]

Y

yield (yēld), **1** give; grant: *Her parents yielded their consent to the plan.* **2** give up; surrender. *v.,* **yield·ed, yield·ing.**

you'd (yüd; *unstressed* yùd), **1** you had. **2** you would.

you're (yùr; *unstressed* yər), you are.

Z

Zip Code (zip′ kōd′), Zone Improvement Plan Code (system of numbers, each number of which identifies one of the postal delivery areas into which the United States and its larger cities have been divided). [*Zip* was formed from the first letters of the words *zone improvement plan.*]

zoo (zü), place where animals are kept and shown. *n., pl.* **zoos.**

a	hat	ī	ice	ù	put	**ə stands for**	
ā	age	o	not	ü	rule	a	in about
ä	far, calm	ō	open	ch	child	e	in taken
âr	care	ò	saw	ng	long	i	in pencil
e	let	ô	order	sh	she	o	in lemon
ē	equal	oi	oil	th	thin	u	in circus
èr	term	ou	out	ᴛʜ	then		
i	it	u	cup	zh	measure		

Writer's Thesaurus

Introduction

Many of your spelling words have synonyms, words with similar meanings. This thesaurus lists those spelling words alphabetically, defines them, and provides synonyms. For many words, you can also look up antonyms, words with opposite meanings. This thesaurus can even introduce you to new words.

Understand a Thesaurus Entry

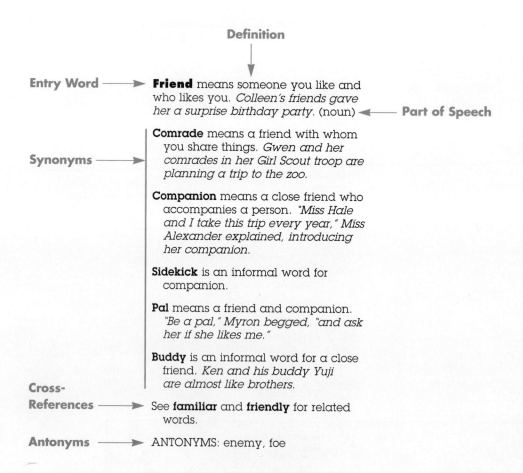

Definition

Entry Word ——▶ **Friend** means someone you like and who likes you. *Colleen's friends gave her a surprise birthday party.* (noun) ◀—— **Part of Speech**

Synonyms ——▶ **Comrade** means a friend with whom you share things. *Gwen and her comrades in her Girl Scout troop are planning a trip to the zoo.*

Companion means a close friend who accompanies a person. *"Miss Hale and I take this trip every year," Miss Alexander explained, introducing her companion.*

Sidekick is an informal word for companion.

Pal means a friend and companion. *"Be a pal," Myron begged, "and ask her if she likes me."*

Buddy is an informal word for a close friend. *Ken and his buddy Yuji are almost like brothers.*

Cross-References ——▶ See **familiar** and **friendly** for related words.

Antonyms ——▶ ANTONYMS: enemy, foe

312

A a

Announce means to make something known to the public. *The manager called a press conference to announce that the team had traded two pitchers.* (verb)

Proclaim is a formal word that means to announce officially. *Mexico proclaimed its independence from Spain in 1821.*

Publish can mean to make something very widely known. *Once the charges of corruption have been published, there will be little anyone can do to stop the investigation.*

Advertise means to make something known to the public by paying for it. *The sale was advertised in the local newspaper.*

Publicize means to make something known to as many people as possible. *The kids publicized their car wash by standing near the road with signs.*

Appearance means the way that someone or something looks. *With its fresh mud wall and new straw roofs, the African village had a prosperous appearance.* (noun)

Look can mean appearance. *Jeremy has the healthy look of someone who works outdoors.*

Air can mean appearance. It often suggests an appearance that causes a feeling. *There was a certain air of mystery about the deserted old house.*

Aspect can mean someone's or something's usual appearance. *The security guard has a watchful aspect.*

B b

Beautiful means very pleasing to the senses or the mind. *These beautiful rugs were made by hand in Turkey 100 years ago, but they still look almost like new.* (adjective)

Pretty means pleasing to see or hear. It is often used to describe girls and women. *Mariko looks really pretty in that hat.*

Handsome means pleasing to see. It is often used instead of beautiful or pretty to describe a man or boy. *Candace thinks Mr. Walking Bear, the science teacher, is awfully handsome.*

Good-looking means handsome or pretty. *My mother always tells my father how good-looking he is because she knows it makes him feel good.*

Stunning means strikingly beautiful. *The model in this picture wears a stunning silk evening gown.*

Elegant means beautiful and graceful. It suggests careful attention. *While Grandpa cooks the holiday turkey, Grandma makes the table elegant with candles and flowers.*

ANTONYMS: ugly, unattractive

Because means for the reason mentioned. *Lyle is late tonight, because he missed the bus.* (conjunction)

Since can mean because. It is used when the cause is explained before the effect. *Since Lyle missed the bus, he is late tonight.*

For means because. This meaning is used mostly in writing. *The people rejoice tonight, for the long war has ended.*

So means with the effect mentioned, or for the purpose mentioned. *Tawana washed the dishes, so you don't have to.*

As a result means with the effect mentioned. *Mickey went around the corner too fast, and as a result the bike skidded.*

Beginning means the time when something first happens or first exists. *The Declaration of Independence marked the beginning of the United States.* (noun)

Start can mean a beginning. *Jason led the sack race from start to finish.*

Creation means the act of making something that did not exist before. *Since the creation of the Cafeteria Committee, we've had better desserts.*

Opening can mean a beginning, especially of a story, music, or other works of art. *The opening of the musical, with its great song and fabulous dancers, really grabbed Mike's attention.*

Introduction can mean a beginning in common use. *Since the introduction of the microwave, cooking habits have changed greatly.*

ANTONYMS: conclusion, end, finish

HAVE YOU HEARD...?

"Beauty is in the eye of the beholder."

—Margaret Wolfe Hungerford

C c

Celebrate means to note a special day with proper activities. *Mexicans proudly celebrate their independence with two days of colorful fiestas.* (verb)

Commemorate means to show respect for a memory, often on a special day. *In January, the United States commemorates the birth of Rev. Martin Luther King, Jr.*

Observe can mean to show respect on a particular day. *The Jewish faith observes Yom Kippur with fasting and prayer.*

Keep can mean to observe or to celebrate. *The Larsens keep Thanksgiving by having a family reunion—all 68 of them.*

Honor can mean to show respect, often at a particular time. *At this morning's ceremony, the city will honor those firefighters who have died in the line of duty.*

ANTONYM: ignore

WORD STORY

Commemorate comes from a Latin word meaning "to bring to mind." The English word *memory* comes from the same Latin root.

Center means a point equally distant from each side or end. It is often used to mean the most important point of activity. *There was a bowl of oranges in the center of the table. Jorge was the center of attention as he described his trip to Puerto Rico.* (noun)

Middle means the central or halfway part of something. *Ms. Gustavson is the one in the middle of the photograph. The bell rang when Kenneth was right in the middle of a story.*

Heart can mean the innermost or most important part of something. *Public buildings like the City Hall and the Board of Education are often in the heart of the city.*

Hub can mean the center of activity. *After school, the Youth Center is the hub of our neighborhood.*

Focus can mean hub. *On market day, the village square is the focus of trade for miles around.*

Choose means to decide to do or take something. *Nestor chose to give his report on the life of Manuel Quezon y Molina, first president of the Philippine Commonwealth.* (verb)

Pick means to choose from many things just what you want. *Robin picked the gray kitten because it was the liveliest of the four.*

Select means to choose from many things after thinking carefully. *"We're only going to rent one movie, Deke, so be sure about the one you select," his mother advised.*

Prefer means to like something better than something else. *My folks want Grandma to stay with us, but she prefers having her own home.*

Elect means to choose, especially by voting for a person. *United States citizens elect a President every four years. When my family went fishing at dawn, I elected to stay in bed.*

Pick out means to choose with extra care. *Mr. Johnson picked out the biggest catfish in the tank.*

SEE **decide** for related words.

ANTONYM: reject

Command means to tell someone officially to do something. *The Emperor of Persia commanded his armies to conquer the cities of Greece.* (verb)

Order can mean to tell someone forcefully to do something. *If kids act up, Mr. Tyler orders them to behave or get detention.*

Direct means to tell someone officially to do something. It is not so strong a word as command. *The police officer directed Mr. Cornell to show his driver's license.*

Instruct can mean to tell someone to do something. *Bertha's parents have instructed her to call whenever she will be late.*

Tell can mean to give someone an order in an informal way. *Freddie, tell your brother to get ready for bed.*

Ask can mean to give someone an order in a polite way. *Mom asked me to set the table for supper.*

Conquer means to defeat someone or something by great effort. *Scientists are attempting to conquer cancer.* (verb)

Overpower means to conquer completely by great strength. *Pirates overpowered our ship.*

Subdue is a formal word that means to bring under control. *The rodeo rider was able to rope and subdue the calf within half a minute.*

Continue means to go on. *World War II continued from 1939 until the defeat of Germany and Japan in 1945.* (verb)

Last means to continue. *The parade lasted for an hour and a half.*

Remain and **linger** can mean to continue. *Lisbet remains in poor health, with a cough that has been lingering for weeks now.*

Persist can mean to last for a long time. *The weather service expects the drought to persist all summer.*

Endure is a formal word meaning to last for a long time, especially when it is hard to do so. *Although they now live thousands of miles apart, the two women's friendship has endured since their schooldays in Moscow forty years ago.*

Keep on means to continue. *George kept on getting taller until he was nearly twenty.*

ANTONYMS: cease, stop

Create means to bring something into being. *The Johnsons created a study area for their children by putting a large table and some bookshelves in one corner of the dining room.* (verb)

Invent means to think up something completely new and bring it into being. *Thomas Edison invented the phonograph in 1877.*

Originate means to start new ideas or methods. *The ancient Greeks originated the concept of democracy.*

Devise means to invent, especially in a clever way. *Using two boards, Manuel devised a ramp to get Elena's wheelchair up the steps.*

Criticize means to point out what is wrong with someone or something. *I hate to go to the movies with Pete because he criticizes everything he sees.* (verb)

Condemn means to criticize strongly and openly. *Everyone condemns cruelty to animals.*

Censure is a formal word meaning to criticize. It is used most often about public affairs. *Representative Guthrie was censured by her own party for mishandling public funds.*

Find fault means to look for what is wrong and point it out. *I asked Don to read my report because he's so good at finding fault.*

ANTONYMS: compliment, praise

D d

Decide means to make up your mind. *It was such a hot day that we decided to go to the city swimming pool.* (verb)

Determine means to decide firmly, often from several choices. *Jolene is still trying to determine which hairdo looks best on her.*

Resolve means to decide firmly. *In Gone with the Wind, a starving Scarlett O'Hara resolved never to go hungry again.*

Conclude can mean to decide after thinking it over. *The police concluded that the driver who caused the accident had been drinking.*

SEE **choose** for related words.

President Harry Truman

HAVE YOU HEARD...?

You may have heard someone say that "the buck stops here." The person who says this means that he or she is the person who decides about something and takes responsibility for it. President Harry Truman is famous for using this phrase to show that as head of the United States government, he had to decide what to do for the country.

More than a hundred years ago, people playing cards used a coin or other marker to show whose turn it was to deal the cards. This marker was called a buck, and it moved around the table as people took turns. Where the buck stopped, that player was responsible for the next deal. "Passing the buck" is still used to mean trying to avoid responsibility for deciding.

Decorate means to make something look good by adding things to it. *Liam's classroom was decorated with flags from all the countries that once were home to the students' families.* (verb)

Adorn is a formal word meaning to decorate. *Archaeologists have discovered ancient paintings adorning the walls of caves.*

Beautify means to make something more beautiful. *Reverend Samson asked everyone to help beautify the chapel by painting the walls and polishing the brass.*

Garnish means to decorate something, especially food. *In the Middle Ages, cooks garnished foods with marigolds and roses.*

Definite means clear and exact. *"Molly needs a definite answer: Will you buy her guitar or not?" asked Jim.* (adjective)

Clear-cut can mean definite. *Daley has a clear-cut choice—he can apologize, or he can forget about coming to my party.*

Decided means definite and unquestionable. *Georgia's smile faded, and her eyes took on a look of decided annoyance.*

Distinct can mean definite and unmistakable. *Since Jonah had played the game before, he had a distinct advantage over me.*

Explicit means clearly and fully stated. *Sonya gave us explicit directions for getting to her house.*

Sonya gave us **explicit** directions for getting to her house.

Destroy means to put an end to something, often by breaking or pulling it to pieces. *The buffalo stampede destroyed the cornfield.* (verb)

Demolish means to smash to pieces. *An earthquake can demolish buildings.*

Wreck means to break something so completely that it cannot be fixed. *During last night's storm, lightning wrecked the gas station sign.*

Ruin means to make something worthless or useless. *If Paul doesn't stop sliding around in the dirt like that, he's going to ruin his jeans.*

Spoil means to ruin. *We should take the rug out of the basement before the damp floor spoils it.*

Tear down means to demolish. *Mr. Lu's company will tear down the old barn and build a theater there.*

ANTONYMS: create, make

Different means not alike. *Edgar and Edwin try hard to be different, because they don't want to be known as "the twins."* (adjective)

Various means different. It is used when there are many different things. *Every morning, Babur opens his family's shop and sets out the thirty baskets of various spices.*

Miscellaneous means of many sorts, not all the same. It may suggest no effort to choose. *My sister collects only clear marbles, but she keeps some miscellaneous ones to trade.*

Assorted means mixed. *I always choose assorted jellybean flavors because I can never decide on just one flavor.*

ANTONYMS: alike, identical, same, similar

Discount means costing less than the regular or listed price. *The Tombas got a discount fare because they took a late-night flight.* (adjective)

Reduced means lower in price than before. *Arnetta bought her heavy coat at a reduced price in February.*

Budget can mean sold at low prices that help save money. *Tori says this budget shampoo is as good as more expensive brands.*

On sale means sold at lowered prices. *Everything in the store was on sale that day.*

Jim glared at the old pirate with a sullen look of **distrust.**

Doubt means a feeling of not believing something or not being sure. *Ashley has made up her mind and doesn't feel any doubts.* (noun)

Uncertainty means a feeling of not being sure. *After a moment's uncertainty, Nestor recognized the path back to his family's farm.*

Suspicion means a feeling of not trusting someone. *The car moving down the dark alley with its lights off raised Deena's suspicion.*

Mistrust means suspicion. *The way Colin avoided answering questions filled Leroy with mistrust.*

Distrust means strong suspicion or a serious lack of trust. *Jim glared at the old pirate with a sullen look of distrust.*

Skepticism means unwillingness to believe or trust. *David feels some skepticism about the account his excited cousin gave of the accident.*

Take something with a grain of salt is an idiom that means to have doubt about something. *DeWayne tells so many extraordinary stories that I tend to take them all with a grain of salt.*

ANTONYM: belief

E e

Elementary means first and simplest. *Rona is learning how to use tools in her elementary carpentry class.* (adjective)

Primary means first. *In the primary grades, schoolchildren learn to read and write.*

Basic means first and necessary for everything that follows. *A basic part of judo is learning how to fall.*

Fundamental means basic. It emphasizes how necessary something is. *The most fundamental part of cooking is using fresh, good-quality ingredients.*

Emergency means a sudden and dangerous situation that calls for quick action. *The Kims had an emergency last night—Myung had an asthma attack and had to go to the hospital.* (noun)

Crisis can mean a dangerous situation, especially the most dangerous part of a story or set of events. *The crisis in the movie came when all six of the explorers fell into the river.*

Predicament means a difficult or dangerous situation that is hard to get out of. *Trapped in a burning building, the hero is in a terrible predicament.*

Enemy means someone who hates someone or something. *The enemies of civil rights tried to keep African Americans from voting. The United States and Japan were enemies in World War II.* (noun)

Foe means an enemy. It is used mostly in books. *The famous detective and his criminal foe stood face to face at last!*

Archenemy means a main or special enemy. *In this computer game, your archenemy is the Zork, who can wipe out your score.*

Invader means an enemy who enters a country by force. *As the invaders approached our city, we could see the flash of their guns and missiles against the sky.*

ANTONYMS: ally, friend

WORD STORY

Enemy comes from a Latin word meaning "friend." How can this be true? The Latin word began with the letters *ami-.* You can see the same letters in *amigo* and *amiable.* If you wanted to say that someone was not your friend, you might call that person your "un-amigo." Try saying that several times fast, and you'll see where *enemy* came from.

Especially means more than others or in a special way. *Luis likes to eat fruit, especially papaya. Mary Ann was especially glad to see Philip, since he had been away all summer.* (adverb)

Particularly means especially. *"I hate getting out of bed," Minh yawned, "particularly on dark, rainy days like this."*

Specifically means with attention to a single item or detail. *Isabel wants to be a nurse, specifically to help old people.*

Primarily means more than others or mainly. *Hilary's mother is primarily a children's doctor, but she sees grownups on occasion.*

Principally means more than others or mainly. *On vacation, Mr. Shelby is principally interested in fishing.*

In particular means especially. *Carly loves to shop, in particular for new clothes.*

Example means one thing or person that shows what others are like. *"On your left," said our guide, "is a perfect example of French armor from the Middle Ages."* (noun)

Instance means an example. *George Washington and Dwight Eisenhower are instances of generals who became President.*

Case means an example. It is often used for an event, or for someone's life. *The farmer recalled a case several years ago of a fox attacking his chickens.*

Illustration can mean an example used to explain something. *"Today,"* said Mr. Blau, *"we will focus on manufacturing states, using Ohio as an illustration."*

Sample means a part that shows what the whole is like. *Gary asked for a sample of the chocolate cherry ice cream before buying a cone.*

Specimen means one thing taken and used to show what others are like. *Jamie's class went on a trip to collect specimens of pond life.*

Excellent means having very high quality. *When it was Barry's turn to cook dinner, he made excellent tacos.* (adjective)

First-rate means excellent. *Suit Yourself sells first-rate clothing.*

Fine and **first-class** mean excellent. *"Why, Daniel, this drawing isn't just good, it's fine!" the art teacher cried. "You're becoming a first-class artist!"*

Superior means having very high quality, especially compared to others. *"Now that you have seen the others," Mr. Bartholomew murmured, "I will show you a truly superior diamond."*

Outstanding means so excellent as to stand out from others. *You have to be an outstanding athlete to be considered for the Olympic team.*

Exceptional means very outstanding of its kind. *The teacher said that Stan's composition showed exceptional writing ability.*

ANTONYMS: bad, poor, terrible

Exercise means repeated activity that increases strength, endurance, and skill. *Jan and Lou get exercise by skating two miles every day.* (noun)

Training can mean the development of strength, endurance, and skill by exercise. *Jenny's former gym teacher went into training for the Pan American Games.*

Workout means a period of exercise. *Tina ran a mile during her workout this morning.*

Calisthenics and **aerobics** are kinds of exercise. Calisthenics especially increases strength and gracefulness; aerobics especially increases endurance. *Ricki does slow calisthenics to get warmed up and then fast aerobics to raise her pulse.*

Jan and Lou get **exercise** by skating two miles every day.

Expensive means costing a lot of money. *Luis decided not to buy those expensive sneakers.* (adjective)

Costly can mean expensive. *Dad gave Mom a bottle of costly perfume for her birthday.*

High can mean expensive. *Mr. and Mrs. Parks like the apartment, but the rent is too high for their budget.*

Overpriced means costing more than it is worth. *Gina says those tropical fish are really overpriced.*

Steep can mean very expensive. *The little grocery on the corner had steep prices compared to the supermarket.*

Sky-high can mean very expensive. *I can't believe anyone pays these sky-high rates for a motel room.*

Cost an arm and a leg is an idiom that means something is extremely expensive. *Marnie wants a computer with a color monitor, but they cost an arm and a leg.*

ANTONYMS: cheap, inexpensive

Experience means to have something happen to you. *Our team has experienced some bad luck this year, but we played fairly well for much of the season.* (verb)

Undergo means to experience something, often something unpleasant. *Mario has to undergo a serious operation to repair the damage to his arm.*

Feel can mean to experience. *Yoko felt great sadness when her best friend moved to California.*

Have can mean to experience. *Kerry had an accident on her bike last weekend.*

Suffer can mean to experience something unpleasant. *The President of the PTA suffered defeat in her bid for re-election.*

Sustain can mean to suffer. *Mrs. Restrepo's house sustained minor damage during the flood.*

F f

Familiar means very friendly and able to share ideas and feelings like members of the same family. *The Burches and Seebergs have become familiar since they set up a car pool together.* (adjective)

Chummy is an informal word that means very friendly, as chums are. *Jerome and Carol got really chummy during the second hockey season they played together.*

Intimate means completely familiar. *Iris has become intimate with one of the women she reads to at the nursing home.*

Close can mean intimate. *Max couldn't believe that his close friend Baram would be moving soon to a city far away.*

Inseparable means so intimate that they seem to be always together. *Conchita and Lisa have been inseparable since they learned how much they both love horses.*

SEE **friend** for related words.

ANTONYM: formal

Friend means someone you like and who likes you. *Colleen's friends gave her a surprise birthday party.* (noun)

Comrade means a friend with whom you share things. *Gwen and her comrades in her Girl Scout troop are planning a trip to the zoo.*

Companion means a close friend who accompanies a person. *"Miss Hale and I take this trip every year," Miss Alexander explained, introducing her companion.*

Sidekick is an informal word that means companion. *"Well, Jed," Prairie Pete told his sidekick, "seems we've cleaned up this old town mighty well."*

Pal means a friend and companion. *"Be a pal," Myron begged, "and ask her if she likes me."*

Buddy is an informal word that means a close friend. *Ken and his buddy Yuji are almost like brothers.*

Amigo means a close friend who understands you well. *"Let's go, amigo," said David, grabbing his skateboard and Damian's arm at the same time.*

Playmate means a person you play with often. *When my kid brother and his playmates are around, I try to be someplace else.*

SEE **familiar** for related words.

ANTONYMS: enemy, foe

AROUND THE WORLD: FRIENDSHIP

A friend in need is a friend indeed.
— **English proverb**

A good friend is revealed on a bad day.
— **Turkish proverb**

On the day of poverty you know who is a true friend.
— **Ghanaian proverb**

He who helps you in need is a true friend.
— **Swahili proverb** (East Africa)

Know a friend when you are in trouble.
— **Tamil proverb** (India)

G g

Guard means to keep someone or something safe. *Secret Service agents guard the President at all times.* (verb)

Defend means to guard, especially from an attack. *Ute warriors gathered to defend their village against the Navajo.*

Protect means to guard, especially from danger. *Jorge wears goggles while welding in order to protect his eyes.*

Shield means to protect. *Sondra wears a cap with a long bill to shield her face from the sun.*

Guide means to show the way to a place by actually going there. *People with severely impaired vision may have dogs that are trained to guide them around.* (verb)

Lead means to show the way by going with or ahead of someone. *When the lights went out during the storm, Mrs. Tucker helped lead the patients down the corridor.*

Direct can mean to show or tell the way. *Ted was lost downtown until a woman directed him to the library.*

Steer can mean to direct someone, or to make something go in a particular direction. *When we moved in, our new neighbor steered us to the cheapest grocery store.*

Usher means to guide someone, especially to or from a door. *Students ushered the audience to their seats for the band concert.*

H h

Honest means not stealing, cheating, or lying. *We chose Ting-Wei for class treasurer because we need a really honest person.* (adjective)

Truthful means telling the facts, not lying. *"Be truthful, Sesha—does this skirt make me look fat?" asked her sister.*

Honorable means knowing and doing what is right. *An honorable scientist like Dr. Blake wouldn't dream of stealing an invention!*

Upright can mean honest and good. *Tom might still be getting in trouble if his boxing coach weren't such a strong, upright man.*

Trustworthy means honest and keeping your word. *Everyone in the movie thinks she's trustworthy, so it's easy for her to steal the plans.*

ANTONYM: dishonest

I i

Important means mattering a lot or making a big difference. *Getting a new job is really important to Luann's mom.* (adjective)

Major means important, especially more important than others. *The steel mill used to be a major employer in this town.*

Significant means important, especially in meaning. *The birth of Graham's first grandchild was a significant event in his life.*

Vital can mean extremely important. *Often Kayonga must spend hours collecting the firewood vital to his family.*

Momentous means very important. *The breakup of the Soviet Union is among the century's most momentous political changes.*

SEE **value** for related words.

ANTONYMS: insignificant, unimportant

Informal means for everyday use, not following rules of public and official behavior. *"For a family picnic, Loretta, informal clothes will do better than that good dress," said her grandmother.* (adjective)

Casual can mean informal. It suggests just letting things happen. *Darshon is a fierce competitor who hates losing even the most casual game with his friends.*

Offhand can mean informal. It suggests not giving something much thought. *Max really hurt Carmelita's feelings with that offhand comment about her science project.*

Spontaneous means acting or done without plan or control, from impulse. *Denise was so happy that she did a spontaneous cartwheel.*

Free and easy is an idiom that means informal and natural. *"No plans," Mr. Madison told the neighbors, "just a free and easy weekend at the beach."*

L l

Late means not on time, especially a scheduled or expected time. *Sara was so anxious not to be late for her first baby-sitting job that she got there a half hour early.* (adjective)

Tardy means not arriving on time. It is often used to mean late for school. *The traffic jam made everyone on the bus tardy.*

Belated means later than should be, especially because of delay. *Uncle Griff sent me a belated birthday card with apologies.*

Overdue means promised for a particular time, but not arrived or delivered. *The drugstore clerk says the October issue of* Teen Health *magazine is overdue.*

ANTONYMS: early, prompt, punctual

Legal means permitted by law or according to law. *Calvin said he would do anything to help his older brother—as long as it was legal.* (adjective)

Lawful means legal. *Since Mr. Torres made no will, his only cousin is his lawful heir.*

Rightful means according to law. *A military government has imprisoned the rightful president.*

Legitimate means rightful. *Ms. Littledog's insurance company ruled that her claim was legitimate and paid her $2,000.*

Licensed means permitted by official license. *Only licensed boats are allowed on Lake Waupaukee.*

ANTONYMS: illegal, unauthorized, unlawful

Level means with the same height all over, so that round things don't roll by themselves. *Forrest put some cardboard under one table leg to make it level with the others.* (adjective)

Even means level. *Undisturbed by wind, the snow lay even on the windowsills and rooftops.*

Flat means level. It often suggests something low. *During the last Ice Age, glaciers scraped the prairies flat.*

Horizontal means level and parallel with the horizon. *The carpenter checked the windowsill to be sure that it was perfectly horizontal.*

Likely means having a good chance of happening. *Richie is likely to spend Saturday helping his father make deliveries.* (adjective)

Probable means almost sure to happen. *When she felt the first drops of rain, Ms. Porter knew it was probable that the picnic would be canceled.*

Liable means likely to have something bad happen. *Scientists know that earthquakes are liable to strike again where they've struck before.*

Apt means likely, especially because of the way someone or something is. *Tamara can do most of the problems, but she's not apt to help us.*

Prone means apt to have something bad happen. *Grace's father's illness makes him prone to periods of bad temper.*

ANTONYM: unlikely

Love means a strong and tender feeling of liking or being fond of someone. *Mrs. Hightower held the sleeping child with love.* (noun)

Mrs. Hightower held the sleeping child with **love.**

Affection means a kind, warm feeling for someone or something. It is not as strong a word as love. *Whitney has a special affection for the elderly couple upstairs and often visits them.*

Fondness means liking or affection. *Grandma's fondness for Pooch is obvious from the way she crawls around on the floor with him.*

Devotion means a very loyal feeling of love or affection for someone or something. *Rocco saved that puppy from drowning, and it gives him total devotion.*

Adoration means devoted love and admiration. *Allen's feeling for his favorite rock group amounts almost to adoration.*

ANTONYMS: hate, hatred

M m

Measure means to find the size or amount of something. *When Yin measured her room, she found it was nine feet wide and ten feet long.* (verb)

Weigh means to find out how heavy something is. *Since Herb went on a diet, he weighs himself the first thing every morning.*

Survey can mean to measure land for its area, boundaries, and shape. *The Wilcox farm must be surveyed before it can be sold.*

Gauge means to measure. It is mostly used in discussing science. *We gauged the amount of rain that fell yesterday as half an inch.*

Quantify means to measure an amount of something. *It is mostly used in discussing science. Aboard the space shuttle, the astronauts record quantified scientific information.*

Aboard the space shuttle, the astronauts record **quantified** scientific information.

O o

Opposite means completely different from each other. *The ships are headed in opposite directions through the canal.* (adjective)

Contrary means opposite. *The Sedlacek sisters hold contrary opinions about which of them started the fight.*

Reverse means exactly opposite, especially in direction or position. *How fast can you say the alphabet in reverse order?*

Contradictory means saying something opposite to what was said before. *The candidate has made several contradictory statements about raising or not raising taxes.*

ANTONYMS: alike, same

Origin means the thing or place that something comes from. It often suggests the reasons for the new thing. *This huge traffic jam had its origin in one flat tire.* (noun)

Source means the person or place where something comes from. It often suggests a steady supply. *Rachel's new cat is a constant source of amusement.*

Root can mean a source or a cause. *The root of Lamar's interest in trains is that his grandfather was a railroad engineer.*

Spring can mean an origin. *"Our ancestors," Jae Choi told his children, "are the spring from which our whole family flows."*

Derivation can mean an origin, especially of words. *The derivation of "Halloween" is two words meaning "holy evening."*

SEE **beginning** for related words.

ANTONYMS: end, finish

P p

Patient means to be able to put up with trouble, hard work, or long delays, without complaining. *Grandpa is always patient with Grandma, even when she gets impatient with him.* (adjective)

Tolerant means able to put up with people whose ideas or behavior are not what you are used to. *"We should not just be tolerant of other cultures," explained Mr. Koenig, "we should learn from them."*

Long-suffering means patient. It is an old-fashioned word, found mostly in books. *Thrifty and long-suffering, the young carpenter's apprentice grew to be a famous architect.*

Forbearing can mean patient and with strong self-control. *The struggle for civil rights was kept nonviolent by forbearing people.*

ANTONYMS: impatient, irritated, exasperated

Perfect means having no faults or being the best. *The swimmer made a perfect dive on her first attempt. Vladimir found the perfect gift for his grandmother.* (adjective)

Ideal means perfect, or as wonderful as you could imagine. *When Saturday came, it turned out to be an ideal day for the carnival.*

Flawless means not having any defects. *On the slender fingers of her right hand, the countess wore two flawless diamonds.*

Faultless means flawless. *Although Javier has been in this country for only three years, he already speaks faultless English.*

Pure can mean perfect. It suggests that something contains no bad parts. *Ronald prides himself on his homemade candy, made with pure chocolate and fluffy coconut.*

Impeccable means so faultless that no one can find anything wrong. *He had such impeccable manners that no one guessed the "prince" was really a swindler.*

SEE **excellent** for related words.

ANTONYM: imperfect

Piece means a small part of something larger, or one thing among others like it. *Della swept the pieces of the broken glass into a pile. The platter was the largest piece of china on the Serra's dinner table.* (noun)

Bit means a small piece of something larger. *Caroline tore the letter into bits.*

Particle means a very little bit. *Dust particles from the volcano make the sunsets very colorful.*

Scrap means a little piece, especially a piece left over. *Andrea cut the picture to fit into the frame and then threw away the paper scraps.*

Lump means a small, solid piece of material. *Darryl gave the carnival pony a lump of sugar.*

Chunk means a thick lump. *Tillie's mother makes stew with chunks of meat, carrots, and potatoes.*

Fragment means a piece that has been broken off. *A fragment of the plane landed more than 500 yards from the crash site.*

Chip can mean a thin, small piece. *The dirt around the rosebushes is covered with wood chips so that the soil stays moist.*

The dirt around the rosebushes is covered with wood **chips** so that the soil stays moist.

Polite means having or showing good manners. *You may not like what Ebony says, but she's always polite in the way she says it.* (adjective)

Courteous means polite and thoughtful. *"How courteous!" Mrs. Taylor exclaimed, when the bus driver got out to help her lift the stroller.*

Gracious means courteous, pleasant, and kind. *Even with the nine unexpected guests, Ms. Nuñez remained calm and gracious.*

Tactful means able to say and do the things that are best suited to other people's feelings. *Richard wondered if there were a tactful way to tell John he should wash his hair more often.*

Diplomatic can mean tactful. *Even when she's criticizing someone, Debbie remembers to be diplomatic.*

ANTONYMS: impolite, rude

Power means the ability to do something or to make something happen. *Paul has the power to motivate people with his eloquent speeches.* (noun)

Energy can mean power. It often suggests power stored up, ready to be used. *The creative energy of the students really comes out in the school's weeklong Festival of Brazil.*

Strength means the amount of power that someone or something has. *Most ants have enough strength to lift ten times their own weight.*

ANTONYM: weakness

Promise means to give your word to someone that you will or will not do something. *The hotel clerk promised to hold a room for us.* (verb)

Agree can mean to promise to do something that someone else wants. *Miriam agreed to wait for me if I was late.*

Pledge means to promise something in a sincere, solemn way. *Next, we will pledge allegiance to the flag.*

Guarantee means to promise, especially to fix, replace, or take back an item sold. *On this used tape deck, everything is guaranteed for ninety days.*

Vouch for means to promise that someone or something is good, true, or valuable. *The auto dealer vouches for the good condition of the used car's engine and brakes.*

R r

Reliable means worthy of being counted on or trusted. *Mr. Koenig told us to use only reliable sources for our research papers—no supermarket tabloid newspapers.* (adjective)

Dependable means reliable. *Ms. Bailey says that Tomás is dependable enough to manage the store on Sundays.*

Responsible can mean reliable and sensible in making decisions. *We always make Tazu referee because we need the most responsible person for that job.*

Tried and true means known by experience to be reliable. *With his tried and true dog guide, Buck, Mr. Nulty walks fifteen blocks to and from work each day.*

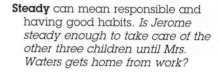

With his **tried and true** dog guide, Buck, Mr. Nulty walks fifteen blocks to and from work each day.

Steady can mean responsible and having good habits. *Is Jerome steady enough to take care of the other three children until Mrs. Waters gets home from work?*

Reluctant means not wanting to do something. It suggests trying to avoid or resist. *Austin has been wrong so often that his friends are reluctant to follow his advice.* (adjective)

Hesitant means holding yourself back from doing something. It suggests doubt or fear. *Peering over the edge of the diving board, Janice felt hesitant about jumping.*

Unwilling means not willing to do something. It suggests an attempt to refuse. *"I am unwilling to spend seventy dollars just because you think the shoes are cool," May's father said.*

ANTONYM: eager

Remember means to call something back to mind. *"Remember!" shouted the captain. "We meet tomorrow in Spyglass Bay!"* (verb)

Recall means to remember. It is often used when an effort is required. *Can you recall when we asked the janitor to fix the sink?*

Recollect means to recall something, especially something from long ago. *"I can recollect when this neighborhood was mostly woods," Mr. Rosewater told his granddaughters.*

Reminisce means to remember and talk about people and events from the past. *Mom and her brothers like to reminisce about their childhood in Cuba.*

Retain can mean to hold something in mind. *As people grow older, they often find it harder to retain new information.*

ANTONYM: forget

Rich means having a lot of money or a lot of expensive things. *Scrooge was rich, but lonely and poor in spirit.* (adjective)

Prosperous means successful, especially with money. *The Itos live in a prosperous middle-class neighborhood.*

Well-heeled is an informal word that means prosperous and not needing more money. *That resort is for well-heeled vacationers.*

Ridicule means to make fun of someone or something. *"Just because I'm taller than anybody in my school,"* Alice sighed, *"do people have to ridicule me all the time?"* (verb)

Mock means to ridicule, especially by imitating. *The clown mocked the lion tamer by pretending a trained poodle was ferocious.*

Kid means to tease someone playfully. *"Bill kids you about your clothes because it's the only way he knows how to be friendly,"* said Mrs. Fredriks.

Josh is an informal word that means to make fun of someone in a good-natured way. *Aunt Prue joshes Uncle Al about what a mistake she made in marrying him.*

Razz is a slang word that means to make fun of someone, especially with rude noises. *After Joanne tripped and was tagged out between first and second, her teammates razzed her all the way back to the dugout.*

S s

Send means to cause to move from one place to another. *Mother sent Vanessa on an errand to the store.* (verb)

Transmit can mean to send signals or programs from one place to another. *Communications satellites transmitted television coverage of the Olympics around the world.*

Dispatch means to send quickly. *The hospital dispatched an ambulance as soon as the news of the accident came in.*

Forward can mean to send on further. *The post office will forward the Jiangs' mail to their new address.*

Export means to send something out of one country to be sold in another. *Honduras exports bananas, coffee, timber, and other products.*

ANTONYM: receive

Separate means to keep things apart or take something apart. *The highway separates these apartment buildings from the neighboring houses. Separate dark and light clothes before you wash them.* (verb)

Divide means to separate. *Ms. Polanak divided the class into teams for a softball game.*

Part means to separate. It is often used about things that were strongly joined. *Parted by war, the sisters met again by accident, years later.*

Split can mean to divide something as if by cutting. *Tom and Dave split the money they got for the empty cans.*

Sever can mean to break a connection or to separate a part from the rest. *Mr. Dankworth's finger was severed in a farming accident.*

ANTONYMS: unite, join

Severe means following the rules without gentleness or sympathy. *Mr. Turner's severe boss refused to let him leave work early on the day of his daughter's piano recital.* (adjective)

Strict means very careful of the rules. *A space shuttle launch is carried out with strict attention to detail.*

Stern means severe and firm in control or judgment. *The vice-principal is stern with students who make trouble.*

Harsh can mean severe and pitiless or even cruel. *"Turning away sick poor people?"* asked Mrs. Palmer. *"How can a hospital be that harsh?"*

Similar means much the same, but not completely the same. *The twins have similar haircuts, but Andy's hair is a bit longer than Jack's.* (adjective)

Like and **alike** mean similar. Like is used before or after things it describes. Alike is used only after the things it describes. *Marcy's wheelchair is like Ted's, but smaller. If they were any more alike, it would be hard to tell them apart.*

Comparable means similar enough to be compared. *The two cars are comparable in many ways—it's the price that makes the difference.*

Corresponding means similar. It suggests that two people or things have related places in their separate systems. *Plug the cord from your CD player into the corresponding sockets on your stereo.*

Of a piece is an idiom that means similar, as if cut from the same piece of fabric. *"We are tired,"* stormed Mrs. Cowan, *"of having millions of widely different senior citizens treated as if they were all of a piece."*

Single means one and no more. *Felipe was the single student with a perfect test score.* (adjective)

Lone means single. It suggests that others may exist, but that this one is alone. It is often used in poems and stories. *As night fell, the travelers directed their steps toward the lone house in the empty valley.*

Solitary means lone. *A solitary horse stood on the horizon.*

Unique means one of a kind, unlike any other. *Lola likes the unique sweaters her grandmother knits for her each year.*

A **solitary** horse stood on the horizon.

T t

Trial means a process of learning the facts about something by attempting to do or use it. *After repeated trials, the boys have discovered how to make fudge just the way they like it.* (noun)

Experiment means a carefully planned trial, especially to learn scientific facts. *Lydia and Carmen will be doing an experiment next semester to see how strong their electromagnet is.*

Test means a thorough trial, often an official one. It suggests very definite results. *Government tests show that the meat is safe to eat.*

Audition means a trial to see how well a person performs, especially an actor, singer, or musician. *"Auditions for the choir are open to all members of the congregation," announced Reverend Parkton.*

U u

Understand means to get the meaning of something. *After years of work, scientists are beginning to understand the writing carved on this stone by an ancient people.* (verb)

Comprehend means to understand. It suggests complete understanding. *Mr. Dunne says his kids comprehend their computer programs so much better than he does that he has to ask for advice.*

Grasp can mean to understand. It suggests taking hold of an idea with the mind. *Most people have trouble grasping how far it is from the sun to even the nearest star.*

Catch on is an informal phrase that means to understand. It often suggests not understanding at first. *Once Mrs. Park caught on to what we were planning, she offered to help with all the phone calls.*

Usual means most commonly seen, found, or happening. *In Chicago some snow is usual in winter. We'll meet for lunch at the usual time.* (adjective)

Customary means usual or according to custom or habit. *It is customary for me to get up at seven o'clock. For the Bedouins of Saudi Arabia, the customary way to travel is by camel.*

Regular means usual and according to custom or rule. *Sarah was late and missed her regular bus.*

Ordinary means usual and regular. *Visiting and helping out friends who are sick is an ordinary part of my grandmother's life.*

ANTONYMS: peculiar, rare, unusual

V v

Value means what something is good for or how much people want it, usually thought of as its price. *Harvey bought the lamp in the antique store for ten dollars, but its actual value is at least fifty dollars.* (noun)

Importance means how much something matters to people. *The discovery of penicillin was of great importance to medicine.*

Worth means value, especially something's usefulness or importance. *The owners recognized Delgado's worth to the team and gave him a salary of a million dollars.*

The Word List in English and Spanish

A

a little (29)	poco, poca
a lot (29)	mucho, mucha
a way (29)	una forma
a while (29)	un rato
absolute magnitude (CC)	magnitud absoluta
absolutely (4)	absolutamente
accept (14)	aceptar
access (14)	acceso
accomplish (9)	lograr
according (9)	según, de acuerdo a
achieve (3)	lograr
activate (26)	activar
additives (CC)	aditivos
address (9)	dirección
adjusted (1)	ajustar (pasado)
admire (2)	admirar
admiring (CC)	admirando
affectionate (26)	afectuoso, afectuosa
afford (9)	tener con qué pagar
Africa (CC)	Africa
aftershocks (CC)	temblores secundarios
afterthought (34)	pensamiento posterior
again (29)	de nuevo; nuevamente
agility (CC)	agilidad
agreement (CC)	acuerdo
air conditioner (11)	máquina de aire acondicionado
all ways (29)	en toda dirección
allergens (CC)	alergénicos, alergénicas
allergy (CC)	alergia
alligator (23)	caimán
allowance (9)	dinero de bolsillo
always (29)	siempre
amber (CC)	ámbar
American (31)	americano, americana
amphitheater (CC)	anfiteatro
anatomy (CC)	anatomía
android (CC)	androide
announce (9)	anunciar
answered (5)	contestar (pasado)
answering (5)	contestando
antibodies (CC)	anticuerpos
apiece (3)	cada uno, cada una

apologize (31)	pedir disculpas
apologized (CC)	pedir disculpas (pasado)
apparent (33)	aparente
apparent magnitude (CC)	magnitud aparente
appearance (33)	apariencia; presencia
appetizer (20)	aperitivo
aquarium (19)	acuario
arc (CC)	arco
archaeologist (CC)	arqueólogo, arqueóloga
architecture (CC)	arquitectura
arena (CC)	arena; rondel
around (29)	por
artifacts (CC)	artefactos
artificial (13)	artificial
artisans (CC)	artesanos, artesanas
artist (CC)	artista
aspires (CC)	aspira
aspirin (25)	aspirina
assume (4)	suponer
asterism (CC)	asterismo
athletic (15)	atlético, atlética
atmosphere (19, CC)	atmósfera
attention (22)	atención
attitude (4, CC)	actitud
attorney (21)	abogado, abogada
attractive (26)	atractivo, atractiva
autobiography (35)	autobiografía
autograph (35)	autógrafo; firmar
automatic (35)	automático, automática
automobile (35)	automóvil
autopilot (35)	piloto automático
autumn (8)	otoño
average (25)	promedio
away (29)	lejos
awfully (25)	muy; terriblemente
awhile (29)	un rato
axis (CC)	eje
Aztecs (CC)	aztecas

B

baby-sit (34)	cuidar niños
bacteria (CC)	bacterias
balcony (CC)	balcón
ballet (23)	ballet
banana (23)	banana

banquet (23)	banquete
barbecue (23)	barbacoa; asar a la parrilla
barometer (CC)	barómetro
barricade (9)	barricada
basalt (CC)	basalto
base (CC)	base
basketball (34)	baloncesto; balón
beautiful (1)	bello, bella
because (29)	porque
become (29)	volverse; convertirse en
beginning (25)	principio; comenzando
belief (3)	creencia
below (29)	abajo; debajo
beside (14)	al lado
besides (14)	además de
body fat (CC)	grasa
bomb (17)	bomba
bombard (17)	bombardear
bookstore (34)	librería
boring (CC)	aburrido, aburrida
brief (3)	breve
brilliant (33)	brillante
broccoli (9)	brócoli
brother-in-law (34)	cuñado
buffaloes (16)	búfalos
buffet (23)	bufet
building (1)	edificio
business (31)	negocio

C

cabinet (25)	armario, vitrina
calendar (CC)	calendario
calories (CC)	calorías
cannon (2)	cañón
canyon (2)	cañón
carbon imprint (CC)	huella de carbono
cardiovascular (CC)	cardiovascular
carnival (19)	carnaval
catsup (23)	salsa de tomate
causeways (CC)	calzadas
cautious (13)	cauteloso, cautelosa
ceiling (3)	techo
celebration (15)	celebración
cent (7)	centavo
center (CC)	centro
central angle (CC)	ángulo central
cereal (7)	cereal
certain (CC)	seguro, segura

championship (26)	campeonato
cheerleader (34)	porrista
Chicago (19)	Chicago
chiefs (16)	jefes
chili (7)	chile con carne
chilly (7)	frío
chivalry (CC)	caballerosidad
chocolate (CC)	chocolate
choices (CC)	opciones
choose (14)	escoger
chord (CC)	cuerda
chose (14)	escoger (pasado)
Christmas (31)	Navidad
circling (15)	dando vueltas
circumference (CC)	circunferencia
cities' (10)	de las ciudades
citizen (20)	ciudadano, ciudadana
city's (10)	de la ciudad
city-states (CC)	ciudad-estados
classic (CC)	clásico, clásica
clean (17)	limpiar; limpio, limpia
cleanse (17)	limpiar
clearance (33)	venta
clergymen (CC)	clérigos
clothes (25)	ropa
clumsy (2)	torpe
coach's (10)	del entrenador, de la entrenadora
coaches' (10)	de los entrenadores
coarse (7)	grueso, gruesa; burdo, burda
cobra (23)	cobra
coincidence (33)	coincidencia
cold front (CC)	frente fría
collect (9)	juntar; recoger
collection (22)	colección
collector (20)	coleccionista
college (9)	universidad
colliding boundary (CC)	área de colisión
Colosseum (CC)	Coliseo
column (8)	columna
columns (CC)	columnas
comedy (2)	comedia
command (9)	ordenar; orden
commercial (13)	anuncio publicitario
committee (9)	comité
communicate (19, CC)	comunicar
compass (CC)	compás
compassion (CC)	compasión

competent (CC) — competente
composite (CC) — compuesto, compuesta
conceited (3) — presumido, presumida
condemn (8) — condenar
conferences (CC) — conferencias
confidence (33) — confianza
congruent figures (CC) — figuras congruentes
connect (9) — conectar
conquer (20) — conquistar
considerate (26) — considerado, considerada
consistent (33) — consistente
constellation (CC) — constelación
constructive (26) — constructivo, constructiva
continue (4) — continuar
convenient (33) — conveniente
convention (22) — convención
coordination (CC) — coordinación
corona (CC) — corona
costume (4) — disfraz
council (7) — concejo
counsel (7) — consejo; aconsejar
counselor (CC) — consejero, consejera
courageously (CC) — valerosamente
course (7) — curso
courthouse (34) — palacio de justicia
coyote (23) — coyote
creative (26, CC) — creativo, creativa
critic (28) — crítico, crítica
criticize (28) — criticar
crocodile (23) — cocodrilo
cross-products (CC) — productos cruzados
crust (CC) — corteza

D

daydreams (CC) — ensueños
dead end (11) — callejón sin salida
debt (8) — deuda
deceive (3) — engañar
decided (5) — decidir (pasado)
deciding (5) — decidiendo
decisive (CC) — decidido, decidida
decorate (2) — decorar
deduction (22) — deducción
defective (26) — defectuoso, defectuosa
definite (19) — definido, definida
degree (CC) — grado
deities (CC) — deidades
delayed (5) — retrasar (pasado)
delaying (5) — retrasando

democracy (CC) — democracia
descend (8) — descender
desperate (25) — desesperado, desesperada
destination (22, CC) — destino
destruction (22) — destrucción
determination (22, CC) — determinación, voluntad
determine (21) — determinar
develop (15) — desarrollar
diameter (CC) — diámetro
dictionary (13) — diccionario
diesel (3) — diesel
dietitian (CC) — dietista
difference (33) — diferencia
different (19) — diferente
difficult (31) — difícil
digestion (13) — digestión
dimensions (CC) — dimensiones
dining room (CC) — comedor
direct (28) — dirigir
direction (28) — sentido
director's (10) — del director, de la directora
directors' (10) — de los directores
discount (CC) — descuento
disease (31) — enfermedad
disguise (8) — disfraz
dishonor (20) — deshonra
disputants (CC) — disputadores
dispute (CC) — disputa
distance (2) — distancia
distract (28) — distraer
distraction (28) — distracción
disturb (21) — perturbar
divisible (CC) — divisible
documents (CC) — documentos
doesn't (15) — no (+ verbo)
dominoes (16) — dominós
don't (10) — no (+ verbo)
double (20) — doble
doubt (8) — duda; dudar
doughnut (11) — rosquilla
drawer (15) — gaveta
drive-in (34) — autocinema
dungeon (2) — calabozo

E

earning (21) — ganando
easel (20) — caballete
Egyptians (CC) — egipcios

electric (28)	eléctrico, eléctrica
electrician (28)	electricista
elegant (19)	elegante
elementary (31)	primario, primaria
emergency (CC)	emergencia
emperor (CC)	emperador
empire (CC)	imperio
encounter (20)	encuentro
enemy (1)	enemigo, enemiga
energy (CC)	energía
enormous (21)	enorme
entrance (33)	entrada
entranceway (CC)	portal
epicenter (CC)	epicentro
equal (17)	igual
equation (17)	ecuación
equator (CC)	ecuador
equilateral triangle (CC)	triángulo equilátero
especially (13)	especialmente
everybody (11)	todos, todas
everything (11)	todo
everywhere (34)	por todas partes; en todas partes
evolved (CC)	evolucionado
exactly (15)	exactamente
example (20)	ejemplo
excavate (CC)	excavar
excellence (33)	excelencia
except (14)	excepto
excess (14)	exceso
exclude (27)	excluir
exercise (CC)	ejercicio
exercised (5)	ejercitar *(pasado)*
exercising (5)	ejercitando
exhale (27)	exhalar
exhaustion (13)	agotamiento
expensive (15)	caro, cara
experience (15)	experiencia
experiment (CC)	experimento
expert (21)	experto, experta
exploration (22)	exploración
explore (21)	explorar
exponent (CC)	exponente
exponential form (CC)	forma exponencial
export (35)	exportar
extraterrestrial (CC)	extraterrestre

F

fact (28)	hecho
factors (CC)	factores
factory (19)	fábrica
factual (28)	objetivo, objetiva
familiar (15)	familiar
family room (CC)	cuarto de familia
fascinate (8)	fascinar
fascinating (CC)	fascinante
fat (CC)	grasa
fatigue (8)	fatiga
fault (CC)	falla
favorite (19)	favorito, favorita
feudalism (CC)	feudalismo
fiber (CC)	fibra
fiefs (CC)	feudos
field (3)	campo
finally (14)	por fin
financial (13)	financiero, financiera
finely (14)	finamente
fishhook (25)	anzuelo
fitness (CC)	estado físico
focus (CC)	foco
forever (29)	para siempre
forget (29)	olvidar
forgotten (20)	olvidado, olvidada
fortunate (26)	afortunado, afortunada
forty (21)	cuarenta
forum (CC)	foro
forward (15)	hacia adelante
fossils (CC)	fósiles
fraction (13)	fracción
frantically (CC)	frenéticamente
friendship (26)	amistad
frustrated (15)	frustrado, frustrada

G

garage (19, CC)	garaje
gasoline (19)	gasolina
generation (22)	generación
glacier (13)	glaciar
gladiators (CC)	gladiadores
goal (CC)	meta; objetivo
going to (29)	ir + a
gracious (13)	gracioso, graciosa
granite (CC)	granito
grateful (1)	agradecido, agradecida
greatest common factor (CC)	mayor denominador común
Greeks (CC)	griegos

grid (CC)	coordinadas; cuadrícula
grief (3)	pesar
guarantee (25)	garantía
guardian (8)	guardián
guidance (8)	dirección
guide's (10)	del guía; de la guía
guides' (10)	de los guías
guilty (8)	culpable

H

hallway (11, CC)	pasillo
hardship (26)	dificultad
headphones (35)	auriculares
heavily (19)	pesadamente
helicopter (15)	helicóptero
hesitant (33)	vacilante
hieroglyphics (CC)	jeroglíficos
high-pressure system (CC)	sistema de alta presión
historian (CC)	historiador, historiadora
historical (28)	histórico, histórica
history (28)	historia
homeroom (11)	aula para llamar la lista
honesty (2)	honestidad
household (CC)	casa
hula (23)	hula
human (17)	humano
humane (17)	compasivo, compasiva
humid (4)	húmedo, húmeda
humiliated (CC)	humillado, humillada
hundredth (2)	centésimo, centésima
hurricane (CC)	huracán
husband (2)	esposo
hydrogen (CC)	hidrógeno
hypertension (CC)	hipertensión

I

ice cream (11)	helado
ice pack (11)	compresa de hielo
ice-skated (34)	patinar sobre hielo *(pasado)*
igneous rock (CC)	roca ígnea
ignorant (33)	ignorante
ignore (21)	ignorar
illegal (32)	ilegal
illegible (32)	ilegible
illogical (32)	ilógico, ilógica
illustrate (19)	ilustrar
imbalance (32)	desequilibrio
immature (32)	inmaduro, inmadura

immediate (9)	inmediato, inmediata
immunity (CC)	inmunidad
impatient (32)	impaciente
imperfect (32)	imperfecto, imperfecta
impolite (32)	descortés
import (35)	importar
important (33)	importante
impossible (CC)	imposible
improper (32)	incorrecto
improvement (CC)	mejora
inaccurate (32)	inexacto, inexacta
incapable (32)	incapaz
Incas (CC)	incas
include (27)	incluir
included (5)	incluido, incluida; incluir *(pasado)*
including (5)	incluyendo
incredible (32)	increíble
independence (33)	independencia
indirect (32)	indirecto, indirecta
inexpensive (32)	barato, barata
infection (22)	infección
influenza (CC)	influenza
informal (32)	informal
inhale (27)	inhalar
injury (2)	herida
instance (19)	ejemplo
instrument (1)	instrumento; instrumento musical
insurance (33)	seguro
intelligent (33)	inteligente
interested (31)	interesado, interesada
interfered (5)	interferir *(pasado)*
interfering (5)	interfiriendo
International Date Line (CC)	Línea internacional de cambio de fecha
interrupt (9)	interrumpir
interview (4)	entrevista
intrigue (8)	intriga
inventive (26)	inventivo, inventiva
ionosphere (CC)	ionosfera
irrational (32)	irracional
irregular (32)	irregular
irreplaceable (32)	irreemplazable
irresistible (32)	irresistible
irresponsible (32)	irresponsable
isosceles triangle (CC)	triángulo isósceles
it's (10)	es, está

J

jealousy (31)	celos
judged (1)	juzgar *(pasado)*

K

kindergarten (20)	jardín de infantes
knights (CC)	caballeros
knives (16)	cuchillos
koala (23)	koala

L

later (14)	después
latitude (CC)	latitud
latter (14)	el último, la última
laughter (31)	risa
lava (CC)	lava
leadership (26)	liderazgo
league (8)	liga
leisure (3)	tiempo libre
lemonade (2)	limonada
let's (10)	vamos a
level (20)	nivelado, nivelada
license (1)	licencia
light-years (CC)	años luz, años de luz
likely (CC)	probable
limestone (CC)	piedra caliza
lines of latitude (CC)	líneas de latitud
literature (CC)	literatura
locker room (11)	cuarto de cambiarse la ropa
longitude (CC)	longitud
lord (CC)	señor
low-pressure system (CC)	sistema de baja presión

M

macaroni (23)	macarrones
magazine (31)	revista
magic (28)	magia; mágico, mágica
magician (28)	mago, maga
magnify (2)	amplificar
magnitude (CC)	magnitud
major (17)	mayor
majority (17)	mayoría
man's (10)	del hombre
manor (CC)	señorío
mantle (CC)	manto
marble (CC)	mármol
Maryland (31)	Maryland
masterpieces (CC)	obras maestras
Mayas (CC)	mayas

measles (16)	sarampión
medal (14)	medalla
megaphone (35)	megáfono
membership (26)	socios de un club
men's (10)	de (los) hombres
mention (13)	mencionar
meridians (CC)	meridianos
mesosphere (CC)	mesosfera
metal (14)	metálico, metálica, metal
metamorphic rock (CC)	roca metamórfica
method (2)	método
microphone (35)	micrófono
mirror (9)	espejo
Mississippi (9)	Misisipí
modern (2)	moderno, moderna
mold (CC)	molde
moose (23)	alce
motion (13)	movimiento
mourn (CC)	lamentar
multiply (31)	multiplicar
mummy (CC)	momia
muscle (17)	músculo
muscular (17)	muscular
mustard (23)	mostaza
mustn't (10)	no haber de
myself (11)	yo mismo, yo misma
myths (CC)	mitos

N

national (13)	nacional
natural (17)	natural
nature (17)	naturaleza
negative (26)	negativo, negativa
neighborhood (1)	vecindario
neither (3)	ninguno, ninguna
neutral (CC)	neutral
New York (4)	Nueva York
niece (3)	sobrina
ninety-five (34)	noventa y cinco
nitrogen (CC)	nitrógeno
nutrients (CC)	sustancias nutritivas

O

o'clock (10)	por ejemplo: Son las dos.
obligate (26)	obligar
observatories (CC)	observatorios
occupation (22)	ocupación
occurred (5)	ocurrir *(pasado)*
occurring (5)	ocurriendo

old-fashioned (34) | anticuado, anticuada
omitted (5) | omitir (*pasado*)
omitting (5) | omitiendo
oompah (CC) | sonido musical de contrabajo
opposite (31) | opuesto, opuesta
oral histories (CC) | historias contadas
order (21) | orden; ordenar
orientation (22) | orientación
origin (28) | origen
original (28) | original
originate (26) | originar
orphan (20) | huérfano, huérfana
ourselves (16) | nosotros mismos, nosotras mismas
outcome (CC) | resultado
outside (34) | afuera
overcome (CC) | vencer
overcook (27) | recocer
overflow (27) | rebosar; sobrellenar
overlook (27) | tener vista a; pasar por alto
overpopulated (27) | sobrepoblado, sobrepoblada
overrule (25) | denigar
overseas (7) | ultramar
oversees (7) | supervisa
ownership (26) | propiedad
oxygen (31) | oxígeno
ozone (CC) | ozono

P

pants (16) | pantalones
parallelogram (CC) | paralelogramo
part-time (34) | jornada parcial
Parthenon (CC) | Partenón
partner (15) | compañero, compañera
passport (35) | pasaporte
patience (7) | paciencia
patients (7) | pacientes
patio (CC) | patio
patricians (CC) | patricios
patron (CC) | patrocinador
pattern (19) | diseño; patrón
peer mediation (CC) | mediación de compañeros
penalty (15) | sanción
percent (CC) | por ciento
perched (CC) | posado, posada
perform (1) | ejecutar

performance (33) | función; ejecución
permanent (21) | permanente
persistent (33) | persistente
personal (14) | personal
personnel (14) | personal
perspective (CC) | perspectiva
petrified (CC) | petrificado, petrificada
pharaoh (CC) | faraón
philosophers (CC) | filósofos
philosophy (CC) | filosofía
picnic (23) | comida de campo
pieces (1) | pedazos
pigeon (15) | paloma
plate tectonic theory (CC) | teoría de las placas tectónicas
plates (CC) | placas
plays (CC) | dramas
plebeians (CC) | plebeyos
pneumonia (CC) | neumonía; pulmonía
poem (17) | poema
poetic (17) | poético, poética
poetry (1) | poesía
polka (23) | polca
polka dot (11) | diseño de puntos
pollutant (33) | contaminante
popularity (CC) | popularidad
population (13) | población
portable (35) | portátil
portico (CC) | pórtico
position (13) | ubicación
possess (9) | poseer
possible (CC) | posible
postdate (27) | posfechar
postgraduate (27) | posgraduado, posgraduada
postponement (27) | aplazamiento
postwar (27) | posguerra
potatoes (CC) | papas
power (CC) | poder
prearrange (27) | arreglar de antemano
precaution (27) | precaución
precious (13) | precioso, preciosa
predict (CC) | predecir
prefer (1) | preferir
prehistoric (27, CC) | prehistórico, prehistórica
premeditated (27) | premeditado, premeditada
preservatives (CC) | preservativos
preserved (CC) | preservado, preservada

pretrial (27)	previo al juicio
preview (4)	cortos, avances
primary sources (CC)	fuentes primarias
prime (CC)	número primo
prime factorization (CC)	factorización de números primos
prime meridian (CC)	meridiano de Greenwich
probability (CC)	probabilidad
probably (25)	probablemente
processing (CC)	procesamiento
produce (28)	producir
production (28)	producción
productive (26)	productivo, productiva
promise (25)	promesa
propeller (20)	hélice
property (2)	propiedad
proportion (CC)	proporción
protein (3, CC)	proteína
purchase (21)	comprar
Pyramids (CC)	pirámides

Q

quacking (CC)	grazneando
quadrilateral (CC)	cuadrilátero
quarterback (34)	jugador que dirige la jugada en fútbol americano
quartzite (CC)	cuarcita
question (13)	pregunta
quizzes (16)	exámenes cortos

R

radar (CC)	radar
radii (CC)	rayos
radius (CC)	radio
rate (CC)	razón, proporción
ratio (CC)	radio
reaction (22)	reacción
realistic (CC)	realista
really (31)	realmente
receipt (3)	recibo
receiver (3)	receptor; auricular
recent (14)	reciente
reception (22)	recepción
recess (9)	recreo
recommendation (22)	recomendación
recycle (20)	reciclar
reduce (4)	reducir
reefs (16)	arrecifes
reflection (22)	reflejo

register (19)	matricularse
relationship (26, CC)	parentesco; relación
relaxation (22)	relajación
reliable (CC)	confiable
relief (3)	alivio
remedial (28)	terapéutico, terapéutica
remedy (28)	remedio; remediar
remembered (5)	recordar (pasado)
remembering (5)	recordando
reminiscent (8)	evocador, evocadora
remodel (1)	remodelar
Renaissance (CC)	El Renacimiento
renew (4)	renovar
report (21)	informe
rescue (4)	rescatar
research (21)	investigación; investigar
resent (14)	resentir
reside (CC)	residir
resign (17)	renunciar
resignation (17)	resignación
respiratory (CC)	respiratorio, respiratoria
restaurant (25)	restaurante
reunion (4)	reunión
review (4)	repasar
rhombus (CC)	rombo
Richter scale (CC)	escala de Richter
ridge (CC)	cordillera
ridicules (CC)	ridiculiza
rift (CC)	grieta
ring (7)	anillo
robots (CC)	autómatas
roller coaster (11)	montaña rusa
roller-skating (34)	patinar
Roman (CC)	romano
root beer (11)	refresco hecho de raíces
roughly (25)	bruscamente

S

sale price (CC)	precio de liquidación
sales tax (CC)	impuesto sobre la venta
sandstone (CC)	piedra arenisca
satellite (CC)	satélite
satisfied (5)	satisfecho, sastisfecha
satisfying (5)	satisfaciente
saxophone (35)	saxofón
scale drawing (CC)	dibujo a escala
scalene triangle (CC)	triángulo escaleno
scarfs (16)	bufandas
scenic (8)	pintoresco, pintoresca

scent (7) — aroma

schedule (25) — programar; horario

scholar (CC) — erudito, erudita

science (8) — ciencia

science fiction (CC) — ciencia ficción

scissors (16) — tijeras

secondary sources (CC) — fuentes secundarias

sediment (CC) — sedimento

sedimentary rock (CC) — roca sedimentaria

seismic waves (CC) — ondas sísmicas

seismograph (CC) — sismógrafo

seismologist (CC) — sismólogo, sismóloga

seize (3) — capturar

self-control (34, CC) — dominio de sí mismo, dominio de sí misma

senate (CC) — Senado

sense (14) — sentido

sensitive (31) — sensible

sent (7) — enviar (pasado)

sentence (19) — oración

separate (25) — separado, separada

serfs (CC) — siervos

serial (7) — en serie

service (21) — servicio

sewer (4) — alcantarilla

she'd (10) — ella había; (condicional)

shelves (16) — estantes; anaqueles

sheriffs (16) — sheriffs

shield (3) — escudar

similar (15) — similar

similar figures (CC) — figuras similares

since (14) — desde

single (20) — solo, sola

sinusitis (CC) — sinusitis

site (CC) — lugar

situation (22) — situación

skateboard (11) — patineta

skiing (25) — esquiar

slogan (20) — lema

snickering (CC) — riéndose

social (13) — social

solar eclipse (CC) — eclipse solar

solar flare (CC) — luz solar

solar system (11) — sistema solar

solar wind (CC) — viento solar

soldier (1) — soldado

solemn (8) — solemne

solos (16) — solos

solution (22, CC) — solución

something (34) — algo

sparkling (15) — centelleante

sphinx (CC) — esfinge

spreading boundary (CC) — área de separación de platos tectónicos

stadium (CC) — estadio

staffs (16) — los personales

starch (CC) — fécula

stationary front (CC) — frente estacionario

stereos (16) — equipos estereofónicos

stereotypes (CC) — estereotipos

stratosphere (CC) — estratosfera

strengths (CC) — fuerzas

stress (CC) — tensión; estrés

strict (2) — estricto, estricta

studios (16) — estudios

subducted plate (CC) — placa tectónica sobre otra

subtle (8) — sutil

suggestion (13) — sugerencia

summertime (34) — verano

sunspots (CC) — manchas solares

swimming (2) — nadando

sword (21) — espada

symphony (35) — sinfonía

T

tape recorder (11) — grabadora

tar pit (CC) — pozo de brea

teammate (11) — compañero de equipo, compañera de equipo

technology (CC) — tecnología

teenage (11) — adolescente

telecast (35) — transmisión por televisón

telegram (35) — telegrama

telegraph (35) — telégrafo

telephone (35) — teléfono

telescope (35) — telescopio

television (22) — televisión

temperature (25) — temperatura

temple (CC) — templo

Tennessee (9) — Tennessee

term (CC) — término

terraces (CC) — terrazas

that's (10) — eso es, esa es

their (7) — su (de ellos, de ellas), sus (de ellos, de ellas)

themselves (11) — ellos mismos, ellas mismas

therapist (CC) — terapeuta

there (7)	ahí; allí; allá
there's (10)	hay, hay un, hay una
therefore (21)	por lo tanto
thermosphere (CC)	termosfera
they're (7)	ellos son, ellas son; ellos están, ellas están
thieves (16)	ladrones, ladronas
thirteen (1)	trece
thorough (21)	total
thousand (1)	mil
through (1)	a través de; terminado, terminada
tickling (15)	haciendo cosquillas
time machine (CC)	máquina del tiempo
time zones (CC)	husos horarios
tissue (2)	pañuelo de papel
together (29)	juntos, juntas
tomato (23)	tomate
tomatoes (CC)	tomates
tomb (CC)	tumba
tomorrow (29)	mañana
tone (CC)	tono
tongue (1)	lengua
tonight (29)	esta noche
tornado (CC)	tornado
tournament (CC)	torneo; certamen
toward (31)	hacia
tractor (20)	tractor
transport (35)	transportar
trapezoid (CC)	trapezoide
trembling (15, CC)	temblando; tembloroso, temblorosa
trench (CC)	zanja
trials (CC)	ensayos, pruebas
troposphere (CC)	troposfera
tsunami (CC)	marejada
tunnel (20)	túnel
twelfth (25)	doceavo, doceava
twittering (CC)	gorjeando

U

undercover (27)	secreto, secreta
undernourished (27)	desnutrido, desnutrida
understand (19)	entender
underweight (27)	de bajo peso
uniform (4)	uniforme
unique (CC)	único, única
unite (17)	unir
United States (4)	Estados Unidos
unity (17)	unidad
universe (4)	universo
unusual (1)	raro; rara
unwritten (25)	no escrito, no escrita
urban (20)	urbano, urbana
usually (31)	usualmente
utopia (CC)	utopía

V

vague (8)	vago, vaga
value (4)	valor
vanilla (23)	vainilla
vanished (CC)	desaparecer (*pasado*)
variety (19)	variedad
vassals (CC)	vasallos
vegetable (31)	legumbre
vertex (CC)	vértice
viewpoint (4)	punto de vista
virus (CC)	virus
vitamins (CC)	vitaminas
volcanoes (16)	volcanes

W

waltz (23)	vals
want to (29)	querer (+ verb)
warm front (CC)	frente cálida
water vapor (CC)	vapor de agua
water-skied (34)	esquiar en agua (*pasado*)
we'd (10)	habíamos; (*condicional*)
weaknesses (CC)	debilidades
wolves (16)	lobos
wondering (25)	preguntándose
woolly mammoth (CC)	mamut lanudo
worst (21)	el peor, la peor, lo peor
worth (21)	valer
wring (7)	escurrir

Y

yield (3)	ceder
you're (10)	tú eres, usted es, ustedes son; tú estás, usted está, ustedes están